ADVANCES IN CONNECTIONIST AND NEURAL COMPUTATION THEORY

Volume 1

John A. Barnden, Series Editor

High-Level Connectionist Models

edited by
John A. Barnden and Jordan B. Pollack

ABLEX PUBLISHING CORPORATION
NORWOOD, NEW JERSEY

Printed in the United States of America

Library of Congress Cataloging-in-Publication Data

High-level connectionist models / [edited by] John A. Barnden & Jordan B. Pollack.
p. cm. — (Advances in connectionist and neural computation theory ; v. 1)
Includes bibliographical references and index.
ISBN 0-89391-687-0
1. Connection machines. 2. Neural networks (Computer science)
I. Barnden, John A. II. Pollack, Jordan B. III. Series.
QA76.5.H4815 1990
006.3—dc20 90-47674
CIP

Ablex Publishing Corporation
355 Chestnut Street
Norwood, New Jersey 07648

Table of Contents

LIST OF CONTRIBUTORS

Richard Alterman, Computer Science Department, Brandeis University, Waltham, MA.

John Barnden, Computing Research Laboratory & Computer Science Department, New Mexico State University, Las Cruces, NM.

Lawrence Birnbaum, Institute for the Learning Sciences & Department of Electrical Engineering and Computer Science, Northwestern University, Evanston, IL.

Lawrence Bookman, Computer Science Department, Brandeis University, Waltham, MA.

Eugene Charniak, Department of Computer Science, Brown University, Providence, RI.

Garrison Cottrell, Department of Computer Science and Engineering, University of California San Diego, La Jolla, CA.

Mark Derthick, MCC, Austin, TX.

Joachim Diederich, International Computer Science Institute, Berkeley, CA.

Michael Dyer, Computer Science Department, University of California, Los Angeles, CA.

James Hendler, Department of Computer Science, University of Maryland, College Park, MD.

Jiawei Hong, Department of Computer and Information Science, University of Massachusetts, Amherst, MA.

Wendy Lehnert, Department of Computer and Information Science, University of Massachusetts, Amherst, MA.

Jordan Pollack, Department of Computer and Information Science, The Ohio State University, Columbus, OH.

Eugene Santos, Jr., Department of Computer Science, Brown University, Providence, RI.

Lokendra Shastri, Department of Computer and Information Science, University of Pennsylvania, Philadelphia, PA.

Xiaonan Tan, Department of Computer and Information Science, University of Massachusetts, Amherst, MA.

David Touretzky, Computer Science Department, Carnegie Mellon University, Pittsburgh, PA.

Fu-Sheng Tsung, Department of Computer Science and Engineering, University of California San Diego, La Jolla, CA.

Foreword

How do the hundred billion neurons in the human nervous system combine their activities to produce cognition and intelligent behavior? How can we model such emergent properties with artificial networks? These questions are at the heart of this book, which represents the leading edge of thought on this topic. The researchers in this volume come predominantly from computer science backgrounds, but have been strongly influenced by results in neuroscience, psychology, philosophy, mathematics, and physics.

Such an interdisciplinary synthesis is rare today in computer science (and probably in most fields). However, at one time, in the 1940s and 1950s, when the foundations of both computer science and the computing industry were being laid, there was no clear boundary between computing machinery and models of the nervous system. The interests of the eclectic pioneers of the fruitful period—McCullough and Pitts, Turing, von Neumann, Wiener, and many others—encompassed natural and artificial computation, intelligence, learning, and self-reproduction. They may have been too successful: the apparent universality of the von Neumann architecture and early successes with symbolic computation led to the institutionalization of their paradigms in both industry and academia. These paradigms did not begin to break down until the 1980s, in part due to the efforts of researchers represented in this volume. In attempting to reformulate the foundations of computational science to include interconnected massively parallel systems, these researchers have adopted a broad perspective reminiscent of that of the founders of the field.

Both neural networks and symbol systems were proposed very early as approaches to achieving artificial intelligence; a number of researchers made contributions to both paradigms. Computation concepts were frequently compared with mental phenomena, and offered as explanatory mechanisms: garbage collection was proposed as an explanation for the forgetting of unimportant details, possibly during dreaming; interpreted vs. compiled programs were proposed as analogous to the differences between unskilled and skilled actions; semantic nets and "pandemonium" models were inspired by neural structures.

But as time passed, the eclecticism of the field declined, and specialized groups split off. Neural net researchers focused prematurely on single layer "perceptrons," and when the serious limitations of these systems became evident in the late 1960s, the whole neural net field collapsed. AI early became nearly synonymous with heuristic search, and, starting in the 1970s, mainstream AI, in search of commercial success, became overwhelmingly dominated by rule-based "expert" systems. While such systems have found useful applications, they could not possibly match the wildly optimistic predictions of their proponents, and a backlash against AI set in in the 1980s. Moreover, the similarities between expert systems and ordinary high-level programming language methodologies seem far more striking than any parallels between expert systems and human intelligence. Vision, speech, and robotics, which were not able to benefit much from the development of symbolic AI, split off from (or were rejected by) AI.

Meanwhile, "neural" nets reemerged in the 1980s. Alas, in a short time much of the field became fixated on one of a handful of narrow paradigms (typically variants of "backpropagation"), and proponents began to endorse claims and promises that make even expert system claims look moderate.

Fortunately, not everyone has jumped on these various lurching bandwagons. In particular, the researchers represented in this volume have managed to resist simple, limited paradigms, and have persisted in asking deep, foundational questions: What are the computational properties of neurons and neuron assemblies? Can they implement standard computational actions and constructs (e.g., variable binding, recursion, rules, logical inference, unification)? If so, how? Is human cognition based on such functionality? Will we therefore have to implement such constructs and actions in order to build intelligent systems?

This book, which is filled with fascinating experiments and informed speculation on such questions, is based on the papers delivered at the workshop on high-level connectionist models held at New Mexico State University, Las Cruces, in April 1988. The participants, many of whom are less than 10 years out of graduate school, offer hope of continuing progress toward the goal of truly understanding and modeling cognition and intelligence.

David L. Waltz
Cambridge, MA

July, 1989

Preface

Most of the chapters in this volume resulted from a Workshop on High-Level Connectionist Models held in April 1988 at the Holiday Inn de Las Cruces, New Mexico. The workshop was funded in part by grants from the American Association for Artificial Intelligence and the Office of Naval Research to the Computing Research Laboratory of New Mexico State University.

Jordan Pollack was in the process of organizing a workshop on Connectionism and Artificial Intelligence (AI) when John Barnden joined the faculty at New Mexico State University with a mandate to produce a book in the same area. We (almost) independently and simultaneously wrote letters of invitation to an identical set of scientists. Happily, we joined forces, merging the workshop and book.

The participants at the workshop, shown in the photograph, were predominantly computer scientists specializing in AI and interested in the technical problems blocking the achievement of high-level cognitive processing (reasoning, planning, natural language understanding, and so on) in connectionist and neural networks. The bulk of this volume therefore has this theme, and addresses in particular the controversial issue of the relationships between symbolic processing and connectionist processing. The work should be of interest to connectionists, neural net researchers, cognitive psychologists, philosophers, AI researchers, and computer scientists. Although a full understanding of all the articles may require some familiarity with connectionism, AI, and computer science, the majority of the material should be comprehensible to cross-disciplinary readers.

The book is the first volume in the series entitled *Advances in Connectionist and Neural Computation Theory*. Each book in this series will bring together papers on the computational abilities of connectionist, neural and "neurally inspired" systems. The series is distinctive in its main emphasis, which is on the question of how one can get connectionist or neural-network models to perform rapid, short-term types of computation that appear useful in higher-level cog-

* Certain portions of this book are the result of work supported by Department of Navy grant N00014–88–J–1066 issued by the Office of Naval Research, and the U.S. Government has specific license rights herein. The Computing Research Laboratory is funded in part by the New Mexico State Legislature through its Scientific Technical Commission.

The participants in the workshop on High-Level Connectionist Models. *Seated, from left to right:* Dan Fass, Garrison Cottrell, and James Hendler. *Standing, from left to right:* Lawrence Birnbaum, Mark Derthick, Wendy Lehnert, Tony Plate, Lokendra Shastri, Lawrence Bookman, David Touretzky, Jordan Pollack, Jeffrey Elman, Michael Dyer, John Barnden, and Roger Schvaneveldt. *Hidden Unit:* Joachim Diederich.

nitive processes. The phrase "Computation Theory" in the series title should *not* be taken to indicate that the articles in this or later volumes are intended to be mathematically rigorous treatises in the foundations of computer science. While this line of investigation is extremely useful (and is represented by one of the contributions in the present volume), we feel that connectionism is not yet ready for complete formalization. Our primary intent behind the use of the word "computation," then, is to emphasize an orientation towards the computational aspects of neural networks, rather than the electronic, psychological, or biological aspects. Our use of the word "theory" is to emphasize an orientation away from the straightforward application of well-known connectionist techniques to particular problems, and toward the development of new concepts and hypotheses.

We wish to acknowledge the aid of many people. Firstly, we must thank all the workshop participants and authors, who ultimately had to pay for their three days of freewheeling discussion with the hard work of writing. Yorick Wilks, director of the Computing Research Laboratory at New Mexico State University, encouraged and supported the meeting. Our students Michael Angerman, Imre Balogh, Tony Plate, and Kankanahalli Srinivas spent many hours transporting the visitors and running the audio-visual equipment. Helen Flechsenhaar, Pat Puckett, Tom Puckett, and Jeannine Sandefur aided in budgeting and administration. Roger and Ann Schvaneveldt hosted the reception at their house. Jeffrey Chu, Don Dearholt, Christopher Fields, and Hing Leung provided useful comments on various chapters. Finally, Kankanahalli Srinivas worked tirelessly to help us get this book completed.

J.A.B, Las Cruces, New Mexico
J.B.P, Columbus, Ohio

November, 1989

1
Introduction: Problems for High-Level Connectionism

John A. Barnden
Jordan B. Pollack

1. PREAMBLE

Typically, a connectionist system is a *large weighted network* of processing units that communicate with each other by means of *simple numeric messages*. A unit transforms incoming messages by a *simple function* which may depend on the unit's *state*. Units operate in a *massively parallel* fashion. In response to an environment, the weights in such networks can often be *slowly adapted* by local modification rules.

We preceded the above definition by the term "typically" because such systems do not form a precise class, but hold family resemblances to each other. Furthermore, our definition is completely framed in computational terms, and lacks the conceptual vocabulary of psychology and biology. In fact, preceding the word "network," we henceforth use the adjective "connectionist," rather than "neural," in order to signal that the systems we are interested in are not (necessarily) biologically realistic.[1]

The focus of this book is a specialized but nevertheless important area within the study of connectionist networks. Much of the successful work in connectionism has been applied to "low-level" perceptual tasks, such as pattern recognition and motor control, and to underlying faculties, such as associative memory. Most conferences and books on the subject view it from a biological, a psychological, or an applied physics perspective. Our focus is on the use of connectionist networks in "high-level" cognitive tasks, such as natural-language processing and logical or commonsense reasoning, that have traditionally been

[1] "Connectionist" is also more neutral than "parallel distributed processing," since we are not confining our attention to systems with "distributed" representations.

attacked with the symbolic representation and processing techniques of Artificial Intelligence (AI). We view the subject of connectionism unabashedly from the perspective of computer science and AI.

Of course, many connectionist models have made inroads into some high-level areas—for example, into certain restricted semantic/pragmatic elements of language processing such as context-sensitive lexical disambiguation (e.g., Waltz & Pollack, 1985; Cottrell, 1985) and case-role assignment (McClelland & Kawamoto, 1986). By and large, however, connectionist attempts to build models of higher-level cognitive processes continually come up against certain technical difficulties concerning processing and representation. These difficulties revolve around the question of achieving the complexity and sophistication of processing that is traditionally obtained, in cognitive psychology and artificial intelligence, by the rule-based manipulation of complex symbolic representational structures. The problems for connectionism that are raised by this question have received preliminary discussion over the last few years by a number of researchers, including Barnden (1984), Pollack (1987), Fodor and Pylyshyn (1988), and Smolensky (1988).

On the other hand, certain features of connectionism (e.g., associative memories, slow adaptation, "distributed" representations, simplicity of messages between units) seem to provide, or at least to promise, properties that are difficult to achieve in the symbolic framework. The advantages most usually claimed by connectionists are forms of fault-tolerance, robustness, flexibility, pattern completion, approximate matching of representations, generalizing ability, avoidance of sequential search of memory, simultaneous handling of multiple and diverse constraints, context-sensitivity, exception handling, fast evidence weighing, and graceful degradation (whereby moderate loss of information or knowledge still allows the system to continue producing results, albeit of somewhat degraded quality). These highly interrelated properties are central in much of the connectionist literature, and an explanation of what they are or how they arise is not attempted here. However, we note that no single connectionist model actually fulfills a majority of these promises. Perhaps sustained research will eventually produce networks which fulfill them all.

Meanwhile, we are faced with the issue of determining how connectionism can, in a reasonably natural way, continue to provide the properties just mentioned (or can fulfill its promise of providing them) while also achieving something like the information-processing capabilities provided by traditional symbolic processing. This book is directed mainly at this issue.[2]

Some people do not see the significance of the issue, arguing that we already have computational architectures able to achieve traditional symbol processing,

---

[2] The book is not to be regarded as a completely representative survey of work on the issue, and the reader striving for greater completeness will at the very least want to consult the works of Hinton and Smolensky (e.g., their papers cited in the bibliography at the end of this Introduction).

so that it is misguided to use connectionist systems to effect such processing, or some approximation to it. This point of view fails to take account of several considerations.

First, if one is interested ultimately in explaining how the brain works, then, on the working assumption that the brain's information processing is to be understood at the level of neural networks, one is led to wonder how neural networks can perform tasks that are conventionally cast as being performed by traditional symbol processing, or tasks such as natural language understanding that obviously involve symbols at some point.

Second, if one considers the possibility that mind emerges from many layers of information processing architecture built "on top of" the brain architecture, then high-level connectionism can be seen as the study of a "middle-level" mental architecture, and the question remains of how symbol processing could emerge from this middle level. The idea of studying such a level of mental architecture as broadly similar to the underlying neural architecture is certainly as justified as the AI view of the ubiquity of serial symbolic processing.

Third, the issue is important in a different way even for connectionists who are not interested in the brain or mind, but rather in engineering useful computing artifacts that are able to perform cognitive tasks. Suppose one wishes to engineer a system that can perform both high-level tasks like reasoning and low-level tasks like perception. One route would be to create a "hybrid" system combining connectionist networks for the low-level tasks with pieces of mechanism that effect traditional symbol processing for the high-level tasks, where no connectionist implementation is specified for those pieces. Chapters 6 and 7 (Hendler and Lehnert, respectively) in this book describe hybrid systems. However, this approach might limit the possibilities for interaction between the connectionist and symbolic aspects of the system. A much tighter and richer interaction could arise by specifying a connectionist implementation *also* for any symbolic processing that the system effects.

Finally, the investigation of how connectionism can emulate traditional symbol processing could lead to new connectionist encoding and processing techniques. These techniques might turn out to be useful or illuminating even in the context of the "nonsymbolic" tasks that connectionist systems have predominantly been applied to.

2. ISSUES

Earlier we alluded to the existence of difficulties that continually show up in connectionist modeling attempts directed at high-level cognitive processing. Many of the specific problems that arise in particular models seem to go away in other models, giving place to new problems. Because the centrally highlighted aspects of connectionism change over time,[3] the same two leading culprits can keep returning in different clothing. The first of these is the inadequacy of naive connectionist representations. The second is connectionism's very limited stock of procedural controls. Below, however, we break these two difficulties into the more particular emergent problems that have been repeatedly identified in the field, and that we proposed to the participants as central questions for the Workshop on which this book is based (see Preface).

2.1. Levels of Description

Is connectionism trying to model brain or mind, and, if so, is it arrayed somehow above, below, or at the same level as symbol processing in a geometric metaphor of abstract levels of mental architecture?

One way of implementing high-level cognitive processing in connectionist systems would be to explain the processing in terms of traditional symbol processing, and implement the latter in connectionist terms. This is the "implementational connectionism" route, whereby the connectionist system would be seen as actually performing traditional symbol processing.[4] This route might seem uninteresting or even incoherent to the more revolutionary connectionist, one with a vested interest in viewing connectionism as being fundamentally in opposition to traditional symbolic processing. As should already be apparent, we ourselves do not take such a revolutionary stance; instead, we allow implementational connectionism as a valid research strategy. However, this does not mean that we are rigidly committed to this route: the idea that there is a path from high-level cognitive processing to connectionism that bypasses traditional symbol processing is also of interest to us. Someone following this route (e.g., Smolensky, 1988) would typically take the view that traditional symbol processing (at the information-processing level) is at best merely an *approximate,* relatively superficial description of the deep, underlying connectionist reality. Typically, the view is that when people appear to be following traditional rules (rules straightforwardly encodable with the tools of traditional symbol processing), the following of the rules is generally not exact, and the rules are merely a descrip-

---

[3] For example, the early 1980s pushed parallelism and analog relaxation, whereas, since the popularization of back-propagation in 1986, the elements of pattern association and learning have been in fashion.

[4] More exactly, the connectionist system would be seen as performing traditional symbolic information processing at the so-called "information-processing" level of description normally used in cognitive psychology and AI. We mention this qualification to guard against the objection that there is a sense in which any connectionist system whatsoever can be viewed as doing symbol processing. For instance, the signals on connections could be regarded as symbols, and the node input/output functions could be regarded as rules. Some existing notions of "symbol" and "rule" are broad enough for this move to be made. However, such symbol processing would not be at the level of description usually assumed in symbolic accounts of cognition.

tive tool. On this view, achieving something like the capabilities of traditional symbol processing does not necessarily imply implementing such processing.

Thus, an overarching problem that each researcher faces is to decide between the two routes described, or to propose a new one.

2.2. Complex Representational Structure

Human cognition appears to involve the rapid creation and manipulation of novel propositions or other structures that can have considerable complexity, such as the proposition conveyed by the sentence "John believes that Pat is angry whenever Tom talks about going to Tibet." On one view, to understand the sentence *is* to construct a manipulable representation of its content. Such representations are quite problematic for naive connectionist models for several reasons:

- It is difficult to see how—given their structural complexity—they are to be embodied at all, by means of the representational tools (features, weights) provided by connectionist research.
- Each new utterance can be quite novel, and the system may never have encountered anything closely resembling a particular piece of information before. If connectionist generalization to novelty rides on existing simple notions of pattern similarity, the systems may be too weak.
- In order to manipulate the representations, powerful and efficient procedural mechanisms will be needed (e.g., for creating them, modifying them, analyzing them, inferring from them)—mechanisms which are not obviously available in the literature.
- Structural similarities between representations should be reflected in similarity of the processing that can applied to them. This is almost identical to Fodor and Pylyshyn's (1988) notion of "systematicity": if a system believes that "if two people hate each other then they are constantly trying to injure each other," then it should be able to apply this rule to the specific case of any two people who hate each other, not just a precoded set of hater/hatee pairs.

This is not the place to go into the complex matter of why these features cause technical difficulty (see Barnden, 1984, and Fodor & Pylyshyn, 1988, for some arguments). The root cause of the problems appears to be that the single most powerful influence on present connectionist encoding and processing techniques has been the continual attempts to achieve visual pattern-recognition in neural networks. (And, it is this application domain that appears most responsible for the growth of interest in associative memory and slow adaptation, which are the other two main concerns for connectionists currently.) In the typical connectionist pattern-recognition system, there is no attention paid to the need to reason about, or to apply other significant types of short-term cognitive processing to, novel combinations of complex objects; thus, the types of problem listed above simply do not arise in any serious form.

In an implementational-connectionism approach to high-level cognitive processing, in which cognitive processing is achieved by the manipulation of (something like) traditional symbolic structures, the difficulties noted in the present subsection take the particular form of problems about how to implement and manipulate computational entities such as rules, formulas, frames, schemata, semantic network fragments, lists, stacks, and trees that are familiar from computer science, artificial intelligence, and cognitive psychology.

2.3. Multiple Instantiations

The problem is worse than that of just achieving the ability to represent complex structures. We must realize the potential importance of attending to *multiple instantiations* of such representations. For instance, if there is a "person" frame or schema on which the representation of individual people can be based, then the representation of a situation involving several people is much aided by an ability to maintain several instantiations of the frame or schema simultaneously. Similarly, a point familiar from the use of rule-based systems in artificial intelligence is that a given rule might apply in several distinct ways to a given situation, each way giving rise to a separate "instantiation" of the rule. So, it might be advantageous to have several such instantiations simultaneously present in some sort of short-term memory.

Now, we are not making an absolutely definite claim for the need for multiple instantiations, since we wish to allow that it may be in principle be possible to represent, say, a multiperson situation by only entertaining one schema instantiation at any one time. However, we do not have a clear idea of how such a system would work, and it would seem that anyone putting forward a schema-based system that did not allow multiple instantiations would bear the considerable burden of proving its usefulness.

The consequence for connectionism is that one cannot say one is anywhere near to solving the problem of embodying such things as schemata in connectionist systems (cf. Rumelhart, Smolensky, McClelland, & Hinton, 1986) until one has addressed the question of multiple instantiations. The question is difficult for connectionism (though easy for the traditional symbol processing paradigm) because, again, it involves the need to rapidly construct and manipulate complex information structures of some sort. At the very least, each individual instantiation would have to specify particular values for the various parameters/slots/roles that did not have default values in the particular case at hand, and to simultaneously maintain several such sets of specifications simultaneously without too much confusion. This last issue is commonly known as the "crosstalk" problem.

2.4. Temporary Associations

The construction of instantiations of frames, schemata, and so on is usually referred to as being in part an exercise in "role-binding," and the construction of instantiations of rules or other types of processing module is usually referred to as being in part an exercise in "variable binding." These terms are largely interchangeable, since a role (slot, etc.) in an instantiatable frame or schema can be regarded as a sort of variable, and a variable in a rule (etc.) can be regarded as a sort of role.

It is difficult to allow the binding of values to variables while avoiding an explosion of units and connections, in the more standard sorts of connectionist systems. Interestingly powerful binding capabilities are, however, provided in less standard systems such as the DCPS system of Touretzky and Hinton (1988), the system of Shastri and Ajjanagadde (1989), which is briefly described in Chapter 10, and the Conposit system described in Barnden's chapter. Note that the variable binding problem is in essence a special case of the problem of ensuring systematicity (see Section 2.2).

Role/variable-binding is a special case of the general problem of dealing with "temporary associations" between items of information, processing entities, and so on. A role/variable-binding is a temporary association between the role/variable and the particular value that is being entertained for it. For example, the idea that John loves Mary involves a temporary association between some notion of loving, some concept of John, and some concept of Mary. Now, although the notion of a role or variable might be at home at a high, abstract level of description of a particular connectionist system, there is a danger that talk of "role/variable-binding" might suggest that a role/variable exists in some clear form at the *low,* concrete level of network description—for example, that it exists in the form of a particular piece of network. One reason why this suggestion might arise is that we are accustomed in computer science to thinking of high-level variables as being realized as concrete things at a low level of system description (e.g., as particular locations in the computer memory). Certainly, one might wish to propose an analogously straightforward concrete realization of roles and variables in a particular connectionist system one is designing, but in general it seems to us preferable to talk in the more neutral terms of temporary associations. These are conceived at a high level of description, and manifest themselves *in some way or other* at the concrete level.

The difficulty of dealing with temporary associations in connectionist systems is worsened by the arbitrariness of possible associations that may need to be accounted for. Although we (and our connectionist systems) may believe that plants do not love, we must still have the ability to put plants in agent position in love propositions: after all, we have just entertained the negation of the proposition that plants love; and we might want to think about someone's believing that plants do love. On these lines, it is not difficult to see that there can be very little in the way of "selectional restrictions," to borrow a linguistic term, that would limit what can be associated with what; and this conclusion holds even without going on to a consideration of restriction-confounding matters such as metaphorical modes of thought. The problem at hand is best described, therefore, as being that of "arbitrary temporary associations."

In connectionist terms, if temporary associations existing at an abstract level are mapped in some way onto facilitated concrete connection paths between subnetworks representing the associated terms—and this is a typical approach—the arbitrariness of temporary associations has the consequence that there must be a connection path between practically every two subnetworks that can represent something. But the difficulty is not just to ensure that the machinery is available for supporting the abstract associations, but also to ensure that they can be *rapidly* set up, deleted (or forgotten or deactivated), and used in reasoning and other activities. It is especially noteworthy that this rapidity must prevail in the face of the possible *novelty* of the associations for the system: in the Tibet example given above, the system may never before have come across the idea of someone being angry at someone else talking about going somewhere.

2.5. Meta-Level Reasoning

An issue that is hardly ever discussed in the connectionist literature is that of a system having information about and reasoning about its own knowledge, reasoning, and so on. There is good reason to think that such meta-level information and reasoning is important in conscious human thought, and perhaps in unconscious thought as well, and it has long played an important part in traditional artificial intelligence research. Meta-level considerations may make a major difference in one's view of how the representation and processing in a connectionist system should be organized. Suppose, for instance, that base-level information (i.e., nonmeta-level information, such as the idea that John loves Mary) is represented in a very "distributed" way in a connectionist system. Then it may be especially hard for the system to realize *that* it has a particular piece of base-level information, and to reason about it *as* a piece of information, because of the difficulty of isolating, as an entity in its own right, its representation of it. The point being made here is linked to the common claim in artificial intelligence that meta-level representation and reasoning is much aided by the use of *simple* representations at the base level (cf. Davis & Buchanan, 1977).

2.6. Procedural Control

Despite the concentration on parallel processing in connectionist systems, it is nevertheless widely recognized that the modeling of high-level cognitive processing is inevitably going to have to address sequential processing. For instance, it is frequently stated that a total system might be composed of specialized subnetworks that trigger each other into operation, leading to sequencing of operations at a gross level of behavior. This is despite the fact that an individual subnetwork might internally be a highly parallel processing entity.

Once sequences of operations have been let through the door, it is difficult to deny entry to branching, iteration, subroutine calling, and possibly recursion, if only because we are so used to these as concomitants of sequential processing in computers. This is not to say, however, that a connectionist system must necessarily have as general a repertoire of sequential control features as we are used to in conventional computational systems. For instance, it is commonly proposed that a connectionist system might only allow some very shallow extent of nesting of "subroutine calls." Whether these proposals will work remains to be seen.

2.7. High-Level Parallelism

Despite, again, the concentration on parallel processing in connectionist systems, there has been little serious work on introducing a large degree of parallelism at a *high* level of chunking of system behavior. Returning to the idea in the previous subsection of having a set of subnetworks that operate in sequence, it may be also be advantageous to allow parallelism, possibly massive, *between such sets*. Thus, parallelism could exist at several different levels of system description, not just at the bottom level of individual units. It could even be that relationships of sequentiality and parallelism between subnetworks arise dynamically in the course of processing rather than being fixed by the total network architecture.

The higher-level types of parallelism may have to involve resource-contention resolution, synchronization, and other complex forms of control that are familiar from the extensive study of parallelism in conventional computer science, but that hardly appear at all in current connectionist systems.[5]

2.8. Rapid Learning

The idea that connectionist systems are capable of "learning" seems to have obscured the fact that they mostly perform only slow adaptation, which requires thousands of training events. Of course, human beings do learn some things rather slowly, and learn them in a way that seems promising as a target for explanation by current connectionist adaptation ideas. However, it is difficult to escape the conclusion that these ideas are not well suited to some very important types of learning, such as those being extensively investigated in the machine

---

[5] "High-level" parallelism is high-level simply by virtue of the level of lumping of system processes, and is not necessarily related to "high-level" cognitive processing.

learning subarea of artificial intelligence. These types include learning by being told, learning by *rapid* generalization over a small set of instances, analogy-based learning, and "explanation-based learning" (Mitchell, Keller, & Kedar-Cabelli, 1986; Dejong & Mooney, 1986). Moreover, the reason that current connectionist learning techniques are not well suited to these types of learning is that the latter involve some of the problems alluded to above, such as the ability to process complex, novel data structures rapidly.

3. CHAPTER DESCRIPTIONS

The issues discussed above provide the general context for the contents of this volume. Different chapters address different subsets of these problems in one way or another. However, the authors usually cast the general problems for connectionism, and their own research contributions, in domain-specific ways.

In order to help the reader manage the flow of ideas, we have tried to organize the volume along these domain lines. Given the breadth of the discussion above, it is not surprising that within each grouping the authors show a broad variation in their view of connectionism and its problems, as well as the assumptions underlying their own contributions. Chapters 2 and 12 move from Natural Language Processing, through Reasoning, to Learning. Chapters 13 and 14 present computational and AI challenges to the connectionist view. The concluding chapter is devoted to discussion, derived mainly from transcripts of interchanges that took place at the workshop on which this book is based.

The following summarizes the thrust of Chapters 2 to 14, and also mentions the topics the authors addressed at the workshop if significantly different from what is in their chapters.

3.1. Natural Language Processing (NLP)

Chapter 2 (Touretzky) presents a system for prepositional phrase attachment in natural language understanding (following on from Touretzky, 1988). In his workshop presentation, Touretzky expressed dissatisfaction at the abundance of trivial models coming out of the connectionist field. He argued that certain ideas had already reached their limit of usefulness and could stagnate the field. He placed lateral-inhibition networks, winner-take-all networks, associative memories and 3-layer back-propagation systems in this class. He sketched several projects apart from the one described in the chapter, including the DUCS system for representing frames (Touretzky & Geva, 1987), and a new, ambitious project on connectionist metonymic reasoning.

Chapter 3 (Dyer) is concerned with almost all of our issues on the boundary between connectionist and symbolic systems. Dyer lays out his general philosophy on "symbolic neuroengineering," through which traditional AI tasks, especially in NLP, are decomposed into modules that can be implemented using connectionist techniques, yielding more robust and flexible systems. He describes work by his group on reconstructing the case-role assignment work of McClelland and Kawamoto (1986), including the process of discovering distributed representations for the elements of the lexicon, and on devising distributed representations for semantic networks, among other things. The chapter sketches interesting approaches to the binding problems, as well as providing a good summary of the contrasts between and relative advantages of current connectionist systems and traditional symbolic systems.

Chapter 4 (Bookman and Alterman) presents a connectionist approach to the complex issue of schema selection in semantic and pragmatic NLP. They greatly refine and extend Waltz and Pollack's (1985) microfeature vector to create a truly useful concept. At the workshop, Bookman argued that connectionism needs better forms of modularity in order to scale up. He described developments in his work on Network Regions (Chun, Bookman, & Afshartous, 1987), which are a hierarchal abstraction over spreading activation networks. This work is therefore bound up with the issue of levels and modes of description. There was an extended discussion at the workshop about the detailed connectionist implementation of network regions and about the advantages and disadvantages of using them.

Chapter 5 (Charniak and Santos[6]) describes a quasiconnectionist system for parsing natural language. It is said to be quasiconnectionist because it is not specified as a detailed network, but instead at a slightly higher level of abstraction; however, one can easily envisage how the system could be given a connectionist implementation. Their system is similar to Barnden's Conposit system in solving the temporary association problem largely by using adjacency encoding in an array of register-like components.

Chapter 6 (Lehnert) makes a strong case for "hybrid" modeling, taking the best of both worlds (standard symbol processing and connectionism) for building useful systems. CIRCUS is a sentence analysis system, and uses a stack and a copy mechanism for control, marker passing for prediction, and connectionist numerical spreading-activation for smooth decision making. She shows how the system can give a unified account of parsing and prepositional phrase attachment, flexibly implementing the "no crossing of branches" constraint on the latter. An interesting feature of the connectionist subnetworks in her system is that they are dynamically constructed in the course of processing a sentence. This is a relatively rare idea in the connectionist field, since networks are usually taken to have a fixed set of connections, but it is, of course, a straightforward notion to implement in a system that also contains standard facilities for symbol processing.

---

[6] who were not at the workshop.

3.2. Reasoning

Moving into the question of flexible reasoning systems, Chapter 7 (Hendler) mounts the hybrid horse and makes it gallop. Hendler's workshop presentation focused on this issue, and led to a lively discussion on levels of description that is recaptured in the Conclusion (Chapter 15). The work presented in his chapter combines symbolic marker passing with subsymbolic connectionist processing, where the latter effects the traversal of microfeature-based similarity associations.

Chapter 8 (Barnden) describes a system called Conposit. This system shows how complex symbolic data structures can be conveniently and rapidly manipulated by rules in connectionist networks. Barnden's work exploits two useful methods, "Relative-Position Encoding," and "Pattern-similarity Association," for structuring and accessing symbolic data structures in connectionist models.

Chapter 9 (Derthick) describes an "energy" minimization approach to generating plausible truth assignments for possibly-inconsistent propositional logic theories. He argues that his approach is better than classical theorem proving because, in addition to being able to reason from partial and inconsitent information, his system also provides a formal probabilistic theory of common-sense reasoning. He describes some special constraints and energy-difinition techniques for shaping the energy surface so as to improve the search for a minimum.

Chapter 10 (Shastri) takes on the question of what contribution connectionism can make to AI. He describes his previous work on knowledge representation and reasoning in a more general framework of discovering fast and tractable means of performing specialized but extremely important forms of inference. One success has been the complete compilation of default reasoning using property inheritance into a spreading activation connectionist network. The network acts rapidly because of the avoidance of time-consuming iterative relaxation processes. Towards the end of the chapter he describes recent work on connectionistically implementing deductive inference with more freedom of variable binding than has been achieved in various other systems. By means of a time-sharing technique, the system can maintain multiple bindings of sets of variables, and performs deductive inference in optimal time.

3.3. Learning

The preceding chapters on reasoning certainly demonstrate how connectionist ideas can contribute directly to the efficiency concerns of more traditional AI. A major question for this type of work is how the systems that are constructed by hand could possibly be developed by some automatic learning process.

Chapter 11 (Diederich) presents work on the rapid learning of concepts in networks of the type studied by Shastri. At the workshop, Diederich described his research on various different types of spreading activation.

Continuing on the theme of learning, Chapter 12 (Cottrell and Tsung) describes some recent work on developing a connectionist system capable of learning, by slow adaptation, how to add arbitrary long numbers together. Of the issues listed above, this work is focused mainly on the issue of control, including looping and branching. The chapter also shows the benefits of adopting a staged approach to slow adaptation. At the workshop, Cottrell presented a number of ideas on the encoding of information in connectionist systems.

3.4. New Challenges

In the final group of chapters, Chapter 13 (Hong and Tan[7]) is a mathematical study of the formal computational relationships between connectionist networks and networks of simple logic gates. The chapter is representative of a growing body of work on such relationships (see also Parberry & Schnitger, 1988, and Judd, 1987). The authors prove that certain typical varieties of connectionist network have similar computational power to logic networks, in a certain technical case of "similar." Such research is theoretically important, not least in reminding us that connectionist models are not in a distant, isolated region of the universe of computational models, but are in fact close to other more traditional models. The chapter therefore serves to underscore a general theme of this book, namely that a rapprochement should be sought between connectionism and more traditional styles of computation.

We give the penultimate word to the workshop attender who was specifically invited as an "anti-connectionist." Chapter 14 (Birnbaum) discusses some hard problems in planning and understanding that present a challenge for connectionists. His examples involve long-chained inferences over very abstract schemata, such as a schema for "looking inconspicuous" and a schema for "helping." Both involve reasoning about an agent's own internal state, and thus require strong self-referential representational systems.

Several participants in the workshop are not represented by Chapters 2 to 14, namely Geoffrey Elman, Jordan Pollack, and Roger Schvaneveldt. Elman described his work on learning to process and predict sequences (Elman, 1988). His system used a recurrent form of back-propagation (Rumelhart, Hinton, & Williams, 1986) over very long input sequences, training a network in prediction tasks. One task was to predict the next word in a long concatenated sequence of grammatically generated sentences. In learning to do this, the network devised a classification for the words which was revealed through cluster analysis. Another network learned to resolve pronouns in variable-length sentences.

Pollack argued in his presentation that multiplicative connections (also known as Sigma-Pi or high-order connections) would lead to more flexible procedural control. He made the analogy between these connections (whose activity modi-

---

[7] who were not at the workshop.

fies the weights of other connections) and the short-circuit between program memory and data memory which distinguishes the stored-program computer from the Turing Machine. Granted this power of self-modification, connectionist networks would be general purpose, but much more unstable, and would require strong conventions to fight the instability. He also described his work on "recursive distributed representations" of sequences and trees, using a recursive form of auto-association (Pollack, in press). He argued that such representations could be the basis of systems which perform inference using fixed-width pattern association. This work is summarized in the Conclusion (Chapter 15).

Schvaneveldt presented his attempt at replicating the connectionist schema-representing system of Rumelhart, Smolensky, McClelland, and Hinton (1986). He compared and contrasted the densely connected networks of this system with the considerably sparser but behaviorally similar networks generated by the Pathfinder graph-theoretic algorithm (Schvaneveldt, Durso, & Dearholt, 1987; Schvaneveldt, 1989).

It is appropriate to report here, rather than in the Conclusion, some points which emerged during the workshop argumentation periods. Wendy Lehnert noted that it is ironic that as artificial intelligence is finally "coming of age" with its formal paradigm of rigorous computational logics, many neural network pundits are proclaiming that "AI is dead." In fact, as AI solidifies its paradigm, many of its "scruffier" scientists are finding that the questions connectionists have raised are much more exciting than logic! On the other hand, connectionism is undergoing a similar early maturation, in that much of the research that is going on—typified by a multitude of proofs about dynamical systems converging and by attempts to achieve everything by means of the back-propagation technique—is very conservative, and is merely incremental improvement upon existing knowledge. By continuing to focus on the boundary between AI and connectionism, high-level connectionists may find a common ground that each side has been ignoring.

REFERENCES

Barnden, J.A. (1984). On short-term information processing in connectionist theories. *Cognition and Brain Theory, 7*(1), 25–59.

Charniak, E., & Santos, E. (1987). A connectionist context-free parser which is not context-free, but then it is not really connectionist either. *Proceedings of the 9th Annual Conference of the Cognitive Science Society*. Hillsdale, NJ: Lawrence Erlbaum.

Cottrell, G.W. (1985). *A connectionist approach to word-sense disambiguation* (Tech. Rep. 154). Rochester, NY: University of Rochester, Computer Science Department.

Chun, H.W., Bookman, L.A., & Afshartous, N. (1987). Network regions: Alternatives to the winner-take-all structure. *Proceedings of the 6th National Conf. on Artificial Intelligence*. San Mateo, CA: Morgan Kaufmann.

Davis, R., & Buchanan, B.C. (1977). Meta-level knowledge: Overview and applications. *Proceedings of the 5th Int. Joint Conf. on Artificial Intelligence*. Los Altos, CA: Morgan Kaufmann.

DeJong, G.F., & Mooney, R.J. (1986). Explanation-based learning: An alternative view. *Machine Learning, 1,* 145–176.

Elman, J.L. (1988). *Finding structure in time* (Tech. Rep. 8801). San Diego: Center for Research in Language, University of California, San Diego.

Fodor, J.A., & Pylyshyn, Z.W. (1988). Connectionism and cognitive architecture: A critical analysis. In S. Pinker & J. Mehler (Eds.), *Connections and symbols* (pp. 3–71). Cambridge, MA: MIT Press, and Amsterdam: Elsevier. (Reprinted from *Cognition, 28,* 1988.)

Judd, S. (1987). Learning in networks is hard. *Proceedings of the First IEEE Neural Network Conference, II,* 685–692.

McClelland, J.L., & Kawamoto, A.H. (1986). Mechanisms of sentence processing: Assigning roles to constituents of sentences. In J.L. McClelland, D.E. Rumelhart, & The PDP Research Group (Eds.), *Parallel distributed processing: Experiments in the microstructure of cognition* (Vol. 2, pp. 272–325). Cambridge, MA: MIT Press.

Mitchell, T., Keller, R., & Kedar-Cabelli, S. (1986). Explanation-based learning: A unifying view. *Machine Learning 1,*(1), 47–80.

Parberry, I., & Schnitger, G. (1988). Parallel computation with threshold functions. *Journal of Computer and System Sciences, 36,* 278–302.

Pollack, J.B. (1987). *On connectionist models of natural language understanding.* Unpublished doctoral dissertation, University of Illinois, Computer Science Department, Urbana, IL.

Pollack, J.B. (in press). Recursive distributed representations. *Artificial Intelligence.*

Rumelhart, D.E., Hinton, G., & Williams, R. (1986). Learning internal representations by error propagation. In D.E. Rumelhart, J.L. McClelland, & The PDP Research Group (Eds.), *Parallel distributed processing: Experiments in the microstructure of cognition* (Vol. 1, pp. 318–362). Cambridge: MIT Press.

Rumelhart, D.E., Smolensky, P., McClelland, J.L., & Hinton, G.E. (1986). Schemata and sequential thought processes in PDP models. In J.L. McClelland, D.E. Rumelhart, & The PDP Research Group (Eds.), *Parallel distributed processing: Experiments in the microstructure of cognition* (Vol. 2, pp. 7–57). Cambridge: MIT Press.

Schvaneveldt, R. (1989). Proximities, networks, and schemata. *Memoranda in Computer and Cognitive Science* (No. MCCS-89-149). Las Cruces, NM: Computing Research Laboratory, New Mexico State University.

Schvaneveldt, R., Durso, F., & Dearholt, D. (1987). Pathfinder: Networks from proximity data. *Memoranda in Computer and Cognitive Science* (No. MCCS-87-90). Las Cruces, NM: Computing Research Laboratory, New Mexico State University.

Shastri, L., & Ajjanagadde, V. (1989). *A connectionist system for rule based reasoning with multi-place predicates and variables* (Tech. Rep. MS-CIS-8905). Philadelphia: Computer and Information Science Department, University of Pennsylvania.

Smolensky, P. (1988). On the proper treatment of connectionism. *Behavioral and Brain Sciences, 11,* 1–74.

Touretzky, D.S. (1986). Representing and transforming recursive objects in a neural network, or "Trees *Do* Grow on Boltzmann Machines." *Proceedings of the IEEE Conference on Systems, Man and Cybernetics.* Atlanta, GA.

Touretzky, D.S. (1988). Connectionism and PP attachment. *Proceedings of the 1988 Connectionist Models Summer School.* San Mateo, CA: Morgan Kaufmann.

Touretzky, D.S., & Geva, S. (1987). A distributed connectionist representation for concept structures. *Proceedings of the 9th Annual Conference of the Cognitive Science Society.* Hillsdale, NJ: Lawrence Erlbaum.

Touretzky, D.S., & Hinton, G.E. (1988). A distributed connectionist production system. *Cognitive Science, 12*(3), 423–466.

Waltz, D.L., & Pollack, J.B. (1985). Massively parallel parsing: a strongly interactive model of natural language interpretation. *Cognitive Science, 9*(1), 51–74.

2
Connectionism and Compositional Semantics*

David S. Touretzky

1. INTRODUCTION

Natural language is an ideal source of problems for connectionism because the domain is so rich, yet for simple sentences processing takes place nearly instantaneously. Although natural language understanding obviously requires inference, interesting results have been obtained with connectionist models that do not perform what I call true dynamic inference. In the first half of this chapter I define a hierarchy of connectionist models, ranging from categorizers and associative memories through pattern transformers and dynamic inferencers. The second half of the chapter examines a particular natural language problem in detail: prepositional phrase attachment. I show that PP attachment is critically dependent on compositional semantics, and that this in turn depends upon dynamic inference. The search for a connectionist solution to the PP attachment problem must therefore begin with a satisfying account of dynamic inference.

2. A HIERARCHY OF MODELS

Connectionist models can be organized into a hierarchy of classes based on the complexity of the input/output pairs they use as training data. In increasing power, the classes are: categorizers, associative memories, pattern transformers,

* An earlier version of this chapter appeared as "Connectionism and PP Attachment" in D. Touretzky, G. Hinton, and T. Sejnowski (Eds.), *Proceedings of the 1988 Connectionist Models Summer School* published by Morgan Kaufmann. Can Tang implemented the interactive activation PP-attachment network. I am grateful to George Lakoff and Wendy Lenhert for their insights on the PP attachment problem, and to James McClelland, Jordan Pollack, and Paul Smolensky for helpful discussions on other matters. This work was supported by National Science Foundation grant EET-8716324, and by the Office of Naval Research under contract number N00014-86-K-0678.

and dynamic inferencers. Even the simplest class of models has interesting properties, such as parallel operation and use of distributed representations, which we may wish to incorporate into natural language models.

2.1. Categorizers

Categorizers place their input into one of a fixed, disjoint set of categories. They share the following properties:

- The number of output patterns is fixed, and small relative to the number of possible inputs. There is a unique output pattern for each of the *n* categories that must be recognized.
- There are many examples of each category, so each output pattern is encountered many times in the training set.
- The training set densely samples the space of possible inputs. No portion of the space can be safely neglected when a categorization task is nontrivial.

The simplest output representation for a neural network categorizer is a set of *n*-bit vectors with exactly one bit on in each. In competitive learning models with a winner-take-all layer, this output format is intrinsic to the architecture, but in other models it is merely an option. More complex output patterns can easily be derived from a competitive model by adding another layer of output units. Each of the winner-take-all units can then produce an arbitrary fixed output pattern by means of appropriate weighted connections to the new output layer. An example is Hecht-Nielsen's counterpropagation architecture (Hecht-Nielsen, 1987).

Several natural language problems have been posed as categorization tasks. The NETtalk grapheme-to-phoneme system (Sejnowski & Rosenberg, 1987), billed as "a model that learns to read aloud," pronounces text by sequentially processing it in seven-letter chunks. The pronunciation of the middle letter in each chuck is determined by categorizing the entire pattern into one of 55 phoneme classes. Each class has an associated output pattern, 26 bits long, that codes for phonetic features such as voicing and place of articulation. Although NETtalk appears to be addressing two highly complex language tasks, reading and speech production, it is really just learning to solve 26 binary categorization problems in parallel. (Note that the 26 problems are not solved independently because the output units share the same hidden layer.)

Whether a network is a categorizer or a pattern transformer is determined by its input/output behavior, not its architecture. Back propagation (Rumelhart, Hinton, & Williams, 1986) can produce either categorizers or pattern transformers. A network can be taught to simulate the behavior of a simpler class, for example, a pattern transformer can simulate a categorizer, but many architectures are incapable of implementing the more complex classes. Classic perceptrons, for instance, can only be categorizers. Also, models that employ a competitive winner-take-all layer, such as ART (Grossberg, 1987), the Nestor learning algorithm (Reilly, Cooper, & Erlbaum, 1982), and counterpropagation with a single winner (Hecht-Nielsen, 1987), are necessarily limited to categorization.

2.2. Associative Memories

Associative memory models such as Willshaw (1981), and recurrent associative networks such as Hopfield nets (Hopfield, 1982) are really just a special class of categorizers. Consider a hetero-associator that maps input patterns I_j to output patterns O_j. Each stored pair $\langle I_j, O_j \rangle$ forms a class. Given an input I^* that is close to some I_j, the associator produces the corresponding O_j. The output pattern O_j thus serves as a *name* for the class of inputs that are sufficiently close to I_j that they can evoke O_j.

In an auto-associator the i/o pairs are of form $\langle I_j, I_j \rangle$. When the model corrects and completes a partial pattern I^* by settling to the nearest I_j, it is classifying the pattern I^* as belonging to the category I_j.

Associative memories differ from categorizers in the constraints they place on the categories that can be learned. A Hopfield net (Hopfield, 1982) treats inputs that are close in Hamming space[1] as instances of the same class; if a few bits are missing in an input pattern they can easily be filled in by auto-association. Categorizers built by back propagation are not constrained to treat nearby points as similar. They can use their hidden layers to learn difficult discriminations, such as parity, where the output is critically dependent on the value of every single input bit, and points close in Hamming space often do not fall in the same class.

On the other hand, back propagation nets are not as well suited as Hopfield nets to reconstructing stored patterns from a partly corrupted version. In the Hopfield net the stored patterns are energy minima: the net will settle into one of these minima (generally the closest one) from any starting point. So a Hopfield net is predisposed to reproduce exactly the patterns it was trained on. (This is not an absolute constraint; Hopfield nets do exhibit false memories.) In contrast, when a backprop net trained on some input/output pairs is given a partially corrupted input it is most likely to produce a corrupted output, unless it has been explicitly shown how to correct corrupted patterns.

2.3. Pattern Transformers

Pattern transformation tasks are more computationally demanding than categorization. They have the following characteristics:

---

[1] The Hamming distance between two bit patterns is the number of bits of one pattern that do not match the corresponding bits of the other.

- The number of output patterns grows exponentially with the size of the input. It is not fixed as in categorization.
- Only a few of the output patterns the network must produce will be familiar. Most will never have been encountered in the training set.

The ability to produce correct outputs for novel inputs is known as *generalization*. In order for the transformation task to be learnable, the function f that maps inputs to outputs must be inducible (with high probability) from the training data. See Valiant (1984) for a discussion of the conditions under which this is feasible.

Pattern transformation in neural nets is easiest when similar inputs should produce similar outputs. That is, given a novel input I^* that is close to some training exemplar I_j, the network should be required to produce an $O^* = f(I^*)$ that is close to $O_j = f(I_j)$.

One of the classic uses of pattern transformation in connectionist natural language processing is the Rumelhart and McClelland (1986) verb learning model, which transforms the phonetic representation of the root form of an English verb into a phonetic representation of the past tense. The model learns to produce correct regular past tense forms of novel verbs, and can also handle special cases such as "eat/ate" or "sing/sang." The use of a distributed, coarse coded representation for the input and output phonetic sequences helped make the correct transformation function for regular cases easy to induce from the training set.

Perhaps the most interesting application of pattern transformation to natural language is the McClelland and Kawamoto (1986) case role assignment model. In this model the input pattern is a representation of the surface form of a sentence, and the output pattern is a set of fillers for four case roles. Words are represented as vectors of semantic features. The mapping of a surface element is highly dependent on meaning and context. For example, a surface subject can fill either the Agent role (as in "the boy broke the window"), the Patient role ("the window broke"), or the Instrument role ("the hammer broke the window"). The fourth role is called Modifier; an example is the noun "sauce" in "the pasta with sauce."

For novel sentences that are similar to the training sentences (e.g., train on "the girl hit the boy," test on "the boy hit the girl"), the McClelland and Kawamoto model correctly infers the case roles of the various constituents using a combination of semantic feature and word order information. It also performs lexical disambiguation, for example, by mapping the pattern for "bat" to either "baseball bat" or "flying bat" depending on context. A finer sort of discrimination is evident in its handling of "chicken," which may be mapped to either "cooked chicken" or "live chicken" depending on the case role it fills. Finally, the model makes some interesting generalizations by inventing new output patterns. Its training set includes sentences involving balls, which have the semantic feature *soft*, and sentences about breaking things, where the instrument (such as a hammer) is always hard. When the model is presented with "the ball broke the window" it outputs a novel feature vector for "ball" with the semantic feature *hard*.

The problem with pattern transformers is that they require an unreasonable amount of training data in order to generalize correctly. When the transformation function to be induced involves very high-order predicates [in the (Minsky & Papert, 1969) *Perceptrons* sense], so that inputs nearby in Hamming space do not necessarily result in nearby outputs, the training set must include almost every possible input/output pair. Two examples are Allen's models of anaphora resolution and sentence translation (Allen, 1987). These models were both constructed by training a back propagation network on virtually the entire input space. The language translation model, for example, was trained on 99 percent of a set of 3300 English/Spanish sentence pairs generated by a simple context-free grammar. It then showed good (but not perfect) generalization on the remaining 33 sentences.

2.4. Dynamic Inferencers

A scheme that requires training on a substantial portion of all possible inputs can neither explain human linguistic performance nor produce a practical natural language understanding automaton. Training set size is exponential in the length of the input, and it becomes unmanageable extremely quickly.

The way I propose to get around this problem is by abandoning the idea of mapping the surface level representation of a sentence to its meaning in a single parallel step. Instead we need to exploit the compositionality of language: the property that the meanings of complex inputs are composed from the meanings of simpler ones (Fodor & Pylyshyn, 1988). We can exploit this property by building a model that combines portions of its input to produce novel meaning structures as intermediate internal states; these then undergo further processing as they combine with more inputs. We avoid the need to train the model on a sizable fraction of all possible inputs by introducing specialized cognitive primitives that allow it to correctly combine intermediate states never previously encountered.

The nature of these primitives remains a central question of cognitive science. Two candidates are variable binding and pointer following (what Newell [1980] calls distal access). The latter refers to the ability to use a symbol (a compact mental object) to refer to some concept which, in its full detail, is not compact. Given a symbol we must have some way of accessing its meaning, but also, given a concept that is to be composed with others, we must have some way of generating a symbol that points to it. These symbols are meaningful in their own right, so that they can function as "reduced descriptions" (Hinton, 1988).

If this is beginning to look suspiciously like ordinary symbol processing, it may not be such a bad thing. The compositionality issue *has* to be addressed; it will not go away. But this does not mean that connectionist networks are reduced to implementing Lisp-like symbol manipulation primitives. Connectionism still has many distinctive properties that may be important for building natural language understanders. Learning algorithms that develop distributed representations and generalize, flexible matching by parallel constraint satisfaction, and efficient parallel search are some of the things that differentiate connectionist models from ordinary Lisp code.

Formally, dynamic inferencers have the following properties:

- Input patterns are sequences of tokens from some vocabulary V. The number of input patterns is exponential in the length L of the input, i.e., it is $O(V^L)$.
- Training set size is at most polynomial in V.
- The computational process dynamically brings together two or more pieces of information which have not been seen together before in order to derive new information. The model therefore exhibits novel intermediate states in response to novel inputs.

Notice that nothing was said above about the output patterns of a dynamic inferencer. They do not matter: it is the intermediate states that are important. Consider a network with an internal model of a static blocks world scene. Its only task is to output "yes" or "no" in response to sentences such as "Is the blue block in front of the red pyramid a large block." This is just a binary categorization task: sentences are placed either in class "yes" or class "no." But to assure a subexponential training set the problem must be implemented as a dynamic inference task. This allows the *meaning* of the query to be derived on the fly by composing the meanings of its components, producing successively more complex internal states. To summarize:

- Dynamic inferencers can produce an exponential number of internal states, corresponding to their exponential number of possible input patterns.
- The internal states produced for complex inputs are systematically related to those for simpler inputs (compositionality property).
- This systematicity is reflected in the structure of the network, through specialized primitives for things like variable binding and distal access. The actual set of primitives required remains an open question.

There are no connectionist dynamic inferencers yet. However, Touretzky and Hinton's distributed connectionist production system comes close (Touretzky & Hinton, 1988). It has an exponential number of working memory states, it dynamically retrieves elements from working memory and uses their components to construct new states, and it requires no training at all. But its version of compositionality is weak; working memory elements cannot be combined into more complex elements.

Derthick's μKLONE system (Derthick, 1988; see also Chapter 9, this volume) is another close approximation to a dynamic inferencer. It dynamically combines information from its knowledge base with information supplied in a query. This combination is a complex process since parts of the query may conflict with previously stored facts; the network must find a plausible interpretation that violates as few constraints as possible. μKLONE extensively exploits structuring of knowledge: concepts have semantic features and are organized into a hierarchy; concepts have roles whose fillers are other concepts; roles also have semantic features and are organized into a role hierarchy; and the choice of fillers of a role is governed by value restrictions. However, μKLONE answers queries in a single parallel annealing; its internal states do not get composed to produce more complex states.

Barnden's Conposit system (Chapter 8) has a strong version of compositionality, and produces rule-based inferences. But it does not perform parallel constraint satisfaction or approximate matching. It is essentially a classical symbolic representation system with a massively parallel connectionist implementation. Fahlman's NETL system (Fahlman, 1979) is another example of this style of computation.

3. THE PREPOSITIONAL PHRASE ATTACHMENT PROBLEM

To reiterate, the two main points of this chapter are, first, that valuable experiments in natural language understanding can be done with connectionist models that are computationally weak. These models are toys, but are interesting nonetheless because they operate in parallel, are constructed automatically by learning algorithms instead of crafted by hand, generalize successfully to novel inputs, and use distributed representations. But the second point is that implementing a real natural language understander requires more than this. It requires dynamic inference.

To illustrate both points I will discuss in detail a restricted version of an important natural language problem: determining where to attach a prepositional phrase when there are several nouns available. The version of the problem considered here is syntactically trivial but semantically rich. Inputs consist of a head noun phrase NP_0 followed by some number of prepositional phrases PP_i, each of which contains a noun phrase NP_i. Noun phrases consist of a definite article "the" followed by a singular concrete common noun; lexical ambiguity is excluded. A typical example is (1):

(1) the car in the junkyard with the dog

Here NP_0 is "the car" and there are two PPs that need to be attached to NPs.

3.1. Syntactic Constraints on Attachment

An inviolable constraint on English is that PPs may only attach to NPs that precede them, that is, the arrows showing attachment may run to the left but not to the right. Obviously then, in (1) PP_1 can only attach to NP_0. But PP_2 ("with the dog") can attach to either NP_0 or NP_1. A second, weaker constraint on attachment is that in the absence of other influences, PPs prefer to attach to the *nearest* NP to their left. So the preferred attachment for (1) is (2a), but (2b) is also legal, and might be preferred in some contexts.

(2a) the car in the junkyard with the dog

(2b) the car in the junkyard with the dog

Since the first PP of (2a) attaches to NP_0 and the second PP attaches to NP_1, we call (2a) a 0–1 attachment structure: (2b) is a 0–0 attachment structure. We can shift the attachment of "the dog" from "the junkyard" to "the car" by adding a third PP, as in (3):

(3) the car in the junkyard with the dog on the hood

The only reasonable place to attach "on the hood" is "the dog." Since "on the hood" makes an implicit part-of reference to the car, attaching it to the dog ties the dog more strongly to the car than to the junkyard, overriding the nearest-left-neighbor attachment preference.

The most important syntactic constraint on PP attachment is the no-crossing rule, which prohibits lines of attachment from crossing as in (4).

(4) the man with the dog in the picture on the leash

The no-crossing rule is a strong constraint, but it can sometimes be overridden by semantic considerations, as in this example from Wendy Lehnert (personal communication):

(5) John saw the girl with the telescope in a red dress.

(See also Chapter 6 this volume.) Attaching "the dress" to "the girl" prevents "the telescope" from attaching to the verb "saw." People are therefore forced either to attach the telescope to the girl (reluctantly, since it fits much better with "saw"), or else violate the no-crossing constraint in order to pair "girl" with "dress" and "saw" with "telescope." In the latter case they characterize the sentence as poorly worded, indicating that they are aware some grammatical constraint is not being obeyed.

A third possibility would be to attach "in a red dress" to John, but this is ruled out for cultural reasons. (Speakers prefer to violate the no-crossing constraint rather than the "no cross-dressing" constraint.)

3.2. PP Attachment as a Competitive Phenomenon

The competitive nature of the attachment problem can be captured in a simple connectionist network as shown in Figure 2.1. The ith column of units represents the alternatives for attaching PP_i to any of the i preceding NPs. In the figure, the presence of a PP in position i feeds an excitatory stimulus to all the units in column i via the vertical line with associated branches. Inhibitory connections between a column's units form a winner-take-all network that enforces the constraint that the PP may attach to only one NP. The no-crossing rule is implemented by inhibitory connections between units in different columns. A slightly lower threshold (indicated by the double line) for the topmost unit in each column produces a weak nearest-left-neighbor attachment preference. Semantic constraints supplied by other modules provide external input, either excitatory or inhibitory, as shown in the bottom-right corner of the figure.

A version of this network has been simulated as an interaction activation model using equations borrowed from McClelland's Jets and Sharks model (McClelland, 1981). The network prefers simple left attachment structures such as 0–1–2, but will choose other structures if semantics warrant it. With a strong enough semantic influence it can be made to violate the no-crossing rule.

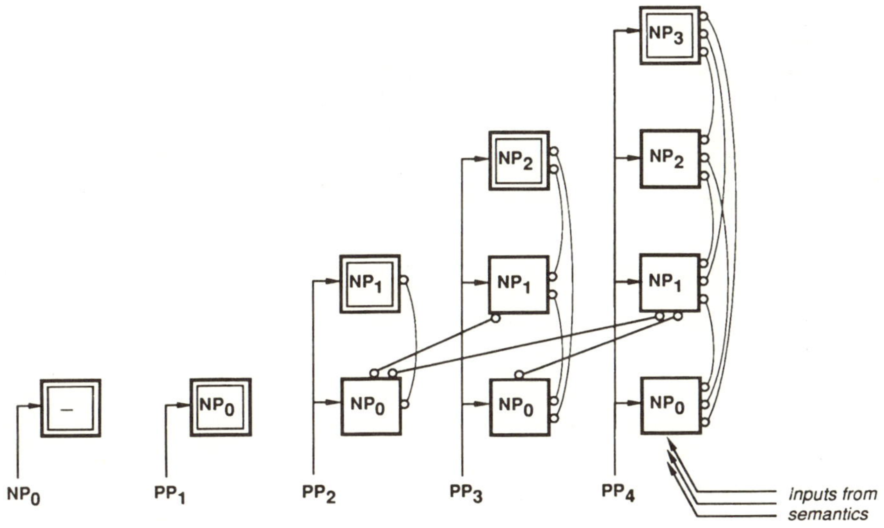

Figure 2.1.
A connectionist network whose stable states correspond to legal PP attachments.

4. THE SEMANTICS OF ATTACHMENT

The competitive attachment network handles syntactic constraints, but it says nothing about how semantic constraints are to be derived. Getting the semantics right, even for this very limited form of the attachment problem, is difficult.

4.1. Naive Associationism

Perhaps the simplest approach to attachment semantics is to rely on an abstract "strength of association" between pairs of NPs. Consider these examples:

(6a) the car with the dog in the cage

(6b) the car with the dog in the garage

The preferred attachment structure for (6a) is 0–1; for sentence (6b) it is 0–0. A black box that predicts the strengths of association between pairs of NPs can solve this attachment problem, as shown in Figure 2.2. The black box can be created by back propagation learning. If concepts are represented as feature vectors, then presumably the black box could generalize from a sufficiently large

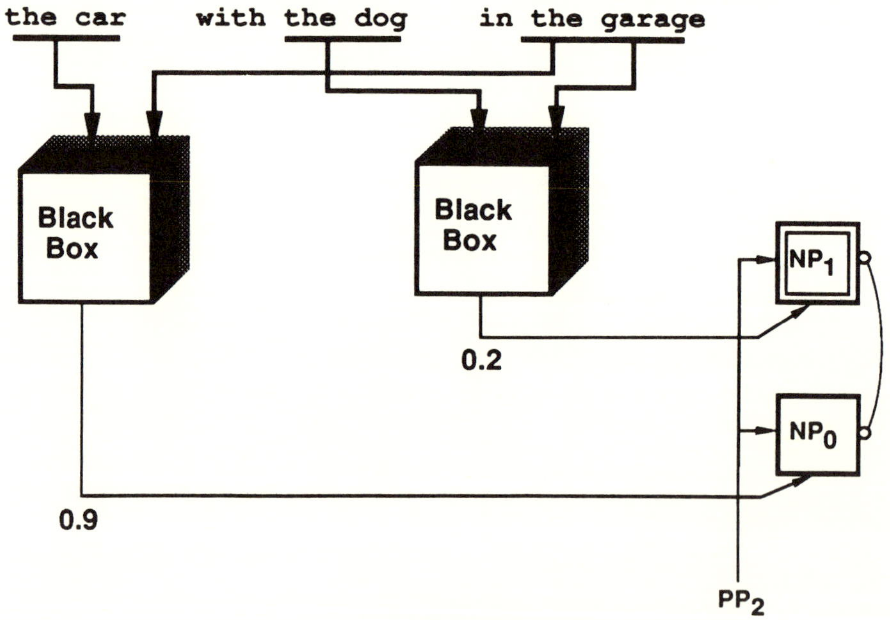

Figure 2.2.
Solving attachment with a black box associator.

training set to handle slightly novel examples, for example, if it learns that "dog" associates with "garage" with a strength of 0.2, it might predict a similar value for "cat."

4.2. Noncompositional Semantics

The reason this associationist approach is deemed naive is that it completely ignores the semantics of the relationship being expressed between the two NPs. Naive associationism therefore gets the following attachment problem wrong:

(7) the car with the dog on the hood

Hoods associate far more strongly with cars than with dogs, but it's not the car that's on the hood in (7). One way to fix this is to train the black box on NP–PP pairs rather than NP–NP pairs. This requires a training set several times larger than before, since each preposition must be treated separately. The output of the black box will now be a measure of plausibility or acceptability, for example, "car on hood" would be rated very low because it violates physical constraints, while "dog on hood" would receive a moderate rating because it is an acceptable physical state, although not a common one.

The black boxes are pattern transformers: they map NP–PP pairs into the unit interval. The competitive attachment net is even simpler; it has a small, fixed number of output states, and is basically doing categorization.

Lehnert is pursuing a variant of the black box approach in the CIRCUS system. She trains a separate black box plausibility estimator for each distinct prepositional sense. This frees the networks from having to determine the intended sense based on the two NPs, and should lead to better generalization behavior as a result.

4.3. Towards a Compositional Semantics

I call the black box approach that takes prepositions into account "noncompositional semantics," because it still ignores the fact that attaching a PP to an NP can change the meaning of the NP. This can in turn affect other attachments. In (3) for example, attaching "on the hood" to "the dog" gives the dog an implicit part-of reference to the car; this causes "with the dog on the hood" to attach to car rather than junkyard. Recognizing the part-of reference in "on the hood" is not enough; the network must transfer that property to "the dog" as a result of the attachment.

A more striking example of the effects of compositionality is (8). We can easily put the dog on the hood or in the car; a black box will happily accept either NP–PP pair in isolation. But the dog cannot be in both places at once because in order to be on the car's hood he must be outside it. As soon as we actually put the dog on the hood, he can no longer go in the car.

(8) the dog on the hood in the car

In the competitive attachment net, the result of attaching "on the hood" to the dog is represented by activity in a single unit, the PP_1-to-NP_0 unit. To achieve compositionality, the attachment must result in something much more complex: the network must somehow *envision* the dog as being on the hood, and thereby in a certain physical relationship to the car, so that when it tries to put dog-on-hood inside the car it detects a spatial violation. This is the essence of compositionality: the dog composed with "on the hood" becomes a different object, with different properties from those of the dog in isolation.

A network with compositional semantics would require expertise in a variety of semantic primitives, such as spatial relations, part-of relations, and accompaniment, in order to know how to compose the meaning of a complex NP from the meanings of simpler NP and PP components. I am not aware of any existing connectionist architecture (other than Nature's own) that can solve this problem.

4.4. Further Observations on Attachment

Long PP chains often correspond to spatial paths that start with a local context and move to a global one. For example, in (9) the reader can picture a path from the book outward to the street.

(9) the book on the shelf in the den in the house at the end of the street

The longer a string of PPs, the greater the pressure to view it as a path of some sort, which implies a simple nearest-left-neighbor attachment structure. Due to limited cognitive capacity, people are unable to handle more complex structures when the PP chains are long, just as they are unable to handle deeply center-embedded sentences. One exception to the nearest-left-neighbor convention for paths is that the last PP can optionally attach to the head NP if it describes the head rather than participates in the path. An example is (10a), which has a 0-1-2-3-4-0 attachment structure. Normally, however, one prefers (10b), whose structure is 0-0-2-3-4-5.

(10a) the book on the shelf in the den in the house at the end of the street on cockatoos

(10b) the book on cockatoos on the shelf in the den in the house at the end of the street

5. RELAXING THE EXCLUSIVITY CONSTRAINT

Up to now we have assumed that each PP attaches to exactly one of the NPs to its left. When sentences are drawn as parse trees this is a strict requirement; otherwise the result would not be a tree. But parse trees are syntactic descriptions; attachment is a semantic phenomenon. Example (3) suggests strongly that attachment relationships between NPs are more complex than syntax acknowledges. To derive the meaning of (3), the hood must participate in two relationships. The PP "on the hood" is attached to the dog, but "hood" must also attach to "car" (by an inferred part-of relation) in order to understand it as a reference to the car, indicating that the dog is on the car. Likewise, the attachment of "in the junkyard" is not exclusive. Besides describing the car, it has an implicit secondary attachment to the dog, since the dog is where the car is.

One of the important contributions connectionism can make to natural language understanding is to encourage fuzzier but richer representations. A connectionist network that could simultaneously represent all the attachment relations in a phrase, both primary and secondary, would be expressing much more of the meaning of the sentence than an exclusive attachment diagram like (3) permits. Rich, fuzzy representations are harder to program, but they are manageable if the programming is done by learning algorithms instead of human experimenters.

6. DISCUSSION

There are several approaches one might take toward solving PP attachment with a more sophisticated network than a pattern transformer. One way would be to use recurrent networks to build up representations for sentences one word at a time. This idea has been pursued by St. John and McClelland (1988) for a much simpler sentence processing task, and also by Allen (1988). But attachment decisions often depend on later words, so the network would have to maintain a representation of the ambiguities in a sentence until it had seen enough of the input to settle on the correct attachment structure. Also, recurrent nets are still very simple architectures. They require huge amounts of training data to learn to recognize and exploit regularity, since they must build all their representational machinery from scratch using iterated pattern transformations. A true dynamic inferencer would start out with primitives like variable binding and distal access already in place; it would not have to construct them via extensive training.

Another approach to attachment might be to build a framelike connectionist representation for concepts, as in DUCS (Touretzky & Geva, 1987). Attachments would be handled as slot fillers. For example, "dog on hood" would be represented by frames for dog and hood; the dog frame would have a slot containing a pointer to hood, and the slot name would include semantic features like "physical contact" and "supports from below." (In DUCS slot names are not discrete symbols; they are feature vectors.) One could build black boxes for reasoning about various primitive semantic relationships between frames, such as spatial, part-of, and support relations. These black boxes would indicate the effects of particular attachments by computing feature vectors for the slots to be added to each frame. We could then develop a competitive architecture for choosing the best attachment based on plausibility ratings. The result of making an attachment would be a modified frame which goes on to participate in further attachments, just as in a conventional symbol processing solution. The drawback to this approach is that we do not want to have to separately enumerate all possible attachments, rank-order them, choose the best, and iterate; it leads to the combinatorial problems that plague conventional symbol processors.

In conclusion, I want to affirm that natural language understanding does require something like symbol processing. Connectionism makes strong, interesting suggestions about the nature of these symbols and the mechanisms that manipulate them. It offers flexible matching via parallel constraint satisfaction; fast associative retrieval; and learning algorithms that construct distributed representations and generalize to novel cases. These models also perform *compositional search,* that is, rather than representing alternative items as separate, discrete entities (combinatorially explosive), they exist simultaneously, with overlapping representations, and they interact competitively. An example is the way rule matching and variable binding behavior emerges from simulated annealing in DCPS (Touretzky & Hinton, 1988).

We should not be discouraged by the limited ability of weak connectionist models like categorizers and pattern transformers to handle symbol processing tasks. Nor should we abandon connectionist representations and retreat to Lisp code. Let us continue to explore the new tools connectionism has to offer, while acknowledging that ultimately dynamic inferencers, not simply pattern transformers, will be required to solve natural language.

REFERENCES

Allen, R.B. (1987). Several studies on natural language and back-propagation. *Proceedings of the IEEE First Annual International Conference on Neural Networks, II,* 287–298.

Allen, R.B. (1988). Sequential connectionist networks for answering simple questions about a microworld. *Proceedings of the Tenth Annual Conference of the Cognitive Science Society,* pp. 489–495.

Derthick, M.A. (1988). *Mundane reasoning by parallel constraint satisfaction.* Doctoral dissertation available as Tech. Rep. number CMU-CS-88-182, Carnegie Mellon School of Computer Science, Pittsburgh, PA.

Fahlman, S.E. (1979). *NETL: A system for representing and using real-world knowledge.* Cambridge, MA: MIT Press.

Fodor, J., & Pylyshyn, Z. (1988). Connectionism and cognitive architecture. *Cognition, 28,* 3–71.

Grossberg, S. (1987). Competitive learning: from interactive activation to adaptive resonance. *Cognitive Science, 11*(1), 23–63.

Hecht-Nielsen, R. (1987). Counter-propagation networks. *Applied Optics, 26*(23), 4979–4984.

Hinton, G.E. (1988). Representing part-whole hierarchies in connectionist networks. *Proceedings of the Tenth Annual Conference of the Cognitive Science Society,* pp. 48–54. Hillsdale, NJ: Erlbaum.

Hopfield, J.J. (1982). Neural networks and physical systems with emergent collective computational abilities. *Proceedings of the National Academy of Sciences USA, 79,* 2554–2558.

McClelland, J.L. (1981). Retrieving general and specific information from stored knowledge of specifics. *Proceedings of the Third Annual Conference of the Cognitive Science Society,* pp. 170–172.

McClelland, J.L., & Kawamoto, A.H. (1986). Mechanisms of sentence processing: Assigning roles to constituents. In J.L. McClelland & D.E. Rumelhart (Eds.), *Parallel distributed processing: Explorations in the microstructure of cognition* (Vol. 2). Cambridge, MA: MIT Press.

Minsky, M., & Papert, S. (1969). *Perceptrons.* Cambridge, MA: MIT Press.

Newell, A. (1980). Physical symbol systems. *Cognitive Science, 4,* 135–183.

Reilly, D.L., Cooper, L.N., & Elbaum, C. (1982). A neural model for category learning. *Biological Cybernetics, 45,* 35–41.

Rumelhart, D.E., Hinton, G.E., & Williams, R.J. (1986). *Learning internal representations by error propagation in parallel distributed processing.* Cambridge, MA: MIT Press.

Rumelhart, D.E., & McClelland, J.L. (1986). On learning the past tenses of English verbs. In J.L. McClelland & D.E. Rumelhart (Eds.), *Parallel distributed processing: Explorations in the microstructure of cognition* (Vol. 2). Cambridge, MA: MIT Press.

St. John, M.F., & McClelland, J.L. (1988). Applying contextual constraints in sentence comprehension. *Proceedings of the Tenth Annual Conference of the Cognitive Science Society,* pp. 26–32. Hillsdale, NJ: Erlbaum.

Sejnowski, T.J., & Rosenberg, C.R. (1987). Parallel networks that learn to pronounce English text. *Complex Systems, 1*(1), 145–168.

Touretzky, D.S., & Geva, S. (1987). A distributed connectionist representation for concept structures. *Proceedings of the Ninth Annual Conference of the Cognitive Science Society,* pp. 155–164.

Touretzky, D.S., & Hinton, G.E. (1988). A distributed connectionist production system. *Cognitive Science, 12*(3), 423–466.

Valiant, L.G. (1984). A theory of the learnable. *Communications of the ACM, 27,* 1134–1142.

Willshaw, D. (1981). Holography, associative memory, and inductive generalization. In G.E. Hinton & J.A. Anderson (Eds.), *Parallel models of associative memory.* Hillsdale, NJ: Erlbaum.

3
Symbolic NeuroEngineering for Natural Language Processing: A Multilevel Research Approach*

Michael G. Dyer

1. BACKGROUND AND MOTIVATION

In the last two decades, the natural language processing (NLP) systems built by artificial intelligence (AI) researchers have been designed under the *Physical Symbol Systems Hypothesis (PSSH)* (Newell, 1980). Under the PSSH, knowledge is assumed to be represented in terms of relationships among symbols, and processes of comprehension, generation, application, retrieval, planning, reasoning, and learning are modeled in terms of the creation and manipulation of symbolic structures (Dyer, 1989). Research by computational linguists has also followed the PSSH, with syntactic knowledge represented as symbolic structures and parsing as various transformations over them. While computational linguists and AI/NLP researchers have often held heated debates over paradigmatic assumptions, such as the role of syntax and universal grammar with respect to a theory of semantics and language acquisition (for example, see Dresher & Hornstein, 1976; Schank & Wilensky, 1977), the shared assumptions of the PSSH have not been seriously challenged by either group.

---

* This research reported here was supported in part by grants from the JTF Program of the DoD (monitored by JPL), the ITA Foundation, ONR, the Keck Foundation and the Hughes Artificial Intelligence Center. Hardware grants in support of this research were supplied by Apollo Computer, Hewlett-Packard, the Keck Foundation, and the NSF. The computer programs described herein were implemented by my graduate students: Sergio Alvarado (now at UC Davis), Charlie Dolan, Michael Gasser (now at Indiana University), Trent Lange, Risto Miikkulainen, Michael Pazzani (now at UC Irvine), Ron Sumida, Alan Wang, and Uri Zernik (now at GE Labs). Helpful suggestions on this paper's content and organization were made by Margot Flowers.

Recently, however, what appears to be a radically new hypothesis for knowledge representation and processing has emerged. Research programs inspired by this new hypothesis vary considerably, which is to be expected, given the early stage of development. These research programs go by many names, including: *Neural Information Processing (NIPS)*, *Parallel Distributed Processing (PDP)* (Rumelhart & McClelland, 1986; Touretzky & Hinton, 1985), *Connectionism (CM)* (Feldman & Ballard, 1982) (Feldman, 1986), *Artificial Neural Systems (ANS)* (Grossberg, 1982, 1988), *Neurocomputing* (Anderson & Rosenfeld, 1988) and *Subsymbolic Processing* (Smolensky, 1988). Here, I will use the term *Subsymbolic Processing Hypothesis (SSPH)* to refer to these related research paradigms in their broadest sense. Below I attempt to enumerate some of the major differences between the PSSH and the SSPH, at times perhaps exaggerating their contrasts, but if so, only to highlight the relevant issues.[1] These contrasts are summarized in Table 3.1.

1.1. Physical Symbol System Hypothesis vs. *Subsymbolic Processing Hypothesis*

(1) *Inspiration and constraints.* Research based on the PSSH is inspired both by introspection and observed problem-solving behavior within a given task/domain. Constraints on symbolic models come mainly from logical and functional constraints of the task/domain. This point of view has allowed AI/NLP researchers to "cut the mind loose from the brain," largely ignoring brain organization and neural mechanisms.

SSPH models are inspired by, and get their major constraints from, brain architectures and neural mechanisms. The approach tends to be more bottom up, with researchers building models whose primitive processing units conform to various aspects of neural behavior. The resulting architectures are then explored to discover what they are capable of computing.

(2) *Data and processing.* In PSSH models, data structures are kept separate from processing structures and processing is realized by one or more interpreters operating over program instructions. Knowledge is explicitly represented in terms of relationships between symbols. Memory is viewed as static and operated on by processes, which are dynamic.

In SSPH models, there is no separation between data structures and interpreters. Long-term knowledge is represented in terms of weighted links between primitive processing units while short-term knowledge is encoded as transient

---

[1] Ultimate computing power is normally not a major issue at the paradigmatic level, since nearly all subsymbolic models are simulated on symbolic architectures. Also, neural networks could be wired up to simulate Turing machines. Therefore, major issues have to do with perspective, that is, which paradigm is most natural for understanding and modeling cognitive function?

Table 3.1.
Symbolic vs Subsymbolic Hypotheses.

PSSH (Symbolic)	SSPH (Subsymbolic)
Constraints are functional/logical	Constraints are brain/neural
Knowledge is distinct/localized	Knowledge is shared/distributed
Distinct tokens and types	Tokens equal types
Memory is static/structured	Memory is dynamic/reconstructive
Storage capacity unlimited	Fixed storage capacity
Separate data and processing	Data and processing merged
Rules are declarative	Rules emerge statistically
Parallelism is peripheral	Parallelism is central
Basic categories supplied	Basic categories emerge statistically
Models fragile to noise/damage	Models are robust/lesionable
Models are programmed	Models are trained or reinforced
Learning by proof and induction	Learning by incremental adaptation

patterns of activation over these processing units. Memory is viewed as fundamentally dynamic.

(3) *Hardware storage and memory management.* In PSSH models, symbols take up distinct locations in hardware memory. Symbols have no special internal structure (i.e., there is an arbitrary encoding, such as ASCII). Memory registers that are used to represent one piece of information are not allowed to represent some other information at the same time. Instances (i.e., tokens) are created by instantiating general templates (i.e., types) and are kept distinct from one another. Multiple tokens and types coexist without interference. There is unlimited free storage, supplied by a virtual memory management system.

In SSPH models, information is distributed throughout a network. Hardware connections are shared, that is, used to represent or contribute to multiple pieces of information at the same time. Knowledge is often stored in terms of microfeatures, which allows the internal structure of symbol-like objects to be directly compared to one another. There is no type/token distinction and as a result of hardware sharing, multiple instances interfere with one another. Storage is limited; all information must reside in a fixed set of connections.

(4) *Representation and interpretation.* Knowledge in PSSH models is represented in terms of predicates and the relationships among them. Inferences are represented in terms of rules which contain mappings between relationships. What is important is to capture functional and logical constraints of the task/domain in terms of inferences among associated symbols and their relationships.

Knowledge in SSPH models is represented in terms of energy landscapes, formed through a statistical analysis of the data. Rule-like behavior is an emergent property of the models, without the existence of explicit rules or rule interpreters. Inference is performed by associative retrieval and/or pattern com-

pletion, via reconstruction of patterns through basins of attraction in the energy landscape.

(5) *Categorization and learning.* The basic categories and relationships in PSSH models are not learned, but are supplied by the programmer or knowledge engineer. Any learning that does occur arises through induction over preexisting symbols and relationships. The result of learning involves: (a) the construction of new instances of existing knowledge structures, (b) the combination of existing structures into novel configurations, and/or (c) the acquisition of new rules to manipulate these structures.

Learning occurs as the result of a stochastic analysis of the data. Rather than learning new rules, SSPH-based models learn through repeated interaction with exemplars. The models cannot be programmed directly via instructions, but rather learn through adaptive modification of weighted links between simple processing elements. Instead of being supplied with symbolic categories, the models form category discriminations automatically, based on feedback, either from a trainer or the internal/external environment.

(6) *Psychological and neurological plausibility.* Since functional constraints are considered most critical, PSSH models do not make a commitment to a particular hardware architecture. All that matters at the architectural level is that fundamental symbolic operations be supplied for traversal, construction, binding, and testing of symbolic structures. Parallelism is considered more an efficiency issue than a theoretical issue.

SSPH models are designed to capture constraints at the neural level. As a result, such models are lesionable and may be compared more directly to biological information processing systems. Massive parallelism is viewed as central, since the distributed nature of the representations requires it.

(7) *Logic and adaptation.* In PSSH models, logic is viewed as both a means for representing knowledge and as a method for analyzing systems. Variables are of central importance and a major function is pattern matching and variable binding (e.g., unification). Knowledge is acquired (or applied) by generating proof chains, with constraints propagated along the chains via variable bindings. With recursive rules and variables, the models have infinite generative capacity.

In SSPH models, associative retrieval and parallel constraint satisfaction are considered basic operations. Variables are not currently available in these models. With a fixed memory, the models currently lack infinite generative capacity.

1.2. PSSH and SSPH Models Currently Inhabit Distinct Processing Niches

If either paradigm were superior along all or most processing dimensions, then one could be easily chosen over the other, but this is not the case. In fact, at this point it appears that purely symbolic and purely subsymbolic (distributed) models inhabit two distinct "niches" in what might be termed abstract processing "ecology." That is, what subsymbolic/PDP models do well, purely symbolic systems do poorly, *and vice versa*. These two niches are summarized in Table 3.2.

In Table 3.2, the set of "+ −" pairs forms one niche, while the set of "− +" pairs forms the other. Here, each "+" represents support for the capability in the rightmost column, while each "−" represents lack of support. These capabilities are described below. The term "purely" is used here since there exist many ways to form hybrid systems, sharing features of both symbolic and subsymbolic. These hybrid approaches are discussed at length in later sections of this chapter.

1.2.1. Natural for the Subsymbolic and Awkward for the Purely Symbolic

1. *Knowledge interaction and integration*—Since all information in subsymbolic models is represented homogeneously, in terms of numerical strengths of activation and weights, it is easy to have many distinct sources of knowledge interact through simple numerical operations, such as summation, multiplication, maximization, and negation. In purely symbolic models,

Table 3.2.
Distinct Processing Niches.

Purely Symbolic	Purely Distributed Subsymbolic	Capability
−	+	knowledge integration
−	+	smooth variation
−	+	intermediate representations
−	+	reconstructive memory
−	+	self-organization
−	+	associative retrieval
−	+	robustness to noise & damage
−	+	associative inference
−	+	adaptive learning
+	−	variables & bindings
+	−	schemas & roles
+	−	constituent, recursive structure
+	−	infinite generative capacity
+	−	defaults & inheritance
+	−	instantiations (types/tokens)
+	−	reference/pointers
+	−	memory management
+	−	intratask communication
+	−	metareasoning
+	−	explanation-based learning
+	−	complex sequential control

specialized rules and procedures must be devised for one kind of knowledge source to communicate or influence another knowledge source.

2. *Smoothly varying knowledge commitment*—By varying the numeric value of a unit, the commitment to an interpretation can also vary in a smooth and continuous fashion. In purely symbolic systems, rules must either be deductive (given: p and p-implies->q, conclude q) or abductive (given: q and p-implies->q, conclude maybe p). In a subsymbolic system, unidirectional links can connect p to q and q to p, with varying weights. If the firing sequence is p followed by q and (a) the weight from p to q is large, then we have deduction, or (b) if the weight from q to p is large, then we have abduction. In addition, we can have all of the smoothly varying possibilities that lie in between these two extremes (Gasser, 1988).
3. *Intermediate representations*—In SSPH models, patterns of activation represent short-term knowledge. Since each activation value can smoothly vary, it allows the entire representation to enter intermediate states. For instance, if a room is represented as activation levels over units representing pieces of furniture and their properties, then a representation for a bedroom can emerge that contains a sofa, small fireplace, a refrigerator and a large dining table in it (Rumelhart & McClelland, 1986a).
4. *Reconstructive memory*—Memory is by definition reconstructive, since the patterns on output are transient behaviors of the long-term memory traces that have been laid down into the interconnection weights. Interference occurs naturally in such memories, since similar forms of knowledge share more interconnection values. Symbolic models that attempt to explain memory confusions do so by assuming that different knowledge structures can point to shared substructures. For instance, a doctor visit and a dentist visit would both point to a generalized office visit (Schank, 1982). Such models have been successful at explaining cross-contextual remindings, but the symbolic approach appears unable to adequately explain how pieces of one memory can get intermingled at a microstructure level with pieces of related memories.
5. *Self-organization*—Through autoassociation (i.e., mapping an input pattern to the same pattern on output) SSPH models can categorize an environment automatically. In contrast, knowledge engineers must supply symbolic models with the fundamental categories needed for forming representations. SSPH models thus have the capacity to form basic categories that were not anticipated by knowledge engineers.
6. *Associative retrieval*—To retrieve information, one need only "clamp" down one or more units on input and the network will settle into a configuration satisfying the largest number of constraints. It is easy to model influence of context in such a model simply by priming (increasing the initial activation of) a set of units before retrieval. Pattern completion results automatically in cases where a complete input pattern is not available. The

pattern that arises is the result of all exemplars that were learned by the system. In contrast, symbolic systems operate by explicitly indexing knowledge and then performing a search to select the most restricted piece of knowledge that best matches the input. As a result, in symbolic models it is difficult to (a) represent the varying influence of experience on decision making, and (b) handle the myriads of exceptions that always arise for any given rule.

7. *Robustness to noise and damage*—Since knowledge in subsymbolic models is distributed over a large number of processing units and weights, destruction of any random subset of units, or modification of a random set of weights, will have little effect on input/output behavior. In some models, noise actually improves function, since it serves to keep the model from retrieving local minima in the energy landscape. When noise or damage does alter I/O behavior, degradation is graceful, with the amount of degradation smoothly increasing as a function of the amount of damage. Since the representations are distributed, removal of processing units does not totally eliminate any specific piece of knowledge. In symbolic systems, the removal of a symbol causes permanent and localized damage to a specific piece of knowledge.
8. *Adaptive learning algorithms*—Most subsymbolic models learn through small, adaptive changes to their interconnection weights. Many learning algorithms operate by calculating an error between the desired and real output of the network. This error is locally computed and causes local adjustments of interconnection weights in parallel, throughout the network. Learning is similarity-based and consists of clustering and/or classifying data by some similarity metric within a very high-dimensional hyperspace. In general, any boolean mapping function can be acquired through learning. Since the learning is by incremental adaptation, it is common to require many weight modification cycles over the training set to arrive at the desired input/output behaviors.

1.2.2. Natural for the Symbolic and Awkward for the Purely Subsymbolic

1. *Variable bindings*—In symbolic models, variables are capable of binding to any type of structure and new symbols can be created dynamically during execution. In subsymbolic models, variables do not (yet) exist and their function can only be partially realized, for example, by specifying ahead of time in the architecture the number of available symbols and their potential range of bindings, for example, Touretzky (1986).
2. *Schemas and roles*—Schemas (frames/scripts) consist of a number of roles and their values, which can point to other schemas. Role bindings supply a

mechanism for propagating information. For instance, when a schema-processing system is told "John entered the restaurant" a restaurant schema (Schank & Abelson, 1977; Dyer, Cullingford, & Alvarado, 1987) is created with John bound to the diner role *throughout the schema*. Later, when the system is told "He showed him the menu." the system binds "him" to the diner role in a <waiter show menu to diner> event in the schema that matches the "show menu" description in the input. Since "him" is bound to the diner role and since the diner role is *already* bound to John throughout the schema, the system can automatically conclude that "him" refers to John. Since subsymbolic models lack variables and bindings, of course they cannot propagate them.

3. *Constituent and recursive structure*—Since symbol systems can keep instances separate and form bindings, it is easy to represent constituency and variable-depth recursive structures, such as "John told Bill that Fred told Mary that . . . ." In this case, each "told" structure can be kept separate, with the object of the inner "told" bound to a role in the structure of the outer "told." Constituency is essential to capture syntactic knowledge, such as the fact that, in passive transformations, the entire subject (noun phrase) becomes the object of "by." This noun phrase can be of variable length, thus causing problems for any PSSH model attempting to map active to passive by being trained on a fixed set of exemplars. Constituency and recursion is also essential in representing semantic information.
4. *Infinite generative capacity*—With variables, bindings and recursion, symbolic models possess infinite generative capacity (Chomsky, 1965). That is, with a finite set of rules, an infinite number of instances can be generated (or recognized). Most subsymbolic models work on a finite number of instances. Subsymbolic models are trained on a finite training set, with a subset of the exemplars reserved. The model's generalization capability is then tested by seeing how well it performs its mapping task on the untested subset. Normally, the percentage of elements in the subset is around 5–20 percent of the entire training set.
5. *Defaults and inheritance*—In symbolic models it is easy to set up "is-a" links from tokens to their types, and from types to supertypes, and so on, in order to form inheritance hierarchies. Information can then be inherited from the higher levels. Subsymbolic models perform inheritance only to the extent that one representation shares features with another. For example, if a person (e.g., John) is represented in terms of features (animate, human, male) and another person (e.g., Mary) is represented as (animate, human, female), then any pattern completion operations over the Mary representation (i.e., processing units with those features) will influence the John representation, simply because the features are shared. But since there is no one place where knowledge about humans *in general* is stored in these

subsymbolic models, it is not possible to add facts about humans in general and then automatically and immediately make this new knowledge available to all instances of humans, as is possible in symbolic models.

6. *Instantiations (types/tokens)*—In symbolic models, multiple instances of knowledge can be kept separate. Without symbols, variable and bindings, subsymbolic models suffer from "crosstalk" (Feldman, 1986), in which additions of the patterns (John loves Mary) and (Fred loves Susan) can lead to the creation of the pseudo-memories: (John loves Susan) and (Fred loves Mary).
7. *Reference and pointers*—A symbol gains its referential capability by maintaining the address of another symbol. The underlying (von Neumann) hardware is capable of retrieving the referenced symbol by accessing information at the desired address. In a symbolic model, the creation and augmentation of a memory for a unique entity consists in adding pointers to/from a unique address in memory. The addition of a pointer allows a symbolic model to dynamically build up virtual structures. In subsymbolic models there are no addresses, since there are no unique locations for information. Consequently, there are no unique building blocks with which to explicitly construct larger structures out of smaller ones.
8. *Memory management*—Symbolic models are supported by a virtual memory, which supplies new, unused storage for the construction of new symbol structures. In subsymbolic models, there is currently no way known to dynamically conscript new processing units and/or layers to allow memory capacity to grow as tasks change.
9. *Intra-task communication*—In symbolic systems, every interpreter is capable of recognizing symbols and manipulating the structures built out of symbols. Consider LISP; in it each function is built out of the primitive, structure manipulating operations: CAR, CDR, CONS, and COND. Thus, the structure built by one function can immediately be traversed, compared and/or used by another function, and for some *other* purpose than that of the function that originally constructed it. Symbolic structures and structure-manipulating functions thus serve as an interlingua for all interprocess communication. In contrast, subsymbolic models live in isolated worlds. The weights formed by adaptation in one associative memory are specific to a given mapping task. It is not currently known how the long-term knowledge encoded in these weights can be interpreted by another subsystem, or applied to a novel task.
10. *Meta-Reasoning*—Since knowledge is composed of globally interpretable symbolic structures, one part of a symbolic system can reason, not only about knowledge produced by another subsystem, but also about itself and it own operations, to the extent they are encoded symbolically. The knowledge encoded in the weights in a subsymbolic model are designed for

rapid, associative retrieval and recognition; however, this knowledge is unique to a specific task and not available for analysis.

11. *One-shot, explanation-based learning*—In symbolic models, associations between pairs can be memorized in one shot, upon entry. The resulting associations, however, do not lend themselves to generalization. In contrast, subsymbolic models require repeated passes through a corpus of data in order to form the distributed representations that support generalization. However, since the generalizations formed by subsymbolic models are basically the result of stochastic processes, their knowledge can be biased by the number of exemplars of a given type. In a rule-based system, an explanation for a novel input can be constructed from a single exemplar, through a process of rule chaining and theorem proving and statistical biasing does not occur.
12. *Complex, sequential control*—No matter how much memory and processing parallelism is available, as long as it is finite, the resulting system will lack infinite generative capacity. Therefore, in addition to virtual memory, feedback loops with sequential control are necessary in symbolic models to give them infinite generative capacity. Symbolic models are supported by programming languages developed over the last 40 years that are designed for specifying extremely complex architectures with modularity, hierarchical organization, feedback, communication and processing control. Currently, subsymbolic models lack high-level programming languages, so descriptions of processing are still very close to the "machine language" level.

1.3. Symbolic vs. Subsymbolic in Man and Animals

Watch a cat chase a rat, or a hawk pick its prey out of the air. Billions of years of evolution have produced neural networks that solve extremely complicated problems in learning to categorize and recognize complex sensory information, and to initiate detailed, coordinated motion. Yet, with all of the complexity of the billions of neurons in the neural circuitry of animals, they cannot engage in an argument over religion or politics; they cannot compare or contrast the meanings of words; they cannot read a newspaper; they cannot play chess or monopoly; they cannot invent a mechanical device or musical composition, and so on. Human language and problem-solving capacities appear to require a qualitative difference in the way the neurons we share with animals are organized. Human brains appear to contain additional "modules," where abstract representations—ones invariant with respect to sensory experience or modality—are formed and linked to one another.

Consider current subsymbolic and symbolic representations for the letter "A" (Figure 3.1). The subsymbolic representation consists of an adaptive network

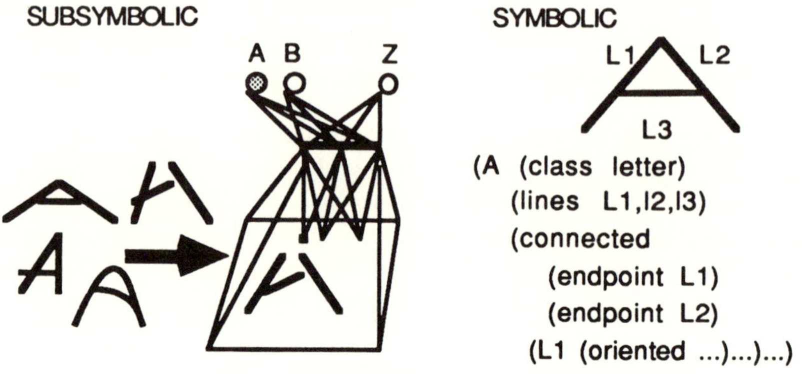

Figure 3.1.
Subsymbolic and symbolic representations for letter "A."

designed for rapid visual recognition and categorization of a widely varying set of exemplars. The symbolic representation cannot begin to handle this kind of variation. However, the symbolic representation captures abstract, structural information.

A symbolic representation of the capital letter "A" consists of symbols representing line segments, their orientations, their regions, and connection relations among them. Thus a symbolic system can communicate what an "A" is to another system, via a symbolic language. A symbolic system can compare representations and answer questions, for example, about how similar or different an "A" is to a "C," "H," or "N," and so on. A subsymbolic model forms a richer sensory representation of "A"s by seeing many variations, but the subsymbolic model can neither represent nor communicate abstractions concerning that representation, for example, that the prototypic "A" contains two line segments joined at their midpoints by a horizontally oriented third line.

Animals definitely have subsymbolic capabilities, but lack symbolic capabilities (or possess them in only the most rudimentary form). Humans clearly have both capabilities. From an evolutionary perspective, symbol processing is a very late development and has evolved on top of neural networks with largely subsymbolic capabilities. As a result, two speculative conclusions can be drawn: (a) symbol processing in humans may be fragile in places, since it has not had a very long evolutionary development, and (b) symbol processing may be computationally complex, since it consists of abstracting and coordinating the complex sensory information supplied by subsymbolic levels.

1.4. Symbolic vs. Subsymbolic in Man and Machines

Current computer models of subsymbolic processing exhibit a very different learning behavior than that exhibited by humans. Psychological experiments, for example, (Bruner, Goodnow, & Austin, 1956; Bower & Trabasso, 1968; Wells, 1963), indicate that people systematically experience different levels of difficulty in discovering conceptual categories, based on (a) the number of attributes (e.g., blue) that are involved, (b) whether the attributes are positive or negative (e.g., not a square), (c) whether the attributes are combined conjunctively or disjunctively. Levels of difficulty are summarized in Table 3.3.

In contrast to human subjects, subsymbolic networks (specifically, PDP networks based on weight adjustment through error back-propagation) show systematic differences in ease of concept identification learning when compared to humans (Pazzani & Dyer, 1987). Major differences are: (a) PDP networks learn conjunctive, disjunctive, and polymorphous concepts with equivalent ease/difficulty; (b) the average number of trials in all cases is much greater for the networks than for human subjects. For example, when using conjunctions/disjunctions of three two-valued attributes, the PDP networks we applied to the concept identification task require eight times as many learning trials as do human subjects.

Concept formation at the symbolic level tends to follow Occam's razor (Pazzani, Dyer, & Flowers, 1987), that is, the simplest hypothesis is pursued first and only later abandoned in the face of conflicting evidence. In contrast, subsymbolic systems entertain multiple hypotheses and follow a gradient descent through a high-dimensional space. While subsymbolic systems can recognize complex, polymorphic categories, they are unable to follow the strategy of Occam's razor. As a result, it takes a subsymbolic system just as long to learn a simple category as to learn a complex one. In contrast, humans can apply prior knowledge to speed up the concept learning task, and, in many cases, learn a concept from a single exemplar (e.g., Pazzani, 1988). Suppose one encounters a single event in which a rich, blond-haired person is kidnapped. Immediately we now that the wealth is relevant and not the hair color. In a subsymbolic system, the importance of the wealth attribute could be represented by biasing the initial weights of the network. However, subsequent events might be about rich, blond-

Table 3.3.
Relative Ease of Concept Identification Based on Number of Learning Trials Required.

Level of Difficulty	Attribute Type/ Combination	Form	Example
Easiest	1. Affirmation	x	squares
	2. Conjunction	x & y	small blue circles
	3. Disjunction	x or y	small circles or large squares
	4. Exclusive OR	x or y, but not both	circles & blue objects, but not blue circles
Hardest	5. Polymorphous	2-out-of-3 (x,y,z)	

haired people getting skin cancer. Now it is the hair color that is relevant. What is needed is a representation that establishes separate causal relationships, between skin cancer and skin color on the one hand, and wealth with attempts at extortion on the other. Symbolic representations are designed for such a task.

It appears that humans use subsymbolic, statistical pattern recognition techniques to form categories in knowledge-poor areas, such as early visual learning in infants. Once some fundamental categories (e.g., colors, shapes) have been formed, humans use these categories symbolically, as building blocks for forming higher-level concepts and generalizations.

1.5. What are Symbols, Anyway?

In the ongoing, symbolic vs. subsymbolic debate (e.g., Dreyfus & Dreyfus, 1988; Derthick & Plaut, 1986; Smolensky, 1988; Reeke & Edelman, 1988; Pinker & Mehler, 1988), there is a spectrum of positions. At one extreme, the argument is made that symbols are not needed and that attempts to recreate them in subsymbolic models are simply imposing over 100 years of ill-conceived notions from symbolic logic (e.g., Churchland, 1986). At the other extreme, the subsymbolic approach is viewed as just a disguised form of the simple associationism of Skinnerian behaviorism, that was laid to rest many years ago with Chomsky's (1959) devastating critique of B.F. Skinner's theory of language, along with the rise of symbol processing models in cognitive psychology and artificial intelligence (Fodor & Pylyshyn, 1988). One model, around which the battle lines have been drawn, is that of Rumelhart and McClelland's (1986b) PDP model for acquisition of the past tense. This model has recently received sharp criticism by Fodor and Pylyshyn (1988b), Pinker and Prince (1988), and Lachter and Bever (1988). These authors have argued that natural language requires symbolic structures to support the infinite generative capacity that it exhibits.

Do we need symbols for natural language processing? The answer to this question depends on what we mean by the term "symbol." If we mean the capacity to relate separate sources of abstract knowledge in a structured way, then clearly symbolic processing is needed. If we mean the implementation of unique bit vectors and addressing operations supplied by von Neumann architectures, then such symbols may very well be just conceptual baggage from the past. Perhaps at some point we may have to invent a new term (e.g., "symboid") to distinguish von Neumann symbols from symbols that are implemented in a distributed fashion. In this paper, however, I use "symbol" in its most abstract sense, to refer to the fundamental capacity for dynamically building and manipulating an unlimited number of abstract structures.

One of the most useful aspects of the symbolic vs. subsymbolic debate is that it forces researchers to more carefully examine their assumptions concerning symbols and symbolic processing. Upon careful examination, it becomes clear that the notion of symbol and symbolic processing is not monolithic, but consists of a configuration of coupled assumptions and capacities. Subsymbolic models show that these assumptions and capacities need not always be so coupled. For example, it is possible to have a subsymbolic model in which reference and recursion is supported but binding capacity is impoverished. It is also possible to incorporate subsymbolic features of spreading activation, thresholds, weighted links, etc., in symbolic models. The construction of hybrid models is important in expanding our understanding of symbolic and subsymbolic processing.

2. SYMBOLIC NEUROENGINEERING: METHODOLOGY FOR SYNTHESIS

What we currently appear to have is a situation in which subsymbolic, distributed processing models exhibit massive parallelism, graceful error degradation, robust fault tolerance, and general adaptive learning capabilities, while symbol/rule-based systems exhibit powerful reasoning and structural and inferential capabilities. If we could embed symbol representations and structure-manipulating operations within a distributed, subsymbolic architecture, then very powerful, massively parallel, fault tolerant high-level reasoning/planning systems could be created. At the same time, by embedding symbolic reasoning in an architecture closer to the level of neural processing, we might be able to shed light on how higher cognitive functions reside in brain mechanisms. These dual possibilities provide powerful motivations for attempting to synthesize symbolic with subsymbolic processing.

To achieve the desired synthesis we must avoid any overly straightforward, direct implementation of symbolic processing; otherwise the result will be a purely symbolic virtual machine. Why bother building a massively parallel architecture, if the symbolic operations that it supports are simply identical to those supported by a standard von Neumann architecture? In such a case, the model would behave exactly like symbolic models and many advantages of the subsymbolic level would be lost. Even the use of massive parallelism does not guarantee increased efficiency at the symbolic level. For instance, Touretzky's BoltzCONS (1986) model is extremely slow at the symbolic level, since it implements some of its primitive LISP list processing functions through simulated annealing (Hinton & Sejnowski, 1986). Drew McDermott has dubbed the problem of the use of massive parallelism at the subsymbolic level, resulting in extremely slow processing at the symbolic level, as the "Touretzky tarpit" problem. Feldman (1986) has criticized PDP models of symbol processing for being overly sequential at the symbolic level, even while remaining highly parallel at the subsymbolic level. A desirable synthesis, therefore, must be more subtle in nature, and result in associative inferential capabilities, with symbolic structures and categories dynamically learned while retaining the best features of distributed representations.

2.1. Need for Complex Architectures

One of the most attractive aspects of subsymbolic, distributed models is their potential for self-organization. Unfortunately, there is a limit to the amount of knowledge a homogeneous, PDP architecture can learn through direct interaction with the data. The more complicated the knowledge and processing, the more architectural structure and stages of development/learning are needed. For instance, we cannot feed 20 years of raw sensory input to a 3-layer, feed-forward, back-error propagation network and then expect a college graduate to result. Even if we succeeded, we would still insist on having a *theory* of knowledge and processing. For example, what architectures support which cognitive tasks? How does changing an architecture or training experience alter the resulting behavior or capabilities of a given model?

Consider the task of recognizing a highly abstract situation, such as natural language descriptions of "irresponsible behavior." Imagine feeding 10,000 paragraphs of text to the input layer of a standard, 3-layer, feed-forward PDP network. Suppose that these texts were broken up into 100 categories, where one category consisted of irresponsible behavior. A PDP network with 100 units on output could then easily "represent" the 100 categories simply by activating a given output unit for a given input text. What is the chance that such a network could discover the conceptual features involved in recognizing irresponsible behavior and generalize correctly to novel texts? One story might involve a babysitter letting the baby fall into the swimming pool. Another story might involve a prosecutor failing to prosecute a criminal. But there could be many other stories involving babysitters and prosecutors that did not involve irresponsibility. If the network did manage to discriminate the desired stories in the training set, the chances would be very high that the network would be simply noticing combinations of very low-level features. Perhaps the stories describing irresponsible behavior in the training set just happen to have more letter "p"s and fewer letter "a"s in their input descriptions than stories in other categories. Clearly, without more existing structure, in a higher conceptual space of goals, agreements, beliefs, and plans, the network could never successfully generalize to novel stories.

The limitation of the generalization capacity of such networks results from two weaknesses: (a) Appropriate levels of conceptual processing must already have been built up within the network architecture, since even humans cannot understand the concept of irresponsibility without first having learned about communication, agreements, agency, goals, and their outcomes; and (b) the architecture must support manipulation of representations that are highly abstracted from sensory data. One reason "irresponsibility" gives such networks a hard time is that it is at a very high conceptual level. That is, there are no specific, low-level features that lead to recognition of that category: *Any* kind of specific behavior may or may not be irresponsible.

The "abstraction representation" problem exists not just in natural language processing, but in any case where the categories are fundamentally conceptual (versus perceptual) in nature. For instance, why is it that, in the visual domain, nonhuman mammals (e.g., pigeons, dogs) can learn to discriminate, say, different images of fish, but cannot learn to recognize images involving humorous, embarrassing, threatening (or other abstract) situations? Imagine a pigeon trying to categorize political cartoons into those that ridicule various kinds of ideological positions. The pigeon could never do it since it lacks the ability to represent the target categories or the abstract features from which they are constructed. Imagine a dog trained to categorize, for example, into a "threat" category, images of a man raising his arm above another man's head while holding a club. What will happen later when the dog sees that man holding a sign above the other man's head in a crowd? The dog will be incapable of correctly categorizing this image because it cannot reason that a sign has a different function than a club and that the man holding the sign, in this context, is raising it simply to make it more visible to view.

2.2. Need for Multiple Levels of Description in Theory Formation

Whatever theory of intelligence we develop, it will have to contain multiple levels of description. There are three general reasons that multiple levels arise:

1. *Complexity*—To manage complexity at lower levels of analysis, higher levels must be created, so that one can focus on and reason about major processes without being overwhelmed by the complexity of detail at the lower levels. Suppose, for instance, that emotional states turn out to be complex "trajectory fluctuations" in some high-dimensional energy "landscape." We will still want to be able to explain, for example, why the victim of a theft is mad at the person the victim believes had stolen the object from him (Dyer, 1987). That is, we will still need a language that describes how a "trajectory fluctuation" representing anger is brought about by a prior "trajectory fluctuation" representing a belief concerning a "trajectory fluctuation" representing a goal and its violation. At some point it will become more efficient and perspicacious to simply drop the repeated term "trajectory fluctuation" and use directly the language of emotional states, goals, plans, and beliefs, with the mapping to the underlying "trajectory fluctuation" calculus understood. As a result, we will end up with languages of description at different levels, along with a theory of how one level maps to the other.

2. *Many-to-many mappings*—In most models, a theory at a higher level can be implemented in many different ways at a lower level. In addition, an implementation at a lower level can represent many possible higher-level constructs. Consider a vector of bits passing through the bus in a von Neumann architecture. Without knowing the exact programming language, compiler and higher-level instruction being executed at that moment, it would be impossible to interpret those bits. They could be an instruction or data; they could be ASCII or EBCDIC or some other, internally managed coding convention. At the same time, consider a higher-level instruction before compilation or interpretation. Depending upon the available compiler and underlying machine, it could be mapped into any one of an arbitrary number of lower-level codes. Thus, although the higher level is implementable in the lower, the *languages* for talking about the higher (or lower) level may not be reducible, where irreducibility means that one cannot interpret or describe one level without simultaneously knowing the current status and context supplied by the other level. If this state of affairs is true for as simple an architecture as a von Neumann machine, with its relatively straightforward mappings between programming languages and machine operations, how much more so will it tend to be true for complex, distributed, dynamically adaptive learning architectures.
3. *Tools versus applications*—When AI researchers developed property lists in LISP, there was great excitement, since it was realized that any kind of symbolic structure could be encoded using such property lists. However, the existence of property lists did not reveal the content of the structures that should be built out of them. Similarly, physicists, for example, Hopfield (1982) and Sejnowski (Hinton & Sejnowski, 1986), have excited PDP researchers by pointing out that memories can be stored as energy minima. But knowing that energy minima are available does not reveal their appropriate content and relationships. This distinction, between the structure of a solution and its content is similar to the distinction between the semantics of a tool and the semantics of the applications developed using the tool. For instance, logic programming can be used to produce an application with a completely distinct semantics from logic, as in the case of building models influenced by emotional states (Dyer, 1987). A related distinction is that of necessary versus sufficient conditions. To explain intelligence we need both. Encoding memories as energy minima may turn out to be necessary for a theory of human and animal intelligence, but it is definitely not sufficient. In some sense, by showing us that memories follow a Hamiltonian equation, we are being told that the brain does not violate any of the underlying laws of physics (something we had assumed anyway). Once we know the underlying tools for structuring memories, the focus of attention naturally shifts to (a) building memory content: which memories get encoded and when, and (b) modeling memory dynamics: how one memory brings about another (e.g., how emotional states are influenced by beliefs and goals).

2.3. Steps Toward Symbolic NeuroEngineering

Symbolic NeuroEngineering (SNE) is a general approach toward building content-oriented theories of knowledge. It receives its inspiration from two sources: (a) *Knowledge Engineering in the AI tradition,* with its emphasis on introspection and constraints from the logical and functional aspects of specific tasks within restricted domains of knowledge, and (b) *Neural Information Processing,* with constraints taken from currently available information about neural mechanisms and brain organization. Symbolic NeuroEngineering takes the following steps: (a) Specify knowledge structures and processes symbolically, using known knowledge engineering techniques in AI; (b) Encode these knowledge structures into a distributed form, using a variety of approaches, to be described below. The encoding may involve mapping symbolic knowledge through multiple levels of description; (c) Use and/or develop adaptive algorithms to reduce or remove the initial fragility of the knowledge structures originally encoded.

This approach allows one to incorporate the synthetic, task-driven orientation of AI knowledge engineering with the bottom-up, analytic approach that dominates in the neurosciences. The symbolic neuroengineering approach allows one to build complex architectures with knowledge encoded by hand, thus bypassing potentially long and complex developmental stages, while at the same time experimenting with how knowledge at a given stage is dynamically modified in the face of experience.

2.4. Four Levels from Mind to Brain

The research path from mind to brain is too complex to be achieved without passing through a number of intermediate levels. Of course, developing any intermediate level constitutes a risk, in that it may not lie on the ultimate path. This risk can be reduced somewhat by entertaining simultaneously a number of possible paths between varying models of processing at different levels of description. Our current research approach in NLP maps mind to brain through four intervening levels, illustrated in Figure 3.2.

There are two major goals of the research: (a) to understand the nature and limitations of models constructed at each level, and (b) to discover methods for mapping from a given level to the levels above and below it. Although the second goal relies on the first, in many ways the mapping goal is more important, since we can validate or judge our theories at one level by how well it supports mappings to, and constraints from, the levels above or below.

1. *Knowledge Engineering Level*—Examination of the structure/content of knowledge/processing needed to support high-level cognitive tasks (e.g., goal/plan analysis for narrative comprehension and belief justification for argument comprehension).

MIND

KNOWLEDGE ENGINEERING (KE)

LOCALIST CONNECTIONIST NETWORKS (LCN)

PARALLEL DISTRIBUTED PROCESSING (PDP)

ARTIFICIAL NEURAL SYSTEMS DYNAMICS (ANSD)

BRAIN

Figure 3.2.
Levels of Research.

2. *Localist Connectionist Network (LCN) Level*—Use of spreading activation, referent structures, thresholds and weighted links over semantic networks to support dynamic reinterpretation of word senses and multi-language generation.
3. *Parallel Distributed Processing (PDP) Level*—Use of PDP models and adaptive learning algorithms to support the development of global distributed representations, recursive structures, role bindings, and propagation of bindings during inferencing.
4. *Artificial Neural Systems Dynamics (ANSD) Level*—Use of artificial neural elements with real-time neural dynamics, for exploring various aspects of the "grounding" problem—that is, how language syntax and semantics can be learned through simulated real-time interaction with other sensory information that contains a temporal dimension.

Our approach is multileveled because each level of research both allows (and/or blocks) functional capabilities available at alternate levels. For instance, at the knowledge level it is easy to implement and bind variables, but difficult to dynamically form generalizations from the input. At the LCN level, it is easy to represent structured knowledge, but difficult to recover gracefully from damage. At the PDP level, it is easy to form distributed representations that are robust against damage, but difficult to represent structure and to implement bindings. At the ANSD level, time dynamics allow sequencing knowledge to be more easily captured than at the PDP level, but the systems are more complex to simulate and analyze.

3. KNOWLEDGE ENGINEERING LEVEL

The knowledge engineering level is needed to specify the kinds of structural relationships and inferences required for high-level cognitive tasks. The constraints supplied by this level are just as real as constraints from the neural level, but perhaps more important in the long run, especially if there turn out to be many different architectures capable of supporting high-level cognitive processing. The NLP systems we have constructed at this level are concerned with (a) the relationship of belief/justifications to goals/planning, for comprehension of arguments and abstract themes, such as irony (Dyer, Reeves, & Flowers, 1990); (b) the organization and acquisition of lexical information; and (c) knowledge content and use within specific domains, such as law (Goldman, Dyer, & Flowers, 1988) and mechanical engineering (Dyer, Hodges, & Flowers, in press). Since the knowledge engineering tradition and its AI technology are well known, the research at this level will just be briefly summarized for two models, along with some of the possibilities and problems these models pose for being implemented at lower levels.

3.1. Argument Units for Editorial Comprehension in OpEd

OpEd (Alvarado, Dyer, & Flowers, 1986) is a editorial text comprehension system designed to read, represent, and answer questions about arguments in the domain of economic protectionism. OpEd's knowledge of argumentation is represented in terms of Argument Units (AUs), which hold abstract belief attack/support structures, where the content of each belief refers to the efficacy of classes of plans and their outcomes. For example, the argument unit AU-NEG-SIDE-EFFECT (Figure 3.3) contains information about multiple goal outcomes of a plan and its effect on competing beliefs.

```
AU-NEG-SIDE-EFFECT:
 x believes [plan P1 should be executed]
          ---supported-by--->
 x believes [executing plan P1 will achieve G1]

y believes [P1 should not be executed]
          ---supported-by--->
y believes [executing plan P1 will achieve G1,
                executing plan P1 (as a side effect) will
                   cause failure of goal G2,
                G2 is more important than G1]
```

Figure 3.3.
An Argument Unit.

This AU commonly appears in economic/political arguments. For example, an economist might argue that printing more money (P1) will initially bolster the economy (G1), but will cause inflation as a side effect, which will hurt both business and consumers more in the long run (failure of G2).

Currently, OpEd can read and answer questions about two single paragraph-length fragments: (a) a Newsweek editorial by Milton Friedman on voluntary limits of Japanese automobiles, and (b) an editorial by Lance Morrow on protection of U.S. motorcycle manufacturers from Japanese competition. A major aspect of the research involves categorizing and representing AUs, along with developing process models for recognizing and instantiating abstract AUs from lexical input.

3.2. Figurative Phrase Acquisition with a Phrasal Lexicon in RINA

The RINA program (Zernik & Dyer 1987; Dyer & Zernik, 1986; Zernik, 1987) is designed to learn novel figurative phrases in context. The RINA lexicon consists of phrasal patterns with associated conceptual and contextual patterns. For instance, given the entries in Figure 3.4, RINA is then told "David took on Goliath."

Since neither of the relevant patterns matches the input, RINA analyzes the resulting discrepancies, at phrasal, conceptual, and contextual levels, and then enters into a dialog with the user to receive more examples of the use of this phrase (e.g., "The researcher took on a hard AI problem"). With each exemplar, RINA refines its syntactic, conceptual, and contextual hypotheses, using knowledge in its episodic memory, such as the major events of the David and Goliath story. As a result, RINA constructs a new entry in lexical memory, where <person 1 "took on" person 2> in a fight context maps to a representation for meeting a challenge.

3.3. Pure Knowledge Engineering: Pro and Con

Currently, abstract structures such as the Argument Units of OpEd cannot be represented for retrieval in a distributed fashion. The main reason is that the information contained in AUs is mainly structural and also highly abstract. For instance, any particular action could be a plan, and any state of affairs could be a goal, so no particular plan, goal or belief can trigger a given AU. What is required is a particular set of *structural relationships* among classes of goals, plans, and beliefs. In distributed models, a vector of features is used to retrieve a memory. But in AU theory, the same specific set of goals, plans, and beliefs will indicate a different AU, depending on how these goals, plans, and beliefs are related to one another.

At the same time, retrieval of an AU from a given set of cues can be viewed as

```
<x "took" y "to" location>  -->  ((ACT PHYS-TRANSFER)
                                   (OBJECT (GROUP x y)
                                   (TO (LOC location)))

<x "on " y>  -->      ((RELATION ON-SURFACE )
                        (OBJECT x)
                        (SURFACE-OF y))
```

Figure 3.4.
Phrasal/Lexical Entries.

a multiple-constraint satisfaction problem, and spreading activation is a very useful technique for satisfying multiple constraints. Therefore, one solution to the problem of retrieval of abstract, structured information is to add spreading activation, thresholds and linked weights to semantic networks, since such networks are already able to represent structural information. This hybrid approach, along with its advantages and disadvantages, is described below (localist connectionist level).

While symbolic models can capture abstract structure, it is difficult to model learning in situations where every piece of knowledge in memory influences every other piece of knowledge. For instance, RINA is currently incapable of learning subtle connotations that arise from related contexts of use. Consider the phrases "David took on Goliath" and "The AI researcher took on a hard AI problem." The meaning of "took on" in these contexts indicate effort and potential risk. Now consider the phrase: "John took on a new worker at the plant." RINA learns to map the phrase "took on" to HIRING in the context where the subject is an employer and the object an employee. However, there appears to remain a hint of a suggestion of effort/risk involved in this description, which is not evident in the phrase "John *hired* a new worker at the plant." In "John *took on* a new worker" there is the additional sense that John may have to spend more time training the new worker than in the more neutral term "hired." This hint of effort/risk appears to come from the influence of past uses of "took on," as in the fighting (David and Goliath) and problem-solving (AI research) contexts. In subsymbolic models, distributed representations support the ability of every memory to influence every other memory, which is extremely difficult to achieve in purely symbolic models. In Section 5 (PDP level) we present a lexical acquisition model potentially able to capture such subtle contextual influences.

4. LOCAL CONNECTIONIST NETWORK LEVEL

Localist spreading-activation networks (Cottrell & Small, 1983; Waltz & Pollack, 1985) have significant advantages over traditional symbolic language understanding systems. Their conceptual knowledge is stored entirely in an interconnected network of simple computational nodes whose activations are calculated using a spreading-activation mechanism. This is opposed to the large collections of sometimes brittle and ad-hoc rules used in purely symbolic systems. More importantly, however, is that many different inference paths can be pursued simultaneously in localist networks, so that disambiguation and semantic reinterpretation can be automatically handled by having each concept providing evidence continuously to related concepts through spread of activation.

4.1. Advantages of LCNs for Word Interpretation

Consider the three major strategies of word sense disambiguation and reinterpretation used by pure symbol processing systems:

1. *Delay*—When an ambiguous word is encountered, interpretation is delayed as long as possible. There are a number of problems with this strategy. Determining how long to delay can be very difficult and in cases where words mutually disambiguate themselves, delaying can cause deadlock, where the interpretation of each word is waiting on the disambiguation of other words.
2. *Commit and backtrack*—In this strategy, a word sense is selected and if it later proves to be incorrect, the system backtracks to that branch point and recomputes an interpretation, using an alternate word sense. The major problem with this approach is that useful work is thrown away. Consider the sentence: "The pot on top of the new stove was smoked by the druggie." Suppose the COOKING-POT meaning of "pot" is first selected. When "smoked by the druggie" is encountered, backtracking will occur and MARIJUANA will be selected for "pot." However, as a result of backtracking, the correctly parsed substructure "on top of the new stove" will be thrown away during backtracking and will have to be reparsed with "pot" interpreted as MARIJUANA.
3. *Commit and error correct*—A more sophisticated approach than backtracking is to commit to an interpretation and upon discovering a discrepancy, instead of backtracking, perform intelligent error-correcting operations. There are two major problems with this approach. First, error correction requires anticipating all of the kinds of errors that might be made, along with specifying their correction strategies. Second, once an error is made, other processes will come into operation, resulting in more errors on top of the original error. By the time the original error is noticed and correction strategies are invoked, a great deal of complex error correction may be required.

An alternative to the above strategies involves spreading continuous positive (and/or negative) activation values in parallel throughout a network of nodes and links. Structures that end up with highest activation values are selected as the correct interpretation. This technique has a number of advantages: (a) An interpretation can be biased or primed for simply by increasing the initial activation values on a selected set of nodes; (b) Each node can smoothly pass activation and/or inhibition to other nodes in a continuous process of feedback, until a stable configuration is found that satisfies the most constraints; (c) Mutual disambiguation can occur without deadlock and the effect of both backtracking and error correction is accomplished as a side effect of the flow of activation; and (d) The mechanism is extremely simple and does not require the use of many ad hoc rules to achieve an integration between different sources of knowledge. Knowledge interaction is handled through simple numerical operations over scalar values.

4.2. Unresolved Problems for LCNs

LCNs also have a number of currently unresolved problems:

1. *Category formation and self-organization*—In LCNs with symbolic nodes and links, whose organization is specified by the knowledge engineer, it is unresolved as to how the primitive node classes and link types were originally learned. It is also unresolved as to how the initial organization of the network could have come about through learning.
2. *Weight adjustment*—In PDP models, a number of general algorithms are now available for automatically adjusting connection weights in response to input/output pairs. No such general algorithms yet exist for networks with semantically interpretable (i.e., symbolic) nodes and links. As a result, in such systems the connection weights must currently be specified by hand.
3. *Variables, pointers, and bindings*—LCN models can be divided into two classes: Network models that allow nodes to store local bindings and to pass pointers among the nodes, and network models that are restricted only to passing activation. The pure LCNs (i.e., activation only) are closer to the neural level, but lack the ability to dynamically create and propagate bindings. The LCNs that are augmented with markers (i.e., structures containing pointers) (Charniak 1983, 1986; Riesbeck & Martin 1986; Rau, 1987) and local memory (i.e., variables) are able to create virtual networks, but are more removed from the neural level, since it is not clear how such symbol processing capabilities would be implemented.

A large portion of the NLP comprehension task involves dynamically building new structures and propagating bindings among these structures. Consider the text: "Mary and her friends were playing baseball. Her mother made her sweep up the broken glass." There are a great many structures of knowledge that must be selected, instantiated, and linked up to build a representation of the conceptual information conveyed here. These structures include: (a) The baseball schema—Mary and her friends are throwing a baseball among themselves; the default location is outside; they have a bat, and so on; (b) Physical causality—Windows break into pieces when hard objects are propelled at them; (c) Object functionality—Brooms are used to collect small pieces of material on the ground; (d) Ownership and goals—The person who owns an object will suffer a goal failure if the object is destroyed; (e) Responsibility schema—The person x who causes a failure for another person y is often the one who must act as an agent for y to recover from the goal failure; and (f) Authority—A mother can request that her daughter perform certain actions without the bargaining required in other agency situations.

These knowledge structures must be selected from among the myriad other, irrelevant structures (e.g., that the mother gave birth to the daughter, that the broom was bought at a store, that baseballs are round, etc.). In addition to selecting them, they must be instantiated with the roles properly bound and these bindings must be propagated into each new structure as it is activated. For example, the one who caused the goal failure is the one obligated to perform recovery operations. In symbolic, rule-based systems, the propagation of bindings is specified by shared variables in the rules, for example, [RESPONSIBLE (x) FOR GOAL-FAILURE (g) OF (y)]—implies—> [AGENT (x) FOR (y) TO-RECOVER (g)]. Pure LCNs are unable to propagate such bindings since they lack the ability to pass pointers and other symbolic information.

LCNs augmented with markers (pointers) are able to propagate bindings and build new structures. They accomplish these tasks by creating virtual networks over the existing network. Consider the simple network in Figure 3.5. By placing markers on the existing nodes, a virtual network can be constructed over the given, fixed network.

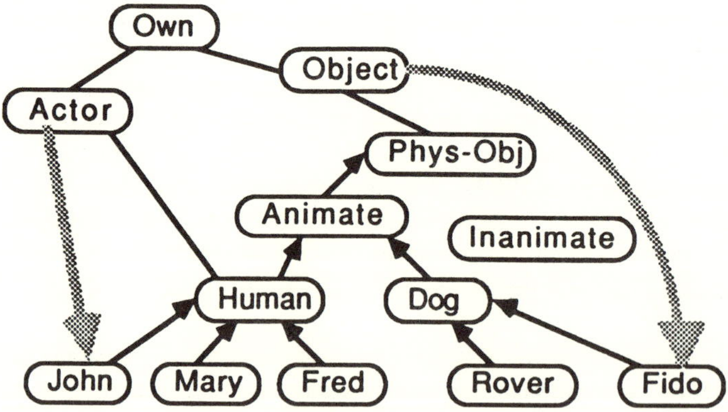

Figure 3.5.
Dark lines represent fixed connections. Virtual connections (gray) are created by placing markers on nodes.

In Figure 3.5, the virtual subnetwork [John <—Own—> Fido] is created by placing a marker on Own:Actor that holds the address of the John node and placing a marker on Own:Object that holds the address of the FIDO node. This allows the creation of virtual nodes, but relies on the location-based addressing scheme supported by von Neumann architectures.

Markers can only be used to represent short-term bindings. For instance, if new markers are placed on the network without either removing (or distinguishing) older markers, then the problem of "crosstalk" can arise. Suppose others markers are placed on the Own:Actor and Own:Object nodes in Figure 3.5, pointing to, say, Mary and Rover, then confusion will result as to whether Mary owns Fido or Rover. It is assumed that, over long periods of time, such transient connections are later turned into long-term memories by adding new instance nodes (Own1) and their roles, as illustrated in Figure 3.6.

In Figure 3.6, the crosstalk problem is solved by creating Own1, a new instance of Own, along with instances (Actor1, Object1) of each role binding. This technique solves the crosstalk problem, since memory confusions can no longer occur. However, humans do exhibit memory confusions. If such confusions are the result of generalization and learning over shared memory structures, then the solution in Figure 3.6 is too localist an approach.

In any case, adding long-term memories at the LCN level requires growing the network and it is currently not known how the creation of new nodes would be achieved at the neural level, but the solution at this level requires that neurons (or ensembles of neurons) be somehow conscripted to act as semantic network nodes/links.

4.3. Dynamic Reinterpretation of Words in CAIN

CAIN (Sumida, Dyer, & Flowers, 1988) is a natural language conceptual analyzer capable of parsing texts that are conceptually and syntactically ambiguous, and that require dynamic reinterpretation. Consider the following text:

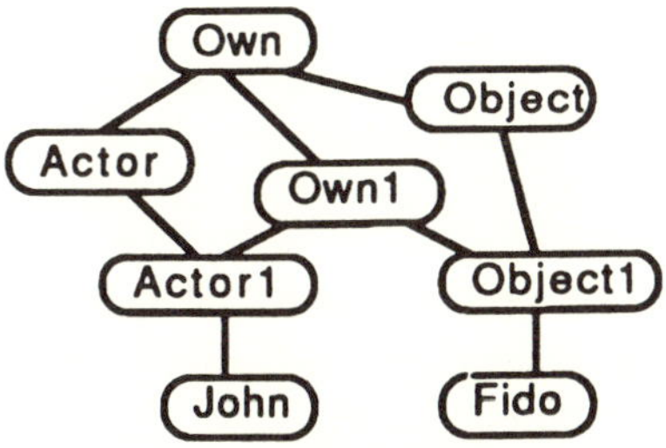

Figure 3.6.
New node instances are indicated by the postfix "1."

John put the pot on the stove. . . . He picked it up and smoked it.

When CAIN reads the first sentence, activation on nodes for "pot" and "stove" cause the COOK-CONTAINER node to receive the highest activation. The subsequent input of "smoked it" spreads activation to MARIJUANA, thus causing "pot" to be reinterpreted.

CAIN operates by passing markers over a semantic network augmented with elements of LCNs, specifically: link weights, continuous activation values, and thresholds. The use of markers allows CAIN to construct virtual bindings between nodes. For example, John can be bound as the smoker by placing a marker on the ACTOR node that connected to the SMOKE node where the marker holds a pointer to the JOHN node. Without such markers, the system must either dynamically build new SMOKE and ACTOR nodes with links to JOHN, or have such a set of nodes already in existence in the network, for every possible combination of bindings. The former approach is not neurally plausible, while the later approach would cause a severe combinatorial explosion.

Conceptual analysis of the input consists of four concurrent operations: (a) Mark lexical items and their associated meanings by spreading *activation markers* (AMs); (b) find knowledge structures that connect marked nodes by spreading *search markers* (SMs); (c) bind the roles of these structures by spreading *role markers* (RMs); (d) find the most specific, connected structures by spreading *descendant markers* (DMs). Different classes of markers are constrained to spread only over specific types of links, thus restricting the search to relevant portions of the network.

AMs propagate from lexical nodes through a lexical/phrasal portion of the semantic network. The nodes in this portion of the network encode the phrasal-concept pairs of the RINA system (see Section 3.2). As a result, CAIN interprets <x "pick" y "up"> as physical-transfer, instead of as initiate-date (e.g., John picked Mary up at the bar) or learn-information (e.g., John picked up tennis quickly).

SMs are propagated over is-a and role links, to activate node configurations representing knowledge structures. SMs receive a different activation strength, depending on the link weights over which they are propagated. Each knowledge representation node has a threshold value. If the incoming activation from the SMs exceeds the threshold, then the knowledge structure is selected, causing RMs to be propagated over role links. When an AM and RM intersect, an AM is placed on the role node. Since an AM holds a pointer back to its source, the role node effectively becomes bound to a concept node originally activated by the input. DMs are propagated down is-a links, to find the most specific nodes for binding. This process allows CAIN to bind JOHN as the ACTOR of SMOKE, rather than binding the more general node HUMAN as the ACTOR.

Figure 3.7 illustrates a portion of CAIN's memory for representing and processing phrases such as <x "pick" "up" y>. Here, each schema (i.e., head plus

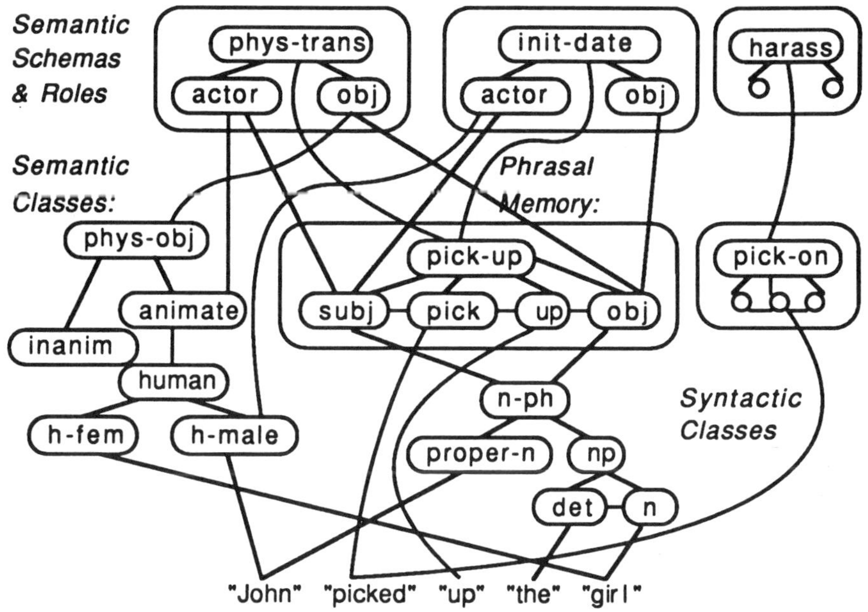

Figure 3.7.
A simplified portion of CAIN's memory structures. (Not shown here are: connection weights, directionality of connections, isa and role connection labels, node thresholds and spread of markers.)

roles) is enclosed in a large oval. Connections between roles represent constraints. For example, the subject role of the pick-up phrase must be the actor of the physical-transfer or the initiator of the date event. In this illustration, the actor of the physical-transfer can be any animate entity and can transfer any physical object, while the actor of init-date must be a male human and can only date a female human. It is important to realize that the labels within nodes in Figure 3.7 are for mnemonic and debugging purposes only—to help set up and analyze the initial network. These labels are not available to CAIN during processing.

As the words in the input are activated (bottom of Figure 3.7), activation spreads both to semantic and syntactic categories and then on to phrasal and semantic schemas. The final interpretation is represented by those schemas with the highest activation. In Figure 3.7, since John and Mary spread activation to h-male and h-female, the init-date schema receives more activation than phys-trans. Once init-date's threshold is exceeded, markers are passed down init-date and its role-nodes end up containing pointers to John and Mary. Phys-trans can also have its role marked (bound) concurrently and, at any point, the bound schema with the highest activation represents the current best interpretation. Thus, as activation levels shift, reinterpretation of the input can occur.

By spreading continuous activation values over weighted links, many nodes can be simultaneously suggested while only those exceeding their thresholds are actually selected. In addition, the use of marker information allows dynamic bindings, thus avoiding combinatorial problems (i.e., pre-existing instance nodes for various instance combinations) while allowing the creation of new structures. For another example of a hybrid (marker passing with spreading activation) system (see Hendler, 1987).

4.4. Automatic Formation of LCNs in Neural Networks

In pure semantic networks, both short-term and long-term information are created by dynamically adding new nodes and links to an existing network. These nodes and links are supplied, for example, in LISP, by selecting new CONS cells from LISP's heap management system and setting the pointer fields of each CONS cell. The resulting structures rely on the underlying addressing-by-location mechanism that von Neumann machines support. In a more neurally realistic model, CONSing is not allowed: New memories do not appear to be constructed in the brain by having neurons sitting "off to the side," unused, and then suddenly becoming "linked up." First, all neurons appear to be active at some level at all times. Second, neurons reside for the most part in a preexisting network of connections and the time scale for growth of new connections is too large to be useful for instantiation of knowledge that occurs on the order of seconds in NLP tasks. Finally, current models of neuronal behavior do not allow single neurons to send or interpret symbols or pointers.

The construction of a long-term, virtual semantic network (VSN) over a preexisting neural network could occur in following way: (a) Each VSN node representing a class (e.g., humans) would consist of an ensemble of neurons (EN), with subsets of these nodes containing connections to different subsets of neurons in other ENs. (b) Novel instances (e.g., John) of a VSN would be created by activating different, distributed patterns of a subset of the neurons in an EN (Figure 3.8). (c) New VSN links would arise by increasing/decreasing the connection weights between ensembles. (d) New VSN class nodes would be created (or destroyed) by increasing or decreasing the connection weights between subsets of neurons within an EN representing a given VSN node (Figure 3.9).

(e) Connection weights between VSN nodes could be learned adaptively, through training and/or reinforcement. For example, in a training situation, a subset of VSN nodes could be "clamped" as input and activation would spread, causing other VSN nodes to become more highly active, serving as output. This output could then be compared with the desired output of the VSN, and connec-

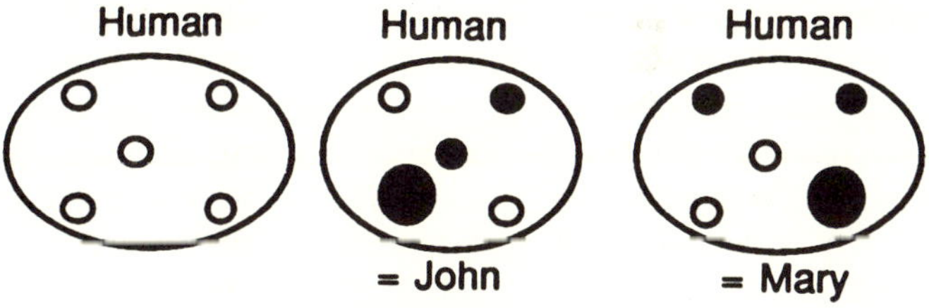

Figure 3.8.
Patterns of activation over the same ensemble of neurons represents different instances of a class.

tions would be adjusted incrementally to increase desired activation paths and decrease undesired activation paths in the VSN. Since each VSN node would consist of an ensemble of neurons, the system would have two major advantages: (a) It would be robust against damage, and (b) it would be highly parallel at the knowledge level. Furthermore, by having instances be distributed as activation patterns over subsets of ENs, we would retain the PDP-level features of automatic generalization and dynamic categorization, while avoiding the limited memory capacity problem inherent in one-neuron-one-concept models.

The model would also exhibit memory interference for within-class objects while avoiding interference across classes. Humans appear to confuse multiple instances while keeping semantic categories separated. The proposed model would not lose a semantic category unless all of the neurons in its EN were destroyed, which would have a low statistical probability (Feldman, 1986). However, destruction of an EN (through stroke or other physical damage) might result in the lose of a specific semantic category, such as relative loss of the ability to comprehend vegetables or small manipulable objects. Some patients exhibit such highly localized deficits (Warrington & McCarthy, 1987). Such results are in keeping with the semilocalist view we have sketched above.

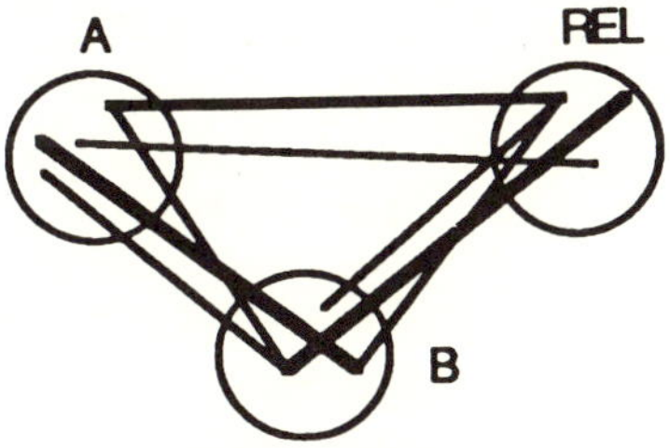

Figure 3.9.
Connection strengths over ensembles establish conceptual relationships over classes.

4.5. Completely Parallel Natural Language Generation in CHIE

In addition to constructing conceptual analyzers for natural language comprehension, we have built an LCN architecture for language generation. The system, CHIE (Gasser & Dyer, 1986, 1988; Gasser, 1988), uses representations that are similar to CAIN. However, CHIE is a pure LCN system; there are no markers and links are not discriminated (e.g., role versus is-a connections). CHIE operates completely in parallel, even during the production of a final sequence of words on output. This sequential behavior is achieved by propagating activation along uni-directional links and using inhibition and special winner-take-all (WTA) networks (Feldman & Ballard, 1982) to determine which word gets selected for output. Let us reconsider more closely the phrase <x "pick" "up">, in Figure 3.10 (first shown in Figure 3.7). First, the phrase must contain sequencing information. We cannot say "Up John Mary picked." Second, optionality in the sequence must be representable, e.g., in addition to <x "pick" "up" y>, the pattern <x "pick" y "up"> is allowed.

Sequencing and optionality is handled by the scheme illustrated in Figure 3.10. Each role-node of the phrase schema contains two nodes (small circles in the figure) for dealing with sequencing. The leftmost circle (LC) in each node represents initiation of this node in the sequence, while the rightmost circle (RC) represents termination. Assume that activation of a semantic schema (e.g., init-date) has spread activation to the pick-up schema for English generation. Activation spreads as follows: (a) Subj:LC spreads activation to generate the subject; (b) When the subject has been generated (not shown in figure), it passes activation back to subj:RC, which now passes activation on to the pick node; (c) Pick:LC spreads activation to "pick," causing this word (if it receives enough activation) to reach threshold and fire, thus producing English output and also passing activation back up to pick:RC. In this way, the entire sequence is produced in

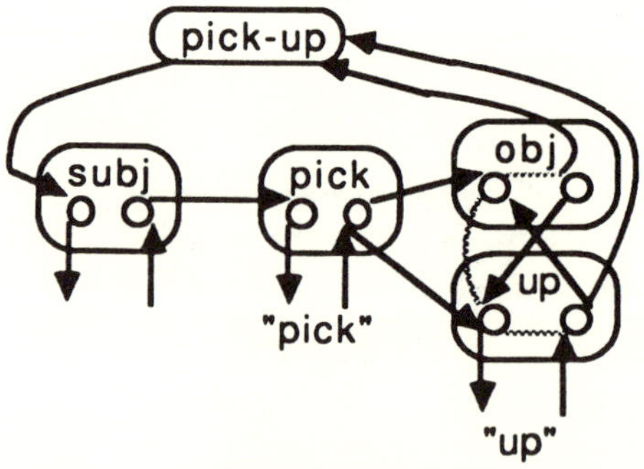

Figure 3.10.
Sequencing in phrasal memory. (Grey lines represent inhibitory connections.)

order by simple spread of activation over weighted connections and nodes with thresholds. Optionality within sequences is handled by alternate paths between LCs and RCs, along with inhibitory links between LCs to force the selection of only one path at a time.

The CHIE system is able to represent multilinguistic constraints and model aspects of language knowledge transfer in humans. For instance, in multilingual speakers, "code switching" can occur, where the speaker inadvertently inserts a word or phrase from language L2 while speaking language L1 (Gasser, 1988).

CHIE does not possess markers, so it cannot hold bindings in the way CAIN does. However, CHIE can hold a kind of temporary binding: by leaving a path of primed nodes as the result of activation. Before these primed nodes decay, if a node along this path receives activation, it will cause enough activation to spread back along this path to refire the primed nodes. This technique is used in CHIE, for example, to influence the selection of pronouns during generation. Instead of generating, "Mary loves John," if "John" is already bound (through a path of primed nodes) to the hearer-role in the conversation, then CHIE can substitute the pronoun "you" for "John" and generate "Mary loves you" (Gasser, 1988).

5. PDP LEVEL

The most common PDP model consists of a network of three layers of simple processing units (input, hidden, output) that operates in a feed-forward manner. During learning, the connection weights are modified through a process of backward propagation of error, that is, a difference between the current and desired output (Rumelhart, Hinton, & Williams, 1986). Tasks in such models are nearly always set up as mapping tasks, where the network is trained on a given corpus of input/output exemplars. The corpus is designed (or assumed) to have some implicit structure and it is the task of the network to discover it. Usually, a percentage of the training corpus is reserved (i.e., not shown to the network during learning). After the network has learned the training corpus, the reserved exemplars are presented to the network. If the network properly maps the reserved exemplars on input to appropriate representations on output, then the network is said to have generalized to novel instances. For natural language mapping tasks, the representations of exemplars on both the input and output layers are usually hand-coded in terms of feature vectors, where one or more units represents a feature, property or class.

5.1. The Syntax-to-Semantics Mapping Task and Semantic Microfeatures

McClelland and Kawamoto (1986) showed how a PDP model could learn to associate a syntactic representation on its input layer with a semantic (case-frame) representation on its output layer, and generalize to novel sentences. The syntax-to-semantic mapping task is non-trivial in English. For example, both sentences S1 and S2 have similar syntax:

S1: The boy ate the hamburger with a fork.
S2: The girl are the pizza with cheese.

However, the semantic representation of S1 assigns "fork" as the instrument of the eating. In S2, although "cheese" is also the object of the preposition "with," its semantic interpretation is as a modifier of the pizza. That is, the girl eats the cheese along with the pizza, but the boy does not eat the fork along with the hamburger.

In addition to similar syntactic cases/roles mapping to distinct semantic roles, distinct syntactic cases will also sometimes map to the same semantic role. Consider sentences S3–S5:

S3: The man opened the door with a key.
S4: The key opened the door.
S5: The door opened.

Here, the words "door" and "key" change in syntactic role. In S3 "door" is the object of the verb; in S4 "key" is the subject; in S5 "door" is the subject. However, in these sentences, "door" must consistently map to the semantic patient (or recipient of the action) while "key" must map to the instrument used to achieve the action.

To obtain several hundred sentences for their training set, McClelland and Kawamoto used sentence templates, such as <HUMAN ATE FOOD WITH UTENSIL> and generated specific sentences by filling in each class in the template with a word from their lexicon. For example, given lexical entries such as "boy," "hamburger," "fork," the above template produces "The boy ate the hamburger with a fork." McClelland and Kawamoto represented the syntax of each sentence in terms of a fixed number of processing units in the input layer, where each group of units represented the syntactic roles: SUBJECT, VERB, OBJECT, and PREP-PHRASE. They represented the semantics of each sentence also in terms of groupings of units (on the output layer), with the semantic case roles being: ACTOR, ACTION, PATIENT, INSTRUMENT, and PATIENT-MODIFIER.

Each syntactic/semantic role was filled in with a word, where each word was represented in terms of a vector of processing units. To represent the meaning of a word, they assigned a semantic interpretation to each unit making up the vector. Thus, each unit represented a "semantic microfeature," such as (MALE, FEMALE, INANIMATE). The semantic microfeature method of representation was used to make sure that words with similar meanings would possess similar representations, thus supporting later generalization after training. For instance, given that the PDP network was trained with S6 below, the network should successfully interpret the novel sentence S7, since the semantic microfeature representation for each pair: (John, Mary), (hamburger, pizza), and (fork, spoon) share active processing units.

S6: John ate the hamburger with a fork.
S7: Mary ate the pizza with a spoon.

For example, assuming that semantic microfeatures include (ANIMATE, INANIMATE, HUMAN, MALE, FEMALE), in that order, with binary-valued units, then representations for "John" and "Mary" would share values on 3 out of 5 units:

John: 10110
Mary: 10101

It is this sharing between vectors that supports generalization of the mapping task for novel inputs. In PDP models, since the connection weights were adjusted to accommodate multiple input/output representations, the memory serves to reconstruct the closest output patterns when presented with noisy or incomplete feature vectors on the input layer.

5.2. Automatic Learning to Distributed Word Representations with FGREP

In McClelland and Kawamoto's model, the semantic microfeature representations of the words were encoded by hand and remained static throughout the training and testing phases. Both of these aspects of the model pose general problems. First, having to encode representations by hand presents a knowledge engineering bottleneck; one even worse than that in AI, since feature vectors are impoverished to the extent that they lack the ability to represent constituent/recursive structure. It is no less difficult a task to decide what a correct set of semantic microfeatures should be than to decide what the correct set of primitive predicates and relations should be in an AI system. Second, by maintaining static representations for the exemplars, there is no way for the system to learn (i.e., form representations) about its environment. In McClelland and Kawamoto's model, this means that the system could not learn about words while learning about the syntax-to-semantic mapping task. Children, however, appear to learn the meanings of words while learning how utterances (with syntactic structure) relate to situations (with semantic significance). In general, PDP models form distributed representations in their hidden layers, but the representations used on the input and output layers remain the same during training and performance. But PDP models must be able to form novel representations of the I/O exemplars if global representations are ever to be formed.

To solve these problems we have developed an extension to back-error propagation, called FGREP (Miikkulainen & Dyer, 1987, 1988), that allows a PDP architecture to automatically discover representations for elements in the input/output layers. The basic approach of FGREP is twofold: (a) to represent the input, not as a pattern of activation on the input units, but as an extra vector of modifiable weights, leading into the input layer (Hinton, 1986), and (b) to extend back-error propagation learning into these representations. Each time the network is trained on an exemplar, the exemplar's representation becomes altered as its weight vector is modified. As a result, the network is, in some sense, "chasing a moving target" since the representations of the exemplars used in the training set are being altered while at the same time the network is attempting to learn the specified mapping task. Thus, the network is learning in a *reactive environment*.

We tried the FGREP method on the McClelland and Kawamoto task, using the same sentence generators and lexical entries. Instead of assigning each word a hand-coded, semantic microfeature representation, we initially assigned to each word a random vector of continuous values. As the FGREP method was applied, these vectors took on new activity profiles. Although the mapping task took a bit longer to learn, when the network reached convergence the lexical entries had formed fully distributed representations. The FGREP architecture for this task is illustrated in Figure 3.11.

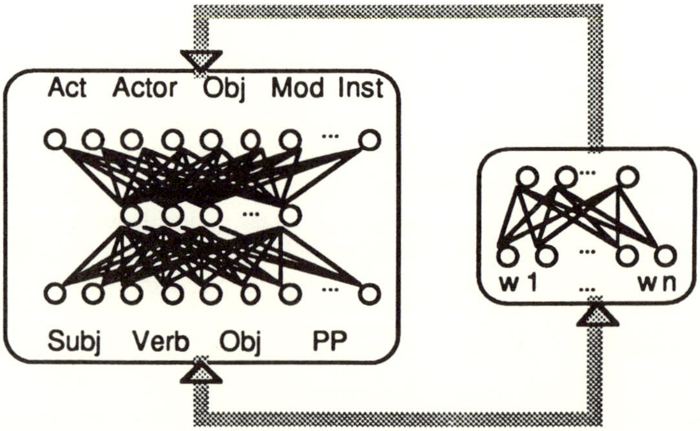

Figure 3.11.
FGREP architecture for lexical acquisition while learning the syntax-to-semantic mapping task.

Here, a sentence is entered on the input layer by taking the weight pattern of a word in the lexicon and spreading activation over their weights to the units for that word's syntactic class (Subj, Verb, Obj, PP) in the specified input sentence. The same operation is performed to encode the word in its correct semantic role (Actor, Act, Obj, Mod, Inst) on the output layer. Back propagation of error is then performed on the connections in the hidden layers, with back propagation extended into the weights for the relevant words in lexicon. Each time the same sentence is presented to the mapping network, it is actually different, since the word representations have been altered as a result of encountering previous sentences containing those words.

Most interestingly, *words with similar semantics* (as defined by word use in the syntax-to-semantics mapping task) *end up forming similar distributed representations in the lexicon.* For instance, similar representations are discovered for words in each of the categories: human, predator, prey, utensil, etc. These are the categories originally used to set up the task, but which represent the hidden structure in the data—initially unknown to the network.

Figure 3.12 shows the initial and final states of distributed representations for four words. Initially, their patterns are random and unrelated. After many iterations, words used identically have identical representations and words used nearly identically have very similar representations.

The resulting theory of semantics contained within the FGREP approach is very different from that of traditional NLP, in which word meanings are represented in terms of symbolic structures and their expectations in terms of inference rules, (for example, Dyer, 1983). In the FGREP model, word representations are automatically formed through use. As a result of learning, *the representation of each word carries a memory trace of all the contexts of use that serve to define it.* If two words are used identically, they representations will converge. However, as their uses diverge, so also will their representations. Ambiguous words end up producing composite representations, sharing activity profiles with both class-

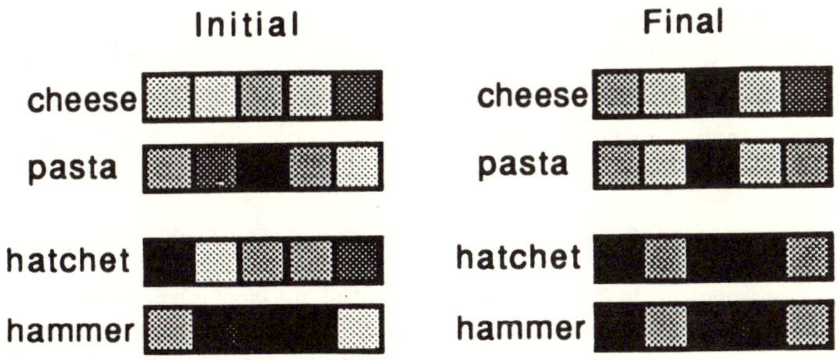

Figure 3.12.
Each word is represented as a distributed pattern of continuous values.

es/uses from which their meanings are drawn. The need to select semantic microfeatures and hand-code word representations is thus eliminated.[2] The representations formed by FGREP are fully distributed and result in a system with better noise handling and generalization capabilities (than in microfeature-based systems), mainly because words with similar meanings have continuously merged representations. At the same time, the concept completion capabilities of PDP networks allows one to place one or more words in the input layer and generate a set of the most likely semantic case-role representations on the output, thus constituting a form of semantic expectations.

We are currently examining how this dynamic lexicon, with such holographically formed representations, can be used for expectation-based conceptual analysis of multi-sentence natural language text.

5.3. Constructing Virtual, Distributed Semantic Networks in DUAL

The semantic network (SN) formalism used by AI researchers to represent knowledge has two major advantages over the "semantic microfeature" vectors used in many PDP models: (a) *SN nodes hold only semantically relevant properties*—A node in a semantic network will have only those few links (properties, features) emanating from it that explicitly point to other nodes. In a microfeature representation, each vector must contain *all* microfeatures, the majority of which will be inapplicable. For example, the microfeature ANIMATE will be present, although inapplicable, when representing a car; the microfeature METAL will be present, but inapplicable, when representing dog, and so on. In general, it is problematic to have a representational formalism in which every feature or property, that something does *not* possess, must be explicitly represented. Such a representational formalism must result in extremely large vectors containing mainly inapplicable microfeatures.

(b) *Representation of constituent and recursive structure*—Properties/features in a semantic network consist of labeled links connecting one node to another, thus allowing constituent and recursive structure (trees and cycles) to be represented. Since semantic microfeatures in PDP models reside in a fixed-width vector, the representation is "flat." Consequently, representations with variable depth, embedded structure cannot be captured directly in the representation. Furthermore, this "flatness" results in crosstalk: the inability to keep rela-

---

[2] One advantage of the system is that it achieves better generalization. In a scheme which does not modify the input representation, one is stuck with whatever generalizations fall out of the handcrafted representations. In the scheme being described, the input is being continuously modified to help do the mapping task. So the task itself imposes similarity on the representations. Certainly, when one introduces the new word into the system, one has to start with a random representation and retrain.

tionships separate. For example, in a vector with features, A, B, C, D, REL1 and REL2, the representation of (A REL1 B) and (C REL2 D) will activate all of the features, thus making it impossible to avoid the creation of phantom structures, such as (A REL1 D) and (C REL2 B).

Many PDP models attempt to represent structure by assigning case-roles to groups of PDP units on the input/output layers. For instance, suppose we designate patterns over 10 units each, say, to represent the ACTOR, ACT, OBJECT, FROM and TO roles of an event; then we can encode with 50 units a case-frame meaning of the sentence "John walked home" as (ACTOR = John, ACT = physical-transfer, OBJECT = John, FROM = unknown, TO = home). But then how do we encode the sentence "Bill believes John walked home"? We could add two more roles (say BELIEF-ACTOR and BELIEF-OBJECT), but this will require changing the width of that layer of our architecture. Even if we do this, then how do we encode "John thinks that Fred wanted Bill to believe that John walked home."? Clearly, what we need is a way to encode variable depth, recursive structures in an architecture with fixed-width layers.

There are a number of ways of achieving this encoding, and all involve the use of recurrent PDP networks (i.e., networks with feedback between layers), where the representations encoded in the hidden units of one PDP network are used to construct novel representations in the input and/or output layers of another (or possibly the same) PDP network. For instance, we can first encode "John walked home" on both the input and output layers (as described in the paragraph above). Once the network is trained on this autoassociative task, we then save the compressed representation, C-R, formed in the hidden layer (Figure 3.13).

We then feed C-R back into the input layer (Pollack, 1988); this time with ACTOR = Bill, ACT = believe and OBJECT = C-R. In this way we can encode variable depth, recursive structures in a fixed-width PDP architecture.

To encode labeled, directed graphs with cycles, we use a related technique, one that involves manipulating the entire weight matrix in one PDP network as an input vector to the input layer of a larger network. That is, *the long-term*

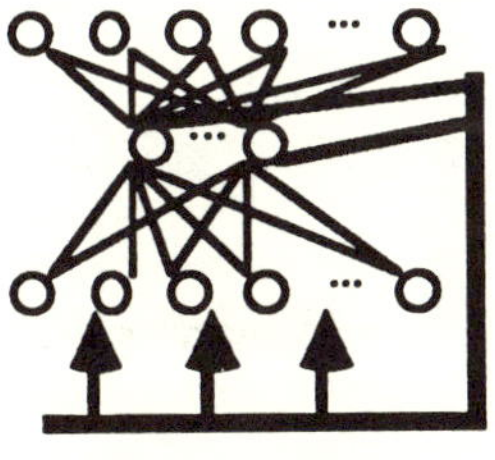

Figure 3.13.
Compressed representation in the hidden layer of units is fed back into one of the groups of units (i.e., case-role) in the input layer.

information in the weights of one network can be transformed into a transient pattern of activation in another network. This technique allows us to rapidly store, retrieve and modify entire networks as patterns of activation.

The architecture we have developed for exploring this technique is called DUAL (Dyer, Flowers, & Wang, 1988) and consists of two PDP networks: STM and LTM. STM is used to represent a single node, Ni, in a semantic network as a set of input/output associations, where each input to STM encodes a semantic link, REL, and each associated output encodes a node Nj such that [Ni -- REL --> Nj] occurs in the semantic network. Once all of the links emanating from Ni are encoded, the entire weight matrix (WMx) formed in STM is transferred to the input layer of LTM. Both STM and LTM are illustrated in Figure 3.14.

The transfer is accomplished through the use of sigma-pi connections (Rumelhart & McClelland, 1986a; Pollack, 1987), that is, weighted links in one PDP network that connect to weighted links (versus units) in another PDP network. LTM is an autoassociative PDP network which stores STM weight matrices as patterns of activation. The hidden layer in LTM is the same length as the input/output layers in STM. Thus, the LTM hidden layer holds a compression of a given STM WMx that can then be fed back to the input and/or output layers of STM.

Assume that we want to encode in DUAL a semantic node representing John, where the John node includes the following link/node associations:

[John —-OWNS—-> Fido]
[John —-GENDER—-> Male]
[John —-JOB—-> Teacher]
[John —-LAST-NAME—-> Dunn]
[John —-WIFE—-> Mary]

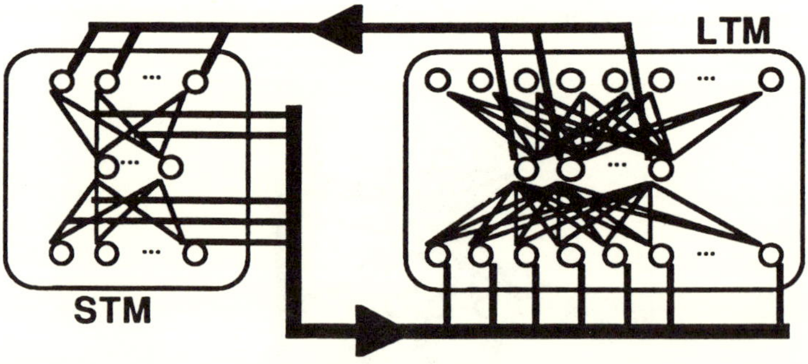

Figure 3.14.
DUAL Architecture. Number of STM weights equals number of input/output units in LTM. Number of hidden units in LTM equals number of input/output units in STM.

Once the WMx for John (W-John) has been formed in STM (by associating semantic properties with their values), we train LTM to autoassociate W-John and then save the compression for W-John formed in the LTM hidden layer. Let us call this compression C-John. By entering C-John in the hidden layer of LTM, we can retrieve the WMx W-John, load it into STM and then, for example, place the representation for WIFE in the STM input layer and retrieve the answer "Mary" associatively on the STM output layer.

Recall, however, that "Mary" is also another node in the semantic network. Thus, Mary is represented as a different WMx (W-Mary) that has to be constructed (at a different time) through weight modification in STM, with its compression (C-Mary) also formed in LTM. Suppose that C-Mary has not yet been constructed at the time that the WMx for John is being constructed; then what is the representation for Mary that the John node should point to for the relation [John —WIFE—-> Mary]? Clearly, when there are cycles between nodes there will always be at least one undefined node Nj at the time that another node Ni is being constructed that has a link to Nj. In such cases in DUAL, the undefined node is initially given a random pattern of activation as its representation. For [John —-WIFE—-> Mary], the WIFE representation on STM input is simply associated with a random representation to STM output. Later, when W-Mary and C-Mary have been constructed, W-John must be updated to associate WIFE on input with C-Mary on output. This update (of the STM WMx for John) will cause all other nodes pointing to John to require updating also. These updates will propagate recursively throughout the entire virtual semantic network until convergence is achieved, at which point the entire semantic network is now successfully encoded. This semantic network can then be traversed via (1) transfer of WMxs from LTM into STM to retrieve a given SN node Ni, and (2) STM associative retrievals to traverse any semantic relation [Ni —-REL—-> Nj].

The process of encoding is described in more detail in (Dyer, Flowers, & Wang, 1988) and causes DUAL to discover distributed representations for all nodes of the virtual, semantic network that is being encoded. As a result, *SN nodes with similar associational links to similar nodes automatically develop similar distributed representations.*

Figure 3.15 illustrates the kinds of activation patterns discovered by DUAL as the result of encoding a simple semantic network. Since both A and C point to the identical nodes with identically labeled links, their representations converge.

The DUAL architecture thus allows us to manipulate a virtual semantic network at the symbolic level, while at the same time retaining many of the robust features (of learning, generalization, graceful error degradation, etc.) associated with PDP networks.

Recently, we have extended DUAL to dynamically discover distributed representations for relations/links connecting similar nodes. In addition to the compressions and generalizations exhibited by such distributed encodings of SN links and nodes, what other purpose might they serve? Consider the use of various

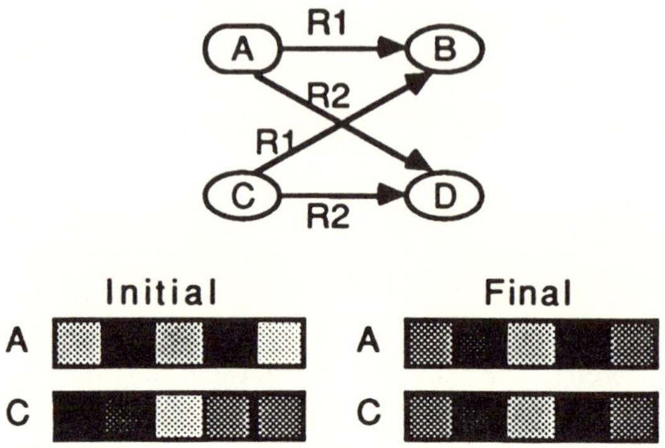

Figure 3.15.
DUAL discovers distributed representations for the nodes of the encoded semantic network.

causal links in semantic networks. Suppose one PDP architecture forms associations between events, where one event caused another. The compression for this entire matrix of event pairs could then become the representation for an abstract CAUSE relation/link at the symbolic SN level. Since the representation of this SN link had been formed via causal experiences, it could then be "opened up" upon demand, resulting in the retrieval of generalizations of all the event pairs that represented experiences underlying the abstract, symbolic notion of causality. Such a system could exhibit symbolic reasoning at one point, by manipulating symbols that are highly abstract and normally "invariant" with respect to experience, while at another point exhibiting associative learning, through the dynamic modification of these abstractions through interactive experience with the world.

5.4. Implementing Role Bindings in CRAM

Currently, we can design PDP networks that dynamically discover distributed patterns of activity to fill roles in the input/output layers. However, representations of schemas in PDP networks still consist of encoding sequences of rules and their fillers (Touretzky & Hinton, 1985). For example, a case-role and filler in the restaurant schema can be encoded as the triple <predicate role-name role-value>. An instantiated restaurant schema might include the triples shown in Figure 3.16.

In a symbolic system, we can bind every diner role in the restaurant simply by binding the diner role anywhere within the schema. In LISP, for example, diner is either a unique atom or a scoped variable, which makes its address unique within the specified binding environment. In contrast, binding all uses of a role

<restaurant1 type restaurant>
<restaurant1 diner John>
<restaurant1 food hamburger>
<restaurant1 init-event event0>
<event0 followed-by event1>
<event1 followed-by event2>
...
<event1 act ingest1>
<ingest1 type ingest>
<ingest1 diner food1>
<food1 value hamburger>
<event2 act trans1>
<trans1 type transfer>
<trans1 diner money1>
<trans1 to waiter>

Figure 3.16.
Encoding a restaurant instance as a set of <pred role filler> triples. (Indenting occurs only for visual clarity.)

in a PDP schema is a nontrivial task, since roles and values are not represented in terms of unique memory addresses, but are transient patterns of activation. If we encode a given pattern of activation for the diner binding in the ingest event, then we must explicitly find every other triple involving a diner and bind these also to that same pattern of activation. For example, if diner is bound to John within an ingest-food event, then we need to explicitly find all other diner-related triples, such as pay-for food, and bind the diner to the correct pattern. How can this be accomplished in a PDP model?

CRAM (Dolan & Dyer, 1987, 1988) is a PDP architecture designed to perform role bindings throughout a schema. Binding and rebinding of roles is accomplished through the use of conjunctive codings, probe networks, and projections.

1. *Conjunctive coding*—This form of encoding is described briefly in (Hinton, McClelland, & Rumelhart, 1986) and differs from the standard implementations of distributed representations in PDP networks, which are termed *coarse codings*. In conjunctive coding, a set of roles are encoded as a conjunction of patterns of activation over N**D units, where D is the number of positions in a relation. For instance, to represent a set of <pred role filler> triples, one allocates a cube of units, where each side of the cube contains N units to represent the patterns of activation that will fill that position in the triple.

Suppose <ingest diner food> were to be represented as a conjunctive encoding, with the following (binary valued) patterns of activation: <ingest = (0 1 0 1), diner = (1 1 0 0), food = (1 0 0 1)>.

Figure 3.17 shows how the triple <(0101),(1100),(1001)> is conjunctively encoded. In this figure, each pattern in one dimension is repeated as the pattern along the next dimension. For instance, the entire pattern (0101) along the x axis is repeated everywhere along the y axis wherever a 1 appears. Likewise, the entire <x,y> plane is repeated everywhere a 1 appears along the z dimension. Although conjunctive coding scales up less well than coarse coding, it retains the advantage that representations are distributed across dimensions, thus supporting merging and generalization of representations. Of course, like coarse-coding schemes, conjunctive coding of too many patterns in memory results in memory interference and creation of spurious memories (i.e., crosstalk).

2. *Probe networks*—A probe network is designed to retrieve all of the concepts from another network that satisfy a certain constraint. For example, if (a) the probe network is a cube of units, in one-to-one correspondence with the source network, where the source network encodes the triple <ingest, diner, food>, (b) the constraint (retrieval cue) is an input pattern of activation across the <x = ingest, y = diner, z = *> where * is unspecified, and (c) each unit in the probe network has a threshold high enough that it will become active only if receiving activation from both the source cube and the input pattern <ingest, diner>, then the probe network will retrieve the triple <ingest, diner, food> from the source network. Thus, conjunctive coding supports a relatively straightforward way of performing pattern completion (i.e., retrieval of complete triples, based on partial triples).

3. *Projections*—Conjunctive coding also supports retrieving all triples, say <x = *, y = role, z = *> from memory and replacing them with triples where x and z are bound to different values. It is this capability that is needed to update every role in a schema by accessing all triples that contain that role and replacing

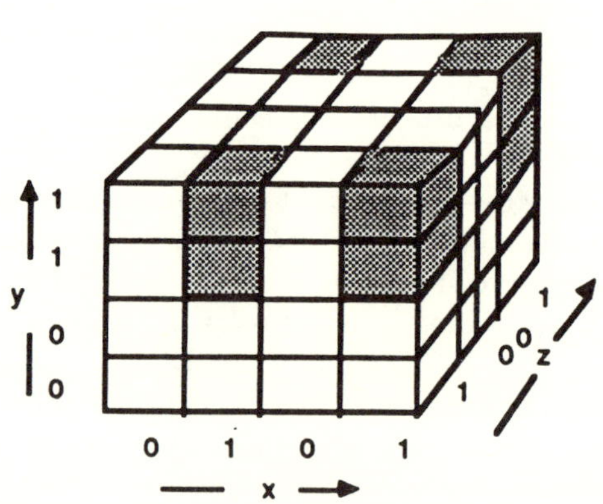

Figure 3.17.
Conjunctive encoding of <ingest diner food> along the axes <x = pred, y = role, z = filler>.

memory with all triples (with that role) rebound. Updating all triples with a given binding in a given position (dimension) is accomplished by projecting n-dimensional networks onto networks with higher (or lower) dimensions. The process of projection is depicted in Figure 3.18.

3-D to 2-D projection is accomplished by taking a 2-D plane of units in the 3-D network and mapping them onto a 2-D network. Thus projection is equivalent to mapping triples into duples. Mapping from a duple to a triple simply requires the inverse projection, but with the pattern from the missing dimension filled in.

Rebinding is thus accomplished by: (a) projecting 3-D onto 2-D (this replaces all triples with the desired duples), and (b) projecting the 2-D image, plus the desired 3rd value, onto a 3-D network. Finally, to decide which value to use as an index during projections, probe networks can be used to retrieve portions of existing triples from memory.

6. ARTIFICIAL NEURAL SYSTEMS DYNAMICS LEVEL

There are two major weaknesses that are exhibited by nearly all current NLP systems:

1. *Lacking of grounding*—Current NLP systems are not grounded in the physical world. That is, NLP systems do not have representations that relate words to sensory information from/about the world. Both symbolic and PDP models for NLP start with representations consisting of primitive syntactic/semantic case-roles (e.g., SUBJECT, ACTOR, OBJECT, MODIFIER) and relationships (e.g., CAUSE, OWNS, WIFE) and then build up more knowledge by linking up objects and relationships with one another internally. But there is no correspondence in these models between internal conceptual structures and sensory experience from the world. Failure to ground language in sensory experience has made it difficult to model language learning, since language in humans is acquired by forming associations between linguistic utterances and other sen-

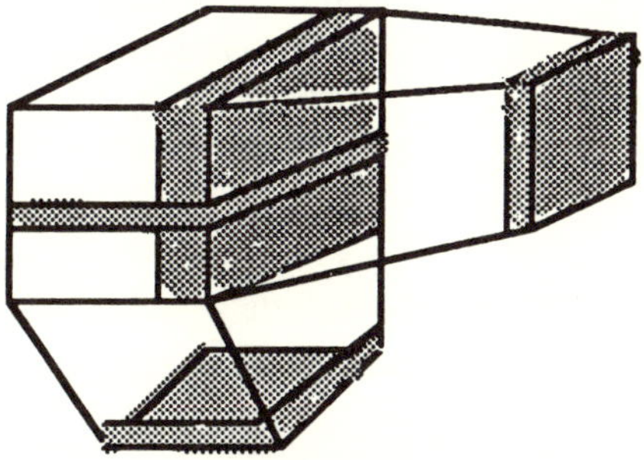

Figure 3.18.
Projecting 3-D network onto 2-D networks.

sory modalities. For instance, small children learn the word "ball" by hearing the word uttered while visually observing and manipulating various examples of balls.

2. *Lack of temporal dynamics*—In symbolic NLP systems, temporal relations may be represented declaratively, but the timing relationships between internal processing and the varying speed of arrival of the input are rarely modeled.[3] However, timing is usually extremely important in NLP processes, such as word interpretation. For example, if we do not read (or hear) one word follow another within a given time window, its interpretation will differ, as in S8 versus S9 below:

> S8: John needs a car jack . . . he intends to ask for it.
> S9: John needs a car . . . [long pause] . . . jack he intends to ask for it.

In S9 we assume that John bought a car rather than a jack, and that "jack" refers to a person who is the subject of the next sentence. Most symbolic NLP systems simply do not deal with such time dynamics.

Most PDP models for NLP also lack time dynamics. The activation levels of PDP processing units are numbers intended to represent an average firing-rate frequency. Standard PDP models (that is, in Rumelhart & McClelland, 1986a) do not actually model the varying patterns of firing of individual spikes nor the time-dependent modification of action potentials. As a result, PDP models are highly abstracted from real neurons; e.g., weight modification during back-error propagation occurs without regard to timing dynamics and the weight update method used during back-error propagation is not directly realizable in real neurons.

Temporal dynamics and sensory grounding become extremely important when building a realistic model for language acquisition at the word and phrase level. Children hear utterances in time-varying temporal sequences while at the same time receiving time-varying information over other sensory modalities. It is by correlating these temporal sequences that sensory invariant abstractions are slowly formed, with knowledge gained by each modality supplying information to other modalities. Thus, visual and tactile knowledge of balls constrains hypotheses for how the word "ball" will be used syntactically and semantically, while knowledge about the use of the word "ball" in language may later supply information that helps in interpreting ambiguous or incomplete sensory information.

6.1. Grounding Language in DETE

The DETE program (Nenov & Dyer, 1988) is designed to explore both the role of grounding and time dynamics in the acquisition of language syntax and seman-

[3] Speech is an exception, but in speech the focus in on word recognition. The focus in NLP is usually at or above the sentence level.

tics. DETE is composed of artificial neurons with temporal dynamics. That is, instead of using a single activation value to represent the average firing rate of a real neuron, the artificial neurons in DETE generate spikes and action potentials over time. The time dynamics of DETE neurons allow the model to associate a temporal sequence of words in its natural language input layer with a temporal sequence of visual images entering its retinal layer. DETE first learns the meaning of "ball" by being presented with different sized circles in different locations in is retinal field. DETE then can learn the meanings of phrases, such as "ball moves up" and "triangle bounced off wall" by associating visual motion sequences of known objects with language input sequences of known words.

Figure 3.19 contains an illustration of the kind of visual/verbal sequences DETE receives as input. The neurons representing a given word may be clamped over the presentation of several visual frames. The model is designed so that the meanings of phrases can be learned even though the phrases are not entered in perfect temporal synchrony with visual motion events. For example, "bounces off" can be entered slightly after the visual event of bouncing and DETE will still ultimately learn the correct visual-to-linguistic mapping.

DETE is composed of four input/output layers:

1. Visual Field (VF)—The VF consists of an array of processing units that act as an input retina. Information enters the retina as a sequence of binary arrays containing one or more simple objects (e.g., circles, squares) that may change position as the next array is entered as input. Information from the VF is passed in parallel to a number of feature extractors, to segment an object from the background and extract shape, size, intensity, location, speed, and direction of motion.
2. Mind's Eye (ME)—The ME is an output array for visual imagination. For example, once DETE has learned the meaning of "ball," by having seen various circles of various sizes, locations, and/or directions of motion, DETE can be given the word "ball" as input and an "image" of a ball-like object will appear in the ME.
3. Sequential Lexicon (SL)—The SL consists of pairs of artificial neurons, each pair connected to a pair of words from the lexicon. Activation of a given neuron in a pair indicates the order of arrival of the word pair in the

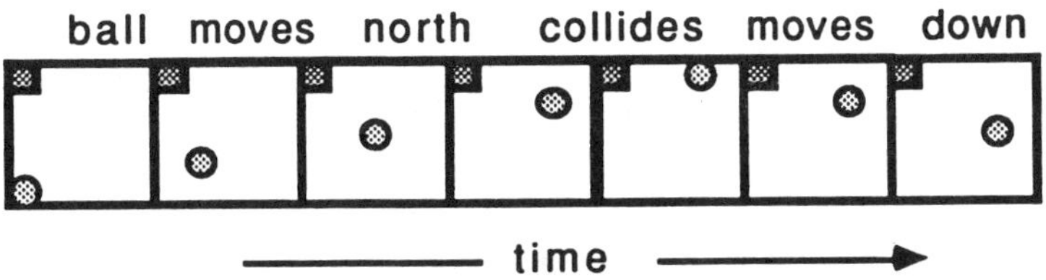

Figure 3.19.
Input sequence of visual/verbal associations.

input. For example, activation of the "left" neuron for the pair (SMALL, BALL) followed by activation of the "right" neuron for the pair (UP, BOUNCE) represents the input sentence: SMALL BALL BOUNCE UP. Figure 3.20 illustrates how two sentences are encoded in a small Sequential Lexicon. The numbers indicate the position of each word-pair in the input sequence while L/R indicates which word of a given word-pair appears first.

4. Hidden Articulation Layer (HAL)—The HAL consists of output neurons connected to lexical entities. Once DETE has learned the meaning of separate words, and then word phrases, DETE can be shown a sequence of a ball moving toward the top of the VF and it will produce the word sequence "ball moves up" in the HAL.

In addition to the I/O layers, DETE contains a number of internal layers, including: (a) A Selective Attention Layer (SAL)—This module allows DETE to attend to a given object in the VF while receiving motion sequences along with word sequences. The design of the SAL and feature extractors are based on the design of the NeoCognitron (Fukushima, 1987) visual recognition and selective attention system. (b) A Visual/Verbal Association Layer (VVAL)—This layer contains connections between neurons in the Sequential Lexicon and neurons in the feature-extraction layers projecting from the Visual Field. For instance, "ball" is represented in the VVAL by forming strong connections between "ball" and the shape extraction neurons for circular shape, with weak connections to position, size, motion and direction-of-motion feature extraction neu-

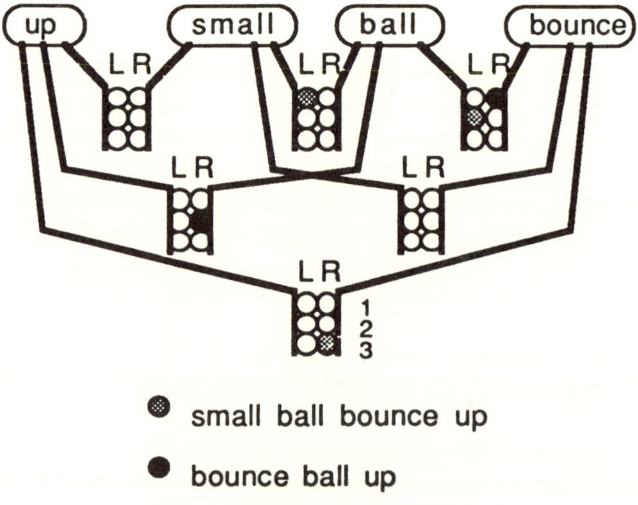

Figure 3.20.
Encoding of two sentences.

rons. As each word (and/or visual object) is input, the corresponding artificial neurons are clamped. Clamping a neuron causes it to generate a burst of spikes and the order and duration of clamping is of particular importance, since associations are formed in the VVAM by the way in which action potentials temporally overlap with one another. For example, if a neuron receives an impulse within a given time duration window of firing, its action potential is boosted.

In some ways the VVAM operates in a manner similar to that proposed by Smolensky (1987). In his model, two (or more) patterns of information are associated by forming tensor products. In the case of DETE, the tensor products formed in the VVAM contain complex timing and nonlinear dynamics which are difficult to analyze, but which allow DETE to associate and generalize temporal sequences across input modalities.

6.2. Future Work on Visual/Verbal Association in DETE

DETE is currently running in *LISP on a 16,834 processor CM2 Connection Machine, acquired by UCLA's interdisciplinary Center for Research in Computational Neurocognition. The Visual Field consists of 1,024 × 1,024 virtual processors. Although DETE contains a visual component for analyzing motion sequences of simple 2-D objects, the focus of our research is not on visual processing, but rather on "the grounding problem"—how the availability of some temporal/visual information can aid in the acquisition of natural language syntax/semantics. To pursue this research we do not have to solve every difficult problem in vision, but must construct a system that is able to extract and apply some of the kinds of visual information that are useful in understanding verbal descriptions. Our current research is proceeding in several directions:

1. *Generalization of word meanings and acquisition of syntax*—DETE learns the meaning of "ball" and "block" by associating these words with circular and square objects in the visual field. A word like "object," however, may sometimes be used to refer to circles; other times, triangles, and so on. DETE can learn the meanings of "object" through training sessions that result in weakening the connections between verbal neurons and neurons in the shape detection layer. However, what about the meaning of a function word, such as "it"? Consider sentences S10–S12:

   S10: The circle collides with the wall and it moves down.
   S11: The circle moves toward the triangle and hits it.
   S12: [The circle is moving slowly toward the square and the square is moving rapidly toward the circle. . . .] It is hit.

   In S10, "it" refers to the circle and not the wall (because the wall is not moving in the visual field). In S11, "it" refers to the triangle (based on syntactic grounds). In S12, "it" refers to the circle, mainly because English usage tends to treat the slower moving object as the recipient of the collision. Clearly, the interpretation of "it" requires a different level of generalization than that required of "circle" and "object."

2. *Learning temporal descriptions*—DETE currently learns to associate "moves" and "bounces" with motion and direction changes in the visual sequence. But consider S13 and S14:

   S13: The circle moved south before it moved north.
   S14: The circle looks like it will collide with the triangle.

   S13 and S14 describe past and future events. Consequently, the visual sequence DETE observes will not correspond with the event sequent currently being described in DETE's word sequence layer. A research issue we are currently exploring is: whether DETE's current architecture can learn the semantics of past and future tense in simple English phrases, and if not, in what way the architecture must be modified to allow the learning of such abstractions.

3. *Use of recurrent networks*—At the present, DETE does not contain recurrent (feedback) connections, such as are needed to handle input sequences in PDP models (e.g., Ellman, 1988). Instead, DETE implicitly encodes sequences in the temporal dynamics of its neurons. In addition, DETE's mainly localist encoding of word sequences (as ordered word-pairs) eliminates much of the need for recurrence. We are currently examining the possible role of recurrent connections in DETE's architecture.

6.3. Future Research in Dynamic Binding through Temporal Patterns

PDP researchers have focused on distributed, *spatial* encodings of information. At this point, very little is known about the use of *temporal* encodings. Most PDP models simply pass a single number (i.e., activation) that represents the average firing rate of a neuron. There is some evidence, however, that specific "pacemaker" neurons (Segundo, Perkel, Shulman, Bullock, & Moore, 1964; Segundo & Kohn 1981) generate unique, preferred temporal patterns (Dayhoff, 1988) over time and that these patterns are used to encode information. Recently, B. Richmond and L. Optican have concluded that spike-train patterns in the visual cortex are nonrandom and carry information encoded as compound, frequency-modulated signals, transmitted in a multiplexed fashion (reported in Vaughan, 1988). If these conclusions are true, then perhaps ensembles of neurons are sending "tagged" information along with general activation values. Such tags could play the roles that markers play in LCN models.

Recently, we have designed a system, ROBIN (Lange & Dyer, 1989), in which numbers are passed along paths in a LCN network. We term these numbers "signatures," since each number represents a unique identification of a node that is imagined to maintain a uniquely identifying activation (or firing pattern) over time. By passing signatures along connections, we can propagate markers. A dynamic binding is created when a node has a signature activation that matches the bound concept's signature. Most importantly, signatures can be passed in the model over very long paths of nodes to handle the nonlocal bindings necessary for inferencing in natural language understanding.

In general, it appears that high-level cognitive processing with neural networks will continue to pose very difficult practical and theoretical problems until equivalently powerful replacements for symbol-like variables and binding operations are found (Touretzky, 1988).

7. CONCLUSIONS

The fact that the symbolic and subsymbolic paradigms have generally non-overlapping strengths and weaknesses is a strong motivator toward finding a synthesis. The approach we have presented here consists of generating hybrid systems at multiple levels of description. At each level, the models constructed both gain and lose capabilities with respect to the levels above and below. Research is then directed toward mapping capabilities from one level to another. The mapping techniques we are currently employing are summarized below:

1. *Mapping KE to LCN Level:* (a) integrating marker passing with spreading activation, thresholds and weighted connections, to perform disambiguation and dynamic reinterpretation of word senses, (b) priming of paths to represent temporary bindings without markers, and (c) spread of activation over unidirectional, asymmetrical weights and node-pairs to handle sequencing in a parallel fashion for NL generation.
2. *Mapping LCN to PDP Level:* (a) using reactive environments with extended back error propagation to discover distributed representations at the input/output layers, thus eliminating the use of semantic microfeatures, (b) transforming weights into patterns of activation in order to encode labeled, directed graphs, and (c) applying projections to conjunctive codings in order to perform role bindings within schemas.
3. *Mapping PDP to ANDS Level:* (a) using action potentials and spike trains to encode temporal information, in order to associate verbal sequences with motion sequences, and (b) design of activation signatures for passing markers, without requiring symbol processing mechanisms.

In pursuing these multiple levels of research, we have: (a) constructed completely parallel language generation and comprehension systems, based on LCNs, (b) developed methods for automatically discovering distributed representations for semantic networks and lexical entities in PDP architectures, and (c) implemented an architecture for exploring the grounding problem by acquiring language syntax and semantics through visual/verbal association.

REFERENCES

Alvarado, S., Dyer, M.G., & Flowers, M. (1986). Editorial Comprehension in OpEd through Argument Units. *Proceedings of American Association of Artificial Intelligence (AAAI-86)*. Philadelphia, PA.

Anderson, J.R., & Rosenfeld, E. (Eds.). (1988). *Neurocomputing: Foundations of research*. Cambridge, MA: Bradford Book/MIT Press.

Bruner, J.S., Goodnow, J.J., & Austin, G.A. (1956). *A study of thinking*. New York: Wiley.

Bower, G., & Trabasso, T. (1968). *Attention in learning: Theory and research*. New York: Wiley.

Charniak, E. (1983). Passing markers: A theory of contextual influence in language comprehension. *Cognitive Science, 7*(3).

Charniak, E. (1986). A neat theory of marker passing. *Proceedings of the Fifth National Conference on Artificial Intelligence*, pp. 584–588. Philadelphia, PA.

Chomsky, N. (1965). *Aspects of a theory of syntax*. Cambridge, MA: MIT Press.

Chomsky, N. (1959). A review of B.F. Skinner's *Verbal Behavior*. *Language, 35*(1), 26–58.

Churchland, P. (1986). *Neurophilosophy: Toward a unified science of mind-brain*. Cambridge, MA: MIT Press.

Cottrell, G.W., & Small, S.L. (1983). A connectionist scheme for modeling word sense disambiguation. *Cognition and Brain Theory, 6*(1), 89–120.

Dayhoff, J.E. (1988). Temporal structure in neural networks with impulse train connections. *Proceedings of IEEE Second International Conference on Neural Networks, II*, 33–45.

Derthick, M., & Plaut, D. (1986). Is distributed connectionism compatible with the physical symbol system hypothesis? *Proceedings of the Eighth Annual Conference of the Cognitive Science Society*, II, 287–298.Amherst, MA.

Dolan, C., & Dyer, M.G. (1987). Symbolic schemata, role binding and the evolution of structure in connectionist memories. *Proceedings of the IEEE First Annual International Conference on Neural Networks*, II, 287–298.

Dolan, C.P., & Dyer, M.G. (1988, January). *Parallel retrieval and application of conceptual knowledge* (Tech. Rep. UCLA-AI-88-3). (Prepared for *Proc. of AAAI Spring Symposium Series*. Parallel Models of Intelligence: How Can Slow Components Think So Fast? Stanford, CA, March 1988.)

Dresher, B.E., & Hornstein, N. (1976). On some supposed contributions of artificial intelligence to the scientific study of language. *Cognition, 4*, 321–398.

Dreyfus, H.L., & Dreyfus, S.E. (1988, Winter). Making a mind versus modeling a brain:

Artificial intelligence back at a branchpoint. *Daedalus: Journal of the American Academy of Arts and Sciences* (Special Issue on Artificial Intelligence), 15–43.

Dyer, M.G. (1983). *In-depth understanding: A computer model of integrated processing for narrative comprehension.* Cambridge, MA: MIT Press.

Dyer, M.G. (1987). Emotions and their computations: Three computer models. *Cognition and Emotion, 3,* 323–347

Dyer, M.G. (1989). Knowledge interactions and integrated parsing for narrative comprehension. In D. Waltz (Ed.), *Advances in natural language processing* (pp. 1–56). Hillsdale, NJ: Lawrence Erlbaum Associates.

Dyer, M.G., Cullingford, R., & Alvarado, S. (1987). SCRIPTS. In S. Shapiro (Ed.), *Encyclopedia of artificial intelligence* (pp. 980–994). New York: Wiley.

Dyer, M.G., Flowers, M., & Wang, Y.A. (1988). *Weight-matrix = pattern of activation: Encoding semantic networks as distributed representations in DUAL, a PDP architecture* (Tech. Rep. UCLA-AI-88-5). Los Angeles, CA: Dept. of Computer Science, UCLA.

Dyer, M., Hodges, J., & Flowers, M. (in press). Computer comprehension of mechanical device descriptions. In J. Gero (Ed.), *Knowledge-based systems in engineering and architecture.* Reading, MA: Addison-Wesley.

Dyer, M.G., Reeves, J., & Flowers, M. (1990). A computer model of irony recognition in narrative understanding. In E. Nissan (Ed.), *Advances in computing and the humanities 1.* Norwich, CT: JAI Press.

Dyer, M.G., & Zernik, U. (1986). Encoding and acquiring figurative phrases in the phrasal lexicon. *Proceedings of 24th Annual Meeting of the Association for Computational Linguistics.* New York.

Ellman, J.L. (1988). *Finding structure in time* (Tech. Rep. 8801). San Diego: Center for Research in Language, University of California, San Diego.

Feldman, J.A. (1986). *Neural representation of conceptual knowledge* (Tech. Rep. TR189). Rochester, NY: Dept. of Computer Science, University of Rochester.

Feldman, J.A., & Ballard D.H. (1982). Connectionist models and their properties. *Cognitive Science, 6.*

Fodor, J.A., & Pylyshyn, Z.W. (1988). Connectionism and cognitive architecture: A critical analysis. In S. Pinker & B. Mehler (Eds.), *Connections and symbols.* Cambridge, MA: Bradford Books/MIT Press.

Fukushima, K. (1987). A neural network model for selective attention. *Proceedings of the IEEE First International Conference on Neural Networks, 2,* 11–18.

Gasser, M. (1988, July). *A connectionist model of sentence generation in a first and second language* (Tech. Rep. UCLA-AI-88-13). Los Angeles, CA: UCLA.

Gasser, M., & Dyer, M.G. (1986). *Speak of the devil:* Representing deictic and speech act knowledge in an integrated lexical memory. *Proceedings of the Eighth Annual Conference of the Cognitive Science Society.* Amherst, MA.

Gasser, M., & Dyer, M.G. (1988). Sequencing in a connectionist model of language processing. *Proceedings of Twelfth International Conference on Computational Linguistics (COLING-88).* Budapest, Hungary.

Goldman, S., Dyer, M.G., & Flowers, M. (1988). Representing contractual situations. In C. Walter (Ed.), *Computing power and legal language* (pp. 99–118). New York: Greenwood/Quorum Publishers.

Grossberg, S. (Ed.). (1988). *Neural networks and natural intelligence.* Cambridge, MA: Bradford Books/MIT Press.

Grossberg, S. (1982). *Studies of mind and brain.* Boston: Reidel.

Hendler, J.A. (1987). Marker-passing and microfeatures. *Proceedings of Tenth International Joint Conference on Artificial Intelligence,* pp. 151–154. Milan, Italy.

Hinton, G.E., & Sejnowski, T.J. (1986). Learning and relearning in Boltzmann machines. In J. McClelland & D. Rumelhart (Eds.), *Parallel distributed processing* (Vol. 1). Cambridge, MA: MIT Press/Bradford Books.

Hinton, G.E., McClelland, J.L., & Rumelhart, D.E. (1986). Distributed representations. In D. Rumelhart & J. McClelland (Eds.), *Parallel distributed processing* (Vol. 1). Cambridge, MA: Bradford Books/MIT Press.

Hinton, G.E. (1986). Learning distributed representations of concepts. *Proceedings of the Eighth Annual Conference of the Cognitive Science Society,* pp. 1–12. Amherst, MA.

Hopfield, J.J. (1982). Neural networks and physical systems with emergent collective computational abilities. *Proceedings of National Academy of Sciences, 79,* 2554–2558.

Lachter, J. & Bever, T.G. (1988). The relationship between linguistic structure and associative theories of language learning—a constructive critique of some connectionist learning models. In. S. Pinker and D. Mehler (Eds.), *Connections and symbols.* Cambridge, MA: Bradford Books/MIT Press.

Lange, T., & Dyer, M.G. (1989). *Dynamic, non-local role bindings and inferencing in a localist network for natural language understanding.* In D.S. Touretzky (Ed.) *Advances in neural information processing systems 1,* San Mateo, CA: Morgan Kauffman. (pp. 545–552).

McClelland, J.L., & Kawamoto, A.H. (1986). Mechanisms of sentence processing: Assigning roles to constituents of sentences. In J. McClelland & D. Rumelhart (Eds.), *Parallel distributed processing* (Vol. 2). Cambridge, MA: MIT Press/Bradford Books.

Miikkulainen, R., & Dyer, M.G. (1987, August). *Building distributed representations without microfeatures* (Tech. Rep. UCLA-AI-87-17). Los Angeles: Computer Science Dept., UCLA.

Miikkulainen, R., & Dyer, M.G. (1988, July). Forming global representations with extended backpropagation. *Proceedings of the IEEE Second Annual International Conference on Neural Networks (ICNN-88),* I, 285–292 San Diego, CA.

Nenov, V.I., & Dyer, M.G. (1988, July). DETE: Connectionist/symbolic model of visual and verbal association. *Proceedings of the IEEE Second Annual International Conference on Neural Networks (ICNN-88),* II, 17–24 San Diego, CA.

Newell, A. (1980). Physical symbol systems. *Cognitive Science* 2.

Pazzani, M.J. (1988). *Learning causal relationships: An integration of empirical and explanation-based learning methods* (Tech. Rep. UCLA-AI-88-10). Los Angeles, CA: UCLA. (Ph.D.)

Pazzani, M.J., & Dyer, M.G. (1987, August). A comparison of concept identification in human learning and network learning with the generalized delta rule. *Proceedings of the 10th International Joint Conference on Artificial Intelligence (IJCAI-87).* Milan, Italy, pp. 147–150

Pazzani, M.J., Dyer, M.G., & Flowers, M. (1987). Using prior learning to facilitate the learning of new causal theories. *Proceedings of 10th International Joint Conference on Artificial Intelligence (IJCAI-87)*, pp. 277–279 Milan, Italy.

Pinker, S., & Mehler J. (Eds.). (1988). *Connections and symbols*. Cambridge, MA: Bradford Books/MIT Press. (Special issue of *Cognition: An International Journal of Cognitive Science*, Vol. 28).

Pinker, S., & Price, A. (1988). On language and connectionism: Analysis of a parallel distributed processing model of language acquisition. In S. Pinker & D. Mehler (Eds.), *Connections and symbols*. Cambridge, MA: Bradford Books/MIT Press.

Pollack, J.B. (1987). Cascaded back-propagation on dynamic connectionist networks. *Proceedings of the Ninth Annual Conference of the Cognitive Science Society*. Seattle, WA.

Pollack, J. (1988). *Recursive auto-associative memory: Devising compositional distributed representations* (Tech. Rep. MCCS-88-124). Las Cruces, NM: Computing Research Laboratory, New Mexico State University.

Rau, L.F. (1987). Spontaneous retrieval in a conceptual information system. *Proceedings of Tenth International Conference on Artificial Intelligence*, pp. 155–162. Milan, Italy.

Reeke, G.N., Jr., & Edelman, G.M. (1988, Winter). Real brains and artificial intelligence. *Daedalus: Journal of the American Academy of Arts and Sciences* (Special Issue on Artificial Intelligence), pp. 143–173.

Riesbeck, C.K., & Martin, C.E. (1986). Direct memory access parsing. In J. Kolodner & C. Riesbeck (Eds.), *Experience, memory, and reasoning*. Hillsdale, NJ: Lawrence Erlbaum Associates.

Rumelhart, D.E., & McClelland, J.L. (Eds.). (1986a). *Parallel distributed processing: Explorations into the microstructure of cognition* (Vol. 1 and 2). Cambridge, MA: Bradford Books/MIT Press.

Rumelhart, D.E., & McClelland, J.L. (1986b). On learning the past tenses of English verbs. In J. McClelland & D. Rumelhart (Eds.). *Parallel distributed processing* (Vol. 2). Cambridge, MA: MIT Press/Bradford Books.

Rumelhart, D., Hinton, G., & Williams, R. (1986). Learning internal representations by error propagation. In D. Rumelhart & J. McClelland (Eds.), *Parallel distributed processing* (Vol. 1). Cambridge, MA: Bradford Books/MIT Press.

Schank, R.C., & Abelson, R. (1977). *Scripts, plans, goals and understanding*. Hillsdale, NJ: Lawrence Erlbaum Associates.

Schank, R.C. (1982). *Dynamic memory*. Cambridge, England: Cambridge University Press.

Schank, R.C., & Wilensky, R. (1977). Response to Dresher and Hornstein. *Cognition, 5*, 133–145.

Segundo, J.P., Perkel, D.H., Shulman, J.H., Bullock, T.H., & Moore, G.P. (1964). Pacemaker neurons: Effects of regularly spaced synaptic input. *Science, 145* (3627), 61–63.

Segundo, J.P., & Kohn, A.F. (1981). A model of excitatory synaptic interactions between pacemakers: Its reality, its generality, and the principles involved. *Biological Cybernetics, 40*, 113–126.

Smolensky, P. (1987). *A method for connectionist variable binding* (Tech. Rep. CU-CS-356-87). Boulder, CO: Department of Computer Science and Institute of Cognitive Science, University of Colorado.

Smolensky, P. (1988). On the proper treatment of connectionism. *The Behavioral and Brain Sciences, 11* (**I**).

Sumida, R.A., Dyer, M.G., & M. Flowers. (1988, August). Integrating marker passing and connectionism for handling conceptual and structural ambiguities. *Proceedings of the Tenth Annual Conference of the Cognitive Science Society*. Montreal, Canada.

Touretzky, D.S., & Hinton, G.E. (1985). Symbols among the neurons: Details of a connectionist inference architecture. *Proceedings of International Joint Conference on Artificial Intelligence* (IJCAI-85). Los Angeles, CA.

Touretzky, D.S. (1986). BoltzCONS: Reconciling connectionism with the recursive nature of stacks and trees. *Proceedings of the Eighth Annual Meeting of the Cognitive Science Society*, pp. 522–530. Amherst, MA.

Touretzky, D.S. (1988). *Beyond associative memory: Connectionists must search for other cognitive primitives* (Tech. Rep. AIP-34). Pittsburgh, PA: Psychology Department, Carnegie Mellon University.

Vaughan, C. (1988). A new view of vision. *Science News, 134*(4), 58–60.

Waltz, D.L., & Pollack, J.B. (1985). Massively parallel parsing: A strongly interactive model of natural language interpretation. *Cognitive Science, 9*, 51–74.

Warrington, E.K., & McCarthy, R.A. (1987). Categories of knowledge: Further fractionations and attempted integration. *Brain, 110,* 1273–1296.

Wells, H. (1963). The effects of transfer in disjunctive concept formation. *Journal of Experimental Psychology, 65,* 63–69.

Zernik, U. (1987). *Strategies in language acquisitions: Learning phrases from examples in context.* Doctoral dissertation, Computer Science Department, UCLA, Los Angeles, CA.

Zernik, U., & Dyer, M.G. (1987). The self-extending phrasal lexicon. *Journal of Computational Linguistics: Special Issue on the Lexicon, 13*(3–4), 308–327.

4
Schema Recognition for Text Understanding: An Analog Semantic Feature Approach*

Lawrence A. Bookman
Richard Alterman

1. INTRODUCTION

This chapter presents a connectionist model for schema recognition within the domain of narrative text, proposing parallel computational techniques for schema recognition and the subsequent operations which occur over the recognized schemata. It addresses some problems critical to text understanding such as the capability for revising earlier interpretations based on a changing narrative context, and the capability of finding plausible parallel interpretations—problems which have not been satisfactorily solved by symbolic models. The chapter also describes an architecture consisting of several memory systems, which communicate over a set of "wires," on which *analog semantic patterns* are induced.

Consider the text shown in Figure 4.1:[1] There are many possible interpretations for the connections underlying this text. For example, when one is waiting in an airport for a flight (2 & 5), it is not unusual that one might pass the time by having a drink (3). Yet later we learn that Sam was not passing the time, but rather he was nervous about asking his boss for a raise. There is also some sort of

* This work was supported in part by the Defense Advanced Research Projects Agency, administered by the U.S. Airforce Office of Scientific Research under contract number #F49620-88-C-0058. The first author is supported through a NASA Graduate Student Researcher Fellowship from the Lyndon B. Johnson Space Center, Systems Development and Simulation Division, Intelligent Systems Branch.

*We thank Dave Waltz for critical feedback regarding several of the ideas contained in this chapter, and for comments on earlier drafts. The first author thanks Tim Hickey for his help on the formal analysis of the model. We also thank John Barnden for a careful reading of this chapter.

[1] The events are numbered consecutively in the text.

Sam bought (1) a ticket. While he waited (2) he drank (3) some scotch. It tasted (4) bitter. The plane departed (5) 15 minutes later. The plane landed (6) an hour late. As a result Sam missed (7) the meeting. He decided (8) instead to telephone (9) his boss to discuss (10) his raise. He said (11) to his boss "if you agree (12) to give (13) me a raise, I will consider (14) staying (15) with the company, but if you refuse, (16) I will probably leave (17). Remember (18), I am a great computer hacker." His boss tentatively agreed (19), provided his best engineer agreed to help (20) the younger engineers.

Later that night, Sam talked (21) to his wife. She asked (22) "how did you get the courage (23) to ask (24) for a raise?" He said (25) "it was the alcohol I drank (26) earlier that day."

Figure 4.1.
Sam bargains for a raise.

bargaining taking place: Sam states his bargaining position (14–15); there is some conversation between them (11); and finally there is a tentative agreement (19). Or Sam's position (i.e., his threat to quit) may be genuine, in which case maybe the events can be best described by a *leave-work* schema. The circumstances under which these interpretations are constructed depend on the narrative context. As the narrative context changes, so should the interpretation. Yet what biases one interpretation over another are the constraints implicit in the text, or common-sense knowledge, outside of, but triggered by the text. Determining what the constraints are, the circumstances under which they hold, and their relative degrees of importance is crucial for determining the most plausible interpretations.

Recognition of these constraints plus facts, memories, knowledge, and their connection to a network of relations is critical to the process of understanding the text, that is, the plausible and fluid interpretations that we construct in order to understand it. But how is this recognition achieved?

In contrast to an earlier connectionist approach of Rumelhart, Smolensky, McClelland, and Hinton (1986), where the representation of schemata is quite impoverished in comparison to traditional symbolic representations, this chapter proposes a model of schema recognition for understanding text based on a set of *analog semantic features*[2] that act as a substrate for semantic memory. This chapter does not address the developmental question, that is, how are the relationships between events initially learned? We assume, instead, a semantic memory that contains a preexisting network of event relations.[3] Semantic memory is represented in the form of an ECC network (*event concept coherence*: Alterman,

[2] In the previous work of Waltz and Pollack (1985) and Bookman (1988; cf. Hendler, 1989) these features were called "microfeatures," but they have been renamed here to more appropriately reflect their intended meaning.

[3] Currently, the first author is working on techniques for automatically constructing semantic memory from dictionary sources and an online corpus of text.

1985, 1989). (An ECC network includes both definitional and conventionalized, or pragmatically derived, relationships among the event concepts.) We will show that an analog semantic feature encoding of an ECC network leads to a more enriched notion of schemata. Although features *per se* are not new (they have been utilized for example, in Hinton, 1981, and Rumelhart, Smolensky, McClelland, & Hinton, 1986), a different model is proposed to account for how they function.[4]

There are four issues that are central to schema recognition within the domain of text understanding that are addressed in this chapter:

- Selecting amongst plausible interpretations—There are several plausible interpretations that partly explain what is going on in the first four sentences (events 1–5) of the story above. Determining the contextual influences implicit in the text, or external to, but triggered by the text, and their relative degrees of importance are problems crucial to selecting the most plausible interpretation.
- Dynamic reinterpretation—After reading the initial segment of the above story, one might conclude that Sam had a drink in order to pass the time while waiting for his flight. It is only later that we learn that he had a drink in order to get his courage up to ask for a raise. The original interpretation, although correct, has to be reinterpreted in light of new data. Deciding when this needs to be done, and exactly how the earlier interpretation should be modified are key problems.
- Soft-constraint matching—Constraints on the matching of the *slot-filler* components or the *variables* of a schema are not purely yes-no propositions, but in part depend on the *motivating context* or *background frame*.[5] Thus matching is a question of relative plausibility; a program should be able to determine that 'computer hacker' and 'best engineer' plausibly match in the context of the above story.
- Contextually graded interpretations—Since events can have degrees of existence (e.g., Sam's boss tentatively agreed to give him a raise), and since they can be part of many different schemata depending on the narrative context and the motivating context (i.e., background frame), it is important to be able to ascertain the degree to which relationships hold.

The above issues point to some of the difficulties for symbolic models. Because of their all-or-nothing matches,[6] they have difficulty in recognizing that events may be "more or less" part of an interpretation (or schema) and can have

[4] Since analog semantic features are semantic in nature they differ from the "microfeature" usage in the PDP models (e.g., Hinton, McClelland, & Rumelhart, 1986; cf. Hinton, 1981), since in the PDP models each active feature (i.e., microfeature) has no semantic meaning in and of itself.

[5] Fillmore (1982) defines the motivating context or background frame as some body of understandings, some pattern of practices, or some history of social institutions, against which the particular category is intelligible to the community.

[6] Although fuzzy methods have been integrated with symbol systems with moderate success.

varying degrees of existence, and that interpretations are fluid, changing as the narrative context changes. In each case the decisions that must be made can not be all-or-none, but must vary depending on the narrative context and the setting (or background information) associated with the set of events. Some models which are subject to some of these pitfalls include: Schank, 1982; Charniak, 1983, 1986; Alterman, 1985; Norvig, 1987, c.f. *frame:* Minsky, 1975; *script:* Schank and Abelson, 1977.

The organization of the chapter is as follows. Section 2 provides some background and a brief description to previous approaches to the schema selection/text understanding problem. Section 3 describes analog semantic features and draws some lessons from previous experimentation with them. Section 4 illustrates with examples the capabilities of the proposed system. Section 5 describes a possible architecture that could account for the model's behavior. Section 6 is a general discussion of the advantages of the model and the last section concludes with some comments and directions for future work.

2. SOME BACKGROUND

There have been several computational models that have tried to solve the schema selection problem. One class uses intersection search/spreading activation/marker passing (e.g., concept coherence in text: Alterman, 1985; finding explanatory actions or the problem of finding connections: Charniak, 1983, 1986; Fahlman, 1979; Quillian, 1968; inference in text: Norvig, 1987). The basic technique of this class of models is intersection search usually followed by some kind of constraint checking. For example, in Alterman (1985) the constraints are between deep cases, while in Norvig (1987) the shape of the path is constrained. Thus, to find the relationship or connection between two actions, or the inferences associated with a piece of text, markers are passed (or activation is spread) over some knowledge base between the two actions (in the former case), or from each concept in the semantic representation of the input text (in the latter case). When an intersection is found that satisfies the constraints, it is reported and the path found is returned.[7]

Some of the difficulties associated with this kind of model can be characterized as follows. In Alterman (1985) the connection between two events/states is found via the *shortest* path connecting the events/states that satisfies the semantic constraints. On the other hand, Charniak (1986; see also Hendler, 1986) introduces *zorch,* an energy cost associated with traversing a path, to find

---

Kosko (1986), for example, proposes a fuzzy knowledge combination theory to help decide when two experts disagree.

[7] In the case of the marker passing reported in Fahlman (1979), only the intersection is reported.

connections in the text. Zorch biases suggested paths to ones with the shortest length. The trouble is that the shortest path is not always the *best* path. In fact, path length is quite arbitrary, since it is not easy to construct a semantic network on "first principles" in such a way that distance (i.e., number of links) corresponds to anything real. A second problem occurs during constraint checking. Here a particular constraint either succeeds or fails, thus potentially prematurely short-circuiting a particular path. The use of such "strong" (or "hard") constraints is typically found in constraint-satisfaction searches (e.g., Waltz, 1975) that *must* satisfy any solution. However, in some domains (e.g., image understanding, Ballard & Brown, 1982), many of the criteria are not all-or-none. This is certainly the case for the task of recognizing schemata. Therefore one would like to have "soft" constraints that can vary as circumstances vary. To avoid the complex constraint checking of Alterman (cf. Charniak, 1986), Norvig (1987) restricts the inferencing capabilities of the model, by using a syntactic filter on the form of the path. This simplifies the inference task, but at the cost of making the knowledge representation problem much more difficult. An additional problem is that the marker passing (or spreading activation/intersection search) and constraint checking as implemented in the above models is nonparallel, which leads to some form of backtracking. Yet complex behaviors are carried out in only a few hundred milliseconds by humans. To be a more plausible cognitive model, a program should obey the *100 time step* constraint (Feldman & Ballard, 1982). As the model described below parallelizes the constraint checking process, which caters for soft constraints and context-dependent constraints, it obeys this constraint.

Another class of models that attempt to solve the schema selection problem are the PDP models (e.g., Rumelhart, Smolensky, McClelland, & Hinton, 1986; Sharkey, Sutcliffe, & Wobcke, 1986; Smolensky, 1986; Dolan & Dyer, 1988) and the hybrid connectionist models (e.g., Chun & Mimo, 1987). Although the PDP models avoid the "strong constraint" problem and obey the *100 time step* constraint, they suffer from the "variable binding" problem (Waltz & Feldman, 1988).[8] A consequence is the inability to handle multiple instantiations of concepts and schemata, a task essential to understanding. The hybrid model (connectionist + symbolic) of Chun and Mimo (1987) solves the variable binding problem by augmenting a connectionist system with marker passing capabilities. In their system, the binding lists associated with a case frame are represented by complicated marks. A process called *marker merging* resolves the potential inconsistencies of incoming marks (i.e., binding lists) with the locally stored

[8] Although various solutions to this problem have been proposed, for example, Smolensky (1987), Touretzky and Hinton (1985), none have been generally accepted. One problem is the great expense in performing the operation. Pollack's (1988) work on representing variable-sized recursive data structures has the start of a solution.

binding list associated with the case frame. One problem is that the size of the local binding lists may become unmanageable and result in greatly increased communication overhead, thereby losing the effect of the parallel computation.

3. ANALOG SEMANTIC FEATURES

Analog semantic features (ASFs) are derived from Waltz and Pollack's (1985) notion of "microfeatures." As originally conceived, they were used to partially define concepts and to associate a concept with others that share its microfeatures. The microfeatures functioned as a representation for global contextual influences of competing word senses. More recently, Hendler (1989) used the term "microfeature" to associate a defining set of features with a concept.

ASFs are features which act as intermediate-level units that are intended to capture underlying structural fragments, that is, pieces of semantic structure—but do not specify the entire meaning of the concept. In this regard they are similar to the microfeatures of Waltz & Pollack. Moreover, in contrast to a concept in a semantic network, there is no explicit relationship between the analog semantic features. Rather, their relationship depends on statistical correlations.

In contrast to the microfeature usage, ASFs function in three ways: (a) as a representation of the *background frame* associated with a given concept/schema in an ECC network, and (b) as an extended representation of global contextual influences that includes representations of *episodes* as well as their interrelationships, and (c) as a *dynamic* substrate on which patterns of activity are induced over time. This also differs from Hendler's usage of a "microfeature," as his usage is strictly definitional and allows no internal dynamics that can represent contextual changes over time.

3.1. Kinds of Analog Semantic Features

Below is a description of the ASFs used in this research. Our purpose is only to demonstrate that ASFs are useful. We hypothesize that people probably have idiosyncratic but redundant sets (assuming this is a reasonable cognitive model). For the purposes of exposition, these features are organized into categories, although in *analog semantic feature* space, they are not explicitly connected. The features chosen were broken down into the following categories:

- Perceptual features (Miller & Johnson-Laird, 1976).
- Event-type features: identifies a verb with particular event types (Pustejovsky, 1988).
- Categories based on the structure of Roget's thesaurus. The category structure can be described by eight classes: abstract relations, space, physics, matter, sensation, intellect, volition, and affections.

- Categories common across cultures: e.g., life themes, distinctions needed to survive.

The system now contains approximately 840 ASFs. Each set of features associated with a category can be thought of as representing a tree whose root denotes the most abstract or the most generalized ASF for the tree. Each subtree in the category represents a subcategory. A small subset of these features is described in the appendix.

3.2. A Previous Experiment with Analog Semantic Features

Previous work (see Bookman, 1988), described a connectionist scheme for modeling context that used a distributed short-term memory composed of ASFs to represent the underlying context associated with the processing of sequences of sentences. To test the contextual mechanism, pairs of ambiguous sentences were presented to the model and it was the model's job to determine the correct interpretation, based on the context it had "built up" as it processed the preceding sentence.

For example, given the sentences: "John went to Mary's party. He had a good time." the system was able to resolve the ambiguity present in the second sentence, "settling" into the correct sense of the word *time*. Note, in the context of *party* the second sentence means he had a good experience, but in the context of *track meet*, it means his measured time for the race just run was quite good. An interesting phenomenon that occurred was that if the sentences were input in reverse order (i.e., He had a good time. John went to Mary's party.), the system still resolved the ambiguity, but it took a longer time. This demonstrated that the system's "understanding" of the sentences was gradually refined as the inputs were processed and that the activity patterns that formed in short-term memory (STM) depended on the order of input. Thus the constellations of ASFs in STM that help to constrain the model's behavior also depend on time dependent interactions.

Each sense of an input word above is represented in the algorithmic description below by a unique node. The basic algorithmic process can be described as follows:

- The node's activation level: Computed by taking the sum of the node's weighted inputs. These include (a) lexical nodes—the actual input words of the sentences; (b) other competing word sense nodes; and (c) syntactic nodes—which encode the grammatical structure of the sentence (e.g., part-of-speech).
- The contribution from STM:[9]
  1. Take the product of a node's "semantic" knowledge (e.g., the lower half

[9] STM is represented by an analog vector, where each position of the vector corresponds to an

of Figure 4.11 represents a partial encoding of the node 'depart') with the node's activation level (computed above).
2. Then take the dot product of this result with the semantic feature vector in STM and normalize the result.

- The contribution to STM: Take the product of a node's "semantic" knowledge times the node's activation level (this product is computed as described above) and update STM by adding the sum of all such computations to the old values there.

It can be shown (Bookman, in preparation) that with the addition of an ASF substrate to a model that contains the above three properties, we can construct a network that is more powerful than a feedforward network with self-loops, that is, "restricted ASF-less" networks. A formal analysis of this algorithm shows that the ASFs in STM have the effect of modifying a dynamic "virtual" self-loop link of each of the word sense nodes (i.e., each word that is ambiguous is represented by a different node for each sense). Therefore, the dynamics of the model describe a kind of unsupervised weight modification or "learning" procedure. The overall effect is that the model's dynamics accounts for potentially more shades and degrees of similarity and difference in the word sense nodes than would be possible using "featureless" networks. Intuitively, the analog substrate helps to achieve the right settling dynamics, as it puts additional constraints on the model.

3.3. Lessons Drawn

There are several lessons that can be drawn from previous experience with analog semantic feature-based models. These include:

1. The settling dynamics are different from "featureless" models: It is possible that the ASF substrate is acting like a *hidden layer* allowing one to get conjunctions of several inputs (represented by the horizontal wires) converging on a semantic feature; and only if the conjunction activates the semantic feature will it in turn influence the word sense unit (labelled $w_1 - w_4$—see Figure 4.2).
2. ASFs contribute to picking a common theme for the sentence: for example, the theme for sentences above (John went to Mary's party. He had a good

independent semantic feature, and the numerical value at that position corresponds to the level of activation of that semantic feature.

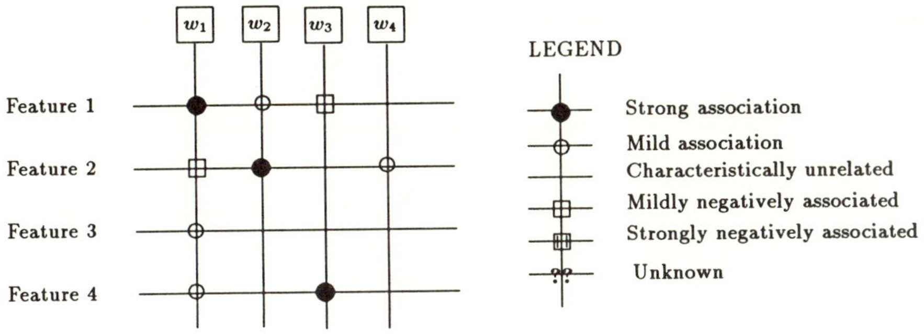

Figure 4.2.
Analog semantic feature substrate acts like a hidden layer.

time.) might be "event/celebration/experience," jointly arrived from "went to" (meaning attended) + "party" + "time." This thematic information would be reflected in the constellation of ASFs that appear in STM. If one had direct competition between the word senses, the theme information could not be derived. See Bookman (1988) for more details.

3. ASFs account for finer distinctions: Figure 4.2 illustrates that many combinations of features (each combination is represented by a vertical wire) can influence a concept (each unit w_i is an instance of a concept)—each combination accounts for a different shade of meaning or distinction, and since wires can have analog values even finer distinctions can be made.

4. SOME ILLUSTRATIVE EXAMPLES

This section illustrates with some examples the benefits of the approach outlined in this chapter. It also describes proposed solutions to these examples and contrasts them with a purely symbolic approach. Note that all of the ASFs used in these examples are among the set of 840 ASFs described earlier.

4.1. Selecting Amongst Plausible Interpretations

Consider the fragment of text from Figure 4.1 shown in Figure 4.3.

Figure 4.4 depicts a partial network of relations from which an event-based interpretation of the above text can be constructed. The network was constructed from the event concept coherence model (ECC) described in Alterman (1989).

Sam bought (1) a ticket. While he waited (2) he drank (3) some scotch. It tasted (4) bitter. The plane departed (5) 15 minutes later.

Figure 4.3.
The airport segment.

Recent work (Alterman & Bookman, 1990a, 1990b) explores the ECC representation in support of several reasoning tasks: determining the conceptual roots, measuring importance, finding the connection between events in the narrative, and narrative summarization.

Figure 4.4 shows several event concepts—for example, a "drink-liquor" concept and a "plane-travel" concept—that can be used to help us understand the airport story shown in Figure 4.3. Each concept is event-wise connected via a set of relations[10] to other event concepts that partly describe what is going on: for example, "drink-liquor" is a kind of "drinking"; drinking has a taste associated with it and "bitter-taste" is one kind of "taste"; and before one can drink-liquor, one has to have the liquor, and after one buys the liquor one also has it. A second set of concepts describes a different set of relations relating to "plane travel," but it is not until one finds the connection(s) between these two event concepts (i.e., "plane-travel" and "drink-liquor") can one really understand the airport segment above. The connection goes something like: when one is waiting in an airport for a flight, one might pass the time by having a drink. In terms of the above network it can be described by the following path:

$$\text{depart} \overset{subseq}{\leftarrow} \text{plane-travel} \overset{subseq}{\rightarrow} \text{wait-in-airport} \overset{subseq}{\rightarrow} \text{drink} \overset{sc}{\rightarrow} \text{drink-liquor}$$

A less plausible connection—as it does not explain the waiting—might be: One of the many things to do at a depot is drink liquor. This can be described by the following path:

$$\text{depart} \overset{subseq}{\leftarrow} \text{plane-travel} \overset{subseq}{\rightarrow} \text{things-to-do-at-depot} \overset{subseq}{\rightarrow} \text{drink} \overset{sc}{\rightarrow} \text{drink-liquor}$$

The question that must be answered is: How does a program find the most plausible interpretation when selecting among a network of equiprobable in-

[10] There are seven such relations: *Class/subclass* is used to indicate property inheritance. *Subsequence* is used to indicate a part of an event which occurs for a subinterval of time. *Coordinate* indicates a part of an event which occurs throughout the interval of the parent event. There are four kinds of temporal relations (*antecedent, consequent, precedent, sequel*) that are differentiated by their time of occurrence (either before or after) and their likelihood (either necessary or probable). Note: *subseq, sc, coord* are abbreviations for the coherence relations *subsequence, subclass,* and

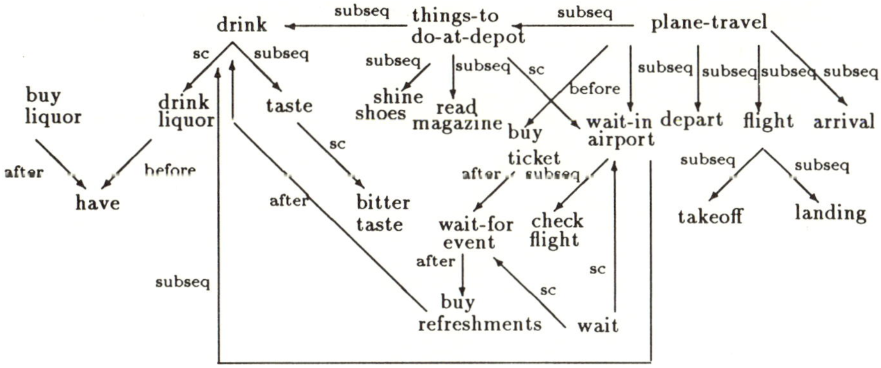

Figure 4.4.
A partial representation for the airport segment.

terpretations? The intersection search/spreading activation/marker passing models (discussed in section 2) find interpretations essentially as a function of network distance only. By favoring shortest paths they place all the burden on the constraint checking phase to eliminate incorrect interpretations. Besides being computationally inefficient, this process is not plausible, for every situation we experience is influenced by thousands of contextual shades and degrees of similarity and thus there are too many plausible interpretations. Hence, interpretations favoring shortest paths are not necessarily more probable. What we propose instead is a model that can dynamically bias the interpretation in one direction or another, depending on contextual influences, and that keeps track of all plausible interpretations. A contextual biasing mechanism is introduced to address the question of finding the most plausible interpretations.

Consider the interpretation that would be constructed from the story fragment shown in Figure 4.3 above using "shortest path":[11]

Interpretation 1

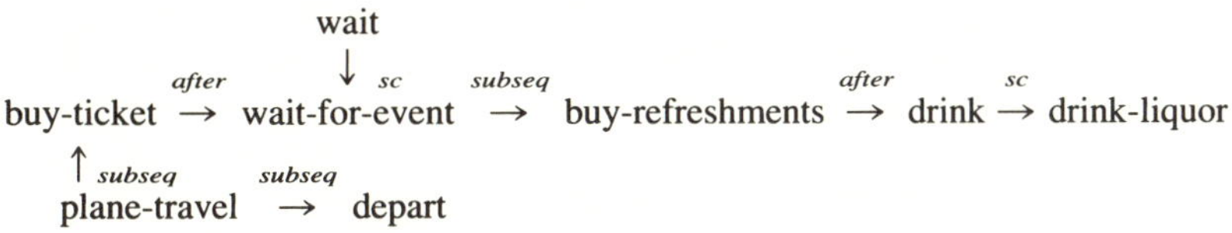

The basic algorithm finds a connecting path between the new event and any

coordinate, respectively. Roughly, the reader can think of these relations falling into one of three classes: taxonomic, partonomic, or temporal.

[11] The event *taste bitter* was purposely left out of this analysis and the analysis in interpretation 2, as it has no effect on the discussion that follows.

preceding, currently active, events in memory. Essentially three paths are found that relate the input events of the story fragment above. The paths are listed below in the order they are found.

1. buy-ticket $\xrightarrow{after}$ wait-for-event $\xleftarrow{sc}$ wait {connects events 1 & 2}
2. wait-for-event $\xrightarrow{subseq}$ buy-refreshments $\xrightarrow{after}$ drink $\xrightarrow{sc}$ drink-liquor {connects event 3}
3. buy-ticket $\xleftarrow{subseq}$ plane-travel $\xrightarrow{subseq}$ depart {connects event 5}

A more plausible interpretation—as it explains the waiting as a waiting in an airport, rather than waiting for some unspecified event (which may be a ball game for all we know)—is:

Interpretation 2

$$\begin{array}{ccccccccc} \text{depart} & \xleftarrow{subseq} & \text{plane-travel} & \xrightarrow{subseq} & \text{wait-in-airport} & \xrightarrow{subseq} & \text{drink} & \xrightarrow{sc} & \text{drink-liquor} \\ & & \downarrow {\scriptstyle subseq} & & \uparrow {\scriptstyle sc} & & & & \\ & & \text{buy-ticket} & & \text{wait} & & & & \end{array}$$

This interpretation also consists of three paths:

1. buy-ticket $\xleftarrow{subseq}$ plane-travel $\xrightarrow{subseq}$ wait-in-airport $\xleftarrow{sc}$ wait {connects events 1 & 2}
2. wait-in-airport $\xrightarrow{subseq}$ drink $\xrightarrow{sc}$ drink-liquor {connects event 3}
3. depart $\xleftarrow{subseq}$ plane-travel {connects event 5}

However, since the length of path 1 of interpretation 1 is less than the length of path 1 of interpretation 2, and subsequent input events are first integrated into existing interpretations (i.e., the input events *wait* and *depart* would result in paths 2 and 3 of interpretation 1 being connected with the active events of path 1—and *not* the shorter path, path 1 of interpretation 2), interpretation 2 would not be found using a shortest path algorithm. Furthermore, in the case of interpretations where the path length is the same, the shortest path algorithm may not choose the more plausible interpretation. Because shortest path is non-deterministic with regards to paths of equal length, it will pick the first interpretation that it discovers, rather than choose the best interpretation.

Figure 4.5 describes what short-term memory might look like after processing the airport segment. It describes a set of active features and schemata, classified

Affections	*Volition*	*Time*	*Space*	*Intellect*
nervousness	habit	lateness	airport	uncertainty
excitement		regularity	public place	
pleasure		changeableness	motion:travel	
content			motion:aircraft	
relief				
comfort				

Figure 4.5.
A snapshot of a portion of active features and schemata for the airport segment.

by category, which can be thought of as representing a portion of the motivating context (or background). In general, the constellations of ASFs that persist over time are used to dynamically constrain the formation of new schemata. It is these constellations that help determine which sets of events co-occur and thus which events get eventually incorporated into a schema. Thus, the features active under the category *space* would cause the event *wait-in-airport* to be activated more strongly than the *wait-for-event* concept, since its *ASF encoding*[12] is more highly correlated with the feature set in STM (i.e., its association with the features: *airport, public place, motion:travel,* and *motion:aircraft*). Now assuming all the other events (depart, plane-travel, buy-ticket, buy-refreshments, drink, drink-liquor) are also active (probably with varying degrees of activation), all these events (assuming the semantic constraints between the events have been satisfied—see Figure 4.12 for an example) are incorporated into a schema, along with the set of features active in STM (i.e., its context, which is denoted by A_s). This set of events represents two possible interpretations, (1) and (2) above. The model keeps around all active interpretations.

Now, as the story is processed, one of the interpretations may weaken due to new information. (An outline of this computation is described in the next section). If not, at the story's finish, the most active interpretation in STM is selected. The connecting relation between each pair of activated events is strengthened based on how well the semantic constraints are satisfied. Thus, those interpretations (i.e., paths) which have best satisfied the constraints will be the most active.

In this model, the contextual biasing mechanism is represented by the short-term memory patterns over the "wires" depicted in Figure 4.11. Each pattern is represented by a vector, where each position of the vector corresponds to an independent semantic feature, and the numerical value at that position corre-

[12] The encoding captures a part of the event's lexical entry and the background frame associated with the event—Figure 4.11 describes a typical encoding.

sponds to the level of activation of that feature. On each relaxation cycle the model accumulates evidence by finding correlations between the semantic features held by different assemblies (i.e., the event plus its case role information—see Figure 4.11) and the current active ASFs and schemata in STM. These correlations, denoted by $C_{E,STM}$, are stored with the event assembly. In effect some of the burden of constraint checking is now distributed to the contextual biasing mechanism via *ASF space*, where evidence accumulates, thus reinforcing or biasing the system's interpretation, forcing it to consider the more plausible interpretations.

4.2. Dynamic Reinterpretation

It is symptomatic of the symbolic models described above, that as the story progresses and thus the narrative context potentially changes, the old interpretations remain fixed, whereas in the model proposed here, old connections may weaken due to changing contextual influences, allowing more plausible ones to form. Consider the last part of the story in Figure 4.1 shown here in Figure 4.6.

We now know that drinking liquor at the airport had nothing to do with Sam having to pass the time. Instead, it was to enable him to get his courage up to ask his boss for a raise. In light of this new information, the previous interpretation (interpretation 2 in Section 4.1) has to somehow change. Now on each relaxation cycle, the activity of each of the event assemblies is recomputed based on the current activity in short-term memory. As schemata are composed of assemblies, this implies that as the narrative context changes, those collections of ASFs in STM relevant to the assemblies and to the schema itself (each schema also has a record of the active features when it was created—the vector A_s), will affect the activation of the assemblies contained therein, potentially changing the structure and content of the schema. This may occur because of two factors: (a) the semantic feature encodings of the particular event assemblies contained in the schema are not as correlated with the ASFs in STM (i.e., the value of $C_{E,STM}$ has decreased; and (b) the context features (i.e., the vector A_s) are not as correlated with the features in STM (i.e., the value of $C_{A_s,STM}$ has decreased).[13] In the former case, those event assemblies which are not as correlated will decrease in activation and in the latter case, the schema itself will decrease in activation, causing the event assemblies contained therein to uniformly decrease in activation. This fluidity is achieved without backtracking, and occurs as a natural byproduct of the settling process. No external mechanism is needed to make these decisions. The decision to reinterpret is an emergent property of the model.

Of course, the interpretation described above (i.e., Sam drank the liquor in order to get his courage up to ask his boss for a raise) could have had a dual

---

[13] When a schema is created the value $C_{A_s,STM}$ is computed and stored as an internal parameter.

Later that night, Sam talked to his wife. She asked "how did you get the courage to ask for a raise?" He said "it was the alcohol I drank earlier that day."

Figure 4.6.
The courage to ask for a raise segment.

purpose, or it could have been that Sam drank, got angry, and thus found his courage and desire to call his boss after drinking. In any event, as the model keeps around all possible interpretations, each of these possibilities is given a chance to survive.

Now this ties in with the reinterpretation example: "He had a good time. John went to Mary's party." discussed earlier in Section 3.2. As the first sentence is ambiguous, after it was processed, the system settled into an ambiguous state in which the two senses of *time:* "duration" and "experience" were both equally active. When the system was then presented with the second sentence, it settled into the correct sense of *time*—"experience"—by revising its earlier interpretation.

4.3. Soft Constraint Matching

Consider the following fragment from the story in Figure 4.1:

Remember, I am a great computer hacker. His boss tentatively agreed, provided his best engineer agreed to help the younger engineers.

How would a program determine that *computer hacker* and *best engineer* match? In traditional symbolic models, where the decision process is all-or-none (i.e., something earlier matches or not), somewhere in the database it must be asserted, or alternatively it must be inferred from the database that the "computer hacker" and "best engineer" are the same person, for how else would the program "know" they are the same. But, it might also be asserted that "computer hacker" and "professor" are the same. Thus the matching should also in part depend on the motivating context or background, as discussed in the previous sections. For example, "computer hacker" could plausibly match "best engineer" in the context of an engineer who works for a computer firm, in which case the engineer might know something about programming.

The soft matching is achieved by determining the feature overlap of the slot-fillers (each slot-filler has a semantic feature encoding—see Figure 4.11), which is computed by taking a normalized product of their common features minus their distinctive features (i.e., features that belong to one slot-filler, but not to the other), weighted by the filler's strength of association. Short-term case role memory (which represents a primitive attention mechanism for case information) is used to suggest a possible filler, if one of the slot-fillers has none. Thus the encodings shown below for the above fillers are sufficient to determine that "computer hacker" and "best engineer" plausibly match.

A "computer hacker" could be encoded using the following ASFs: sentient:+1, eccentricity:+1, intelligence:+1, curiosity:+1, caprice:+1, skill:+1, success:+1. The 'best engineer' could be encoded as: sentient:+1, eccentricity:−0.5, intelligence:+1, curiosity:+0.5, caprice:−0.5, skill:+1, success:+1.[14]

4.4. Contextually Graded Interpretations

In the introduction we asked, how one gets a machine to recognize that events may be "more or less" part of a schema and can have varying degrees of existence? That is, schemata are graded just as categories are (e.g., small boat) and membership is a matter of degree (see Rosch, 1975). Consider another fragment of text from Figure 4.1 shown here in Figure 4.7.

In the prototypical bargaining schema depicted in Figure 4.8, there is an offer, a refusal, an agreement, and some conversation throughout the bargaining. But in the text above, is Sam's threat a negotiating ploy or is he really planning to quit? If it is a negotiating ploy, then the *bargaining schema* is an appropriate representation of the text. If it is a genuine threat to quit, then the *leave-work* schema would be more appropriate. A third possibility is that neither of these schemata are appropriate, but some combination of both is.

Yet the decisions that are necessary for determining which schema is more appropriate cannot be yes-no decisions, since events have degrees of reality (e.g., his boss's agreement is tentative as opposed to firm). To account for this, each connection between events has a weight associated with it that indicates the relation's likelihood of occurrence. Thus, a small weight on the connection (link) between "bargain" and "agree" is suggestive of a tentative agreement. The calculation to determine the weight is based on the correlation of activity of the event's semantic feature encoding with the contents of short-term event memory. The higher the correlation the more likely it is that the relation holds.

Since the text in Figure 4.7 does not have any evidence indicating that Sam would have left (and this would be reflected by the activity in STM), it is probably the case that the bargaining schema is a more appropriate representation for explaining the connection between the events. Now according to Fillmore (1982), words give us categories of meanings which can be used in many different contexts, this range of contexts being determined by the multiple aspects of

---

[14] The −0.5, 0.5, +1 indicate respectively, a mild negative association, a mild association, and a strong association of the semantic feature of the concept. For example, eccentricity:+1 indicates that computer hackers are strongly associated with being eccentric.

He decided instead to telephone his boss to discuss his raise. He said to his boss "if you agree to give me a raise, I will consider staying with the company, but if you refuse, I will probably leave. Remember, I am a great computer hacker." His boss tentatively agreed, provided his best engineer agreed to help the younger engineers.

Figure 4.7.
The bargaining segment.

its prototypical use. The activity in STM is a reflection of the changing contextual influences. These influences help to determine which schema an event is a part of and to what degree; and when the ASFs associated with the motivating context more or less match the defining prototype (represented by the semantic context, i.e., the network of active event relations), then this determination can be made. The matching is based on the semantic features active in STM.

Unfortunately, the decision when to accept a schema, despite a weak match, versus when to create a new one is a difficult unsolved problem. Possibly by associating a *threshold* with each relation, which can be adjusted based on the frequency of occurrence of the events it connects, a partial solution can be obtained. For if the threshold is high, than a lot of evidence would be needed to obtain a match, and if the threshold is low, very little evidence would be required. Here, a high threshold intuitively means that the relation is not as likely to occur based on the model's experience to date.

The above process produces contextually graded interpretations, that is, the interpretations have information that indicates the likelihood of each of their relations, along with a set of ASFs that indicates the motivating context or background. For example, Figure 4.9 describes a set of active features, classified by category, which could represent a portion of the background information. A small link weight in conjunction with appropriate weightings of these features could indicate that the above "agreement" was tentative.

In the symbolic models where the decisions are all-or-none, the above interpretation (i.e., the bargaining schema) could also be accepted, but with none of the above detailed information—information which can be extremely useful to other processes. It is also possible that an interpretation may fail when it should

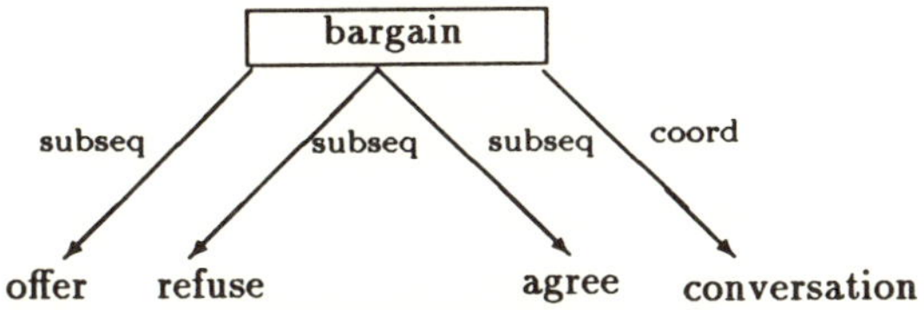

Figure 4.8.
The bargaining schema.

Volition	*Communication of Ideas*
willingness	misrepresentation
desire	indication
indifference	
eagerness	

Figure 4.9.
A snapshot of a portion of short-term memory indicating a tentative agreement.

not, because the constraint checking in these models is not sufficient to handle the complexity of nuances inherent in narrative text.

5. TOWARDS AN ARCHITECTURE

The overall architecture of a system that responds to the issues discussed in Sections 2 and 4 is described in Figure 4.10. It consists of six components: semantic memory, episodic memory, short-term memory (STM), an underlying ASF layer (represented by the intersecting horizontal and vertical "wires"), outside processing modules that interface to the ASF layer (see Figure 4.13), and a bus structure (represented by the horizontal "wires").[15] Each of the large rectangular boxes (i.e., those marked with an *E* and containing three smaller boxes) represents an event/state in either semantic or episodic memory. Each event/state node can be thought of as a *vertical event assembly* that has an associated set of deep case roles (e.g., agent, theme, etc.—the case roles are indicated by the small boxes inside the assembly), which in turn have links to a set of potential fillers (i.e., the ASFs). The assembly relates a high-level concept (e.g., an event) to its "parts" (e.g., the case roles associated with the event) which in turn are associated with their "parts," the ASFs. The vertical assemblies thus relate information at different levels of abstraction (as opposed to a horizontal assembly where the information is at the same level of abstraction).

The division of memory into "episodic" and "semantic" memory is due to Tulving (1983). Episodic memory refers to memory of specific past events, while semantic memory refers to generalized knowledge of the world. Here, semantic memory (i.e., long-term memory) represents the system's conceptual knowledge, whereas episodic memory represents the actual details of particular events

---

[15] The actual division is not as sharply drawn as the figure indicates, for as the system develops new schemata based on the events it has processed, these schemata will be eventually incorporated into semantic memory—a form of long-term learning.

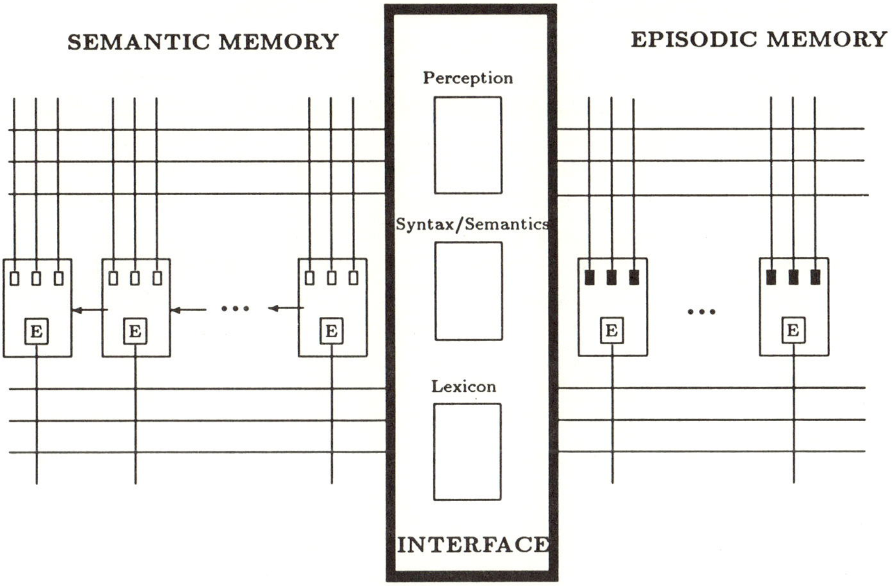

Figure 4.10.
System Architecture.

in the text. For example, consider the sentence "The plane departed 15 minutes later." The sentence refers to a particular instance of *departing*, represented in episodic memory, in contrast to the relevant conceptual notion of *departing*—to go away from, to leave—that is represented in semantic memory.

The system also contains two "short-term memory systems" (STM's) to represent different kinds of contextual information. The first, a short-term event memory (STEM), models the dynamically changing event/state context. The second, a short-term case role memory (STCM), models the dynamically changing roles associated with the event.[16] Actually STCM is segmented into 13 segments, one for each of the case roles, where each segment (portion of the vector) represents its encoding. Note the case role slots for the vertical event assemblies in semantic memory are initially unfilled (the unshaded rectangles), in contrast to the assemblies in episodic memory (the darkened rectangles). The STEM and STCM serve as "changing viewports" or windows into both long-term semantic memory and episodic memory, with information shuttling between the memories based upon their storage capacities and other time dependent properties.

[16] Evidence from neuroscience suggests the existence of multiple short-term memories, each for different information processing systems, for example, visual, spatial (see Squire, 1987).

5.1. The Analog Semantic Feature Layer

The ASF layer contains a distributed set of "analog semantic features," which act as intermediate-level units. The intermediate-level units in conjunction with an ECC network represent the background frame associated with a given concept/schema. The ASFs are used to encode the event assemblies in both semantic and episodic memory (see Figure 4.11) and to encode the semantic constraints between event assemblies (see Figure 4.12). This encoding captures a part of the event's lexical entry and the background frame associated with the event assembly. Each semantic feature is connected to all event assemblies that share that semantic feature and each event assembly is connected via bi-directional links to only those ASFs that are associated with it. Currently there are six levels of association between the ASFs and the components of the event assemblies: strong, mild, characteristically unrelated, mild negative, strong negative, and unknown (cf. Waltz & Pollack, 1985). The latter is intended to be used as a "learning" site.

Since event assemblies potentially share ASFs (the same set of ASFs encodes all assemblies), the activation that is spread through the network from a new incoming event causes a clustering of the shared ASFs in *ASF space,* that

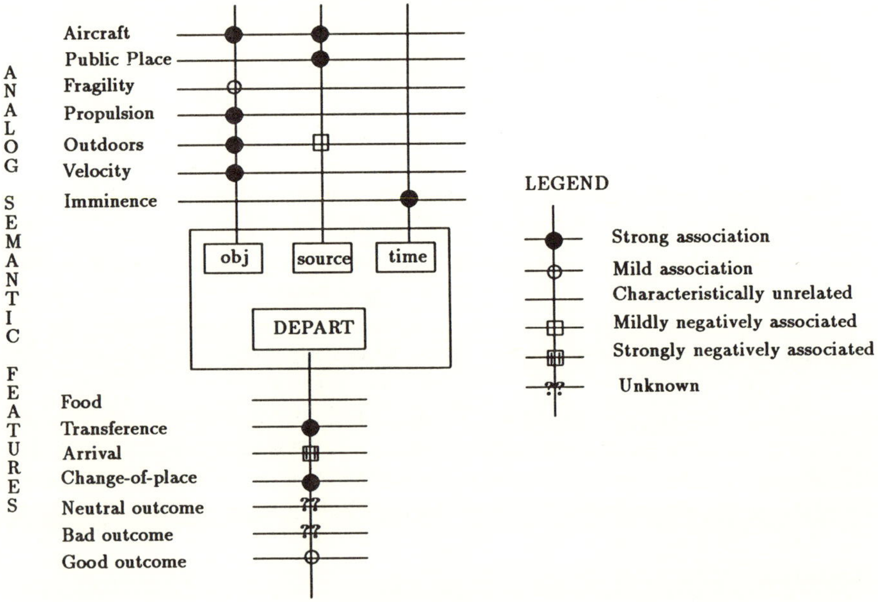

Figure 4.11.
A sample encoding of an episodic event—The plane departed 15 minutes later.

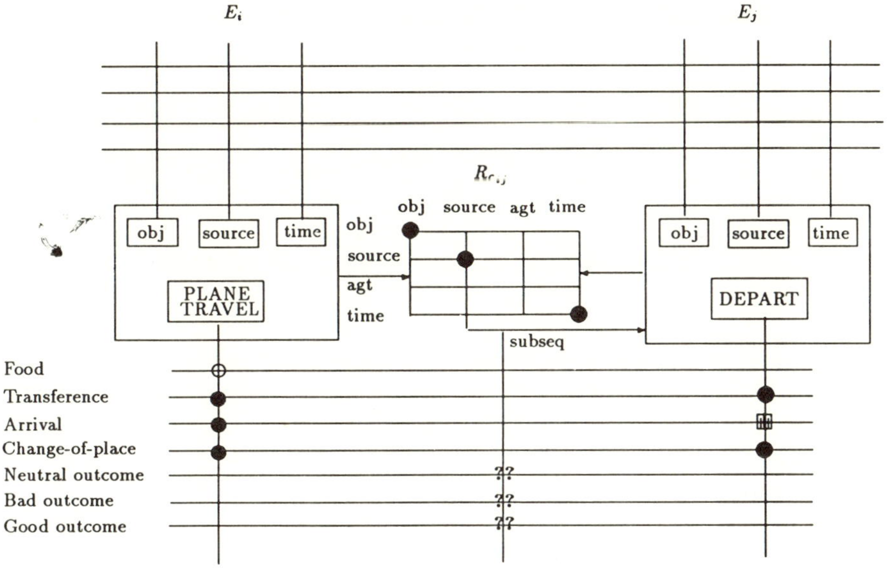

Figure 4.12.
The link between the vertical assemblies *depart* and *plane-travel.*

constrains the system's behavior causing it to 'settle' into different states. This is analogous to clustering in a high-dimensional space.

The patterns of activity over the "wires" in Figure 4.10 form the basis of the short-term memories, STEM and STCM. These memories act as conduits through which information flows, is deposited, and decays over time. Each active feature in the memories corresponds to an independent ASF, and the numerical value at that position corresponds to the level of activation of that feature. The information flow into and out of these memories is actually carried by separate channels of the bus—the upper channel for STCM and the lower channel for STEM. This is depicted in Figure 4.10. One use of the STCM is to potentially fill the default case slots of event assemblies in semantic memory.

Figure 4.11 shows a more detailed description of an encoding in one of the assemblies shown in Figure 4.10. It describes a particular episodic event: "The plane departed 15 minutes later." The lower part of the figure shows part of the actual encoding of the event ***depart*** forced by outside processing systems acting in conjunction with the underlying ASF substrate (see Figure 4.13). Thus the event ASFs: *transference, change-of-place,* are strongly associated with the event ***depart,*** while the semantic feature *arrival* has a strongly negatively association with the event ***depart*** and the semantic feature *good outcome* has a mild association with it. The upper half of the figure shows part of the encoding of the case role fillers *plane, airport, 15 minutes later* associated with the slots *obj,*

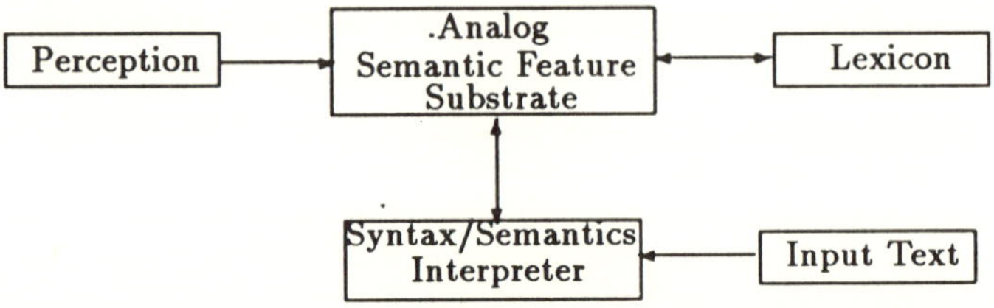

Figure 4.13.
The interface to the analog semantic substrate.

source, and *time* respectively, of the event ***depart.*** For example, the semantic features *aircraft, propulsion, outdoors* and *velocity* are strongly associated with the role filler *plane* of the *obj* slot of the ***depart*** event.

Semantic memory can be best thought of as represented by sets of triples of the form: (R_{cij},E_i,E_j). Each triple is an encoding of an ECC relation. The triple describes a relationship R_{cij} between the vertical assemblies E_i and E_j, where c_{ij} represents an encoding (a bit matrix) of the semantic constraints between E_i and E_j, with the elements E_i, E_j each encoded by a vector of ASFs. A detailed description of a constraint encoding is shown in Figure 4.12. Here each marked intersection of horizontal and vertical wires represents a semantic constraint. For example, Figure 4.12 indicates three semantic constraints:

1. the *object* of the **departing** must match the *object* of the **plane-travel**
2. the *source* of the **departing** must match the *source* of the **plane-travel**
3. the *time* of the **departing** must match the *time* of the **plane-travel**

One additional point to note is that ASFs can be computed by the system (e.g., after relaxation settles) and attached at the relation level. Figure 4.12 indicates that the semantic features: *neutral outcome, bad outcome,* and *good outcome* are initially unknown, that is, to be "filled in" as that knowledge became available from higher-level schemata. This information could be computed by taking the average of each slot's value (i.e., each active semantic feature) in each assembly of the schema.

An important difference between this model and the intersection search/marker passing/spreading activation models mentioned previously in Section 2, is that here the constraints are represented by ASFs, whereas there the constraints were symbolic. It is the "constraints as ASFs," that results in the soft matching property described in the introduction. This occurs because schemata can be activated even though not all semantic features match.

As there are 13 case roles currently in the system, there are 169 possible semantic constraints between a pair of vertical event assemblies. Figure 4.12

only shows 16 of the 169 possible constraints. In the current version of the system each semantic constraint is initially hard-wired. Each link also has a label and a weight attached to it. The weight indicates the strength of connection between vertical event assemblies and the label a relational dependency. (As described earlier there are seven such relations.) Thus the relation *subsequence* in Figure 4.12 indicates that the event **depart** is a part of the event **plane travel.**

5.2. The Interface Layer

This section provides a more detailed picture of the overall architecture. It describes how memory could interact with the outside world, thus forming a more complete model for understanding text.

Figure 4.11 described a particular encoding of the episodic event—The plane departed 15 minutes later. Several different modules are needed for a system to recognize and represent this episodic event. Figure 4.13 depicts these modules. They include:

- Perception—This module could be used to further constrain the possible combinations of features in the ASF substrate.
- Lexicon—Each entry would have wires to the ASF substrate. Work by Lesk (1986) suggests that the encoding of each entry could be done automatically using statistical methods on large volumes of text.
- Syntax and semantic interpreter—This module also has a bundle of connections to the ASF substrate, but in addition, it would contain links to each incoming event. Its interaction with the lexicon and the ASF substrate would produce a representation of an episodic event, that is, an encoded vertical event assembly.

5.3. The Representation of Context

The three kinds of memory described above (semantic, episodic, and STM) represent different sources of contextual information as patterns over ASFs in *ASF space,* with each information source having a different *contextual* influence. These include:

- Episodic context—Represents a specific event, some examples are: The plane departed 15 minutes later; Sam's talking to his wife or his drinking scotch at the airport. Episodic context is related to the notion of episode in story schemas (e.g., *story grammars:* Rumelhart, 1975; *schema/narrative trees:* Simmons & Correira, 1980).

- Semantic context—The conceptual network (see for example, Figure 4.4) provides a context for interpreting the relationships between the event concepts used in the text. In the proposed system this takes the form of an ECC network.
- Background frame or Motivating context—Represents some body of understandings, some pattern of practices, or some history of social institutions, against which the particular category is intelligible to the community (Fillmore, 1982).
- Narrative context—Represents the ongoing interpretation, that is, across episodes.

The interactions between the analog patterns over the ASF wires result in the emergence of a representation of the model's current "understanding." Figure 4.14 depicts this interaction. Here episodic memory reflects the episodic context, where each episode is encoded by the processes described in the interface layer (see Figure 4.13), while semantic memory reflects both the narrative, semantic, and motivating contexts. The motivating context is represented by an ASF encoding of the model's initial set of event relationships; semantic context is represented by the network of active relations (a kind of high-level "semantic trace") that currently reside in semantic memory (each circle in Figure 4.14 is an event assembly, with the link representing the relation R_{cij} between assemblies); and the narrative context is represented by the collection of active schemata (indicated by the rectangular shapes in Figure 4.14) that are constructed from this conceptual network.[17] The information from both episodic and semantic memory is accumulated over time into the STMs, which is fed back in the next cycle of processing. The feedback from STM helps to determine which features in both memories should remain active and which should decay.

What's interesting here is that the above interaction enables the model to construct more plausible and fluid interpretations that can potentially reflect more shades and degrees of similarity and difference than would otherwise be possible, for it incorporates the contextual influence from four different sources of information.

5.4. Prediction/Schema Completion

The set of examples previously discussed in Section 4 were concerned with the interpretation process, that is, explaining how the new events fit into the model's current "understanding." Thus "understanding" was represented by the patterns of activity over the various memories and these patterns included representations

[17] The size and color of the objects correlate with degree of activity of an assembly, a schema, or strength of connection between assemblies.

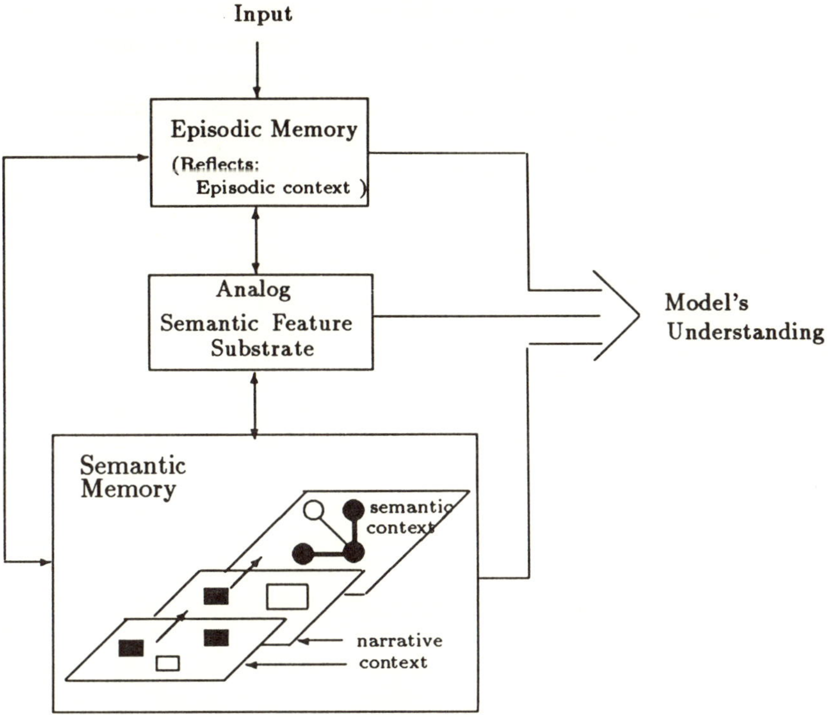

Figure 4.14.
The emergence of a representation of the model's current "understanding."

of the contextual influences discussed in Section 5.3 (i.e., episodic, semantic, motivating, and narrative influences). It is possible to use the same mechanisms for prediction. Consider turning off all outside inputs (a kind of sensory deprivation), that is, all the wires from the modules in Figure 4.13 to the ASF substrate are cut.

As the model contains a "trace" of its behavior, the patterns of activity on the memory wires above, it can make a prediction as to what the next event should be by using the "trace" as its input. Consider the airport segment example previously discussed in Section 4.1:

Sam bought a ticket. While he waited he drank some scotch. It tasted bitter.
The plane departed 15 minutes later.

A snapshot of the STM trace is shown in Figure 4.5 and a high-level "semantic trace" (produced when the text was originally input) is described by interpretation 2 in Section 4.1. If this trace is fed back as input to the system, then the pattern of activity that it induces over the ASF wires, given the contents of STM, could enable it to predict that Sam also did some reading while he waited, or one of a number of things one does at a depot. Since the event "things-to-do-at-depot" is closely related in ASF space to the event "plane-travel," there is evidence for the connection between them, thus enabling this prediction.

5.5. Neurophysiological Motivation

Some of the ideas that underlie this model come from suggestions from neuroscience:

- The idea of a vertical event assembly is inspired by von der Malsburg (1981), according to which a cell at a higher level in the brain is associated with[18] one at a lower level, and these, in turn, may be associated with those at a still lower level. Without such vertical assemblies, von der Malsburg claims it would be rather difficult to unite the higher level with their low level details in a rather short time.
- Von der Malsburg and Bienenstock (1986) propose that the events which underlie brain function are best described by compound states, which they characterize as stable *activity-connectivity* states. In these states there is a good match between activity and connectivity, that is, between successful events and activated synapses, and between failures and deactivated synapses. The relaxation process is modelled after this computation. Here an excitatory signal can only be successful if there are other active signals converging on the same target event assembly and few or no inhibitory signals have just fired—in our model a signal is composed of information from the link connecting two event assemblies (see Figure 4.12) and information from the ASF signals emanating from STM. All such signals that successfully pass the constraint relaxation cycle[19] are strengthened, thus making the target event assembly more active and hence its associated ASF encoding more likely to occur.

The association of a higher level concept with one at a lower level[20] is a powerful idea, for it solves the combinational problem of how the brain can respond to an unlimited number of distinct sentences, passages of music, visual scenes, and schemata.

---

[18] Here "associated with" means that the cells fire approximately simultaneously.

[19] Determines which currently active event assemblies satisfy their semantic constraints.

[20] For example, the general notion of a "face" is a high-level concept that can be associated with the its parts (e.g., nose, eyes)—its lower-level details.

> The brain's solution is to use *temporary* combinations of a subset of a much more limited number of units (the 10^{12} or so neurons in the central nervous system), each combination being brought into action as the circumstances demand and then largely discarded. (Crick, 1984)

The solution proposed here uses the above ideas to develop a computational model of schema recognition for understanding text. The vertical assemblies described here relate a high-level concept (i.e., an event or state, case roles) with its low level details (i.e., collections of ASFs which instantiate the event or state's filler slots). This is achieved through the use of two representations: (a) a weighted semantic (ECC) network of relations, and (b) an underlying substrate of ASFs. Thus the "meaning" of a concept/schema comes in part from its relative position in the ECC network and in part from its ASF encoding. It is this dual representation that imbues our model with its representational power. In our model this results in collections of interrelated, structured k-lines (Minsky, 1980, 1986)—which are sets of event assemblies with context information—which we propose as a more structured and detailed representation for textual understanding.

6. DISCUSSION

6.1. Advantages of the Approach

The spreading activation/marker passing approach versus PDP (see Rumelhart & McClelland, 1986) continues the debate as to whether one should use a local or a distributed model. (See Bookman, 1988, for further discussion as it pertains to natural language understanding.) The local model offers the advantage of internal clarity. The distributed model allows for adaptability and "grace under degradation." The model proposed here captures the advantages of both of these models. For example, an analog semantic feature-based encoding of the semantic constraints between concepts is used. This avoids the "brittle constraint" problem whereby a particular constraint either succeeds or fails. In addition, the ASFs capture many of the underlying details associated with the schema. This accounts for contextually graded interpretations and the dynamic reinterpretation properties discussed in the examples section. A strength of local spreading activation/marker passing models is that underlying conceptual knowledge is easy to manipulate and understand. As mentioned earlier, we have used one form of these conceptual structures (ECC) for summarizing text and determining importance. The manipulation of conceptual structure is a much harder task for the PDP models previously mentioned in Section 2. The problem is the lack of internal structure.[21] The solution proposed here, structured assemblies as build-

[21] Hinton's (1988) notion of a reduced description and Pollack's (1988) RAAM's, which are compositional distributed representations, are attempts to deal with this problem.

ing blocks, with a shared pool of ASFs is an attempt to deal with this issue within the domain of narrative text (cf. Dolan & Dyer, 1988).

An additional problem related to the previous one is that of representing multiple instantiations of concepts and schemata. In the model described here, it is the use of the two combined representations—a localist semantic network and an underlying pool of distributed ASFs—that help in its solution. Here role information is bound within each schema. As a result, if a concept appears two or more times with different role information, each concept instance (i.e., the vertical event assembly plus its role information) would be "recruited" (Feldman, 1982) into a new schema and thus a new instantiation of the concept along with its current role fillers would be created. The localist representation stores relational dependencies between concepts, while the ASF substrate determines which slots get filled. The slots as features helps to determine which dependencies get strengthened (or weakened if the satisfaction of the semantic constraints falls below a given threshold or the concepts are uncorrelated). Thus this model attempts to draw on the strengths of both classes of models and is put forward as a more suitable replacement then either pure localist or pure PDP models.

The use of the distributed set of ASFs gives the model one additional advantage: It enables the system to find the *best match* between memories (i.e., on the patterns over the ASF "wires") versus the *shortest path* joining two concepts. One reason that this can happen, is that each node in semantic and episodic memory acts like a *demon,* "shouting" to short-term memory if it is applicable (i.e., if its semantic encoding is relevant), as opposed to following predetermined pathways in a network. In addition by performing relaxation on the semantic feature set, we get constellations of ASFs that persist over time, that can be used to dynamically constrain the formation of new schemata.

The weighted links in memory allow dynamic modification of semantic memory. After processing a piece of text the system will develop a bias, thus making it easier to process the same or similar texts on successive times, and possibly enabling the system to recognize that it has seen the same text before. Currently, no use has been made of the latter feature, but a future version will attempt to do so. Another potential use of weighted links is cue recall. Here some aspects of a previous event are presented as recall cues (cf. Halgren, 1984), and since some of the connections between assemblies have been previously strengthened, excitation of the cue causes aspects of the original experience to become excited. As a result, this can lead to the reconstruction (or recall) of the activity pattern present at the original experience.

It is important to note that most of the computation here is local to each node and thus the schema recognition algorithm can be efficiently performed by massively parallel hardware. As noted before, most intersection search/spreading activation/marker passing models have implementations that are not truly parallel, due to their sequential constraint checking, whereas the link constraint relaxation computation outlined here can be performed in parallel.

In summary the model offers the following advantages:

- An enriched dual representation—accounts for contextually graded interpretations and the dynamic reinterpretation property
- Overcomes brittleness of constraint checking
- Selects plausible interpretations
- Best match versus shortest path
- Memory is dynamically modifiable
- Massively parallel computation

6.2. The Analog Semantic Feature Contribution

The overall effect of the ASF substrate is that it accounts for the recognition of schemata that can have varying degrees of existence, with potentially more shades and degrees of similarity and difference between them, than would otherwise be possible (i.e., using "featureless" networks). A key point is as each active feature in STM corresponds to an independent semantic feature, a mere 30 semantic features could specify a billion different contexts—and we surely have thousands of different ASFs (Minsky, 1986, makes the same argument about microfeatures). The above argument assumes the ASFs are binary, but in this model they can have analog values, thus potentially allowing for even finer shades of contextual influence.

The ASFs are serving what Fillmore (1982) calls the motivating context or background. Consider the word *breakfast*. According to Fillmore (1982), "to understand this word is to understand the practice in our culture of having three meals a day, at more or less conventionally established times of the day, and for one of these meals to be eaten early in the day, after a period of sleep, and for it to consist of a somewhat unique menu." Yet as he points out, each of the above three conditions typically associated with it can be independently absent, still allowing a native user to use the word. For example, someone can sleep through the morning, wake up at two o'clock in the afternoon, and sit down to a meal of pancakes, bacon, and orange juice, and still call that meal "breakfast." The category of meanings associated with the word breakfast is thus determined by the conditions of the background situation which can more or less match the defining prototype.

Semantic feature layered networks also require fewer links, because they do not have to have links between all relevant pairs of words, only between a word and its ASFs. Suppose one has 10^6 concepts in one's conceptual network, without a ASF layer, one would need 10^{12} connections between them. If one assumes that approximately 2000 ASFs are needed to represent these 10^6 concepts, then a network with a semantic feature layer would only require $2 * 10^9$ connections.

Alternatively, we can state the above argument in the following form: What is the number of questions one has to ask in order to *automatically* build an unrestricted featureless semantic network, like the one described in this chapter? The answer is N^2 questions, since one has to check the possible relationship between each concept and every other in the dictionary; while the answer is mN questions for semantic feature layered networks, where m is the number of ASFs necessary to represent N concepts, and $m \ll N$ (e.g., $m = 2000$ and $N = 10^6$ as above). In practice if one is going to build such featureless networks by hand, then the complexity is much less than N^2. However, the goal is to build these networks by machine and thus the complexity really is N^2.

6.3. The Symbolic And Subsymbolic

Smolensky (1988) describes the cognitive descriptions associated with the "symbolic paradigm" as "built out of entities that are *symbols* both in the semantic sense of referring to external objects and in the syntactic sense of being operated upon by 'symbol manipulation.'" Whereas in the "subsymbolic" paradigm, *subsymbols* participate in numerical and not symbolic computation.

The ASFs serve as a dynamic substrate from which constellations of ASFs emerge by interacting with higher-level symbolic structures. The feedback between the "symbolic" and "subsymbolic" (the ASFs) lead to the formation of new schemata, which are represented by both "symbolic" and "subsymbolic" parts.

There have been two other recent computational approaches that combine the "symbolic" with the "subsymbolic." One approach (Hendler, 1989) uses symbolic as "tags" to sort out where each concept gets its activation from, which is either from the symbolic markers or the subsymbolic microfeature network. This information is then used to determine similarity between concepts. Another approach (Sharkey, Sutcliffe, & Wobcke, 1986), uses a collection of distributed micro-elements (i.e., the subsymbolic), linked to *Threshold Knowledge Units* (TKUs) (i.e., the symbolic) that correspond to scenes. Then as the system moves from one pattern to the next, in response to an external input, the TKUs activate the associated micro-elements most relevant to that current input based on the structure of the TKUs, that is, the micro-elements that connect to it.

In the approach taken here, incoming events induce analog patterns of activation over a dynamically changing ASF substrate. These patterns are then "structured" into schemata by an ASF encoded symbolic network; the symbolic information helps in the synthesis of new schemata by extracting common patterns from the substrate that are consistent with the input and existing event relations. This is similar in spirit to the TKU model, but differs, as the TKU model is incapable of revising an earlier interpretation in light of new data, and has no mechanism to represent changing contextual influences.

7. CONCLUDING REMARKS

This chapter presents a connectionist model for schema recognition within the domain of narrative text. It addresses some problems critical to text understanding such as the capability to reinterpret a previous interpretation based on changing circumstances and the capability to find plausible interpretations in parallel—problems which have not been satisfactorily solved by the symbolic models discussed in this chapter.

A particularly hard problem for symbolic models is the first one, for how does the program decide when the text needs to be reinterpreted? Usually it is under the direction of a central executive (e.g., in the marker passing/spreading activation models, the executive is the constraint checker) that determines which things might change. In the solution proposed here, there is no central executive, rather the decision to reinterpret is an emergent property of the model. The reinterpretation is determined by the interaction of semantic and episodic memory using short-term memories that dynamically cause a strengthening or weakening of parts in the existing schemata based on STMs changing contextual influences. The reinterpretation is a natural byproduct of the relaxation process. An analogy one might make is to consider each schema to be attached via "rubber bands" to its parts and when the narrative context changes, this is reflected in STM causing the rubber band to "stretch" making the existing interpretation less plausible. A break in the rubber band might correspond to a violated expectation, that is, a surprise. These surprises could form the backbone of new episodes and semantic memories, which could be used as a form of learning or for further examples of previous events. The latter might enable the system to recognize a situation it has encountered before.

Although the solution proposed is an implementation in progress (for more recent progress see Bookman & Alterman, 1990), a portion of the algorithm, however, has been successfully tested for the task of word sense disambiguation (see Bookman, 1988). The model described there also uses a distributed short-term memory composed of ASFs to represent the underlying context. Here via a set of short-term memories, the system provides a way of automatically "indexing" into a network of relations (i.e., semantic memory) to extract plausible interpretations. This is accomplished via a "settling" process, based on a parallel *best match,* that is, where the semantic and contextual constraints are maximally consistent with the input. The set of interpretations (i.e., schemata) constructed by the system along with representation of its *motivating context* (its cache of short-term memory at the time the schemata were formed) is the system's representation of its "understanding." Future work will involve extensive testing of the model and further analysis of its behavior.

Based on the work of Hendle (1990), the first author is developing a method for automatically encoding the ASF knowledge associated with events. This work represents research in progress.

The problem of "long-term" modification to semantic memory was not addressed here, but if one views long-term learning as time-integrated short-term modification (and short-term modification was explored here), it should be possible to investigate its effects as multiple stories are input to the system. This also raises the possibility of the system recognizing when it has already seen a story, hinted at above.

Another direction involves the possibility of learning the semantic constraints between concepts (e.g., the *object* of the **departing** must match the *object* of the **plane-travel**). In previous work on ECC networks, this was an interactive process. We would decide what the constraints were and then run our program and see if the interpretation it produced was reasonable. If it was not, we would change the constraints. Unfortunately, changing just a single constraint could have unforeseen effects. As this process is very time consuming, some automatic process is needed to learn the constraints. Currently, this problem is being addressed by the first author.

In summary, events represent categorizations of experience, where each category has a motivating situation that occurs against a background of knowledge and experience. In systems which do not take into account such information, that are constrained to solely follow predetermined pathways, the most plausible interpretations are not always found, whereas in this system, such information is represented in ASF space, and since associations between events can in addition be based on their closeness in ASF space, more plausible interpretations can be found.

APPENDIX

The appendix describes a set of ASFs associated with the category *affections*. There are 11 categories in total, only one of which is listed here. As stated before, each set of features associated with a category represents a tree whose root (e.g., affections in this case) denotes the most abstract or the most generalized semantic feature for the tree.

Affections: A Category of ASFs

1. personal relations
    - Emotion: feelings, lack of feelings
    - Excitability: excitement, inexcitability, nervousness, patience, impatience
    - Pleasure: pleasantness, unpleasantness, pleasure, displeasure, dislike, content, discontent, cheerfulness, solemnity, sadness, regret,
    - Anticipative emotions: hope, hopelessness

— Concern; anxiety, fear, cowardice, courage, rashness, caution
— Discriminative affections: fastidiousness, taste, vulgarity, ugliness, beauty, ornamentation, simplicity, affection, ostentation
— Pride: pride, humility, servility, modesty, vanity, boasting, bluster, arrogance, insolence
— Esteem: repute, disrepute, an honor, title, nobility, commonality
— Contemplative emotions: wonder, unastonishment

2. Sympathetic Affections
— Social relations: sociability, unsociability, seclusion, hospitality
— Social affections: friendship, friend, enmity, hate, love, lovemaking, endearment, marriage, celibacy, divorce, widow
— Civility: courtesy, discourtesy
— Benevolence: kindness, malevolence, misanthropy, public spirit, benefactor, evildoer
— Sympathy: pity, pitilessness, condolence, forgiveness, congratulation
— Gratefulness: gratitude, ingratitude
— Ill humor: ill humor, resentment
— Selfish resentment: jealousy, envy
— Reprisal: retaliation, revenge

3. Morality
— Morals: ethics, right, wrong
— Moral obligation: dueness, undueness, duty, imposition
— Moral sentiments: respect, disrespect, contempt, ridicule, flattery, disparagement, threat
— Moral conditions: justice, injustice, selfishness, unselfishness, virtue, vice, wrongdoing, guilt, innocence
— Moral practice: sensuality, chastity, unchastity, indecency, temperance, intemperance, gluttony, intoxication, sobriety
— Moral observance: legality, illegality, jurisdiction, tribunal, judge, lawyer, lawsuit, accusation, justification, acquittal, condemnation, penalty, punishment, atonement.

REFERENCES

Alterman, R. (1985). A dictionary based on concept coherence. *Artificial Intelligence, 25*, 153–186.

Alterman, R. (1989). Event concept coherence. In D. Waltz (Ed.), *Advances in natural language processing* (pp. 57–87). Hillsdale, NJ: Lawrence Erlbaum Associates.

Alterman, R., & Bookman, L.A. (1990a). *Reasoning about the semantic encoding of the connectivity of events*. (Tech. Rep. CS-90-141). Waltham, MA: Brandeis University, Computer Science Department.

Alterman, R., & Bookman, L.A. (1990b). Some computaional experiments in summarization. *Discourse Processes, 13*(2), 143–174.

Ballard, D.H., & Brown, C.M. (1982). *Computer vision*. Englewood Cliffs, NJ: Prentice-Hall.

Bookman, L.A. (1988). A connectionist scheme for modelling context. In D. Touretzky, G. Hinton, & T.J. Sejnowski (Eds.), *Proceedings of the 1988 Connectionist Models Summer School* (pp. 281–290). San Mateo, CA: Morgan Kaufmann.

Bookman, L.A. (In preparation). *A formal analysis of ASF networks*.

Bookman, L.A., & Alterman, R. (1990). *An analog semantic feature encoding of memory and context* (Tech. Rep. CS-90-147). Waltham, MA: Brandeis University, Computer Science Department.

Charniak, E. (1986). A neat theory of marker passing. In *Proceedings of the Fifth National Conference on Artificial Intelligence* (pp. 584–588). Los Altos, CA: Morgan Kaufmann.

Charniak, E. (1983). Passing markers: A theory of contextual influences in language comprehension. *Cognitive Science, 7,* 171–190.

Chun, H.W., & Mimo A. (1987). A model of schema selection using marking passing and connectionist spreading activation. *The Ninth Annual Conference of the Cognitive Science Society* (pp. 887–896). Hillsdale, NJ: Lawrence Erlbaum.

Crick, F. (1984). Function of the thalamic reticular complex: The searchlight hypothesis. *Proceedings of the National Academy of Sciences, 81,* 4586–4590.

Dolan, C.P., & Dyer, M.G. (1988). Parallel retrieval and application of conceptual knowledge. In D. Touretzky, G. Hinton, & T.J. Sejnowski (Eds.), *Proceedings of the 1988 Connectionist Models Summer School* (pp. 273–280). San Mateo, CA: Morgan Kaufmann.

Fahlman, S. (1979). *NETL: A system for representing and using real-world knowledge*. Cambridge, MA: MIT Press.

Feldman, J.A. (1982). Dynamic connection in neural nets. *Biological Cybernetics, 46,* 27–39.

Feldman, J.A., & Ballard, D.H. (1982). Connectionist models and their properties. *Cognitive Science, 6,* 205–254.

Fillmore, C. (1968). The case for case. In E. Bach & R. Harms (Eds.), *Universals in linguistic theory*. New York: Holt, Rinehart & Winston.

Fillmore, C.J. (1982). Frame semantics. *Linguistics in the morning calm*. Seoul, Korea: Hanshin Publishing Company.

Halgren, E. (1984). Human hippocampal and amygdala recording and stimulation: Evidence for a neural model of recent memory. In L.R. Squire & N. Butters (Eds.), *The neuropsychology of memory* (pp. 165–182). New York: Guilford Press.

Hendle, D. (1990). Noun classification from predicate-argument structures. *The Twenty-Eighth Annual Meeting of the Association for Computational Linguistics*, pp. 268–275. Pittsburge, PA.

Hendler, J. (1986). *Integrating marker-passing and problem-solving: A spreading activation approach to improved choice in planning*. Doctoral thesis, Brown University, Providence, RI.

Hendler, J. (1989). Marker-passing over microfeatures: Towards a hybrid symbolic/connectionist model. *Cognitive Science, 13,* 79–106.

Hinton, G.E. (1981). Implementing semantic networks in parallel hardware. In G.E.

Hinton & J.A. Anderson (Eds.), *Parallel models if associative memory* (pp. 161–188). Hillsdale, NJ: Lawrence Erlbaum.

Hinton, G.E. (1988). Representing part-whole hierarchies in connectionist networks. *The Tenth Annual Conference of the Cognitive Science Society* (pp. 48–54). Hillsdale, NJ: Lawrence Erlbaum.

Hinton, G.E., McClelland, J.L., & Rumelhart, D.E. (1986). Distributed representations. In J.L. McClelland & D.E. Rumelhart (Eds.), *Parallel distributed processing: Explorations in the microstructures of cognition* (Vol. 1, pp. 77–109). Cambridge, MA: MIT Press.

Kosko, B. (1986). Fuzzy knowledge combination. *International Journal of Intelligent Systems, 1,* 293–320.

Lesk, M. (1986). Automatic sense disambiguation using machine readable dictionaries: How to tell a pine cone from an ice cream cone. *Proceedings of SIGDOC*. New York: Association for Computing Machinery.

Miller, G.A., & Johnson-Laird, P.N. (1976). *Language and perception*. Cambridge, MA: Harvard University Press.

Minsky, M. (1975). A framework for representing knowledge. In P.W. Winston (Ed.), *The psychology of computer vision* (pp. 211–277). New York: McGraw-Hill.

Minsky, M. (1980). K-lines: A theory of memory. *Cognitive Science, 4,* 117–130.

Minsky, M. (1986). *The society of mind*. New York: Simon and Schuster.

Norvig, P. (1987). *Inference processes and knowledge representation for text understanding*. Unpublished Doctoral thesis, University of California at Berkeley.

Pollack, J. (1988). Recursive auto-associative memory: Devising compositional distributed representations. *The Tenth Annual Conference of the Cognitive Science Society* (pp. 33–39). Hillsdale, NJ: Lawrence Erlbaum.

Pustejovsky, J. (1988). Constraints on the acquisition of semantic knowledge. *International Journal of Intelligent Systems, 3*(3), 247–268.

Quillian, R. (1968). Semantic memory. In M. Minsky (Ed.), *Semantic information processing* (pp. 227–270). Cambridge, MA: MIT Press.

Rosch, E. (1975). Cognitive reference points. *Cognitive Psychology, 7,* 532–547.

Rumelhart, D. (1975). Notes on a schema for stories. In D. Bobrow & A. Collins (Eds.), *Representation and understanding* (pp. 211–236). New York: Academic Press.

Rumelhart, D.E., & McClelland, J.L. (1986). *Parallel distributed processing: Explorations in the microstructure of cognition* (Vol. 1). Cambridge, MA: MIT Press.

Rumelhart, D.E., Smolensky, P. McClelland, J.L., & Hinton, G.E. (1986). Schemata and sequential thought processes in PDP models. In J.L. McClelland & D.E. Rumelhart (Eds.), *Parallel distributed processing: Explorations in the microstructure of cognition* (Vol. 1, pp. 7–57). Cambridge, MA: MIT Press.

Schank, R., & Abelson, R. (1977). *Scripts, plans, goals, and understanding*. Hillsdale, NJ: Lawrence Erlbaum.

Schank, R. (1982). *Dynamic memory*. New York: Cambridge University Press.

Sharkey, N., Sutcliffe, R.F.E., & Wobcke, W. (1986). Binary and continuous connection schemes for knowledge access. *Proceedings of the Fifth National Conference on Artificial Intelligence* (pp. 262–266). Los Altos, CA: Morgan Kaufmann.

Simmons, R., & Correira, A. (1980). Rule forms for verse, sentences, and story trees. In N. Findler (Ed.), *Associative networks: The representation and use of knowledge in computers* (pp. 363–391). New York: Academic Press.

Smolensky, P. (1986). Information processing in dynamical systems: Foundations of harmony theory. In D.E. Rumelhart & J.L. McClelland (Eds.), *Parallel distributed processing: Explorations in the microstructure of cognition* (Vol. 1, pp. 194–281). Cambridge, MA: MIT Press.

Smolensky, P. (1987, February). *A method for connectionist variable binding* (Tech. Rep. CU-CS-356-87). Boulder, CO: Department of Computer Science and Institute of Cognitive Science, University of Colorado.

Smolensky, P. (1988). On the proper treatment of connectionism. *The Behavioral and Brain Sciences, 1*(1), 1–74.

Squire, L. (1987). *Memory and brain.* New York: Oxford Press.

Touretzky, D., & Hinton, G. (1985). Symbols among the neurons: Details of a connectionist inference architecture. *Proceedings of the Ninth International Joint Conference on Artificial Intelligence* (pp. 239–243). Los Angeles, CA.

Tulving, E. (1983). *Elements of episodic memory. Oxford Psychology Series No. 2.* New York: Oxford University Press.

von der Malsburg, C. (1981). *The correlation theory of brain function* (Tech. Rep. Internal Report 81-2). Goettingen, West-Germany: Department of Neurobiology, Max-Planck-Institute for Biophysical Chemistry.

von der Malsburg, C., & Bienenstock, E. (1986). Statistical coding and short term synaptic plasticity: A schema for knowledge representation in the brain. In E. Bienenstock, F. Fogelman Soulie, & G. Weisbuch (Eds.), *Disordered systems and biological organization.* Berlin: Springer-Verlag.

Waltz, D. (1975). Understanding scenes of line drawings with shadows. In P.W. Winston (Ed.), *The psychology of computer vision* (pp. 19–91). New York: McGraw-Hill.

Waltz, D., & Feldman, J. (1988). Connectionist models and their implications: Readings from cognitive science. In D. Waltz & J. Feldman (Eds.), *Connectionist models and their implications* (pp. 1–11). Norwood, NJ: Ablex.

Waltz, D., & Pollack, J. (1985). Massively parallel parsing: A strongly interactive model of natural language interpretation. *Cognitive Science, 9,* 52–74.

5
A Context-Free Connectionist Parser Which is not Connectionist, But Then it is not Really Context-Free Either*

Eugene Charniak
Eugene Santos, Jr.

1. INTRODUCTION

This chapter describes CONPARSE, a context-free parser designed in a *connectionist* architecture.

Connectionism has attracted considerable attention of late because it offers a new way of looking at old problems in Artificial Intelligence and Psychology—a way which also has considerable neurophysiological plausibility (Feldman & Ballard, 1982; Rumelhart & McClelland, 1986; Lippmann, 1987). Unfortunately, connectionism, or at least the *distributed* connectionism we will assume in this chapter, has been hard to apply to high-level cognitive tasks. Connectionist parsing has been of interest because of parsing's intermediate role between higher and lower cognitive abilities.

Indeed, there have been several previous attempts at a connectionist parser (Cottrell, 1985; Fanty, 1985; Selman, 1985; Waltz & Pollack, 1985; Allen, 1987; Hanson & Kegl, 1987; Pollack, 1987; Fanty, 1988). The "classic" connectionist approach was taken in the PARSNIP system (Hanson & Kegl, 1987), where a three-layer feedforward network was trained on sentences using back-propaga-

*This work was supported in part by the Office of Naval Research under contract N00014-79-C-0592, the National Science Foundation under contracts IST-8416034 and IST-8515005 and by the Defense Advanced Research Projects Agency under ARPA OrderNo. 4786. Thanks to James McClelland for some encouragement.

tion. Others (Cottrell, 1985; Fanty, 1985; Selman, 1985; Waltz & Pollack, 1985; Allen, 1987; Pollack, 1987; Fanty, 1988) approached this problem by carefully structuring their networks. Some (Allen, 1987; Pollack, 1987) also incorporated semantics to become more of a model for natural language processing.

CONPARSE was designed to be a purely syntactic system. Thus, the systems of (Cottrell, 1985; Fanty, 1985; Selman, 1985; Waltz & Pollack, 1985) are most closely related to it.

All these systems, however, have a major failing—they are strictly speaking, only capable of parsing regular grammars. This is inevitable. Connectionism assumes a large, but bounded, number of units. Thus any connectionist scheme must be finite state.

Nevertheless one can ask if such parsers could approach context-free in the limit (as the number of units is increased) and since the answer for all is "yes" it seems reasonable to call them all (including ours) "context-free."

More interesting though is to ask how the memory limitations show up in the parsing process. The failings of previous parsers have been distinctly *unhuman*. They are limited to fixed length sentences. Ours is more promising in this regard. While it does fine for right branching structures, it is limited in its ability to parse center embedded constructions, a point we will return to later.

Ours does, however, have a distinct failing of its own—it is not a *true* connectionist architecture. But let us say what it *is* first.

2. REPRESENTING A PARSE TREE

The easiest way to visualize the parser, and how it represents a parse tree, is to imagine a parse tree drawn on a white board, as shown in Figure 5.1. Naturally since we are talking about a distributed connectionist scheme, we will break the white board up into many distinct units, each one of which may have one of a small number of distinct values—S, NP, VP, PP, Noun, and so on. This is shown in Figure 5.2.

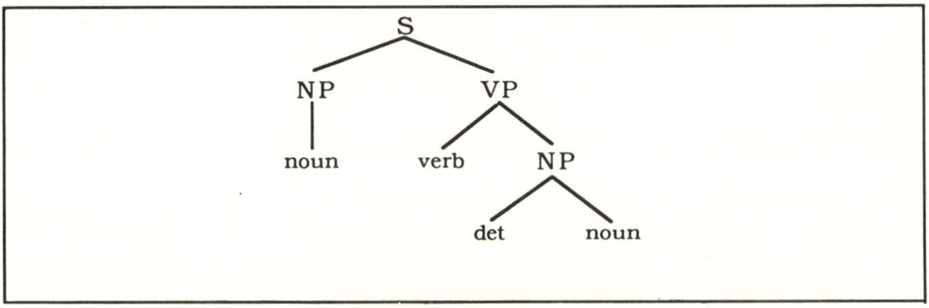

Figure 5.1.
Parse tree on a white-board.

	S		
NP	VP		
		NP	
noun	verb	det	noun

Figure 5.2.
Segmented parse-array.

The scheme shown in Figure 5.2 has several representational inadequacies. For one, the representation does not indicate which constituents dominates which and as such does not distinguish the two PP attachments in Figure 5.3. Furthermore the same parse tree can have many distinct representations. Figure 5.4 denotes the same tree as Figure 5.2, but is quite different.

Thus we indicate a parse tree by including the entire path, from leaf to root, in every column as shown in Figure 5.5. This means that a single constituent, for example, the S in Figure 5.5 will be represented as several units. Nothing indicates that these all denote the same S constituent. There are different ways this could be handled. The one we have chosen is to introduce "binding" units. Each unit denoting a nonterminal (or the lack thereof, represented internally by the symbol e) has a sister unit which states which, if any, of the units in the column to the right is the same constituent. In our figures we will use lines to indicate such bindings (see Figure 5.6). Internally these are values from 0 to the height of the array plus a special value, b, for a "boundary" indicating that we have a right boundary of a constituent and thus there is no corresponding constituent to the right.

As has been implicit in our diagrams so far, the actual input to the parser is not words, but rather their parts of speech, since that is all that is relevant to our task.

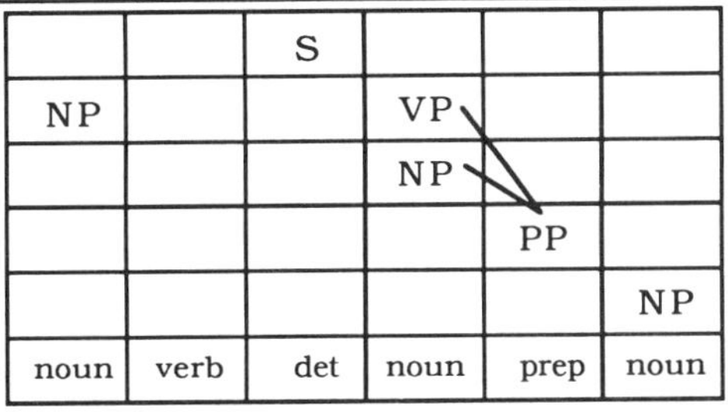

Figure 5.3.
Ambiguous parse array.

S			
NP		VP	
			NP
noun	verb	det	noun

Figure 5.4.
Another representation of Figure 5.2.

Thus parts of speech are the terminal symbols in the grammar. We have distinguished the bottom row of the parser, where the parts of speech appear, from the other rows, since all of the others have nonterminals only. Also the terminal row does not have binding units since we do not admit discontinuous terminal constituents. In what follows we will pretty much ignore the terminal units. So, for example, most rules which apply to nonterminals have special cases for terminals. These are ignored.

3. HOW THE PARSER WORKS

The basic idea is that words (really parts of speech) are read into the parser on the lower right and then shifted to the left as each new word comes in. Thus, the columns are numbered from 0 to N starting from the right.

Initially all NT units are set to e, and all B units are set to b. At the first word the lower-right unit, TR(0), then has its value *clamped* to, say, noun, and all of the NT(i,j) units, recompute their values synchronously (that is, all based upon the values in the previous iteration). Then the B(i,j)'s compute their values (using the new NT values but the old B values).

This is repeated several times. As it turns out, each iteration will roughly

		S	S
S	S	VP	VP
NP	VP	NP	NP
noun	verb	det	noun

Figure 5.5.
Tree-path parse array.

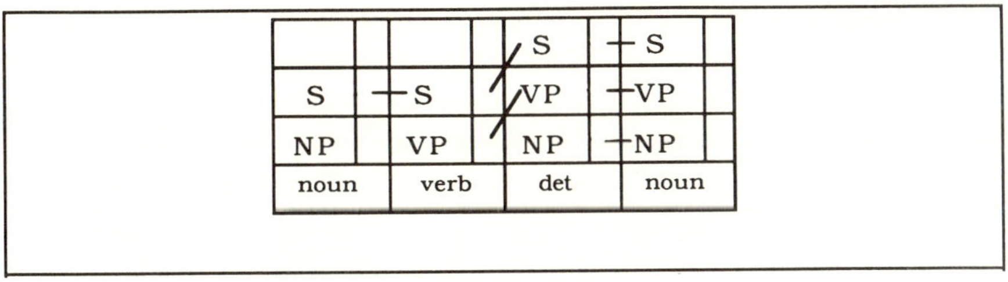

Figure 5.6.
Actual representation of a parse.

compute a level of the parse tree starting from the bottommost level, the terminals (see the section on Rules). Choosing a large number of iterations may lead to wild guesses in the upper levels since there may be important information not yet input to the system from the right (e.g., dealing with left embedded sentences). On the other hand, choosing a small number may lead to incomplete construction of the tree, especially in the case of a rather deep one. Currently, the system will iterate the number of times equal to the height of its matrix. Figure 5.7 shows the starting configuration and that after three iterations. Since a unit will typically have some probability for several different values, each unit in Figure 5.7 has four values for it. If all four are the same it means that value has probability > .75. Three the same indicate a probability > .5, and so on. This is true for lines as well, but we only indicate the most probable to reduce the jumble. In point of fact, however, all the lines in all of the examples go the same place. At this point the entire network is shifted to the left, leaving NT(0,j) = e and TR(0) is clamped to the next part of speech. Figure 5.8 shows a noun and verb following

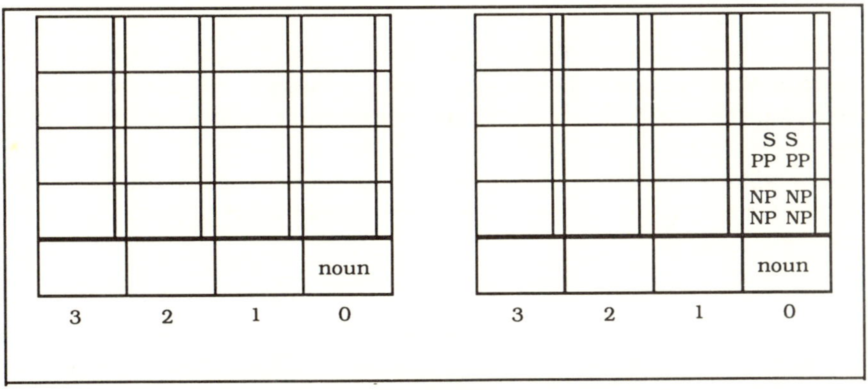

Figure 5.7.
Start of sentence "noun verb noun."

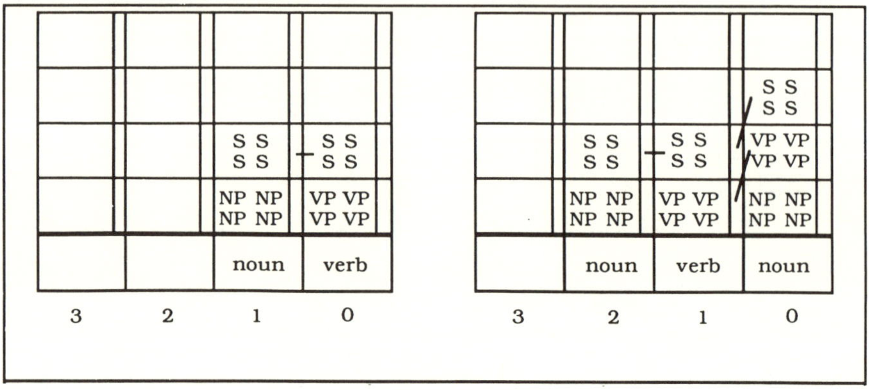

Figure 5.8.
End of sentence "noun verb noun."

on the heals of the input in Figure 5.8. This processing, and all of the other examples, have been done using the following grammar:

S	–>	NP VP
P	–>	verb NP PP*
PP	–>	prep NP
NP	–>	(det) noun PP*
NP	–>	pronoun
NP	–>	propnoun

Shifting words left (and eventually out the left-hand side) allows the parser to handle sentences of unbounded length, at least in principle. Since such shifting is not within the traditional connectionist repertoire, it makes our architecture slightly suspect to a *traditionalist*. It also means that sentences longer than the parser's width will not be completely represented at any one time. In such cases we take the total parse tree to be the *obvious* combination of the trees created during the parse.

4. RULES

Next we describe the actual rules applied at each unit. These will take us still further from connectionist orthodoxy because we allow unit calculations to be much more complex than the typical summing plus threshold. In particular a unit decides what value to adopt by summing the influence of several subrules which apply to it.

The subrules fall into two broad types, *housekeeping* rules, and *grammar* rules.

Housekeeping Rules

Housekeeping rules enforce the basic expectations of how the system is to work and as such remain constant over all grammars. There are three such rules.

Binding consistency. If a binding unit B(i,j) has value k, then NT(i,j) should denote the same constituent as NT(i − 1,k). more formally, the system tries to preserve the following constraint.

$$\{NT(i,j) = NT(i-1,k)\} + \{B(i,j) = k\}$$

This rule is applied in all ways. That is, NT(i,j) tries to make itself equal to NT(i − 1,k), and vice versa, while B(i,j) tries to pick a value which will make its left and right NT's the same.

Tree-consistency. If B(i,j) = k then B(i,j + 1) wants to be k + 1, and vice versa.

$$\{B(i,j) = k\} + \{B(i,j+1) = k+1\}$$

Again this is used both ways, with one exception. When a higher unit, B(i,j + 1), uses it to determine the value of a lower unit, B(i,j), if B(i,j + 1) = k + 1, then B(i,j) = k or b.

Blank-edge. If there is no constituent at a position NT(i,j), then NT(i,j) = e, for empty. In such cases no value of B(i,j) would have any real meaning. It turns out that the machine works better if such B(i,j)'s are assigned to be boundaries, so this rule encourages

$$\{NT(i,j) = e\} + \{B(i,j) = b\}$$

Grammar Rules

The program does not learn a grammar from examples, but must be given the grammar, which is then compiled into four rules, each of which form one aspect of the function computed at each NT and B units (though some only to one or the other).

Up-Down. Given a rule like S −> NP VP, the presence of an NP at position i,j should encourage the presence of an S at i,j + 1, and conversely. More generally assume a rule of the form A −> . . . B . . . then the following combination is encouraged:

$$\{NT(i,j) = A\} + \{NT(i,j - 1) = B\}$$

Left-hand side start rule. Given the rule S −> NP VP the presence of a starting NP should encourage a starting S.

$$\{NT(i,j) = A\} + \{NT(i,j - 1) = B\} +$$

$$\text{forall}(k)[\{B(i - 1,k) \mathrel{!=} j\} + \{B(i - 1,k - 1) \mathrel{!=} j - 1\}]$$

This rule is only applied to the B units, since it is a more restricted version of the up-down rule when applied to NT's.

Left-hand side finish. Given the rule S −> NP VP the presence of a VP which is ending should encourage the S above it to end.

$$\{NT(i,j) = A\} + \{NT(i,j - 1) = B\} + \{B(i,j) = b\} + \{B(i,j - 1) = b\}$$

Right-hand side start finish. The rule S −> NP VP encourages a finishing NP with an S above it to be followed by a starting VP with an S above it. Assuming the rule A −> . . .B_1 B_2 . . .

$$\{NT(i,j) = A\} + \{NT(i,j - 1) = B_1\} + \{B(i,j - 1) = b\} + \{NT(i - 1,j - 1) = B_2\}$$

5. LIMITATIONS AND PSYCHOLOGICAL RELEVANCE

As already noted, the parser escapes the fixed sentence length limitation because it shifts in input into the registers, constructs a parse tree for the section in question, and eventually shifts the input out on the left.

However, parse trees are bounded not only in width, but in height. Thus long sentences will tend to have high trees, and so it is possible that some of the tree will shift up *over the top* and be lost. If we are willing to agree that the system's parse tree is the collection of the partial trees created before they shifted either left and out, or up and out, then it is nevertheless possible for the program to construct arbitrarily wide and high trees.

Figure 5.9 shows the system parsing a modest right embedded sentence which due to the very small parser width and height still overflows the buffer in both directions. (The height and width are parameters one sets).

However, the shifting has effect on what can be parsed correctly. In particular, the depth limitation means that right embedding is fine, but center embedding

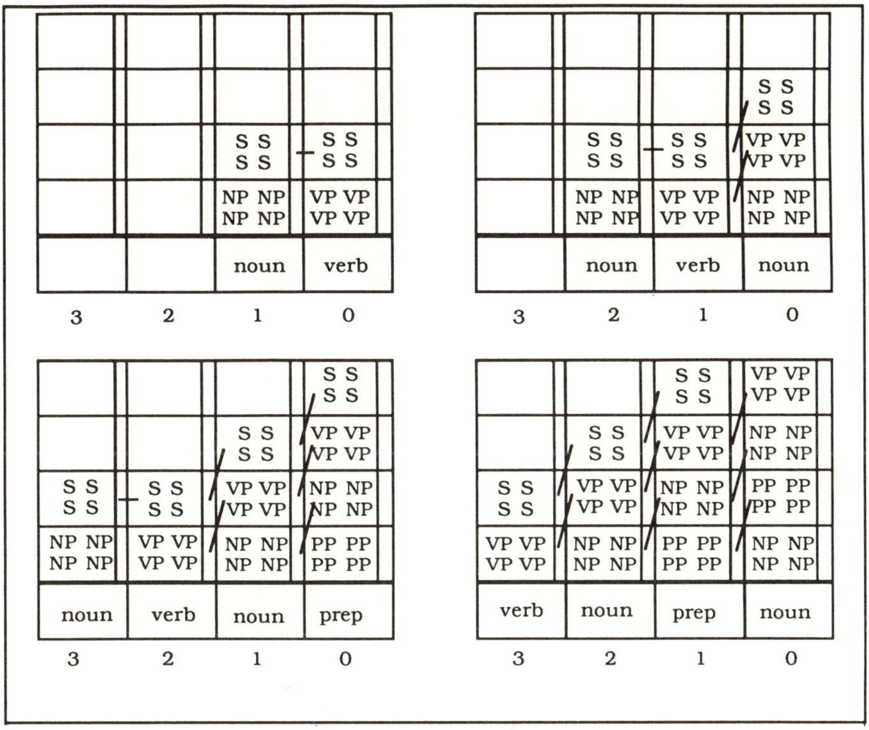

Figure 5.9.
Overflow on "noun verb noun prep noun."

will be difficult. Although the front of the tree is being shifted left and out, and the top of the tree is going over the top, if the sentence is right embedded then the portion of the tree to which the input should attach is always present. For center embedding this will not be true, and thus the parser cannot parse such examples correctly. In Figure 5.10, eventhough the two S's in the matrix represent the one S in the parse tree, it is impossible for the system show it as such.

6. HOW THE PARSER REALLY WORKS

We have described how the parser works in terms of the contributions of rules which we expressed as constraints to be satisfied. We have not specified exactly how the constraint satisfaction works. The actual rules are formalized in terms of array multiplication. We will consider only one of the simplest rules here, the up-down rule.

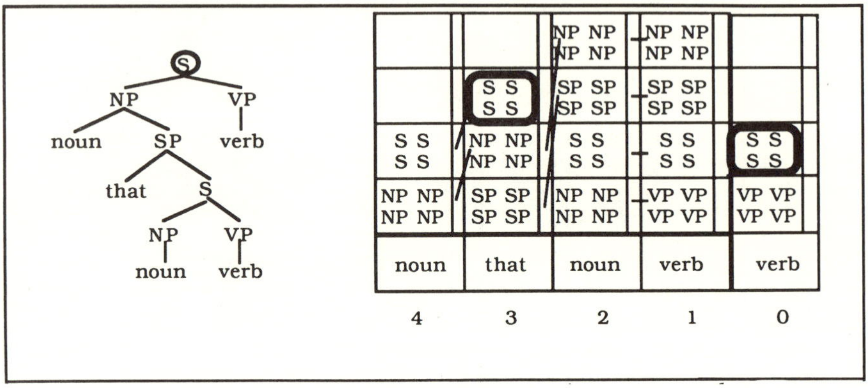

Figure 5.10.
Center embedding with "noun that noun verb verb."

First we need to modify our notation slightly. So far we have denoted unit values with equations like NT(1,2) = S. However, as we have already noted, NT(1,2) may be, say .7 = S, .2 = NP, and .1 = PP, or some such. Therefore, it would make more sense to say NT(1,2) = (.7,.2,.1,0) where we use S = 0, NP = 1, PP = 2, and VP = 3 to indicated vector positions. Alternatively we could use a 3-D array and say NT(1,2,1) = .2. (Arrays start with position 0). In fact, it proves to be most convenient to represent the situation as $NT_1(2,0) = .7$ $NT_1(2,1) = .2$ etc. Here the column number becomes a subscript picking out different two dimensional arrays. Next, we can represent the grammatical information needed by the up-down rule as an array itself.

$$UD(i,j) = \begin{cases} 1 \text{ iff the ith and the jth nonterminals are} \\ \quad \text{found in a rule of the from } i \rightarrow \ldots j \ldots \\ 0 \text{ otherwise} \end{cases}$$

Now consider how we apply the UD rule downward. We look at each position, and consider to what degree the entity at position j suggest what should be at j − 1. We can consider the NT_i array then to be this:

$$NT_i(k,LHS).$$

We then perform the array multiplication

$$NT_i(K,LHS) \times UD(LHS,RHS) = NT_i(K,RHS)$$

The resulting array has at position K the values that the LHS at K induces on the RHS. To get this into the format we want, we then shift down K by 1, so that the values of the RHS for K − 1 appear in the K − 1th position. Thus the up down rule looks like this:

$$NT_i(K - 1, RHS) = \text{shift-K-down-1}(NT_i(K,LHS) \times UD(LHS,RHS))$$

The other rules are similar, but often more complicated.

7. PROBLEMS AND FUTURE RESEARCH

There are many ways in which the parser could use improvement. It currently predicts that center embedding is more difficult than right or left embedding, but does not explain why some forms of center embedding (of Ss) are worse than others (of PPs). If we used a grammar which represented NP's as deep trees, rather than flat ones, this issue would be even more critical.

We have only tried the parser on the simple context-free grammar given earlier, plus a few minor extensions. We have no knowledge of how it works on more complicated grammars. In particular we would like to handle extended phrase-structure grammars. These grammars typically represent categories as collections of features, where each feature can be varied independently of the others, and will result in a different category. In an architecture such as ours, it would seem natural to model this using a unit for each feature, but how well this will work remains to be determined.

The CONPARSE system incorporates no form of learning whatsoever. The entire network, rules, weights, and so on is entirely "hand-constructed" around the grammar it is initially given. Once constructed, the network remains fixed, especially the weights of the connections. So, care must be placed in choosing connections and connection strengths. Thus, this usually leads to many hours of tedious tinkering.

Aside from all this, there is still much motivation for learning. However, due to the "nonconnectionistic" features of CONPARSE, standard learning algorithms like back-propogation are not applicable.

The most troublesome feature to learning is the systems ability to shift. As mentioned earlier, we utilized shifting to avoid restricting ourselves to fixed length sentences. However, this also restricts us to maintaining only a portion of an otherwise overly long sentence. So the problem results in how do we train sentences which are much wider than its buffer. A possible approach would be to do our learning in a fashion similar to our parsing.

In parsing, a word is shifted in one at a time and an attempt is made at building the portion of the tree that corresponds to the portion of the sentence currently in the system. In training, we would also work with one word at a time. Basically, the parse tree for the portion of the sentence in the system is supplied. We can call these "snapshots." Now, the system then attempts to parse as usual but also keeps in mind what its goal should be by using the snapshot. The connection strengths are modified by a punishment/reward system. When a rule "tends" toward the snapshot, it is rewarded by increasing its strength. When a rule "tends" away from the snapshot, it is punished by decreasing its strength. Also, from experience, we believe that we must also take into consideration how the rules interact with one another. (Research in this learning approach can be found in Santos, 1989.)

8. CONCLUSION

We have presented a distributed connectionist architecture for parsing context free grammars. It improves earlier attempts in that it is not limited to parse trees of fixed width and height (i.e., fixed-length sentences). The memory limitations inherent in connectionist architectures comes out in an inability to parse center-embedded sentences, although right-embedding works out fine.

REFERENCES

Allen, R.B. (1987). Several studies on natural language and backpropogation. *Proceedings of the International Conference on Neural Networks, 2,* 335–341.

Cottrell, G. (1985). *A connectionist approach to word sense disambiguation.* Doctoral thesis, University of Rochester, Department of Computer Science, Rochester, NY.

Fanty, M. (1985). *Context-free parsing in connectionist networks* (TR 174). Rochester, NY: University of Rochester, Computer Science Department.

Fanty, M. (1988). *Learning in structured connectionist networks* (TR 252). Rochester NY: University of Rochester, Computer Science Department.

Feldman, J.A., & Ballard, D.H. (1982). Connectionist models and their properties. *Cognitive Science, 6,* 205–254.

Hanson, S.J., & Kegl, J. (1987). PARSNIP: A connectionist network that learns natural language grammar from exposure to natural language sentences. *Proceedings of the Ninth Annual Cognitive Science Society Conference,* pp. 106–119.

Lippmann, R. (1987, April). An introduction to computing with neural nets. *IEEE ASSP Magazine,* pp. 4–22.

Pollack, J.B. (1987). *On connectionist models of natural language processing.* Doctoral thesis, Computer Science Department, University of Illinois at Urbana-Champaign.

Rumelhart, D., & McClelland, J. (1986). *Parallel distributed processing: Explorations in the microstructure of cognition* (Vol. 1). Cambridge, MA: MIT Press.

Santos, E., Jr. (1989). A massively parallel self-tuning context-free parser. *Advances in Neural Information Processing Systems 1* (pp. 537–544). San Mateo, CA: Morgan Kaufmann Publishers.

Selman, B.A. (1985). *Rule-based processing in a connectionist system for natural language understanding* (Tech. Rep. CSRI-168). Toronto: Computer Systems Research Institute, University of Toronto.

Waltz, D.L., & Pollack, J.B. (1985). Massively parallel parsing: A strongly interactive model of natural language interpretation. *Cognitive Science, 9,* 51–74.

6
Symbolic/Subsymbolic Sentence Analysis: Exploiting the Best of Two Worlds*

Wendy G. Lehnert

1. INTRODUCTION

Despite some recent speculation about the changing methodological styles in artificial intelligence, it is still possible to learn something by writing exploratory computer programs. This is especially true when a new processing technique or synthesis of different techniques is being attempted for the first time. In this spirit, we have designed and implemented a conceptual sentence analyzer, CIRCUS, which integrates three distinct information processing architectures.

CIRCUS uses (a) a stack-oriented control for syntactic predictions, (b) a marker-passing design for predictive preference semantics, and (c) numerical relaxation with lateral inhibition for data-driven preference semantics. Semantic preferences are therefore realized by two distinct mechanisms: We use marker-passing for the preferences associated with predictive semantics, and we use numerical relaxation for the preferences associated with data-driven semantics. This makes CIRCUS a blend of symbolic processing techniques (for a and b) and subsymbolic processing techniques (for c).

The distinction between predictive semantics and data-driven semantics is not a new one. For the sentence analyzers designed by the "Yale School," this distinction is usually described as the difference between *predictive* or *top-down slot-filling* versus *bottom-up slot insertion* (Riesbeck & Schank, 1976; Birnbaum & Selfridge, 1981; Dyer, 1983; Cullingford, 1986; Lytinen, 1984). Semantically oriented sentence analyzers that have evolved from other traditions also acknowl-

---

*This research was supported by the Advanced Research Projects Agency of the Department of Defense, monitored by the Office of Naval Research under contract #N00014-87-K-0238, the Office of Naval Research, under a University Research Initiative Grant, Contract #N00014-86-K-0764, and NSF Presidential Young Investigators Award NSFIST-8351863.

edge that the problem of filling existing slots within a conceptual frame is distinct from the problem of creating and inserting new slots into a frame that does not predict such slots. For example, recent work in preference semantics differentiates noun and verb case information from preposition case information (Wilks, Huang, & Fass, 1985).

To our knowledge, CIRCUS is the first system to characterize predictive semantics as a purely symbolic process while data-driven semantics is characterized primarily as a subsymbolic processes. In this chapter we will discuss some example sentences that illustrate the predictive/data-driven distinction and show how CIRCUS handles them. We further contend that any sentence analyzer which does not make a predictive/data-driven distinction must be either finessing a large class of problems, or trying to stretch a single processing mechanism farther than it can reasonably be expected to go.

When viewed in terms of linguistic models that are not process-oriented, we will see that our predictive/data-driven distinction does not carve up the world along the same lines as a linguist might. For example, linguists often view the problem of prepositional phrase attachment (pp-attachment) as a problem that can be resolved in a purely syntactic manner (Frazier & Fodor, 1979). When semantic considerations are introduced, they are usually based on lexical preferences from verbs (Ford, Bresnan, & Kaplan, 1981). In CIRCUS we will see that some pp-attachments are resolved by predictive semantics while others require data-driven semantics. In other words, some pp-attachment problems can be solved by standard symbolic methods, while others are best addressed using subsymbolic techniques.

While we cannot hope to give a full technical description of CIRCUS in this chapter, we will focus on those aspects of CIRCUS which are most interesting from the perspective of "high-level connectionism," and hope that our broad description is sufficient to convey a general sense of the overall system design.

2. SYNTACTIC PROCESSING

Over the years there has been much confusion about the status of syntactic knowledge within conceptual sentence analyzers. Although conceptual sentence analyzers do not produce syntactic parse trees, it is an overstatement to say that these systems never use syntax. What they don't use is a syntactic grammar, but it is nevertheless useful to recognize simple syntactic constituents like nouns and verbs, and so on. The important claim is that syntactic knowledge must be instrumental to semantic interpretation—not just a means for identifying syntactic structure alone.

CIRCUS is consistent with this tradition although it is somewhat more principled about its organization of syntactic constraints. All syntactic predictions associated with dictionary items are isolated in the stack-oriented architecture of

CIRCUS, and therefore kept separate from the processes that consider semantic constraints. This makes it easier to untangle the interactions between syntax and semantics, and it gives us an obvious advantage in constructing dictionary definitions.

Although we will not go into the details here, the syntactic processing in CIRCUS is well documented and available in a popular AI textbook (Schank & Riesbeck, 1981) where it is described as McELI, a micro version of a conceptual sentence analyzer designed by Chris Riesbeck (Riesbeck, 1975). Ironically, we use McELI inside CIRCUS to do nothing but recognize syntactic sentence constituents, and store appropriate sentence fragments inside global buffers that keep track of constituents like the subject of the sentence, direct and indirect objects, prepositional phrases, and so forth. The buffers are restricted to simple syntactic structures with a strongly "local" sense of the sentence: Larger constituents like clauses are not recognized using explicit syntactic buffers.

No attempt is made to resolve all syntactic ambiguities as soon as they are encountered. Syntactic ambiguities will be handled incrementally when the marker passing algorithm interacts with McELI and contributes the constraints it derives from predictive preference semantics. If we see "John gave Mary . . . " we will retain Mary as a possible binding for both the direct object and the indirect object until more information is made available to us. This wait-and-see strategy is necessary since many sentences can resolve themselves in more than one way ("John gave Mary a kiss" vs. "John gave Mary to the sheik"). The marker-passing algorithm described in the next section will generate a semantic preference which gives us a bias for Mary as an indirect object, but the syntactic processing of McELI will not relinquish its multiple interpretations unless the ambiguity can be resolved on the basis of syntactic constraints alone (as would be the case for "John gave Mary to the sheik").

To illustrate the syntactic predictions used by McELI, consider the verb "to give." In its active form, we can expect this verb to predict (1) a direct object, (2) a direct object followed by a prepositional phrase using the preposition "to," (3) a prepositional phrase with "to" followed by a direct object, or (4) an indirect object followed by a direct object. The following sentences illustrate each possibility:

1. John gave a book.
2. John gave a book to Mary.
3. John gave to Mary a book.
4. John gave Mary a book.

These predictions are not unique to the verb "to give," nor do they apply to all verbs in general. Using the request packet mechanism of McELI, it is easy to encode these expectations. When an ambiguity can be resolved on the basis of syntax alone, McELI can handle the resolution without additional help. For example, in processing (2), McELI will initially fill both the direct object buffer and the indirect object buffer with the noun phrase "a book." Three predictions are active at that point. One prediction expects to see a prepositional phrase next (as in 2), and another expects to see a second noun phrase (as in 4). If the first situation is encountered, we empty the indirect object buffer as soon as the prepositional phrase is recognized. If the second situation arises, we overwrite the direct object buffer when the second noun phrase is found. If the sentence terminates (as in 1), we empty the indirect object buffer as before. In any case, the momentary ambiguity is resolved by combining limited nondeterminancy with a wait-and-see strategy.

Because the syntactic constituents recognized by McELI are immediately given to the marker passing algorithm to augment purely semantic constraints and preferences, we cannot describe the role they play without talking about marker passing in CIRCUS. To conclude this section, we will merely point out that while McELI is a severely limited "toy" when viewed as a complete conceptual sentence analyzer, we have found McELI to be quite capable when regarded as a subsystem that is expected to do nothing more than recognize simple syntactic constituents in a deterministic manner. The stack-oriented architecture of McELI is not overwhelmed by this task, and it is easy to encode appropriate dictionary definitions for McELI that describe the simple syntactic predictions needed by CIRCUS.

3. PREDICTIVE PREFERENCE SEMANTICS

The predictive semantics module (PSM) in CIRCUS is responsible for filling slots in predefined semantic case frames. CIRCUS makes no commitment to a particular style of semantic representation, although we favor the "deep" semantic case frames of the sort found in conceptual dependency (Schank, 1975) as opposed to lexical case frames (Simmons, 1984). The more complex case frames are usually associated with verbs, but simple case frames can also be associated with nouns. Semantic dictionary entries for lexical items must list multiple frames to differentiate multiple word senses, although specific word senses can be effectively ignored by excluding them from the dictionary. When two or more word senses are present to compete with one another, preference semantics must try to resolve this competition and determine which word sense is most likely in the context of the given sentence.

PSM interacts with McELI each time a new syntactic constituent is recognized by McELI. Control is passed from McELI to PSM and then back again to McELI. While PSM is active, two primary tasks are accomplished: (a) network construction, and (b) marker passing. If a case frame satisfies certain instantiation criteria, PSM will also "freeze" that case frame with its assigned slot fillers for future access as a part of the conceptual meaning representation CIRCUS derives for the sentence. We will now talk about each of these tasks in more detail.

3.1. Network Construction

Each network constructed by PSM consists of three types of nodes: (a) syntactic nodes, (b) concept nodes, and (c) semantic feature nodes. Different types of information are passed between different node combinations, and different links are used to channel different kinds of information. The basic goal of the network is to activate concept nodes which will contribute to the conceptual interpretation of the sentence. The network is constructed with the following restrictions:

1. Syntactic nodes can only be connected to semantic feature nodes.
   (1a) these may be connected by a *soft constraint link,* or
   (1b) these may be connected by a *hard constraint link.*
2. Concept nodes can only be connected to semantic feature nodes.
   (2a) these may be connected by a *slot-filling link,* or
   (2b) these may be connected by an *enablement link.*
3. Multiple syntactic nodes can be connected to a given semantic feature node.
4. Multiple semantic feature nodes can be connected to a given syntactic node.
5. Multiple semantic feature nodes can be connected to a given concept node.
6. Multiple concept nodes can be connected to a given semantic feature node.

Definitions describing specific concept nodes and semantic feature nodes must be provided to PSM before sentence analysis begins. All semantic dictionary entries are defined in terms of these two node types. Concept nodes are added to the network when a lexical item in the sentence contains a dictionary definition for a concept node, although the presence of such a dictionary entry is not a sufficient condition by itself for network expansion. Semantic feature nodes are added to the network whenever a newly activated concept node references them in its definition. Syntactic nodes are added to the network whenever McELI assigns a sentence fragment to a constituent buffer.

To get a more concrete sense of what is going on during network construction, let's take a look at a specific example. We will take as our example the network constructed by PSM in order to process "John gave Mary to the sheik." After we have described the network construction for this sentence, we will then discuss the marker passing algorithm that uses this network.

The complete network generated by "John gave Mary to the sheik" appears in Figure 6.1. To see how this is incrementally constructed, we'll describe each partial construction as control moves back and forth between McELI and PSM.

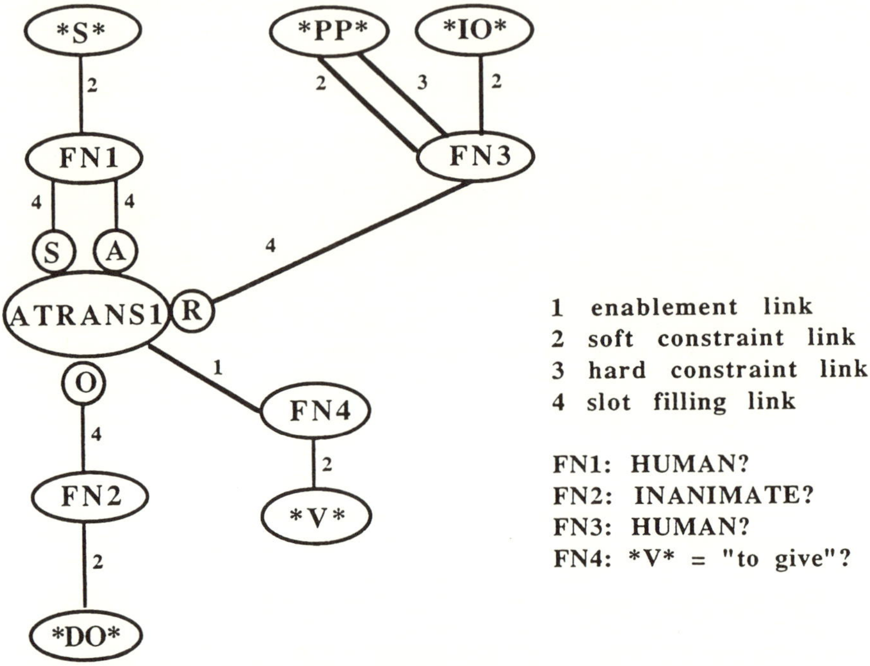

Figure 6.1.
The PSM Network for "John gave Mary to the Sheik."

1. John . . .

At this point McELI hypothesizes a subject for its sentence and places "John" in the *S* buffer. When control passes to PSM, we construct a single syntactic node marked *S* in Figure 6.1. The value associated with this node is the sentence fragment "John." PSM also consults its semantic dictionary to see if there are any concept node entries under John, but finds nothing.

2. John gave . . .

McELI places "gave" in the *V* buffer, and a syntactic node *V* is created for the network. This time, when PSM consults its semantic dictionary, it finds a single concept node under the verb "gave."[1] This concept node describes an ATRANS event[2] which appears as ATRANS1 in Figure 6.1. The concept node

[1]This concept node definition should really appear under an entry for the infinitive "to give" but we do not have any morphology routines hooked up to CIRCUS at the present time.

[2]ATRANS is a primitive act in conceptual dependency (Schank, 1975)

definition ATRANS1 is designed to drive the bulk of our network construction from here on through the end of the sentence. For now, semantic feature node FN1 is added to the network with a soft constraint link between *S* and FN1, and slot-filling links between FN1 and ATRANS1. We also add a second semantic feature node NF4, with a soft constraint link between *V* and FN4, and an enablement link between ATRANS1 and FN4. We will discuss the utility of these semantic feature nodes when we describe the marker passing algorithm.

3. John gave Mary . . .

McELI now passes two buffers to PSM, both of which contain the sentence fragment "Mary." The *DO* buffer hypothesizes that Mary may be a direct object, and the *IO* buffer hypothesizes that Mary may be an indirect object. PSM creates two corresponding syntactic nodes, marked *DO* and *IO* in Figure 6.1. PSM then consults the definition for ATRANS1 and adds the semantic nodes FN2 and FN3 to the network, using a soft constraint link to join *DO* to FN2, a slot-filling link to join FN2 to ATRANS1, a soft constraint link to join *IO* to FN3, and a slot-filling link to join FN3 to ATRANS1. Finally, PSM consults its semantic dictionary to see if there is a concept node definition associated with Mary, but it finds none.

4. John gave Mary to the sheik.

McELI now passes *PP* buffer to PSM which contains the sentence fragment "to the sheik." PSM builds a syntactic node marked *PP* in Figure 6.1. PSM also consults the definition for ATRANS1 and determines that *PP* should be joined to FN3 using both a soft constraint link and a hard constraint link. PSM also consults its semantic dictionary to see if there is a concept node definition associated with "sheik" but it finds nothing.

Each time control passes to PSM, we complete whatever network construction is needed, and then execute the marker passing algorithm. We will now describe marker passing in PSM.

3.2. Marker Passing

In order for the marker passing algorithm to run, we must have at least one concept node present in the network. For our example sentence, this first occurs after we've processed "John gave . . ." As described above, the network at that time consisted of *S*, *V*, FN1, FN4, and ATRANS1. In general, information flows from the syntactic nodes to the semantic feature nodes, and from the semantic feature nodes to the concept nodes. We can think of this spreading activation as a parallel process since there are no order effects or time-sensitive dependencies during marker passing.

When a semantic feature node completes a path from a syntactic node to a concept node, the semantic feature node acts as a semantic constraint checker to see if the concept frame associated with the concept node should fill a slot, or maybe remove itself from the network altogether. Slot filling links are used to channel potential slot fillers, and enablement links are used to sustain concept nodes in the network.

In our example, FN1 is designed to check the head of the subject noun phrase found in *S*, and determine whether or not this noun refers to a human. This determination is made in accordance with whatever memory model is available to CIRCUS, a problem we will discuss later in section 5. For now, we will simply assume that a feature node can pass a value of 1 or 0, depending on whether its test returns true or false. We will refer to these numbers as semantic preference values. In this case, John tests out as a human, and FN1 will pass the slot filler, John, to ATRANS1 along with its semantic preference value of 1. We should note that each slot-filling link into ATRANS1 also specifies the targeted slot for our slot-filler. In this case, we have a pair of slots specifying the actor and the source for the ATRANS frame (the small letters circled at the end of each slot-filling link indicates which slot is being targeted by that link).

The other semantic feature node, FN4, is joined to ATRANS1 by an enablement link which operates to confirm the viability of the concept node as the sentence progresses. In our case, FN4 simply checks that the contents of *V* is a form of the verb "to give," a condition that will test true as long as "gave" is the only verb we encounter in the sentence. In general, enablement conditions are used to dismiss concept frames at any time after they are triggered by dictionary look-up, usually after additional constraints within the sentence appear and prohibit the possibility of a given word sense.

At this point in the sentence (John gave . . .) the marker passing algorithm passes a confirmation on the enablement condition to ATRANS1, and semantic preference values yielding a sum of 2 to the ATRANS concept frame on the basis of John as both an actor and source for the ATRANS. We therefore keep ATRANS1 in the network, and assign it an activation level of 2/4 (we divide by 4 because there are 4 variable slots in the ATRANS frame: actor, object, source, and recipient).

The following concept has activation level .5
event = ATRANS
actor = JOHN
source = JOHN

By the time we reach "John gave Mary . . ." we have added two more syntactic nodes, *DO* and *IO*, and two more semantic feature nodes, FN2 and FN3. FN2 checks to see if the direct object is an inanimate object, and FN3 checks to see if the indirect object is a human. Since Mary is bound to both *DO* and *IO*, FN2 fails and FN3 succeeds. FN2 then passes Mary to ATRANS1 as a candidate for the object slot with preference value of 0, and FN3 passes Mary to ATRANS1 as a candidate for the recipient slot with a preference value of 1. Because these preference values are interpreted as soft constraints (the semantic feature nodes received their potential slot fillers via soft constraint links), the ATRANS frame receives both slot fillers, and adds Mary to the ATRANS frame as both an object and a recipient. However, PSM marks the object slot with a flag to indicate that this slot filler violates a semantic preference, and the activation level rises only to .75, indicating that all is not well as far as the frame instantiation is concerned.

The following concept has activation level .75
event = ATRANS
actor = JOHN
object = MARY <<< semantic violation
recipient = MARY

When the sentence is completed (John gave Mary to the sheik) we have the complete network at our disposal, and the marker passing algorithm completes its frame instantiation using ATRANS1. The only addition to the network is a syntactic node, *PP*, and this node is joined to FN3 via a soft constraint link and a hard constraint link. Given a prepositional phrase to consider, FN3 can now pass new information on to ATRANS1. First recall that McELI will now empty the *IO* buffer that feeds the syntactic node so that *IO* no longer points to Mary. The only channel feeding information to FN3 are now the links joining FN3 to *PP*. The hard constraint link requires that *PP* hold a prepositional phrase using the preposition "to." If this condition is not met, FN3 will not pass any potential slot fillers on to ATRANS1 on the basis of *PP*. Since we pass this test, we then consider the soft constraint link, which asks only that the object of the prepositional phrase be human. As a soft constraint, this test could fail without blocking the slot filler (just as we saw for FN2 above), but this time, the sheik qualifies and is passed to ATRANS1 as a slot filler for the recipient slot with a preference value of 1.

The following concept has activation level .75
event = ATRANS
actor = JOHN
object = MARY <<< semantic violation
source = JOHN
recipient = SHEIK

At this point, we are done with our sentence and we can take our semantic meaning representation from ATRANS1, the only concept node in the network. We have an ATRANS event with actor = John, object = Mary, source = John, and recipient = the sheik. Note that the activation level is still only .75, since the slot filler for the ATRANS object still fails to meet the semantic preference associated with that slot (Mary is not an inanimate object). When PSM returns this instantiation of the ATRANS frame as the conceptual representation for our sentence, it flags this slot filler as one which violated a semantic preference.

3.3. Resolving Competing Word Senses using Predictive Semantics

Before we move on to data-driven semantics, we should point out that some word sense ambiguities can be resolved on the basis of predictive semantics alone. For example, suppose we wanted to understand the sentence "John gave Mary a kiss" as well as "John gave Mary to the sheik." Now we no longer want to interpret the event as an ATRANS event. (No transfer of possession occurs here as it did with the sheik). For lack of a better decomposition, we'll simply characterize it as a kissing event.

However, both sentences start out with the same verb, and we can't reject ATRANS1 as a valid concept node on the basis of any hard enablements. In fact, ATRANS1 will receive the same amount of activation that it had for "John gave Mary to the sheik" since only the object of the ATRANS frame violates its semantic preference for an inanimate object. Indeed, if our dictionary recognized the possibility of a chocolate kiss, we could give ATRANS1 an activation level of 1 and be perfectly confident about this interpretation. Barring, for the moment, the idea of a candy kiss,[3] we can only reject an ATRANS1 interpretation with activation level = .75 if some competing concept node can come up with a higher activation level.

Figure 6.2 shows how a competing concept node can be brought in to establish an interpretation of the sentence based on a kissing event. In this case, the $KISS concept node resides in the semantic dictionary under the noun definition for "kiss." This is the appropriate place to index a possible kissing event, since we don't want to predict a possible kiss every time we see the verb "to give."

Note that $KISS introduces only one new semantic feature node, FN5. The rest of its links hook up to nodes already present in the network because of ATRANS1. $KISS has two enablement links from FN4 and FN5, and two slot-filling links from FN1 and FN3. It shares the same hard and soft constraints used by ATRANS1 to fill its actor and recipient slots, so it can tap into those parts of the network without additional effort. For enablements, it simply requires the verb "to give" (FN4) and a direct object which is an event (FN5). Since the first enablement is shared with ATRANS1, we can once again tap into the existing network structures without further construction. Only FN5 and the two links connecting it need to be added when $KISS is added to the network.

---

[3]We will come back to this problem of lexical ambiguity in section 4.1.

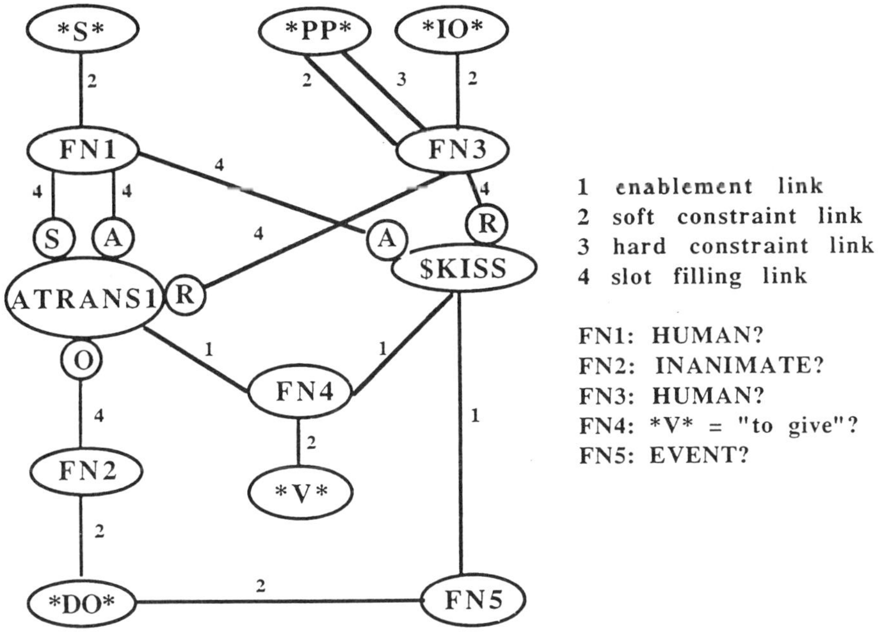

Figure 6.2.
The PSM Network for "giving a kiss."

Now the marker passing algorithm passes slot fillers to both ATRANS1 and $KISS, in which case ATRANS1 arrives at an activation level of 3/4 (we have a preference violation on the object slot), and $KISS determines that John can be an actor and Mary can be a recipient without any preference violations, yielding a concept node activation level of 1. A simple comparison of these activation levels will then tell us which of the surviving concept nodes holds the best interpretation of the sentence.

3.4. Resolving Competing Predictions Across Nested Case Frames

In the last section we saw how multiple concept nodes could compete with one another to settle a word sense ambiguity. In such competitive situations we want to see one concept node win so only one can participate in the final interpretation of the sentence. But it is also possible for multiple concept nodes to create nested case frame instantiations in a final meaning representation. Then we want to see multiple concept nodes cooperate with one another and stay out of each other's way as much as possible. To see how these cooperative situations arise, consider the following sentences:

[S1] John gave Mary the key to the city.
[S2] John gave the key to the city to Mary.

Here we have the ATRANS1 concept node attempting to instantiate an ATRANS frame, while a second concept node associated with the concept of a key is also trying to fill a simple frame describing a key and the object the key opens. To make matters even worse, we'll assume that the KEY concept node has a semantic preference on its single slot (the opens-slot) that the slot filler be something which has a lock, a condition not met by cities. For both S1 and S2, we want to see the KEY case frame instantiated despite the fact that its slot filler does not satisfy the semantic preference associated with that frame. Both S1 and S2 should produce the following meaning representation:

```
event = ATRANS
actor = JOHN
object =
        header = KEY
        opens = CITY <<< semantic violation
source = JOHN
recipient = MARY
```

We will use the ATRANS1 concept node described before, and we can easily define KEY to fill its opens-slot on the basis of a prepositional phrase with the preposition "to" (a hard constraint), and a head noun which can have a lock (a soft constraint). In S1, the ATRANS frame will be fully instantiated as soon as we get to "the key." We need only complete the KEY frame instantiation when the final prepositional phrase arrives.

To recognize the nested case frame relation, we need to add one new link type to the network grammar described in section 3.1. We will now allow a case-frame value link to connect syntactic nodes to concept nodes whenever a noun sense triggers a concept node definition. Figure 6.3 shows the PSM network needed to handle S1 and S2.

A tricker situation arises with S2. Now we have to watch out for the fact that the *PP* buffer is going to get overwritten by McELI when the second prepositional phrase is encountered. This is fine for the ATRANS frame, which should be picking up Mary as its recipient anyway. But it is not so good for the KEY frame, which will lose its pathway to the city and fail to pick up the correct slot filler.

PSM handles this by putting a time limitation on each concept frame to make sure that slot filling constituents which are too far removed from a potential node are not considered by that concept node. Distance is measured by a clock that ticks off the syntactic constituents recognized by McELI. For simple concept nodes triggered by nouns, this heuristic is very effective. For example, the KEY

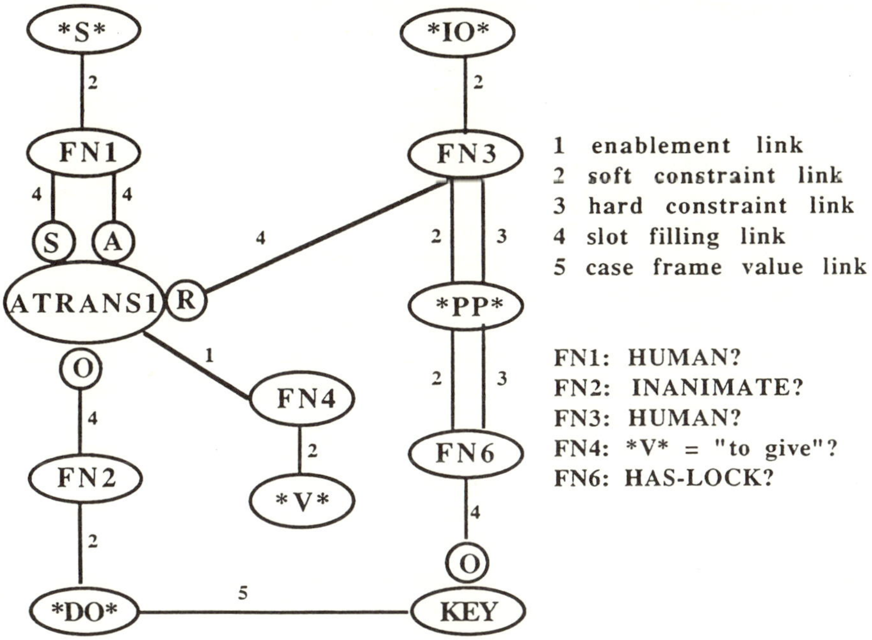

Figure 6.3.
A PSM Network for Nested Case Frames.

frame should never look past the syntactic constituent immediately following the noun "key."

When the time limitation for a concept node is up, a mechanism freezes the current frame instantiation, and procedures that access the concept node from that time on will only see the frozen case frame instantiation no matter what else is happening in the PSM network. In this way, it is possible to overwrite the information within a syntactic node and still retain old information within case frame instantiation as needed.

Now let's look at another trouble maker:

[S3] John gave the key to the city.

In this sentence, we have both the ATRANS case frame and the KEY case frame actively competing for the second prepositional phrase, but neither of them finds their semantic preference satisfied. Who wins? Normally, we look at the semantic preferences to resolve this sort of competition. If John gave the key to the car, we'd want to see the KEY frame win. If John gave the key to Mary, we'd want to see the ATRANS frame win. Because CIRCUS keeps track of slot fillers that violate preferences, it is possible to resolve situations where two frames grab the same constituent, but only one is semantically satisfied. In cases like S3, we allow CIRCUS to remain uncertain about the outcome. Without a strong semantic preference to guide us, S3 remains semantically ambiguous and no further attempt is made by CIRCUS to resolve the problem.

Note that a "key to the city" is just as anomalous as "a key to the chair" if we stick to the KEY frame definition given above. If we had another word sense for key which encoded the ceremonial notion of a symbolic key, we could set up a competition between the multiple concept nodes associated with keys, and resolve the problem that way. This explains why people reading this sentence do have a preference which would swing their interpretation toward some ceremonial understanding of the event in question. CIRCUS can arrive at the same conclusion, but only if we give it adequate knowledge about multiple word senses.

Notice that each of these examples described a problem with prepositional phrase attachment. When two concept frames compete for the same prepositional phrase, we are looking at competing attachment points for the prepositional phrase. The ambiguity in S3 arises from the fact that "to the city" might be attached to either the verb "gave" or the noun "key." In these instances, CIRCUS must rely on predictive semantics alone to make judgment about the best attachment. Given an adequate dictionary of multiple word sense definitions and appropriate semantic preferences within those case frame definitions, we can expect predictive semantics to suffice for these attachment problems. However, other attachment problems associated with prepositional phrases cannot be resolved on the basis of predictive semantics alone. We will consider these problems in the next section.

4. DATA-DRIVEN PREFERENCE SEMANTICS

Each of the following sentences contains a prepositional phrase that cannot be interpreted on the basis of predictive semantics alone. Many verbs and nouns can act as the attachment point for a prepositional phrase describing a locational setting (in the car or in a box). If we treated these modifiers in terms of predicted slots, we would have to duplicate a very large number of predictions for many case frames in our dictionary.

[S4] John gave the key to Mary *in the car.*
[S5] John gave Mary the key to the car *in the car.*
[S6] John gave the key to the city to Mary *in the car.*
[S7] John gave the key to the car to Mary *in the city.*
[S8] John gave the key *in a box.*
[S9] John gave the key to the city *in a box* to Mary.

[S10] John gave the key to the city to Mary *in a box.*
[S11] John gave the key to the car to Mary *in a box.*

Because these prepositional phrases operate with such sweeping generality, it makes sense to interpret them in a more bottom-up fashion, dealing with each instance only as it appears without top-down expectations. The final prepositional phrase in each of S4–S7 attaches to the verb, crossing 2 or 3 intermediate constituents to make the attachment. In S8–S11 we see a prepositional phrase attaching to a noun, with 0, 1, or 2 intermediate constituents intervening. Notice that "in a box" could conceivably attach to "gave" if you are willing to imagine a box large enough to contain John and Mary. But if your prototypical box is somewhat smaller, you will prefer a descriptor that limits its scope to the location of the key.

Although these examples all illustrate attachment points that coincide with conceptual frames (ATRANS1 and KEY), any noun can qualify as a possible attachment point regardless of whether or not it carries a case frame definition (John gave Mary a necklace in a box). In general, any noun or verb preceding a prepositional phrase can operate as a potential attachment point for that prepositional phrase, as long as we don't cross certain clause boundaries (like the main verb). To determine the best attachment point, some mechanism must be invoked that can weigh all the different possibilities and come up with the best interpretation. The constraints that inform this decision are primarily semantic constraints, although we will discuss a syntactic constraint for prepositional phrase attachment in section 4.3.

4.1. The Lateral Inhibition Network

To resolve the problem of bottom-up prepositional phrase attachment, we will first assume that any prepositional phrase claimed by a case frame slot prediction does not require further analysis, even if the slot filler violates a soft constraint as described in the previous section. The network relaxation mechanism we are about to describe only applies to prepositional phrases that are left uninterpreted by predictive semantics.

When such a prepositional phrase is encountered, we construct a network whose nodes are joined by both activation links and inhibitory links. To illustrate the network construction, consider the following sentence:

[S12] John gave a kiss in a box to Mary in the car.

Here we have two prepositional phrases that are unresolved by predictive semantics: "in a box," and "in the car." To make matters even more interesting, we will supply our dictionary with two word senses for the lexical item "kiss."

$KISS_E$ will be an event involving an actor and a recipient. $KISS_C$ will be a piece of chocolate candy wrapped in tinfoil.

Each node in the relaxation network corresponds to (a) an attachment point, (b) a head noun in a prepositional phrase, or (c) a preposition. In fact, we have distinct nodes for each separate word sense associated with (a), (b), or (c), but our discussion of S12 will only incorporate multiple word senses for the kiss (two instances of attachment points). Moreover, copies of prepositional word sense nodes will be made for each possible attachment point associated with a given prepositional phrase. We will therefore refer to nodes of type (3) as relational nodes, since they each describe a relational interpretation between the head noun and a potential attachment point. It follows that if multiple word senses are associated with a given attachment point, separate relational nodes are created for each targeted word sense as well ($KISS_E$ and $KISS_C$ illustrate this situation).

Figure 6.4 shows the relaxation network associated with S12. We can see from this diagram that "in a box" has three possible attachments associated with it: one pointing to ATRANS1, one pointing to $KISS_E$, and one pointing to $KISS_C$. "In the car" has five possible attachment points: the box, ATRANS1, $KISS_E$ and $KISS_C$, and Mary. Notice that this semantic interpretation of the attachment problem does not correspond perfectly to the syntactic notion of prepositional phrase attachment. While $KISS_E$ and $KISS_C$ are both triggered by

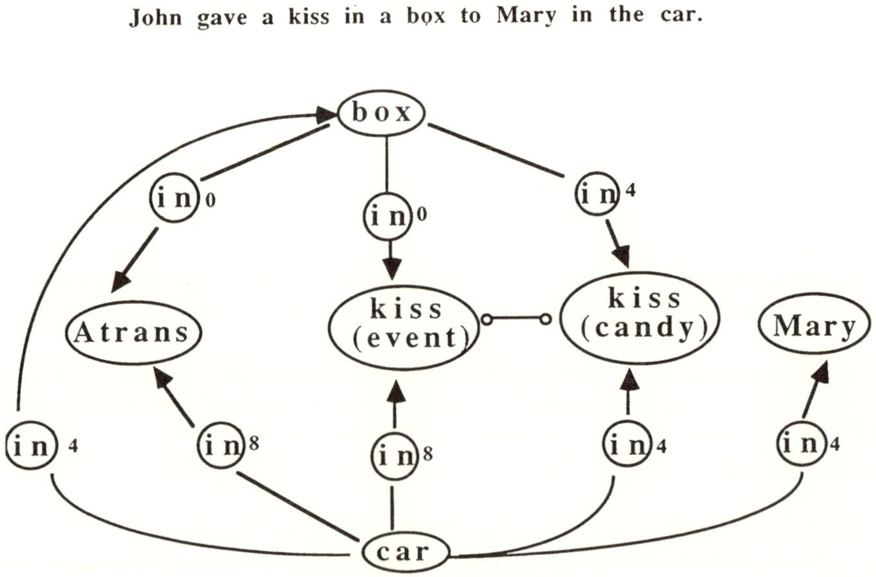

Figure 6.4.
Data-Driven PP-Attachment.

the noun phrase "a kiss," $KISS_E$ serves to disambiguate the sense in which "gave" should be understood. Giving a kiss is not like giving a book. So an attachment to $KISS_E$ is really a syntactic attachment to the verb "gave" rather than the noun "kiss." However, we are not interested in building a syntactic parse tree: our only goal is to find the right case frame for a bottom-up slot insertion. Since our network is created with semantic entities rather than syntactic ones, the notion of a purely syntactic prepositional phrase attachment need not concern us. Syntactic attachments are rather beside the point, and they can be effectively bypassed without any trouble. We are treating prepositional phrase attachment as a strictly semantic problem with purely semantic solutions.

In figure 6.4 we have shown an inhibitory link between $KISS_E$ and $KISS_C$, indicating that these two nodes are mutually exclusive and in competition with one another. All other links shown in Figure 6.4 are activation links. In fact, there are more inhibitory links in this network than we have attempted to show in our figure. Each relational node associated with a given prepositional phrase must inhibit every other relational node created by the same prepositional phrase since all of these relational nodes signify competing interpretations for the given phrase. We therefore have 3 inhibitory links (not shown) connecting the 3 relational nodes associated with "in a box," and 10 inhibitory links (not shown) connecting the 5 relational nodes associated with "in the car." Once this relaxation network has been constructed, we can execute our relaxation algorithm.

Each node in the relaxation network is initialized with a value between 0 and 10. Only the relational nodes can be initialized with non-zero values. The initial value given to a relational node is determined by the available memory model and will be discussed later. For now, we will assume that the following conditional is used to compute initialization values to describe the relation "X in Y":

```
IF X is an event and Y is bigger than a person
THEN return 8,
ELSE IF X is not an event and X is not bigger than Y,
        THEN return 4,
        ELSE return 0.
```

Figure 6.4 shows how the relational nodes are initialized using the above rule. Having initialized the network nodes, we can now apply a simple relaxation algorithm (Feldman & Ballard, 1982) until the network stabilizes and each node settles down to a steady (or near-steady) value. The exact algorithm we use in CIRCUS is the same one we have used elsewhere (Lehnert, 1987a) so we will not bother to go into those details here.

Once the network has stabilized, we can interpret the resulting node values to resolve three separate problems. One relational node should beat out the competition to attach each of the two prepositional phrases, and either $KISS_E$ or

$KISS_C$ should win to resolve the lexical/conceptual ambiguity introduced by "a kiss."

Notice that the ambiguity of the kiss can only be resolved by understanding the constraints associated with "in a box." If this prepositional phrase can attach to $KISS_C$, but not $KISS_E$, then we will receive a preference for $KISS_C$ over $KISS_E$. If the box is big enough to allow either attachment, we will receive no preference for one sense of kiss over the other. "John gave a kiss to Mary in the car," leave us much more undecided about the kiss ambiguity than S12 does.

Although it may not be obvious from the initial node values in Figure 6.4, the relaxation algorithm will eventually stabilize with attachments that describe a piece of candy in a box, and an ATRANS event taking place in the car. The final output from CIRCUS will therefore be:

event = ATRANS
actor = JOHN
object = $KISS_C$
[relational-link = IN (BOX)]
source = JOHN
recipient = MARY
[relatinal-link = IN(CAR)]

In the next section we will explain how results from the relaxation algorithm are used by PSM in order to produce this representation.

4.2. Interactions between Predictive and Data-Driven Semantics

Although the data-driven processing described in the last section is useful in resolving certain ambiguities associated with multiple word senses and prepositional phrase attachment, we must still coordinate these results with the preferences and results obtained by predictive semantics. A dynamic interaction between predictive semantics and data-driven semantics occurs if the relaxation algorithm is invoked after each syntactic constituent is recognized. As we saw earlier, control first passes to predictive semantics which produces its case frame instantiations and preferences without the benefit of any data-driven processing. Then the relaxation network is constructed on the basis of whatever we have seen so far, and the relaxation algorithm passes its results back to predictive semantics in case any data-driven problem resolutions can influence a case frame instantiation or competition between case frames.

There are three ways that data-driven semantics can influence and augment predictive semantics. These are:

1. Bottom-up slot insertion
2. Word sense preferences for predicted slot fillers
3. Enabling conditions for predictive case frames

Bottom-up slot insertion is the simplest example of the data-driven contributions. When a prepositional phrase is not recognized by predictive semantics, data-driven semantics must attempt to find the best relational interpretation for the prepositional phrase. Once that relation has been identified, we simply insert a new slot inside the appropriate case frame which describes the relation in question. For example, if John gave Mary a book on Tuesday, we would insert the slot (relational-link = TIME (TUESDAY)) inside the ATRANS1 instantiation.

Although word sense preferences are addressed by the soft constraints of predictive semantics, we can also benefit from the preferences of data-driven semantics when multiple word senses are involved. In S12 we saw how $KISS_C$ will beat out $KISS_E$ as a result of the relaxation algorithm after "in the box" is encountered. Although ATRANS1 had a soft preference for $KISS_C$ over $KISS_E$, we were not prepared to dismiss $KISS_E$ on the basis of predictive semantics alone (remember that "John gave Mary a kiss in the car" remains ambiguous without the constraints from "in a box" to resolve the word sense of kiss). But once data-driven semantics has given us a strong preference for $KISS_C$ over $KISS_E$, we can now go back to predictive semantics with the message that $KISS_E$ should not be considered as a possible slot filler for any case frames that might have wanted it. In S12, this will suppress an interpretation where ATRANS1 allows $KISS_E$ to operate as a possible object slot filler despite the preference violation that occurs when an event is pushed into the ATRANS object slot.

The final way in which data-driven results can influence predictive semantics is through the enabling conditions associated with predictive case frames. This is how the competition between $KISS_E$ and ATRANS1 is actually resolved in S12. When the $KISS_E$ word sense for "a kiss" is dismissed by the relaxation algorithm, the enabling condition for the $KISS case frame will fail to be met since the direct object of "gave" can no longer describe an event. Once a case frame enablement fails, the case frame is removed from consideration by predictive semantics, leaving only surviving case frames as viable contenders for the final interpretation.

Because enabling conditions for predictive case frames may be sensitive to timing effects as we move through the sentence, this last form of interaction between data-driven semantics and predictive semantics makes it desirable to run the relaxation algorithm periodically as we move through the sentence. If we wait until the end of the sentence to bring in data-driven effects, there is a danger of missing some failed enabling condition which was detectable for only a limited time as we moved through the sentence (most likely because McELI overwrites its syntactic buffers). This suggests that the two processes must operate in a roughly parallel fashion, with frequent communication between them.

It is also important to note that in every interaction described here, information always flows from the data-driven component to the predictive component. We never see information from predictive semantics influencing the relaxation algorithm. For this reason, we can say that predictive semantics operates in a strictly top-down fashion, while data-driven semantics is truly bottom-up. Bottom-up information can influence top-down processing, but top-down processing cannot influence a process that is purely bottom-up. This suggests an important claim about the relationship between symbolic and subsymbolic processes which sounds quite plausible in general: Symbolic processes can be influenced by subsymbolic processes, but the converse does not hold. If we assume that symbolic processes are basically serial while subsymbolic processes are essentially parallel, we have a corollary to this claim: serial processes can be influenced by parallel processing, but the converse does not hold. It is interesting to note that experimental reaction time results on lexical access appear to be completely consistent with this general rule of serial/parallel interaction (Swinney, 1984).[4]

4.3. The No-Crossing-of-Branches Rule

At this point we have outlined the basic mechanism of data-driven processing, but we have not argued for the necessity of network relaxation. If S12 were our only example of data-driven processing, it would seem that simple heuristics based on symbolic memory interactions should suffice. In this section we will present a more compelling argument for the necessity of relaxation algorithms in data-driven processing.

The most striking argument seems to arise from a syntactic constraint called the no-crossing-of-branches rule. This rule accounts for the dissonance that most people experience when reading the following sentence:

[S13] The man saw the woman with binoculars in a green dress.

Most people who read this sentence conclude that (1) the man was using binoculars and the woman was wearing a green dress, but the sentence is poorly worded, or (2) the woman was carrying binoculars and wearing a green dress. The first interpretation is based on semantic preferences which strongly suggest that the binoculars should be an instrument for seeing, and the woman must be the one wearing the green dress. Any discomfort with the wording of the sentence under this interpretation is due to the fact that this semantically valid interpretation violates a syntactic rule about pp-attachment.

The no-crossing-of-branches rule goes into effect when there are multiple prepositional phrases in a sentence. It says that no two attachments can cross each other in going from prepositional phrase to attachment point. (1) violates the no-crossing-of-branches rule because the semantically-preferred pp-attachments for this sentence do cross one another:

[4]Notice also the similarity to Pylyshyn's notion of "cognitive impenetrability" (Pylshyn, 1984).[Ed].

The man saw the woman with binoculars in a green dress.

The second reading (2) of S13 is syntactically more acceptable, but perhaps a bit bothersome semantically since the instrumentality of binoculars to the act of seeing is so strong that we are reluctant to dismiss this attachment option. Unfortunately, the only way that the man can be using the binoculars without violating the no-crossing-of-branches rule is if the man or the binoculars wear the dress. Few readers are willing to entertain these possibilities as acceptable interpretations for the sentence.

As we can see, the no-crossing-of-branches rule is a soft constraint. It can be violated if semantic constraints are strong enough to force an interpretation that renders the sentence poorly worded. But in the absence of any such compelling constraints, the no-crossing-of-branches rule normally contributes to a productive unraveling of multiple pp-attachments.

It has been argued that the no-crossing-of-branches constraint can only be realized by a sentence analyzer which "performs complete syntactic processing of its input" (Tait, 1983). The reasoning here starts with the observation that no-crossing is a nonlocal constraint because a prepositional phrase can cross over an arbitrarily large segment of the sentence to reach its intended attachment point. It follows that any process which can detect a no-crossing violation must access a global representation of the sentence structure (e.g., a syntactic parse tree) in order to exploit the no-crossing constraint. Semantically-oriented analyzers which "deal only with local word-order effects" (Tait, 1983) cannot hope to apply no-crossing to pp-attachment routines because the no-crossing rule is properly concerned with global word order effects.

Although the claim that localized word orders cannot handle essentially global problems is quite correct, it is not true that global constraints like the no-crossing rule require complete syntactic processing. In CIRCUS we have implemented the no-crossing-of-branches rule without any need for a syntactic parse tree or syntactic structures beyond those described in section 2 (which are highly localized). All we need is the lateral inhibition network described in section 4.1, and a time stamp on each syntactic constituent associated with prepositional phrases and attachment points. If we maintain pointers from the nodes in the lateral inhibition network to the time-stamped syntactic constituents underlying them, we can use this simple time stamp to recognize no-crossing violations. The time stamp will give us an adequate sense of the global relationships we need to consider, and no one would characterize a set of time-stamped sentence constituents as much of a syntactic parse tree.

To see how the no-crossing rule is implemented in CIRCUS, consider Figure 6.5 where we have drawn a picture of the lateral inhibition network needed to process S13. Here we see two competing word senses for the preposition "with" and one word sense for the preposition "in." (A serious dictionary would provide us with many more word senses for these prepositions but our picture would only

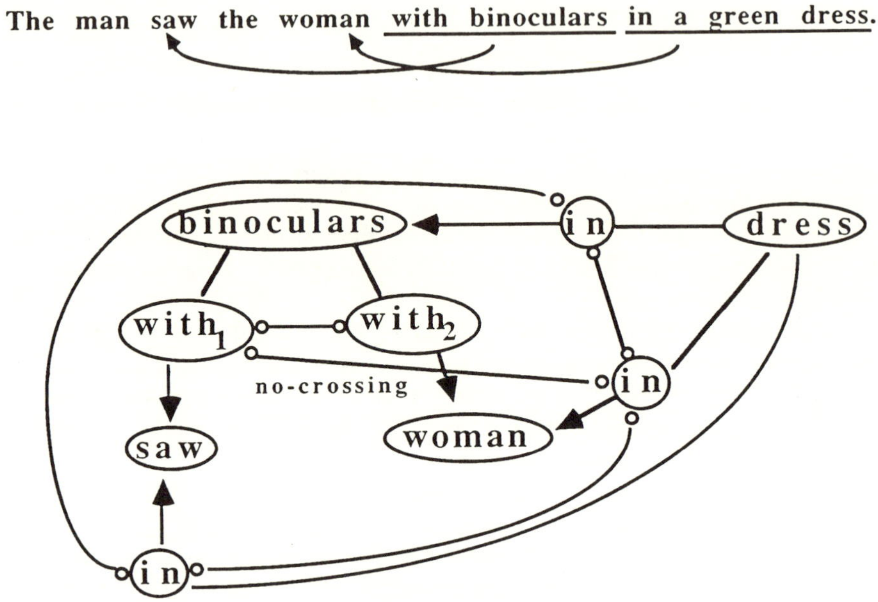

Figure 6.5.
The No-Crossing-of-Branches Rule.

be muddied up by more attachment nodes.) Each of the two word senses for "with" generates two attachment nodes and the single word sense for "in" generates three attachment nodes. (Note that Figure 6.5 does not show all of the attachment nodes associated with "with." Once again, we are only trying to keep the picture simple.)

Each attachment node is associated with a unique prepositional phrase and a unique attachment point. By consulting the time stamps for each pair of constituents affiliated with an attachment node, we can specify a time interval which describes the scope of this particular attachment node. The longer the time interval, the more distance we have between the prepositional phrase and its potential attachment point.

Assume two attachment nodes are given the time intervals [a,b] and [c,d], where $a < b$, $c < d$, and $a < c$. Then these two attachment nodes will violate the no-crossing rule if and only if $c < b < d$. Under no other condition will we see a violation of the no-crossing rule. It is easy to check the pairwise combinations of attachment nodes in our network to determine if any pairs qualify as a violation of the rule. If we find any such pairs, we can then incorporate this information into our lateral inhibition network by adding an inhibitory link between the two offending attachment nodes to indicate that these nodes are mutually exclusive and incompatible with one another.

This inhibitory link will operate as a soft constraint in the sense that a stable network could conceivably settle out with maximal activation on two attachment nodes that cross. In such a case we would simply accept the sentence interpretation that violated the no-crossing constraint, presumably because semantic considerations overwhelmed the no-crossing rule. In any case, the no-crossing rule is implemented using the same data-driven technique for soft-constraints that we use to arbitrate competing word senses and attachment points. Syntactic constraints and semantic preferences then operate within the relaxation algorithm on equal footing, without any opportunity for one constraint type to dominate the other. The various constraints reinforce or compete with one another in a truly heterogeneous manner until a globally optimal interpretation of word senses and pp-attachments is obtained.

Most sentence analyzers which implement the no-crossing rule recognize it as a hard constraint and cannot balance it against semantic considerations as we do with CIRCUS. Since people are willing to violate the no-crossing rule some of the time, but not all the time, it seems obvious that a flexible mechanism is needed to utilize the no-crossing constraint. We believe that numerical relaxation is extremely convenient for problems of this type. Moreover, any purely symbolic technique for the no-crossing rule will be necessarily brittle and arbitrary in trying to balance syntactic sensitivities against semantic preferences. The subsymbolic method of network relaxation is far better suited to the resolution of multiple soft constraints.

5. UNDERLYING MEMORY MODELS

Our overview of CIRCUS has been dominated by descriptions of control structures. We have described interactions between syntactic analysis and the marker-passing algorithm, as well as interactions between the marker passing algorithm and numerical relaxation. We have seen how to construct appropriate networks for both marker passing and numerical relaxation, and we have looked at specific sentences to illustrate all of these ideas. Up until now, we have managed to finesse as much as possible the question of underlying memory structures, although we have explained where memory interactions are needed.

There are three basic types of memory that drive the sentence analysis of CIRCUS. They are:

1. A Lexical Dictionary (LD)
2. Structured Relational Preferences (SRP)
3. Unstructured Relational Preferences (URP)

The LD is used during syntactic analysis and network construction for the marker passing algorithm, SRP are used during marker passing, and URP are used for numerical relaxation. We will describe the role played by each form of memory, and indicate where we stand with respect to our current implementation of CIRCUS.

Of the three memory modules, the LD is the most straightforward and least interesting aspect of memory. Here is where we set up associations between words and word senses, word senses and case frame definitions, word senses and parts of speech. Syntactic predictions are associated with any word sense that assumes a semantic case frame interpretation. In general, there must be at least as many syntactic predictions for a given word sense as there are case frame slots for that word sense.

The machinery for handling dictionary information is fully implemented in CIRCUS and completely adequate for the sorts of sentences we've been discussing in this paper as well as others.[5] We do not mean to suggest that there are no interesting problems in designing LD definitions. One must always make hard decisions about primitive decomposition within a case frame representation, where to draw the line between two distinct word senses, and whether or not a sentence representation should strive to be free of inferences. But all of these problems are primarily problems in representation rather than memory per se. So let us leave the LD and concentrate on the remaining two memory structures needed to drive CIRCUS.

5.1. Structured Relational Preferences

Structured Relational Preferences (SRP) refer to constraints that aid in the identification of case frame slot fillers. These are generally soft constraints, since they can be violated if syntactic considerations force a case frame instantiation that contradicts normal semantic expectations. Most predictive case-frame parsers utilize some form of a slot constraint mechanism, and the standard solution involves semantic feature checking. Indeed, simple semantic features are what CIRCUS is currently using as well.

Each word sense in the LD is associated with a semantic feature vector, and the feature nodes in PSM normally do nothing more than check for the presence of a given semantic feature. We could improve on the current solution a bit by introducing an inheritance tree to organize our semantic features, but there are other problems with semantic features that transcend the question of how cleverly we organize them.

For example, consider the problem of instantiating a case frame for eating. "John ate a hamburger," is fine as long as John is a human, but "John ate some hay," should signal a semantic violation. Then again, eating hay is fine if you're a horse, so we can't hope to nail the preference on the basis of the object slot

---

[5]For example, CIRCUS can simulate garden path effects for reduced relative clause sentences by tracking competing case frame instantiations (via concept node activation levels) within PSM.

filler alone. Here we need to consider both the agent and the object together in order to determine whether or not the object qualifies as food for that particular agent. A simple semantic feature called "food" is not sufficient since the agent doing the eating must be taken into consideration as well.

At this point we have to decide whether or not we are primarily interested in building a practical system for some limited domain, or a system that makes theoretical claims about psychological validity. For the sake of building practical systems, simple semantic features are largely adequate. But if we want to make claims about the correct model for SRP in general, we are more inclined to invoke a model of episodic memory structuring. There are a variety of possibilities here, but they must all incorporate some capability for learning from experience. Some recent attempts in this direction have made tentative steps toward outlining an episodic model of SRP, including the DMAP system (Riesbeck & Martin, 1986), and ELAN (Lehnert, 1987b). We can also imagine a connectionist strategy using a learning technique like back propagation and distributed representations, so we see an opportunity here for either symbolic or subsymbolic SRP models.

By moving away from semantic discriminations into episodic ones, we can set up preferences that may be extremely specific, but nevertheless valid. For example, if we know a particular individual named John, and we also know that John is a vegetarian, we should be concerned to hear that John is eating a hamburger. This constitutes a violation of episodic expectations. If our experience never goes beyond knowledge about one person named John, SRP may effectively take John to be a good representative of all humans. The issue of dynamic generalizations and appropriate levels of abstraction become important for any SRP model that operates on the basis of episodic memory. It necessarily follows that any episodic model of SRP must incorporate a model of similarity-based (inductive) learning as well. The earliest strategy for handling SRP as a dynamic episodic memory structure was illustrated by the IPP system which read stories about terrorism and created generalizations based on those stories (Lebowitz, 1983a, 1983b).

At the present time, connectionist models for inductive learning are currently limited to simple associations or a single relational predicate with two arguments. If a connectionist network could scale up to an arbitrary set of relational predicates with arbitrarily many arguments, we would have the basis for an episodic memory that yields case frame slot-filling preferences. SRP therefore provides us with an opportunity to experiment with high-level connectionism, but the demands of SRP seem to push techniques like back propagation beyond their reasonable limits in terms of training requirements.

5.2. Unstructured Relational Predicates

Unstructured Relational Predicates (URP) are needed by the relaxation algorithm in CIRCUS to provide initial activation levels for relational nodes representing pp-attachments. Although a relational predicate is, in fact, a structured entity, we are calling the memory behind these predicates unstructured because the preferences needed to handle relational node initialization are better described in terms of semantic knowledge instead of episodic knowledge. At some early stage of development, a child might answer the question "Can a person be in a car?" by thinking of specific people getting into a specific car, but this type of knowledge must generalize very quickly to levels of abstraction that drop their episodic origins. In general, we will assume that event-oriented memory remains essentially episodic, while relational memory quickly evolves into semantic memory organization even if its earliest roots are episodic. These assumptions deserve substantial discussion, but we will not digress here to pursue it.

Since data-driven preference semantics requires knowledge about relational constraints, URP is properly addressed by semantic memory models rather than episodic ones. In section 4.1 we saw how CIRCUS could invoke a simplistic conditional statement for the purpose of initializing our relaxation network. For limited applications, this primitive notion of URP might prove to be adequate. However, any extensive application that requires data-driven semantics would probably encounter a difficult obstacle if we have to scale-up by tuning these conditionals in order to handle a large class of attachment interactions.

To address this issue of scaling up, we have been investigating the utility of back propagation as a technique for training a semantic memory model to provide an URP capability. Using examples from a corpus of scientific papers, we've trained networks by presenting triples representing noun-preposition-noun combinations (e.g., "temperature in Fahrenheit") along with one of two possible outcome values: "plausible" or "implausible." Each network consists of 32 input units (16 binary features for each noun), 12 hidden units, and one output unit. We train a separate network for each preposition, but the binary features used for encoding input nouns remain fixed across all networks. Once training is completed, we can produce correct plausibility for 94 percent of the training corpus, and 81 percent of a novel test set. A more detailed account of this experiment can be found in (Wermter, 1989).

Although our hit rate on novel test items may not appear to be overwhelmingly impressive, it is important to note that the novel test set contains nouns which were not necessarily present in the training corpus. To add a new noun to URP, we need only structure its representation in terms of the 16-feature vector. No additional knowledge is required since the backprop network has already encoded the necessary knowledge for making relational plausibility judgments. Substantial training is required to add a new preposition to URP, but in general, we can expect to have more nouns that prepositions, so this requirement does not seem unreasonable. If we can improve the hit rate on novel test items by either restructuring our feature vector or opting for more training, it appears that back propagation may be an effective strategy for scaling up substantial URP memories.

6. CONCLUSIONS

In this chapter we have concentrated on the basic architecture of CIRCUS in an effort to show how (a) stack-oriented syntactic analysis, (b) marker passing for predictive preference semantics, and (c) numerical relaxation for data-driven preference semantics, can operate together in order to take full advantage of each processing strategy. We have also seen how one strictly syntactic constraint is easily handled by the numeric relaxation algorithm, suggesting that syntactic and semantic concerns are not always best served by separate processing strategies (despite our general tendency with CIRCUS to do just that). It might be better to characterize the three modules of CIRCUS in terms of (a) local syntactic constraints, (b) local semantic constraints, and (c) global constraints of either a syntactic or semantic nature. This somewhat more accurate portrayal of the CIRCUS processing modules suggests a useful pattern for understanding the respective roles of symbolic and subsymbolic information processing.

In section 4.2 we have talked previously about the top-down/bottom-up relationship between predictive preference semantics and data-driven preference semantics. We further pointed out that the top-down component of predictive preference semantics was symbolic and serial, while the bottom-up component of data-driven preference semantics was subsymbolic and parallel. Now we can also add a local/global edge to this same boundary line, so the following dichotomies emerge:

predictive	vs.	data-driven
top-down	vs.	bottom-up
symbolic	vs.	subsymbolic
serial	vs.	parallel
local	vs.	global

These contrasting dichotomies are familiar to anyone who has been watching the AI/connectionist debates in recent years, but it is unusual to find a single system where both aspects of each dichotomy are present and operating in concert. In general, AI models tend to be situated in the left column, while connectionist models are more comfortable with the right side. CIRCUS represents a powerful synthesis of symbolic and subsymbolic techniques, utilizing properties from both columns as needed to handle a variety of problems.

Inevitably, people like to understand the claims associated with system implementations. Is the model being proposed psychologically valid, physiologically motivated, or just a clever hack? More importantly, for any claim being made, which parts of the system implementation are meant to be taken seriously, and which should be dismissed as necessary kludges?

In trying to answer these questions about CIRCUS, we must first admit that the exploratory aspect of CIRCUS is a synthesis of many ideas—some new and some old. We were primarily interested in designing a conceptual sentence analyzer that did a few things better than other conceptual sentence analyzers. Ideas were pulled from a variety of places, including the connectionist literature on sentence analysis (especially Waltz & Pollack, 1985), but there was no one theoretical motivation behind the design of CIRCUS. It was, and remains, largely an engineering effort. As such, we believe that CIRCUS has been very successful insofar as it is currently being used to provide natural language processing capabilities for other research projects.

On the other hand, CIRCUS is fully consistent with a number of theoretical claims. Some of these claims are specific to theories about natural language processing, while others are more general in nature. To researchers intent on the pursuit of "high-level connectionism," we are in a position to make one very general claim about the application of subsymbolic techniques to processes associated with "high-level" cognition. Namely, there is no reason to believe that a single information processing mechanism can be held accountable for processes as complex as sentence analysis.

Indeed, we have seen many attempts to reduce sentence analysis to a single computational mechanism fail time and time again. The list is long and thoroughly researched: augmented transition networks, semantic grammars, chart parsers, production systems, expectation-based systems, and more recently, marker passing, back propagation, and spreading activation algorithms. In each case, we see a mechanism with obvious shortcomings and apparently insurmountable problems. In each case, one or two aspects of the problem at hand are addressed effectively and attractively, while everything else remains beyond the scope of the current model. And still the hope lives on that someday we will manage to find the one correct mechanism. This desire to reduce a complex phenomenon to a simple explanation is understandable from the perspectives of elegant science and aesthetic sensibility, but it should not preclude from consideration the possibility that such explanations are simply not in the cards.

Cognitive processes must not be confused with the phenomena of physics or other natural sciences. Cognition is a biological entity which has evolved over a long period of time as an adaptive mechanism. Any system that takes a million years to develop is not likely to be elegant or optimal. On the contrary, we have every reason to believe that there are multiple layers of information processing mechanisms, each contributing to specific aspects of the problem at hand, much as the gross anatomy of the brain layers newer structures over older ones.

At the workshop where CIRCUS was first presented, one participant described CIRCUS as an example of a "grandiose architecture." The import of this characterization seemed clear: No one prefers to go after solutions of this complexity—surely we can do better by persisting in the search for the (one) right mechanism. And indeed, there are lessons to be learned by pushing a single mechanism as far as it will go. But many of these lessons are clearly at odds with the idea of a single processing mechanism. Some aspects of language processing are characterized by memory limitations and serial processing effects (limited syntactic embedding, garden-pathing on certain reduced-relative clauses, the general inability to handle sentences of arbitrary syntactic complexity), while other effects can only be explained in terms of parallel processing (lexical priming phenomena are the most compelling examples here). If we take all the available evidence into consideration, the hope for a single explanatory mechanism seems truly quixotic.

Moreover, we have no reason to feel defeated by solutions that require "grandiose architectures." On the contrary, any computational model of natural language processing that remains extensible and consistent with human information processing capabilities must be welcomed, even if some aesthetic sensibilities need to be sacrificed along the way. So CIRCUS is presented here without apology, but with some defensiveness. We are not too proud to propose a grandiose architecture for natural language processing: Natural language is a complicated problem. When we have competing explanations of equal power and breadth, we will happily invoke Occam's razor and allow simplicity to dominate. Until then, it is better to worry about extensibility first, and aesthetics later. If "high-level connectionism" is going to flourish and succeed, this shift in research priorities may be a crucial first step.

REFERENCES

Birnbaum, L., & Selfridge, M. (1981). Conceptual analysis of natural language. In R.C. Schank & C. Riesbeck (Eds.), *Inside computer understanding* (pp. 318–353). Hillsdale, NJ: Lawrence Erlbaum Associates.

Cullingford, R. (1986). *Natural language processing*. Totowa, NJ: Rowman & Littlefield.

Dyer, M. (1983). *In-depth understanding: A computer model of integrated processing for narrative comprehension*. Cambridge, MA: MIT Press.

Feldman, J.A., & Ballard, D.H. (1982). Connectionist models and their properties. *Cognitive Science, 6*(3), 205–254.

Ford, M., Bresnan, J., & Kaplan, R. (1981). A competence-based theory of syntactic closure. In J. Bresnan (Ed.), *The mental representation of grammatical relations*. Cambridge, MA: MIT Press.

Frazier, L., & Fodor, J. (1979). The sausage machine: A new two-state parsing model. *Cognition, 6,* 191–325.

Lebowitz, M. (1983a). Memory-based parsing. *Journal of Artificial Intelligence, 21*(4), 363–404.

Lebowitz, M. (1983b). Generalization from natural language text. *Cognitive Science, 7*(1), 1–40.

Lehnert, W.G. (1987a). Case-based problem solving with a large knowledge base of learned cases. *Proceedings of the Sixth National Conference on Artificial Intelligence*. Seattle, WA.

Lehnert, W.G. (1987b). Learning to integrate syntax and semantics. *Proceedings of the Fourth International Workshop on Machine Learning*. Irvine, CA.

Lytinen, S. (1984). Frame selection in parsing. *Proceedings of the National Conference on Artificial Intelligence*. Austin, Texas.

Pylyshyn, Z.W. (1984). *Computation and cognition*. Cambridge, MA: MIT Press.

Riesbeck, C. (1975). Conceptual analysis. In R.C. Schank (Ed.), *Conceptual information processing*. Amsterdam: North-Holland.

Riesbeck, C., & Martin, C. (1986). Direct memory access parsing. In C. Riesbeck & J. Kolodner (Eds.), *Experience, memory and reasoning* (pp. 209–226). Hillsdale, NJ: Lawrence Erlbaum Associates.

Riesbeck, C., & Schank, R. (1976). *Expectation-based analysis of sentences in context* (Research Report #78). New Haven, CT: Department of Computer Science, Yale University.

Schank, R.D. (Ed.). (1975). *Conceptual information processing*. Amsterdam: North-Holland.

Schank, R.D., & Riesbeck, C. (1981). *Inside computer understanding: Five programs plus miniatures*. Hillsdale, NJ: Lawrence Erlbaum Associates.

Swinney, D. (1984). Theoretical and methodological issues in cognitive science: A psycholinguistic perspective. In W. Kintsch, J. Miller, & P. Polson (Eds.), *Method and tactics in cognitive science* (pp. 217–233). Hillsdale, NJ: Lawrence Erlbaum Associates.

Tait, J.I. (1983). Semantics-directed parsing. In K. Sparck Jones & Y. Wilks (Eds.), *Automatic natural language parsing* (pp. 169–177). New York: John Wiley & Sons.

Waltz, D., & Pollack, J. (1985). Massively parallel parsing: A strongly interactive model of natural language interpretation. *Cognitive Science, 9*(1), 51–74.

Wermter, S. (1989). Integration of semantic and syntactic constraints for structural noun phrase disambiguation. *Proceedings of the Eleventh International Joint Conference on Artificial Intelligence*. San Mateo, CA: Morgan Kaufmann.

Wilks, Y., Huang, X., & Fass, D. (1985). Syntax, preference and right attachment. *Proceedings of the Ninth International Joint Conference on Artificial Intelligence*, pp. 779–784.

7 Developing Hybrid Symbolic/Connectionist Models

James Hendler

1. INTRODUCTION

A persistent theme in Western cognitive research has been that of spreading activation. In this view, "mental energy" spreads through the brain in response to a sensory input, much as waves propagate from a pebble thrown into a pond. This tradition begins as long ago as Aristotle, and continues into American psychological tradition through the work of the British associationist school and the American behaviorists. In recent years this notion of activation spread has again been gaining popularity and acceptance particularly in the computational cognitive modeling community.

Two very different schools of thought have been developing based on different approaches to this phenomena. One of these schools has given rise to neural network and connectionist models. This work holds that low-level entities, connected through a network of weighted links, spread activation between input sensors and output effectors. Nonlinear functions and networks of unconnected "hidden" nodes are suggested to explain cognitive phenomena as "emergent behaviors." A second school, however, argues that spread of activation is not a low-level, subsymbolic activity, but rather that activation flows among conceptually related items in a semantic network in which both the nodes and links have specific meanings. This approach has given rise to both the work in marker-propagation (Fahlman, 1979) and symbolic marker-passing.

Psychological experimentation in spreading activation has produced much evidence as to how the human cognitive mechanism works. We believe this evidence makes a rather compelling argument for one of two solutions: either a new mechanism differing from both marker-passing and connectionism which can account for both sets of results or a hybrid model, in which both connectionist and symbolic models cooperate. While the first of these is always a possible solution, the latter seems a more manageable research agenda. In this chapter we review this evidence and briefly describe our own work which takes some first steps at developing a model aimed at helping to bridge this gap.

2. SPREADING ACTIVATION

One often cited argument for the connectionist methodology is that its models account for many of the spreading activation effects demonstrated experimentally, particularly recent results in reaction time studies of priming. These results show priming affects on items which are perceptually or categorically similar. Examples include rhyming priming, in which words that rhyme cause priming ("cow" primes "now"), lexical priming, in which all word senses, regardless of meaning are primed by an input string ("c-o-w" primes both the nominal "animal" and the verbal "fear"), and spelling primings, in which words spelled similarly can prime each other ("cow" priming "caw"). A full list of references on "low-level" priming is beyond the scope of this paper, however Anderson and Bower (1979) present a discussion of the history of associationism and many of the earlier results in the field, Rumelhart, McClelland, and the PDP Research Group (1986) discuss many of the activation spreading results as related to the PDP connectionist model, and (Hendler, 1987a) presents a long discussion of priming results related to marker-passing as discussed below.

The marker-passing types of models, which are motivated largely by the work of Quillian (1966) who is credited with coining the term "spreading activation," represent knowledge as a set of interconnecting nodes related by semantically interesting links. By propagating energy along these links, semantic relations can be found. Marker-passing models have been proposed to account for cognitive tasks such as natural language processing (Charniak, 1983; Granger, Eiselt, & Holbrook, 1984; Hirst, 1983; Norvig, 1987) and planning (Hendler, 1987a). This approach also accounts for a set of experimental results from the psychological literature.

While the work of Collins and Quillian (1970), Collins and Loftus (1972), and others is often used by the connectionists as more evidence in their favor, these experiments demonstrated priming effects that are hard to account for using a paired association framework.

In these experiments priming was shown to occur between semantically related, but neither physically co-occuring or perceptually related primes. An example of this is the priming of "milk" from "cow"—while it is possible that a country-bred person might have often seen the milking of cows, it seems unlikely that a city-bred child will be using other than a semantic relation such as "milk comes from cows." Although there is some evidence that this type of priming spreads through less of the network and takes longer than the priming of perceptually and categorically related items (DeGroot, 1983), the effect is nevertheless evident in many experiments.

These two different approaches to the spread of activation have very real repercussions when it comes to the issue of massive parallelism and its correlate, explaining the performance of the human cognitive mechanism. For the connectionist approaches, models with fast numeric computations modeling the spread of energy in the brain are sufficient. Such models allow parallel distributed computing and try to directly model neuron-like computing with a large network of highly interconnected, relatively simple, processing units. The marker-passing school, however, requires the need for the passing of discrete messages between nodes (or groups thereof) representing distinct concepts. These messages can be simple bits (as in Fahlman's, 1979, NETL system) or complex markers (as in Quillian's, 1967, Semantic Memory program or our own marker-passing system, Hendler, 1986). While computer architectures can be designed that permit both types of processing, a reconciliation of the two approaches seems necessary if we are to understand the cognitive computing performed by the human brain.

We believe that the seeds of a reconciliation between these disparate approaches can be found by examination of some other psychological results, particularly the work of Posner and Snyder (1976). These results demonstrate a fairly reliable effect showing two types of activation spread. The first, automatic spread of activation (ASA), occurs without conscious control. It starts quickly, with onsets typically less than 50 milliseconds, and rapidly falls away, typically disappearing by 200–300 milliseconds. The second form of activation appears to be under conscious control, and starts just prior to the decay of the ASA. This spread seems to be less pervasive, but effects can linger much longer, even making their way into the long-term memory and showing up after days or weeks[1].

We have tried to base our own work on developing models that might help explain these two types of activation. Initially we demonstrated that a massively parallel marker-passing algorithm, the "most connectionist" of many of the modern symbolic approaches, could be combined with a local connectionist model, the most "symbolic" of the connectionist approaches. Using the notion of microfeatures, we embedded a local connectionistlike network into a symbolic network, and used the marker-passing technique to provide "energy" into the lower-level network. Hendler (1987b) described this model and presented an example of using it to solve a planning task which required that an object be recognized to be perceptually similar to another object.

Our more recent work is focusing on a system which uses a stronger notion of microfeatures in the above model. A back propagation network is trained on an encoding of objects corresponding to some of the nodes in a semantic associative network. Using the marker-passing technique a traditional symbolic reasoner is able to use the hidden nodes of the connectionist representation to reason about the perceptual similarity of objects. A small version of this model has been

---

[1] See, for example, Granger and Holbrook (1983).

implemented, and we are presently exploring several domains for practical problems on which to test the model. In the remainder of this chapter we discuss reasoning about perceptual similarity and show how the more complex model addresses this issue.

3. PERCEPTUAL SIMILARITY

Many phenomena needing to be explained by the cognitive scientist have their roots in the perceptual similarities between various objects as viewed by the human cognitive apparatus. Some examples include:

Categorization, where humans can classify objects as better and worse examples of some category (for example, "sparrow" is consistently rated as a better "bird" than "turkey").

Priming, where the priming occurs for perceptually similar objects. An example of this is "rhyming priming" in which words which rhyme demonstrate priming effects.

Functional identification, in which objects which have perceptual features in common are used to perform functions associated with each other (for example, substituting a rock for a hammer due to a similarity in mass).

Traditional symbolic modeling, in the AI and cognitive psychology communities, has been unable to offer an explanation of these effects.

Connectionist approaches appear to have shed some light on a mechanism (or set thereof) which can be used to explain the recognition of perceptual similarities. Distributed connectionist models can be trained so as to develop an internal representation that roughly corresponds to a set of nonsymbolically identifiable features which are used to determine such similarity over a set of inputs. Such features, often called *microfeatures,* are an important reason for the success of parallel distributed models (McClelland & Rumelhart, 1981; Rumelhart & McClelland, 1986).

Examples of the types of microfeatures learned by connectionist networks can be seen in examining a clustering analysis of the hidden network units of the NETTALK system (Sejnowski & Rosenberg, 1986). NETTALK, a 3-layer network with an input layer, one hidden layer, and an output layer, was trained with letter strings and the corresponding phonemic encoding of the central letter of the string. A clustering analysis of the hidden unit weights developed during the running of the program indicated that certain input patterns caused greater activations of certain weights. An example would be a set of unit weights which was maximized when presented with most occurrences of "A E I O and U." This set of weights would thus be said to encode what we call vowels, and thus we could refer to "vowel" as a microfeature learned by the system. Other microfeatures discovered could not be as easily described. For example, in one run of the program a set of weights might be discovered which maximizes letters such as T and D when appearing near the end of words, but not at the front. This has no easily described symbolic label, it might most closely described as "letters whose pronunciation hardness changes in conjunction with nearness to a right hand space."

Connectionist models are usually associated with learning algorithms that enable them to create these microfeatures from a set of training examples. The networks can then produce output values for elements they were not trained on by, in essence, finding items with the most elements in common. This is particularly useful to networks which are trained as "classifiers," that is, the training set is used to get the network to have the behavior of differentiating a set of objects based on, for example, some sort of acoustic or other signals.

Unfortunately, while present connectionist models do allow this type of classification and recognition of perceptual similarity, they have not yet been made to perform the complex reasoning tasks that have been the forte of symbolic AI approaches. While such tasks as expert reasoning, natural language analysis and planning can be handled fairly easily (although primarily only in limited domains) by the rule-based approaches of traditional fifth generation computing systems, those neural network programs attempting these tasks have had limited success. Those connectionist systems which have been most successful in these traditional domains, structured connectionist systems (Feldman & Ballard, 1982; Shastri, 1985), have not had the property of learning the types of microfeatures described earlier.

While it may not be inherently impossible for purely connectionist approaches to handle complex reasoning tasks someday, it will require significant breakthroughs for this to happen. Similarly, getting purely symbolic systems to handle the types of perceptual-similarity-based reasoning that connectionist networks perform well would require major advances in AI. In this chapter we present an approach in which a hybrid system, a semantic network merged with a backpropagation learning network, is used to provide complex reasoning about perceptual similarities. The next section will describe this model, following which we give an example of its use, and provide a discussion of some of the ramifications of such hybrid models.

4. THE HYBRID MODEL

The hybrid model described in this paper is an extension of an earlier system described elsewhere. The original system, called SCRAPS, used a marker-passing algorithm to find information of use to a planning system.[2] In extending the SCRAPS model to do some simple similarity based reasoning we demonstrated that a massively parallel marker-passing algorithm, the "most connectionist" of

[2] This work is described in detail in Hendler (1987b).

many of the modern symbolic approaches, could be combined with a local connectionist model, the most "symbolic" of the connectionist approaches. This work focused on the embedding of a local connectionist-like network into a symbolic network, and used the marker-passing technique to provide "energy" into the lower level network. Hendler (1989) describes this model and presents an example in which merging these approaches enables us to deal with a task which neither approach, alone, has yet been able to solve.

Our recent work, however, has focused on a more powerful integration of the symbolic and connectionist techniques. A distributed network is trained on an encoding of objects corresponding to some of the nodes in a semantic associative network. Using the marker-passing technique a traditional symbolic reasoner is able to use the hidden nodes of the connectionist network as microfeatures for performing similarity-based reasoning.[3]

A diagram of the system is shown in Figure 7.1. The rectangle labeled "semantic network" represents a small segment of the symbolic knowledge-base used by the program: Nodes represent symbols while links represent relationships between them. The distributed network, contained in the lower rectangle of the figure, is a three-layer network with a single layer of hidden units. The dark rectangle, labeled *Microfeature Network,* represents a section of the model in which the microfeatures learned by the distributed network are accessed by an activation spreading algorithm. It is this interaction which we will be discussing throughout the remainder of this chapter.

The system works by first training the distributed network as a classifier over the perceptual encoding of the items corresponding to the leaves of the semantic network. The classifier is trained using a version of the back propagation learning algorithm based on Rumelhart et al. (1986). The hidden unit layer develops a distributed internal representation (similar to the NETTALK encoding discussed in the introduction) in which the microfeatures serve to correlate the encodings to the objects.

Once the training phase is completed, the links between the hidden and output units contain a weight space that can be used for performing the similarity-based reasoning. The mechanism used to provide the communication between the two networks is that of marker-passing. Essentially, symbolic activation spreads through the symbolic network. When a link to the distributed network is encountered, numeric activation, with strength corresponding to the activation energy of the symbolic marking, is passed into the distributed network. This energy propagates to the hidden units and then back to the output units. Those symbolic items most closely related, where closeness is now defined as similarity over the perceptual encoding, gain energy and are able to propagate symbolic information. Paths between activated items can now be found and evaluated by the

[3] Where similarity is defined with regard to the encoding scheme used.

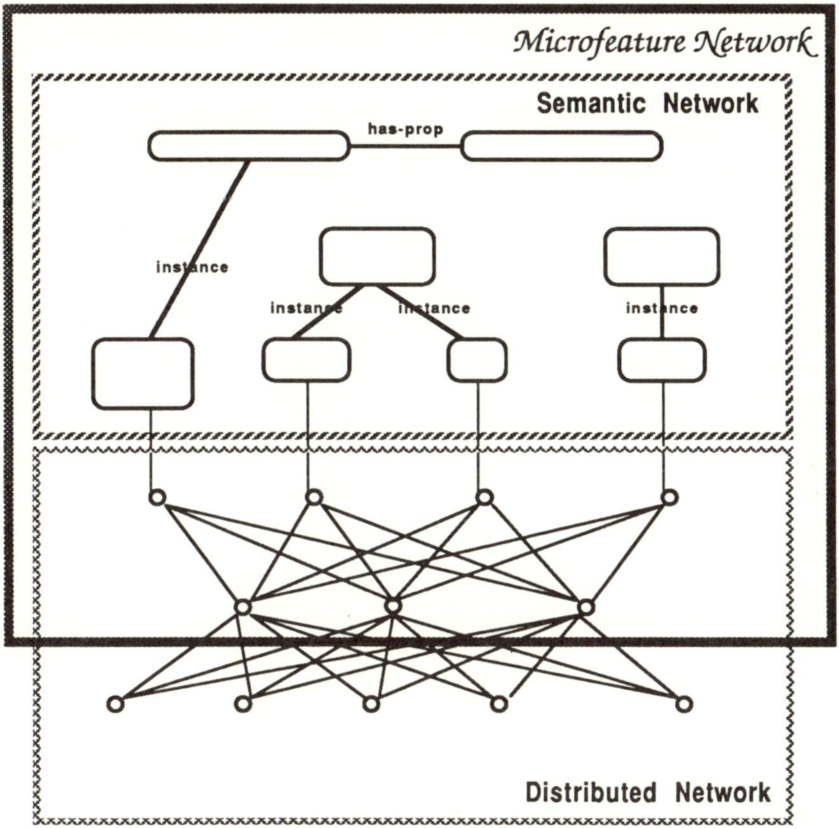

Figure 7.1.
A hybrid network model.

symbolic mechanism. A detailed example of this mechanism and a description of the marker-passing algorithm are presented in the next section.

4.1. Details of the Hybrid Model

To understand the model in more depth, it is important to understand the basic marker-passing approach being used and how the energy levels that pass through the back-propagation network are computed. In this section we will first discuss these issues and then present some examples of the use of our model.

4.1.1. Marker-passing. One approach to certain AI tasks is that of using an activation spreading algorithm which passes symbolic information through a traditional associative network (one in which the arcs between nodes represent symbolic information rather than link strengths or the like). These "marker-passing algorithms" can pass very simple information (Fahlman, 1979) or complex marks which include various amounts of control information for use in the marker-passing process (Charniak, 1986; Hendler, 1986; Quillian, 1966). Such systems have been shown to integrate gracefully with the standard AI technologies for natural language processing (Alterman, 1985; Norvig, 1987; Charniak, 1983, 1986; Hirst, 1983) and planning (Hendler, 1987a). A detailed discussion of the various forms of these algorithms and their past use can be found in Hendler (1986).

The marker-passer used in our hybrid model is based on one first proposed in Charniak (1983) and later extended in Hendler (1987a). This algorithm works by spreading activation, in the form of symbolic markers, throughout a knowledge base. When these markers encounter other markers an intersection is found. The paths meeting at this intersection are then returned to a path evaluation mechanism. This mechanism checks each path for information which can be used to help guide the natural language or planning component. If no such information is found, the path is ignored.

As an example consider the case of the use of this marker-passing approach in helping to identify a correct solution to a problem with several alternatives. For example, if we are attempting to plan

Trying to commit suicide while holding a gun.

the system needs to choose between each of the possible ways of performing the suicide plan. The planning system would start by passing markers to each of the alternatives, these in turn mark their subplans, etc. While this goes on we the system would also be passing markers starting with the frame *gun*. The path

SUICIDE → to do SUICIDE(x) KILL (x,x) → KILL → method of KILL(y,x) is SHOOT(y,x) → SHOOT → precondition of SHOOT(y,x) is possess (y,GUN) → GUN

is found by the marker-passer and is reported to the path evaluator. This path presents a potential solution to the task which has been posed, committing suicide and the path evaluator causes the problem solver to prefer the *shoot* plan for achieving the *suicide* goal. A similar path could be used by a natural language system in understanding the story:

Jack wanted to commit suicide. He picked up a gun.[4]

Again, to summarize, the marker-passer works by spreading activation

[4] Based on Charmiak (1983).

through a network starting form several initial nodes. When activation from one origin reaches activation spreading from another origin, a path is reported. This path is then examined by a path evaluation mechanism which determines whether the information reported is of use to the NLP or planning module. If it is appropriate actions are taken, if not the path is ignored.

One of the most important features in the design of a marker-passer is a mechanism which can limit the number of nodes marked and of paths returned. If too many paths are found by the marker-passer we lose efficiency since the evaluator must examine all those paths which are reported. If too few paths are reported the correct information can be missed. The marker-passer must be designed so as to constrain the number of paths reported.

The simplest form of such an attenuation mechanism can be built into the algorithm in the form of a length limitation. In a complex network all the nodes are connected to each other. Some of these paths are long and tortuous—they require that a large number of inferences hold true. If one holds the breadth of activation spreading to a set limit, these long paths can be avoided. Most marker-passing systems to date have used such a limitation. Another commonly used limitation is to check the outbranching of the nodes being marked. If the branchout goes above a certain number no marks propagate. This is to avoid very common nodes, such as *Animal* from marking all of their exemplars (*Cat, Dog, . . . Platypus,* etc.).

The attenuation mechanism used by our marker-passer was designed to limit both the length and branchout of paths found without violating the locality constraints needed for massively parallel computing. This is done by using a numerical constant to represent activation strength, and by dividing this strength by each node's outbranching as marking proceeds. If we start at a highly branching node enough energy is available for it and all of its children to be marked. If, however, we hit such a promiscuous node late in processing, its children are not marked as the activation strength will have diminished based on the outbranching of the nodes in the path prior to the current node.

It turns out that designing the attenuation mechanism in this way has many desirable features. In particular it can be shown that this mechanism fits nicely into a massively parallel implementation of marker-passing where it can serve as a feedback mechanism between the marker-passer and the planning component of SCRAPS. Further, by using a computation based on the attenuation numbers reaching a node of intersection, a path strength can be efficiently computed for use by the path evaluator. Finally, it appears that such an attenuation mechanism accounts for certain cognitive findings better than either a length or promiscuity limitation. (For a discussion of all of these see Hendler, 1987a.)

4.1.2. Details of the Hybrid Model (Continued). The hybrid mechanism works by using the activation strength of markers to provide the numeric activation necessary in the microfeature network. When a node connected to the back-propagation network is encountered, the activation strength of the symbolic mark is used as activation energy over the distributed network's links. Since these are weighted links (with the weights learned by the back-propagation algorithm), the activation is divided by weight as it passes down the links and is recombined as it leaves the network. As other nodes of this network gain activation they start passing symbolic marks with activation strength based on the amont of energy reaching them through the network. Marking then proceeds as normal, paths are found, and the path evaluator is invoked as usual.

As an example of what occurs when the symbolic activation energy encounters the connectionist network, consider the case where the output and hidden units of a simple network have been learned (via training over some input set) to be connected by the weights shown in Figure 7.2. Activation from the symbolic network enters a node (say *N1*) with an initial strength of ψ. This activation strength is divided by the outbranching of the node and then multiplied by the weight of each link to the hidden units. Thus activation flows from *n1* to *h1* with a strength of $\psi \times 1/3 \times Weight(n1,h1)$. A similar computation is made to each of the other hidden units. This activation now spreads to each of the other output nodes in turn. Thus, *n2* would gain activation of

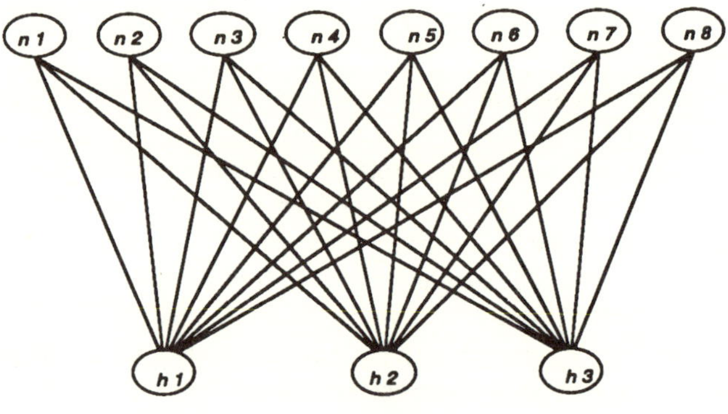

Weights

	h1	h2	h3
n1	-4.98	4.40	-2.82
n2	-6.99	-4.99	-2.23
n3	-6.11	3.49	0.30
n4	-6.37	-4.68	2.53
n5	4.36	3.73	-5.09
n6	4.38	-5.97	-3.67
n7	0.89	1.07	3.32
n8	3.88	-6.95	1.88

Figure 7.2.
Weights learned (input units omitted).

$$
\begin{aligned}
&Activation(h1)\times Weight(n2,h1)/8+ && \psi\times Weight(n1,h1)/3\times Weight(n2,h1)/8+\\
&Activation(h2)\times Weight(n2,h2)/8+ \quad = && \psi\times Weight(n1,h2)/3\times Weight(n2,h2)/8+\\
&Activation(h3)\times Weight(n2,h3)/8 && \psi\times Weight(n1,h3)/3\times Weight(n2,h3)/8
\end{aligned}
$$

which works out to an activation of $.8\psi$. Table 7.1 shows a graph of the activation spread between the output units. The table, which is symmetric, can thus be read as showing the output at each of the other units when an activation strength of 1 is placed at the named node.

4.1.3. Using the hybrid system. In this example we describe how the hybrid system can be used to solve a simple (and, we admit, quite contrived) problem. Figure 7.3 shows the hybrid knowledge as it would be used to represent some simple facts such as: *Rex is a doberman, dobermans chase mailmen. Spot is a tabby cat, tabby cats are petted by mailmen.* We will now consider the hybrid system being used by a natural language component to fill in the blank in the sentence:

Fido ____________ the mailman.

where *Fido* is known to be a poodle. Since no direct connection can be found in the semantic system (we have not explicitely encoded, for example, that "dogs chase mailmen"), the system will have to use similarity-based reasoning to decide if *Fido* is more like *Rex,* in which case we would assume that the blank would be filled with "chased," or if *Fido* is more like *Spot,* in which case the blank would correspond to "is petted by."

In testing our hybrid model we used a simplified encoding that was biased in one of two ways. In an 18–3–4 three-layer network each of the output nodes,

Table 7.1.
Activation Spread Between Output Units in 6-3-8 Network.

Multiply Ψ by:

	n1	*n2*	*n3*	*n4*	*n5*	*n6*	*n7*	*n8*
n1	•	.80	1.03	.17	.38	−1.57	−.38	−2.30
n2	.80	•	1.02	2.60	−1.57	.31	−.79	.14
n3	1.03	1.02	•	.97	−.63	−2.03	−.03	−1.97
n4	.17	2.60	.97	•	−2.42	−.38	−.09	.52
n5	.38	−1.57	−.63	−2.42	•	.64	−.38	−.77
n6	−1.57	.31	−2.03	−.38	.64	•	−.60	2.14
n7	−.38	−.79	−.03	−.09	−.38	−.60	•	.09
n8	−2.30	−.14	−1.97	.52	−.77	2.14	.09	•

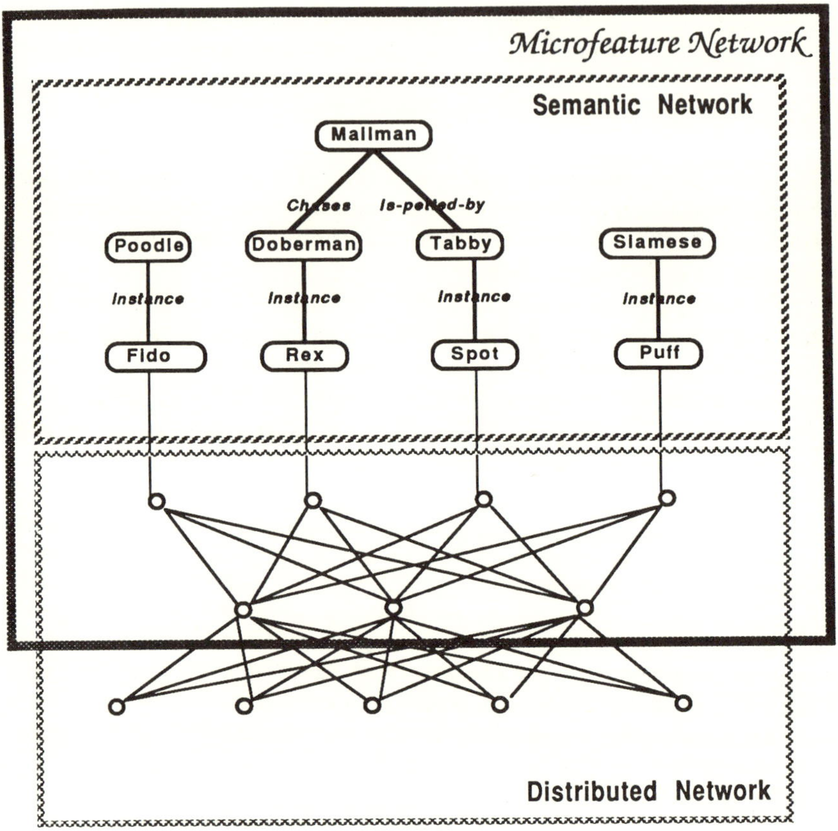

Figure 7.3.
The sample hybrid knowledge base.

corresponding to, *Rex, Fido,* etc., was associated with four input patterns. In one set of training exercises these inputs differed only in one set of features such that *Rex* and *Fido* shared the common set. In a second trial series only *Rex* and *Spot* shared these features. The other features were randomly assigned. (We should make it clear here that no actual significance should be associated with this particular encoding. That is, this example is not derived to show that a network could make the correct decision based on such simple inputs, but rather to have an example which shows the behavior of the hybrid system. As we will briefly discuss in the conclusion section, more realistic testing of the hybrid system is currently being undertaken.)

In each case the system was started by passing markers from *Fido* and from *mailman*. An initial activation energy was chosen to start marking.[5] When the marks from *Fido* encountered the distributed network, they were propagated as described in the previous section. If the markers from the output nodes which shared activation continued through the semantic network to reach "mailman" a path was returned. If the activation proceeded through several nodes several paths would be returned.

In the first case, where *Fido* and *Rex* shared features, the activation spread from *Fido* to the hidden units and back to the output. As expected, only *Rex* was able to continue activation. This activation spread to mailman, and the path

Fido → *(Similar Fido Rex)* → *Rex* → *(Inst Rex Doberman)*
→ *Doberman* → *(Chases Doberman Mailman)* → *Mailman*

was found. In the second case the shared microfeature is between *Fido* and *Spot*, so the path

Fido → *(Similar Fido Spot)* → *Spot* → *(Inst Spot Tabby)*
→ *Tabby* → *(Pets Mailman Tabby)* → *Mailman*

is found instead.

5. CONCLUSIONS

In this chapter we have described a simple hybrid mechanism which can be used in certain limited cases to perform similarity-based reasoning. The system contains both a semantic network and a distributed connectionist (neural) network in which the leaves of the semantic network are put in one-to-one correspondence with the output units of the distributed network. The distributed network is then trained to classify these nodes based on an input encoding. The weights learned in this training are used by a marker-passing component to recognize perceptual similarities.

It is important to realize that the microfeatures used in this model are distributed patterns. They may not correspond to single concepts, but rather as an ensemble they serve to correlate objects. It is also important to note that this similarity is, as previously stated, *similarity over the perceptual encoding*. Thus, if the encoding does not capture the appropriate similarities, inappropriate symbolic activations may result. As a rather extreme example of this, consider using "spelling" as the encoding. If the network were trained, as was NETTALK, to

[5] The actual number is an empirically determined constant having to do with the average branchout in the network and the desired path lengths. Details can be found in Hendler (1987a).

associate letter strings to the objects, then *Fido* would be found to be most closely similar to *Puff* due to the shared feature "f." While this would not be incorrect, it would clearly not provide a useful encoding. This is a general problem for neural network-based computing. The general solution is to use naturally occurring encodings, such as sonar signals, acoustic waves, pixel intensities, and so on, as input to the networks.

Finally, as should now be evident to the reader, our work is also founded on a belief that the "warring camps" philosophy currently dominating the relationship between connectionists and traditional AI and cognitive modeling researchers is a considerable hindrance to reconciling the two different types of psychological results described in the introduction. A more cooperative partnership is needed if we are to solve the basic mysteries of human cognitive processing and to gain an understanding of the overall cognitive architecture, rather than simply the underlying physical structure, of human thought.

REFERENCES

Alterman, R.A. (1985). A dictionary based on concept coherence. *Artificial Intelligence, 25*(2), 153–186.

Anderson, J.R., & Bower, G.H. (1979). *Human associative memory*. Hillsdale, NJ: Lawrence Erlbaum Associates.

Charniak, E. (1983). Passing markers: A theory of contextual influence in language comprehension. *Cognitive Science, 7*(3), 171–190.

Charniak, E.C. (1986). A neat theory of marker-passing. *Proceedings of the 5th National Conference on Artificial Intelligence,* pp. 584–588.

Collins, A.M., & Loftus, E.F. (1972). A spreading-activation theory of semantic processing *Psychological Review, 6,* 407–428.

Collins, A.M., & Quillian, M.R. (1969). Retrieval time from semantic memory. *Journal of Verbal Learning and Verbal Behavior, 8,* 240–247.

DeGroot, A.M.B. (1983). The range of automatic spreading activation in word priming. *Journal of Verbal Learning and Verbal Behavior, 22,* 417–436.

Fahlman, S.E. (1979). *NETL: A system for representing and using real world knowledge*. Cambridge, MA: MIT Press.

Feldman, J.A., & Ballard, D.H. (1982). Connectionist models and their properties. *Cognitive Science, 6,* 205–254.

Granger, R.H., Eiselt, K.P., & Holbrook, J.K. (1984, September). *Parsing with parallelism: A spreading-activation model of inference processing during text understanding* (Tech. Rep. #228). Irvine, CA: Artificial Intelligence Project, University of California, Irvine.

Granger, R.H., & Holbrook, J.K. (1983, May). *Perseverers, recencies, and deferrers: New experimental evidence for multiple inference strategies in understanding* (Tech. Rep #195). Irvine, CA: Artificial Intelligence Project, University of California, Irvine.

Hendler, J.A. (1986). Issues in the design of marker-passing systems. In R. Jernigan, B. Hamill, & D. Weintraub (Eds.), *The role of language in problem-solving—II.*

Hendler, J.A. (1987a, October). *Integrating marker-passing and problem solving: A spreading activation approach to improved choice in planning.* Hillsdale, NJ: Lawrence Erlbaum Associates.

Hendler, J.A. (1987b, August). Marker-passing and microfeatures. *Proceedings of the 10th International Joint Conference on Artificial Intelligence*, pp. 151–155. Milan, Italy.

Hendler, J.A. (1988, March). Activation spreading inconsistencies: On the need for hybrid symbolic/connectionist models. *Working Notes; AAAI Symposium on Parallel Models of Intelligence.*

Hendler, J.A. (1989). Marker-passing over microfeatures: A cautious step towards the subsymbolic *Cognitive Science, 13*(1), 39–106.

Hirst, G.J. (1986). *Semantic interpretation and the resolution of ambiguity.* Cambridge, England: Cambridge University Press. (Original work published 1983).

McClelland, J.L., & Rumelhart, D.E. (1981). An interactive activation model of the effect of context in perception: Part I. An account of basic findings. *Psychological Review, 88*(5), 375–407.

McClelland, J.L., Rumelhart, D.E., & the PDP Research Group (1981). *Parallel distributed processing* (Vol. 2). Cambridge, MA: MIT Press.

Norvig, P. (1986). *Unified theory of inference for text understanding.* Doctoral Dissertation, Computer Science Department, University of California at Berkeley. (Available as: Report No. UCB/CSD 87/339, Department of Computer Science, University of California—Berkeley, 1987)

Posner, M.I., & Snyder, C.R.R. (1975). Attention and cognitive control. In R.L. Solso (Ed.), *Information processing and cognition.* Hillsdale, NJ: Lawrence Erlbaum Associates.

Quillian, M.R. (1966). *Semantic memory.* Doctoral Dissertation, Carnegie Institute of Technology, Carnegie-Mellon University, Pittsburgh, PA. (Published as Report 2, Project 8668, Bolt, Baranek, and Newman Inc.)

Rumelhart, D.E., McClelland, J.L., & the PDP Research Group. (1986). *Parallel distributed processing* (Vol. 1). Cambridge, MA: MIT Press.

Sejnowski, T.J., & Rosenberg, C.R. (1986). *NETTALK: A parallel network that learns to read aloud* (Tech. Rep. JHU/EECS-86/0). Baltimore, MD: Johns Hopkins University, Electrical Engineering and Computer Science.

Shastri, L. (1985, September). *Evidential reasoning in semantic networks: A formal theory and its parallel implementation.* Doctoral dissertation, Computer Science Department, University of Rochester, NY.

8
Encoding Complex Symbolic Data Structures with Some Unusual Connectionist Techniques*

John Barnden

1. INTRODUCTION

The introduction to this volume mentions some computational problems that must be dealt with in applying connectionism to high-level cognitive processing. In this chapter I describe some representational techniques that go a long way towards solving many of the problems. These techniques are called "Relative-Position Encoding" and "Pattern-Similarity Association." They are realized in a particular way in a model called "Conposit," which will be described, but there are potentially many other ways of realizing them. Conposit itself will go through future developments that will significantly alter the way in which the techniques are realized.

The techniques are unusual for connectionism but can straightforwardly be viewed as extrapolations from conventional data structuring techniques in computers. Despite this strong relationship to conventional computation, Conposit is definitely in the connectionist/neural-net camp because of its use of massively parallel processing over classical connectionist/neural units. I anticipate that the ultimate form of Conposit will also include distributed representations, "reduced descriptions" (Hinton, 1988), connectionist-style, spreading-activation-based in-

* This work was supported in part by grant AFOSR-88-0215 from the Air Force Office of Scientific Research, to Barnden, and grant NAGW-1592 under the Innovative Research Program of the NASA Office of Space Science and Applications, to Barnden and C.A. Fields. I am indebted also to NASA for supercomputer support through the MPP Working Group. I am grateful to Kankanahalli Srinivas for suggestions and for assistance with simulations.

dexing of long-term memory items, and possibly some degree of slow learning by connection weight adaptation.

Conposit currently exists in several simulated versions with different capabilities, although the versions use the same techniques and could easily be amalgamated. These simulations are only of limited versions of Conposit. The extensions now being effected are summarized in the concluding section of this chapter. One Conposit version, which will be the main focus of attention in this chapter, effects simple inferences, such as those obtained by applying the rule:

if one person loves another person who in turn loves a third, then the first person is jealous of the third.

Such inferences are fairly trivial by the standards of traditional AI, but few connectionist systems have anything like an adequate ability to make them. Apart from Conposit, these few include the systems of Shastri and Ajjanagadde (1989), Touretzky (1986), and Touretzky and Hinton (1988). The central problem is that of avoiding the massive quasiduplication of circuitry to handle the many different particular situations to which a given rule applies. Conposit is general in being able to handle any such situation, and does so by using essentially the same piece of conclusion-forming circuitry for each situation to which a given rule applies. In sum, Conposit solves the variable-binding problem—and indeed the arbitrary temporary association problem in general (see volume Introduction)—in a satisfactory way.

A second version of Conposit was constructed as an exercise to demonstrate that the model is capable of processing that is at least as complex as that in Touretzky's (1986) BoltzCONS system. One of the primary exercises to which that system was applied was the conversion of a simple sort of parse tree for an active-voice sentence into the corresponding passive-voice parse tree. This mainly involves reattaching the subject noun-phrase subtree of the active-voice parse tree as the object noun-phrase in a "by" prepositional phrase in the passive-voice tree. There is no difficulty in getting Conposit to perform such manipulations.[1]

A third version of Conposit embodies many key features of Johnson-Laird's "mental model" theory of syllogistic reasoning (Johnson-Laird, 1983, 1988; Johnson-Laird & Bara, 1984). According to this theory, a human being performs (or fails to perform) a syllogism by constructing one or more "mental models," where in the present context a mental model is essentially a collection of tokens divided up into groups that correspond to the classes mentioned in the syllogism. For instance, in concluding that "some A are C" from "some A are B" and "all B are C," the person would use the premises (the latter two statements) to construct a mental model in which there are some A tokens, some B tokens, and

---

[1] Neither BoltzCONS nor the corresponding Conposit version was intended as an account of human natural language processing, but only as an exercise in complex data structure manipulation.

some C tokens, where some of the A tokens are linked to some B tokens by identity relationships, and all of the B tokens are similarly linked to some C tokens. The person can "read off" an appropriate answer about A and C from the model. In essence, the model is used as a highly abstracted example situation conforming to the premises. In general, a syllogism will require several models to be constructed, and some human errors in syllogistic reasoning can be ascribed to a failure to consider enough models. The theory involves complex information processing of the sort that presents a challenge to connectionism, because of the need to create temporary tokens, the need to create the identity links between those tokens, the need to traverse these temporary links, and the need to perform complex sequences of actions. Nevertheless, it is *straightforward* to realize the theory in Conposit. No special techniques are needed, nor do the techniques evolved for the first version mentioned above need to be applied in an unnatural or unduly complex way. An initial syllogistic version of Conposit is reported in Barnden (1989b), and a much-extended version has recently been simulated.

Both Relative-Position Encoding (RPE) and Pattern-Similarity Association (PSA) are described in Section 3, but it is useful to mention here that both have strong links to methods that have been used in other connectionist systems or hypothesized as being used in biological neural networks, and also to basic data-structuring methods used in computers. RPE is related to "topographical" encodings, in which some notion of location in a connectionist/neural network corresponds to some notion of location in a represented "space" of some sort, in such a way that "neighboring" locations in the network correspond to "neighboring" locations in the represented space. The most frequently discussed type of topographical encoding is retinotopic encoding, whereby position on the retina is mapped fairly directly onto position within a region of visual cortex. What RPE abstracts from topographical encoding is the general idea that *relative position* of locations within a connectionist/neural network can be used as a substrate for the representation of relationships—that is, structure—within a represented domain (which need not be a space in any usual sense). In Conposit, RPE is applied to the representation of *abstract* relationships, such as that between an action and the agent of the action. The quasiconnectionist parsing system of Charniak and Santos (Chapter 5, this volume) uses a closely related form of RPE, as it uses relative position in a network to support the representation of syntactic relationships. As for RPE's relationship to computer data structuring methods, the technique can be seen as a version of the notion of "sequential allocation" of data structures in computer memory.

PSA is related to a variety of previously used techniques. Essentially, PSA uses similarities of patterns of activation in different parts of a network to encode structure. PSA is most clearly related to the "reduced descriptions" technique (Hinton, 1988), but, as Section 5 shows, it can also be regarded as being a complex form of the "binder node" technique for representing temporary associations between pieces of data. PSA is very similar to content addressing (associative addressing) in computers.

Granted that RPE and PSA have such relationships to other connectionist research and to computer data structuring methods, the space of possible versions or realizations of them has not been explored. Part of the point of my research on Conposit is to show that particular, novel versions of RPE and PSA can be used to tackle the computational problems mentioned above, and to show therefore that it is worth studying the techniques in a general, systematic way and seeking further realizations of them.

Conposit's processing of symbolic data structures is largely effected by a form of marker-passing operating within the structures. This is a somewhat unusual form of marker-passing, in that these structures are highly temporary, whereas in the connectionist literature marker-passing is usually over a (relatively) static network. See Chapter 6 in this volume for another system using marker passing over dynamically constructed data structures.

The rest of the chapter is organized as follows. Section 2 explains some important aspects of research strategy that need to be appreciated during the rest of the exposition. Section 3 briefly explains the general nature of the RPE and PSA techniques. Section 4 is an overview of Conposit at an intermediate level of description just above that of detailed connectionist/neural networks; at this level, Conposit is described as a machine based on groups of registers that can hold symbols. Sections 5 and 6 discuss in detail the form that RPE and PSA take in Conposit and the way in which Conposit accomplishes variable binding. Section 7 is the conclusion, and mentions some ongoing work on extending and improving Conposit. An Appendix briefly sketches the implementation of the Conposit register machine as a connectionist network.[2]

2. RESEARCH STRATEGY

2.1. Conservative and Radical

Typically, a connectionist or neural net researcher wishing to develop an approach to high-level cognitive processing will adopt a "conservative" strategy of trying to deploy *existing* connectionist techniques for representation and process-

---

2 (a) Except in one respect, discussed in the Appendix, it is fairly trivial to map the register machine down to detailed circuitry, in a number of different ways. (b) This chapter is in part an abridgement of Barnden (1988b). Some other articles and presentations in which aspects of Conposit have been discussed are Barnden (1985, 1986, 1987, 1988a, 1988b, 1989a, 1989b) and Barnden, Srinivas, and Dharmavaratha (1990). However, the system was only named "Conposit" in early 1988.

ing, more or less as they stand. The motivation for this, apart from the mere desire to stay within his or her view of the connectionist/neural-net paradigm, is to preserve certain advantages that existing connectionist systems have and which are held to be difficult to obtain in traditional symbol-processing systems. The advantages most frequently cited are: graceful degradation of performance in the face of failure of some nodes; similarity-based generalization; and the ability to learn to perform the required tasks.

Certainly, it is worthwhile to try to retain such advantages.[3] However, there is a "radical" strategy which could also allow their retention in the long run. Conposit is being developed according to this strategy, which has two stages:

Stage 1. Develop connectionist systems for high-level cognitive processing that use representation or processing techniques that may be novel from the point of view of connectionism, and that are specifically geared towards solving the computational problems alluded to in Chapter 1 (e.g., the problem of arbitrary temporary association). In doing this, do not try very hard to retain connectionist advantages such as the ones mentioned above (but allow the desire for such advantages to influence choices that would otherwise be left open).

Stage 2. Either (a) modify the systems developed in Stage 1 so as to ensure graceful degradation, and so on, or (b) use those systems as heuristic guidance for the development, on more "conservative" lines, of other connectionist systems for high-level cognitive processing, which do exhibit graceful degradation, and so on.

The obvious question is: Why follow this radical strategy as opposed to the conservative one?[4] Isn't it dangerous to assume that step (2) of the radical strategy could be effected? The answer lies in the fact that there is a counterbalancing danger in the *conservative* strategy: the danger of assuming that the familiar connectionist techniques can indeed be deployed effectively for high-level cognitive processing, while preserving the capability for graceful degradation, etc. Those techniques were originally designed primarily with the objectives of coping with visual pattern-recognition, associative memory, and adaptive learning, and *not* with any appreciable sensitivity to the computational issues raised by high-level cognitive processing. There is therefore no a priori cause for hope that the conservative strategy will succeed.

What the issue comes down to, then, is the question of which of the two

---

[3] To the extent that existing connectionist systems actually *have* the advantages in the first place. Fodor and Pylyshyn (1988) place some doubt on them doing so. Although I am not as doubtful as they are, it is true that connectionist claims for the advantages are often sparse in argument and evidence.

[4] One might question the choice of the terms "conservative" and "radical," in that the "conservative" strategy is the one that would tend to be adopted by the more radical connectionists. But "more radical" in this sentence means more opposed to traditional symbolic processing, whereas my usage of the terms "conservative" and "radical" appeals only to what is, respectively, more and less standard *within* connectionism.

strategies faces the greater danger. It seems to me that there is not very much evidence either way. Certainly, there have been some interesting pieces of work guided by the conservative strategy. However, the authors of such systems are often the first to admit that their approaches only go a limited distance towards coping with the computational problems mentioned in Chapter 1. It is by no means self-evident that the systems will be able to cope effectively with greater task complexity and variety. On the side of the radical strategy, I claim that Conposit not only goes further towards a satisfactory solution of the computational problems but also shows much more *evident* promise of being extensible to greater task complexity and variety (though of course there are no guarantees here either). And, the work on the extensions described in the concluding section of this chapter suggests that there is good cause to hope that step (2) of the radical strategy can indeed be effected.

A danger with the conservative strategy is that it may lead one to overlook useful novel techniques that nevertheless stay within the connectionist paradigm (and have just as much biological plausibility as familiar techniques, supposing that one is interested in this issue). Indeed, the conservative strategy could even lead one to overlook techniques that are in some sense logical extensions or generalizations of the familiar techniques, if they are far enough removed from the latter. Conposit's representational techniques are a case in point.

It might be objected that the conservative strategy is a necessary concomitant of connectionism—that a system is only connectionist if it uses the familiar techniques. Such an objection betrays an artificially restricted notion of connectionism. To me, a system is connectionist if it is a network of relatively simple processing units that communicate by means of simple values, where, furthermore, major portions of the processing rely on massive parallelism over a significant subset of the units. There is a case also for requiring that the system's long-term "knowledge" reside in the network's strength-modulated connectivity, rather than in, say, informational structures within or attached to individual nodes or connections—and many people do impose this requirement. With connectionism so characterized, Conposit is perfectly connectionist, despite the fact that it has—currently—no provision for graceful degradation, similarity-based generalization, or adaptive learning.

As regards the choice of tactic in step (2) of the radical strategy, I am moving towards (a) in my own work—that is, I will be modifying Conposit as developed so far—while maintaining the hope that the system could serve as heuristic guidance to other connectionists interested in high-level cognitive processing but who wish to follow a more conservative strategy.

2.2. A Multi-Span Bridge

Conposit is aimed at bridging the gap between high-level cognitive processing and neural networks—a gap between a high level and a low level of description.

An attempt to build such a bridge could either seek to cross the gap with one span, or could seek to use a series of spans, touching down at intermediate levels of description. Now, one of the major features of modern computer science, and traditional AI in particular, is that gaps between high and low levels of description are bridged with a series of spans: passing from high-level task description down to electronic bit manipulations through a succession of levels, such as the high-level programming language level, the assembly-language level, and the machine-code level. However, connectionist systems have generally not availed themselves very much of multiple levels of (explicit and detailed) description. It is therefore worthwhile to rehearse some of the benefits of a multispan approach involving explicit, detailed system descriptions at each level.

First, the complexity and sophistication of the ultimate mapping derived from the highest to the lowest level is likely to be greater the more spans are used. If it turns out, as seems likely, that the mapping from high-level cognitive processing to neural networks needs to be complex and sophisticated, then a many-span approach may be the only practical way for us to design the mapping. To put it another way, an approach with too few spans may lead the researcher to come up with excessively direct correspondences between aspects of the top level and aspects of the bottom level. An example of this phenomenon is the strong tendency in connectionism to think of binding (of values to variables, of fillers to roles, etc.) in terms of the facilitation of connection paths, where facilitation typically involves connection-strength changes within the path or activity-level changes on intermediate nodes on the path. There may be nothing intrinsically wrong with this general idea, but the current dearth of spans in connectionism encourages excessively simple versions of it. On the other hand, in Conposit, which as we will see rests on more spans than is usual, there is indeed a sense in which binding can be seen to be realized ultimately by the facilitation of connection paths, but this realization is relatively complex when viewed as a single leap. Yet, the realization is a conceptually simple one when broken down according to the sequence of spans adopted.

A second advantage of having more spans, familiar from ordinary computer science, is that it allows a system-design effort to encompass more alternative mappings from top level to bottom. There is the potential for varying the nature of an individual span without affecting other spans very much. Ideally, if there are two spans between one level and another and one considers m different versions of the first span and n different versions of the second, then one is implicitly considering $m \times n$ different cases altogether (although, in practice, interactions between the spans may reduce this number). In a logically equivalent approach with a single span between the two levels in question, these different cases would have to be explicitly and separately considered, and the systematic relationships between them would be less perspicuous.

The use of intermediate levels should not be taken to imply that upper-levels are *insulated* from lower ones. That is, it is perfectly possible for design decisions taken at one level to influence or constrain design decisions taken at the next higher level and so on up. Thus, the advocacy of levels should not be construed as a claim that cognition can be explained at a relatively high level untainted by connectionist or neurophysiological considerations. One of Conposit's intermediate levels has been significantly affected by the neural-net level.

2.3. Implementational Connectionism

The design of Conposit has so far proceeded through two intermediate levels of description, as illustrated in Figure 8.1. From this one can see that Conposit supplies, more or less, a neural net implementation of traditional high-level symbolic processing in the form familiar from AI: for instance, propositions are typically encoded at this symbolic level as fragments of semantic network.[5] This level is viewed as an intermediate level below that of high-level cognitive processing. There is a another intermediate level interposed between the high-level symbolic processing level and the neural net (connectionist) level. At this lower intermediate level, Conposit is described as a machine that manipulates the symbolic contents of a set of "registers." These registers are somewhat akin to registers in a computer, insofar as the latter are conceived of abstractly as holders of symbols (rather than as holders of bit-strings). At the connectionist level, Conposit is a connectionist implementation of the register machine.

All in all, therefore, Conposit in its current form can be viewed as an exercise in "implementational connectionism," to use Pinker and Prince's (1988) term. This type of connectionism is one (even perhaps the only one) with which Fodor and Pylyshyn (1988) find no fault; and this is no coincidence, since many of their criticisms are related to considerations in Barnden (1983, 1984b). This is not the place for a proper discussion of the Fodor and Pylyshyn critique. I am in general agreement with many of their arguments, while parting company with them on some issues. The crucial point of agreement is on the importance of systematicity and of the sensitivity of processing mechanisms to representational structure.

The inclusion of the higher symbolic-processing level should be seen as a temporary research tactic that is open to being abandoned at a later stage. That is, it could well turn out to be advantageous ultimately to map high-level cognitive processing down through a different route to the register-machine level or the neural-net level. However, the tactic allows methods and techniques from traditional AI to be exploited. My hope is that experience gained through mapping the higher symbolic-processing level down to the register-machine level will provide

[5] It is not, actually, quite true that the higher symbol-processing level of Conposit is traditional, since it includes provision for a type of spatial imagery (Barnden, 1985, 1986, 1987). Also, the inclusion of syllogistic reasoning on the lines of Johnson-Laird (1983, 1988) makes Conposit's symbol processing untraditional from the AI point of view.

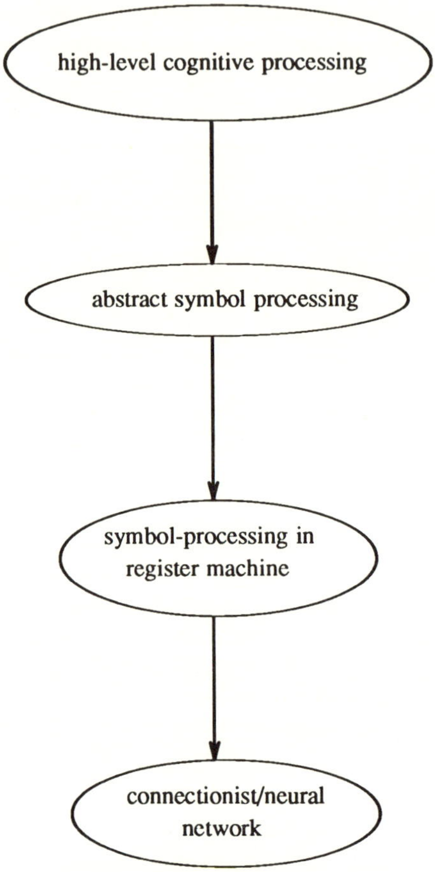

Figure 8.1.
Levels of description.

heuristic guidance for later efforts to map high-level cognitive processing in some other way down to lower levels.

An analogous comment applies to the register-machine level. Conposit as defined at this level is oversimple, and overrigid in its use of registers; and the future developments of Conposit alluded to earlier will considerably modify the nature of this level, perhaps to an extent such that it would be more appropriate to talk of the level being replaced by another one (though still at roughly the same "vertical" position on the high-low axis).

Smolensky (1988) has championed the idea of mapping high-level cognitive processing down to connectionist networks by a route that circumvents traditional symbolic processing—such processing then being viewed merely as an approximate high-level characterization of system behavior that is convenient for some purposes. Although the development of Conposit has not been informed by this view, my comments above should indicate that my long-term program is not antithetical to the view: to repeat the point, I would hope that research on Conposit would be in a good position to inform the future development of systems in accordance with Smolensky-like strategies.

One danger in making a Smolensky-like claim—such as that traditional symbolic processing is merely an approximate, humanly convenient characterization of cognition, and that therefore we should not be in the business of neurally implementing such processing—is that one may then erroneously conclude that the technical issues that would be brought up by such implementation can be avoided by not engaging in it. For instance, one might conclude that one can avoid the issue of arbitrary temporary association, or its special cases such as variable binding.[6] Certainly, one might avoid the *particular forms* of the issues that arise in neurally implementing traditional symbolic processing. However, it is important to realize that the issues are not so much an artifact of such processing, but are rather a feature of the high-level cognitive processing tasks themselves. For instance, the fact that we can reason with the information in a novel, complex sentence like "Tom is angry whenever Sally talks about going to Tibet," which may involve concepts never before brought together, shows that we must have the ability to bring the appropriate internal representations, processes or whatever together in an inference-facilitating manner, however untraditional those representations/processes/ . . . may be. Again, consider variable binding: although this term does strongly suggest the simple computer science idea of linking an atomic, discrete symbol to some neat, traditional, symbolic value, the *real* point is that the cognitive system must have some way of applying substantially the *same* inferential mechanism to many *different* appropriate situations—to avoid massive duplication of mechanism for all the different situations that are conceivable. Suppose, for example, that we generally infer that X is jealous of Z when we hear that X loves Y and Y loves Z, *whoever* X, Y and Z are (as long as X is not Z, of course). At some stage in our brains the processing of these cases must come down to using (more or less) the same piece of mechanism. *This* is really what the issue dubbed "variable binding" amounts to.

Thus, a Smolensky-like approach may be appealing, but it does not of itself absolve one from the computational problems emphasized in Chapter 1. If anything, the problems are liable to be magnified because of the relative unfamiliarity and inchoateness at the present time of cognitive accounts that do not rely on traditional symbolic processing. One tool for combating this magnification is the heuristic guidance provided by the development of systems which, like

[6] Discussions with some connectionists have left me with the impression that such conclusions have been drawn, although Smolensky himself is not at fault in this respect, as far as I know.

Conposit, involve the neural net implementation of traditional symbolic processing.

2.4. Conposit as Heuristic Guidance for Brain Theory

So far, I have cast Conposit as potentially providing heuristic guidance of two sorts: guidance to connectionist researchers who adopt the "conservative" strategy defined above; and guidance to researchers who wish to map high-level cognitive processing to neural networks while circumventing traditional symbolic processing. But there is a third form of heuristic guidance that I intend Conposit to supply: guidance to the development of theories of how *biological* neural networks in brains could perform high-level cognitive processing. That is, I propose that *something recognizably like* Conposit, or using versions of the techniques that Conposit uses, could be a viable brain theory of some aspects of cognition. I am not putting Conposit forward as it stands as a brain theory; at most, it is a tentative, approximate, simplified and highly partial version of a future brain theory. Although my claim of a link to brain theory may seem weak to the point of cowardice, it is merely an expression of the most that any biologically oriented connectionist *should* claim about his or her model, unless it has a very tight, detailed connection to neurophysiology.

I do propose two positive things. First, I hold that it is well worth looking at versions of the "Relative-Position Encoding" and "Pattern-Similarity Association" representation techniques (described later in this chapter) in devising brain theories. Second, I propose that there is still *heuristic* value in proceeding as if Conposit were a serious brain theory in its present form. The idea here is to seek implementations of the register-machine Conposit as a biologically reasonable neural net, and to measure the time that Conposit then takes to perform various tasks, assuming reasonable values for such parameters as signal-transmission speeds. If Conposit so implemented runs at acceptable speeds, then that gives us reason to hope that a serious brain theory analogous to Conposit could be viable; if it does not run at acceptable speeds, it behooves us to seek brain theories that avoid the features that make it slow.

Simulations of Conposit have in fact incorporated implementational assumptions and parameters that appear to be biologically reasonable. These assumptions are at a coarse level of description, rather than at the detailed level of biological neuron modeling, so that there is no premature commitment to detailed neural circuitry. For instance, reasonable assumptions are made about how far apart in the brain various modules of the system would be, and about how fast signals would travel between them. The results are encouraging: for instance, Conposit as reported in Barnden (1989b) can work a syllogism by means of Johnson-Laird mental models in about two and a half seconds of simulated brain time, which compares well with the performance of the faster human subjects in experiments (Bara, personal communication).[7]

2.5. Research Strategies: Summary

In developing Conposit I have adopted a "radical" strategy of trying to deal with the computational problems in the volume Introduction by means of relatively novel connectionist techniques, postponing the question of reclaiming the standard connectionist advantages of graceful degradation, similarity-based generalization, adaptive learning, and the like. This strategy was adopted to free the research from conceptual limitations encouraged by familiar connectionist techniques.

Conposit's bridging of the gap between high-level cognitive processing and neural networks is achieved in three spans, going through a high level of traditional symbolic structures (though not necessarily used for reasoning in a traditional way), then through a register-machine level, to rest finally at the neural-net level. The motivation for adopting a multispan strategy was to facilitate the development of a relatively sophisticated overall bridge, and to allow a more economical and systematic study of the space of possible systems. The motivation for using a traditional high-level symbolic structures level was to exploit past work on knowledge representation in AI and to simplify the task of dealing with the computational problems mentioned in the volume Introduction. These problems are a feature of high-level cognitive processing itself, not particularly of the traditional symbolic approach to such processing. In that Conposit provides a connectionist/neural implementation of traditional symbolic processing, it can be viewed as an effort in "implementational connectionism."

The techniques used in Conposit could serve as heuristic guidance to connectionists proceeding according to other strategies. Conposit is also intended as heuristic guidance in the development of brain theories of high-level cognitive processing. In particular, the RPE and PSA techniques are promising from the point of view of brain theory.

3. TWO ENCODING TECHNIQUES

A major thesis of the research is that a promising way to approach high-level cognitive processing in connectionist systems is to encode complex temporary

---

[7] Some types of syllogistic inference can be seen as a sort of inheritance-based inference, and then the two and a half seconds figure may seem alarmingly high, in view of the common supposition that fast human cognition is rife with inheritance-based inference. I should therefore mention that Conposit has a simple wired-in form of inheritance-based inference (see Section 4.10) that operates on a much smaller time scale—measured in a few tens of milliseconds of simulated brain time.

data structures by means of two techniques called "Relative-Position Encoding" (RPE) and "Pattern-Similarity Association" (PSA). These are answers to the following basic question, which lies at the heart of the technical difficulties summarized in Chapter 1:

3.1. The Temporary-Association Question

How are pieces of information put into temporary association with each other in a connectionist system? For instance, how are the different parts of a complex temporary proposition put together? How are variables bound to values?

In this section, I give a general description of RPE and PSA, placing each of them within a more general category that also includes techniques proposed by other researchers.

Representational techniques in a system only take on real meaning in the context of the operational features of the system that rest on those techniques. The relevant features of Conposit will be summarized in Section 5.

3.2. Pattern-Similarity Association (PSA)

An (excessively) simple example of the general PSA idea is as follows. Imagine two subnetworks *h* and *j*, each divided into two parts called the Information Part and Associator Part. See Figure 8.2. The temporary proposition that John is hungry could be encoded by letting the Information Parts of *j* and *h* contain activity patterns JOHN and HUNGRY representing John and the property of being hungry, respectively, and letting the Associator Parts of *h* and *j* contain the same activity pattern X. The subnetworks *h* and *j* are deemed to be temporarily associated by virtue of this equality of their "associator" patterns (X). In more sophisticated versions of the PSA idea, the required similarity of patterns would not have to be equality, and, in principle at least, there would not have to be separate Associator and Information subnetworks—associator patterns could be mixed in with information patterns, or similarity could be defined directly on patterns that also act as information patterns representing John, the being-hungry property, and so on.

PSA is therefore a class of techniques differing on what they take pattern similarity to be and on the degree to which there are separate Associator and Information subnetworks. Also, PSA is a subclass of a more general category of "*pattern-relationship*" techniques. In these, the temporary association consists of the exploitation of some given relation on activation patterns, where this relationship could, but need not, be usefully cast as some sort of similarity. An example is provided by the "reduced descriptions" technique (Hinton, 1988) whereby an activity pattern representing some piece of information can be "pointed to" within another information item by means of a "reduced" version of that activity pattern. Reduced descriptions are produced from full representa-

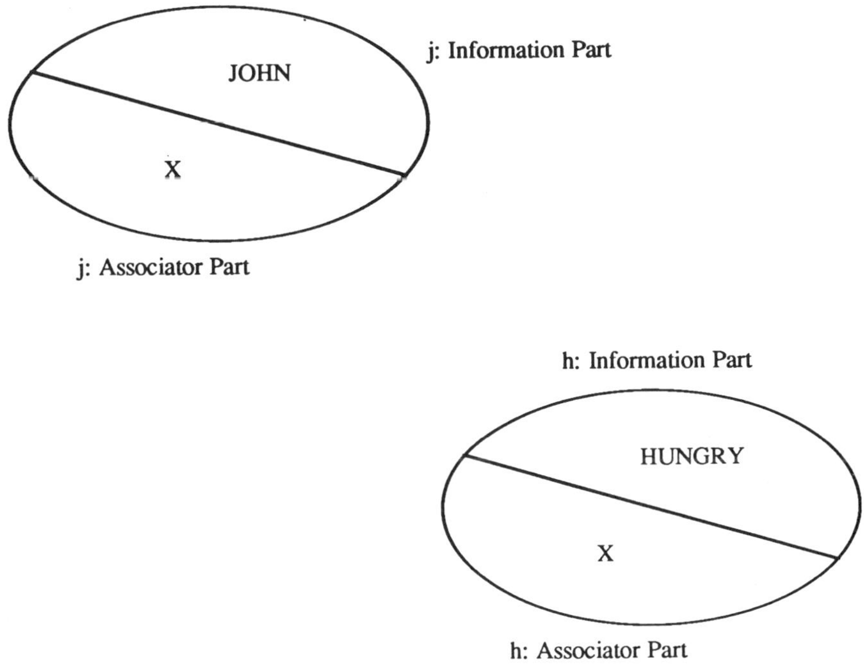

Figure 8.2.
Pattern-Similarity Association.

tions and vice versa by some encoding/decoding network. The purpose of the reduction is, essentially, to allow automatically generated "pointers" of severely limited size.

The version of PSA used in Conposit is very like the form assumed in the simple example above. However, instead of there being separate Information and Associator subnetworks, there is a set of registers any of which can be temporarily used to hold an activity pattern acting as an associator pattern and/or an information pattern. Similarity of associator patterns is just equality.

The way the registers acting temporarily as associator registers enter into useful data structures will become apparent in the next section. In fact, this entering-into is mediated by RPE, and Conposit's RPE would not be adequate without the PSA, so that the two techniques are highly intertwined in Conposit.

3.3. Relative-Position Encoding (RPE)

Again, an excessively simple example of the general idea is as follows. Imagine a network that can be viewed as a two-dimensional array of subnetworks (see Figure 8.3). Call each such subnetwork a "register" for convenience. Assume

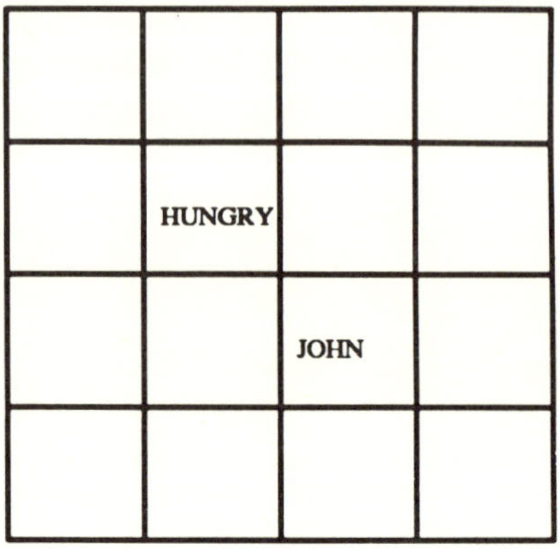

Figure 8.3.
Relative-Position Encoding. Each square stands for a register.

that there is a set of activity patterns any of which can be temporarily installed in any of the registers. Suppose then that at some moment two subnetworks *h* and *j* that are adjacent in the array hold, respectively, an activity pattern HUNGRY representing the idea of being hungry and an activity pattern JOHN representing John. Finally, take this subconfiguration of activity patterns to encode the temporary proposition that John is hungry. It could also have been encoded by using any two other adjacent registers in the array in a similar way.

The version of RPE used in Conposit is much like this, but the subconfigurations of activity patterns are a little more complex, as we will see. A two-dimensional array of registers is used, and register adjacency in the array is indeed the relative position relationship that is exploited in the encoding of symbolic data structures.

More sophisticated versions of the idea could depart from Conposit's version in a number of directions. The closest departure would be to have an array whose number of dimensions was not two. A further departure would be to have a network with a non-array structure while still providing a useful notion of relative position. On the other hand, keeping to the idea of an array, it could be more like a TV screen on which patterns can appear in any position on a quasi-continuous range, rather than being confined to discrete registers.[8] In any array-based version of RPE, one could allow relative-position relationships other than

[8] In early work leading to Conposit I adopted arrays like this (see, e.g., Barnden, 1984a). I changed to arrays of discrete registers so as to allow a system that could be more easily simulated and analyzed. However, I still think that there *may* ultimately be more future in a TV-screen version, especially from the point of view of brain theory. This shows one respect in which Conposit is to be viewed as heuristic guidance for the development of future, more sophisticated systems.

strict adjacency to have associational significance. In particular, in a TV-like array, different degrees of adjacency could conceivably be used to encode different degrees of association. In fact, versions of Conposit that have not yet been simulated do exploit non-adjacency relationships, for special types of image-like data structure (Barnden, 1985, 1986, 1987).

An array in a connectionist or neural system is a mathematical conception, and need not in principle be reflected in the geography of a physical realization of the system. Fodor and Pylyshyn (1988) make a related observation. However, there could be advantages in such a reflection. In fact, in the hypothesized biological neural net implementation of Conposit, an abstract register array *is* mapped out as a physical array. This is because the main interaction among registers is neighbor-neighbor, so that the realization of *functional* adjacency of array elements as *physical* adjacency has advantages of efficiency and of simplicity of "wiring." Actually, a Conposit array is conjectured to correspond to a cortical column, in the context of the heuristic pretence that Conposit is a partial brain theory (see Section 2 above on research strategy). The array registers form subcolumns within the overall column for the array. This idea provides one motivation for taking an array of dimension two in Conposit, and constitutes one of the ways in which implementational considerations have had an effect on the design of Conposit at the register-machine level.

Just as PSA is a subclass of the more general "pattern-relationship" category, the RPE class of techniques is a subclass of a more general category of "*positional*" techniques. Limited forms of positional technique crop up in many connectionist systems and neural networks, especially those concerned with visual perception. The general idea is best approached by means of a simple prototypical example. Consider a word-perception system that has a separate register-like subnetwork for each letter position in words. A particular pattern of activation distributed over the *ith* subnetwork represents the presence of a particular letter at position *i*. Implicitly, therefore, the patterns of activation in the subnetworks encode *temporary associations*—relative positions—of letters in a word. Thus, the technique is termed "positional" because temporary association is achieved *merely by placing suitable activation patterns, encoding the information items to be associated, in suitable "positions" in the total network.*[9] There is no weight change, activation of binder units, or use of special associator patterns. Similarly, retinotopic encodings in the brain are positional, as indeed are somatotopic and tonotopic encodings (although in the last case the position encodes sound frequency, not position in a visual field).

The quasiconnectionist sentence-parsing system of Charniak and Santos (Chapter 5, this volume) uses an interesting and advanced positional technique which can be classed as an RPE technique. The model is centered on a two-

---

[9] The name of the positional technique does *not* derive from the fact that what is encod*ed* in many applications is position in words or some other type of space.

dimensional array of registers, which could in principle be implemented as connectionist subnetworks. By putting the registers into suitable states representing syntactical categories, the array can hold parse trees. The tree structure is encoded to a large extent by the relative positioning of states in registers, although this is refined by another device that can be viewed as a very limited sort of pointer. The model's use of RPE makes it Conposit's closest neighbor in the space of existing connectionist systems.[10]

RPE differs from simpler positional techniques by not having any particular, predetermined roles assigned to particular registers, and by being insensitive to the *absolute* position occupied by activity patterns.

3.4. The Relationship to Conventional Computers

It is useful to realize that PSA and RPE, especially in the straightforward forms they take in Conposit, are strongly related to familiar, basic data structuring techniques in existing computers. PSA is similar to the idea of "associative addressing" in some existing computers, whereby two locations containing the same (sub)string of bits may be considered to be currently associated. And RPE is similar to the "sequential allocation" technique that can be found to some extent in virtually all data structures as implemented on existing computers, as any introductory text on computer data structures will reveal. For instance, a standard way to implement an abstract one-dimensional array (vector) of numbers is to place them in their natural order in some series of consecutive locations in main memory. Or, a record describing an employee might occupy a sequence of consecutive locations, different locations holding information about different features of the employee, with the position of each location relative to the start of the record conveying the significance of that location. Sequential allocation therefore relies on exploiting relative-position relationships among memory locations, with adjacency as a special case, and is therefore reminiscent of Conposit's RPE.

4. CONPOSIT AS A REGISTER MACHINE

Conposit exists in a number of simplified, simulated versions and also as a more elaborate, "full" version that is under continuous development and has not yet been simulated. This Section and the next two confine themselves to describing the nature of the simulated versions of Conposit. A general characteristic of these versions is that they are *entirely* concerned with *short-term* data structures and

[10] Conposit was developed independently of the Charniak & Santos system, and prior to it as far as I know—witness Barnden (1984b, 1985, 1986, 1987).

manipulations. There is *no* long-term memory of data (except insofar as the "hardwired rules" described below can be viewed as holding long-term information). Equally, the versions perform no learning, and involve no weight changing. The structure of the system as implemented as a connectionist network is completely and intricately hand-crafted, bearing only a vague relation to the currently popular and highly uniform multilayer neural networks.

This section describes Conposit only at the register machine level. (Recall Figure 8.1, showing the different levels in the overall approach.) The implementational level, at which the system is described as a connectionist/neural network, is sketched in the Appendix. Computer simulations have mostly been limited to simulating Conposit strictly at the register-machine level itself, not at the level of connectionist networks; the simulations can, nevertheless, be viewed as simulating the nets at a somewhat abstract level of description.

One component of Conposit has been simulated, in isolation, at the connectionist level. This component is the main "parallel distributor," which is described below. It is the only aspect of the simulated versions of Conposit that presents any significant problems in the design of a connectionist implementation. Part of the job of the parallel distributor is to arbitrate between and to serialize (i.e., to sequence) messages that are quasisimultaneously being sent through a shared channel. The parallel distributor has significance beyond Conposit, since variants of the connectionist techniques proposed for its implementation could be used in other types of connectionist system that include sequential processing.

4.1. Overall Structure of Simulated Conposits

The overall structure is shown in Figure 8.4, the main flow of information being shown by the arrows. This figure reveals that each version is, at a high level of description, a fairly conventional production system (rule-based system). The productions or rules are shown in the figure as being split into condition parts, bundled up in the Subconfiguration Detection Module, and action parts, bundled up in the Rule Action Parts Module. The rules "detect" and "manipulate" the short-term data structures held in the short-term memory (working memory), which consists of a two-dimensional register array of the sort advertised in the previous section. The register array is also called the Configuration Matrix (CM), since data structure fragments are realized in the CM as "subconfigurations" made up of the temporary contents of bunches of registers.

The rules mentioned in the figure are "hardwired" as permanent parts of the system. A version of Conposit in which data structures in a register array can act as "software rules," executed by hardwired mechanisms attached to the array, is being developed. The rest of this section, however, we will assume only the existence of fixed, hardwired rules.

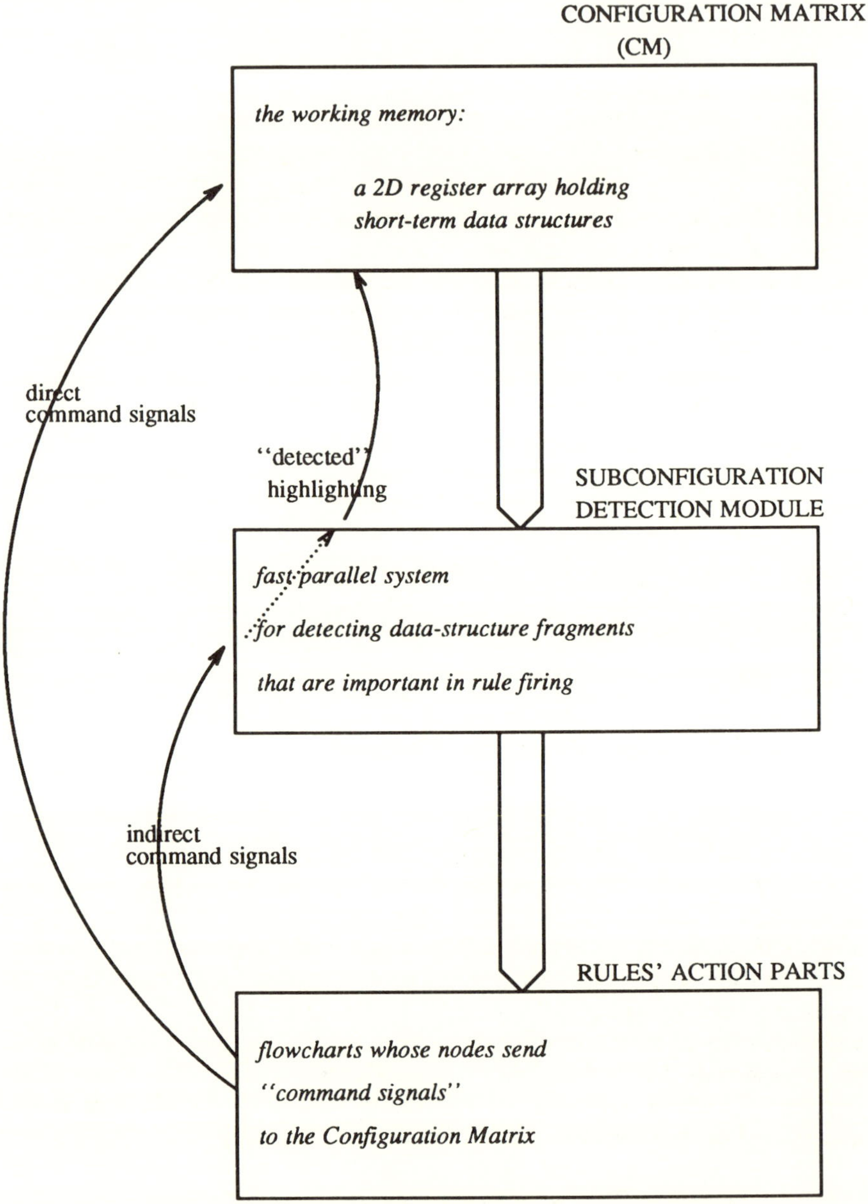

Figure 8.4.
Overall structure of each simulated Conposit version.

The system operates in a cyclic way. In each cycle, the presence of data structures in the working memory causes one rule to fire, changing the contents of working memory. Then another cycle starts.

4.2. The Configuration Matrix

The CM is a 32 × 32 array of registers. In the connectionist implementation of the register machine [see the Appendix], each register is a small connectionist subnetwork. Each register is connected to all its neighbors, and also to a module called the CM's "Parallel Distributor." One of the purposes of the parallel distributor is to allow indirect communication between any two registers. However, no register knows the identity of any other register except for its neighbors, and nonneighborly communication is based on the *broadcasting* of symbols via the parallel distributor. Other functions of the parallel distributor will become apparent below.

The state of a register at any moment has two parts, called its current "symbol" and its current "highlighting state." At the register-machine level, a symbol is a member of a large set of symbols, which are just unanalyzed, atomic objects of some sort.[11] The highlighting state, at the register-machine level, is a collection of ON or OFF values, one for each of a set of "highlighting flags." I refer to the flags by names of various sorts, which I introduce below as needed. Any combination of ON or OFF values is allowable across the highlighting flags of a register. All registers have the same, fixed set of highlighting flags, though of course they generally differ on the ON/OFF values they have for them. Ultimately we would want to settle for a particular number of highlighting flags, but so far different versions of Conposit have had different numbers of highlighting flags.

Thus, the content of the CM at any moment is given by a function σ from the CM registers to a state set β. Each member of β is an ordered pair (s, h), where s is a symbol and h is a function from the set of highlighting flags into the set {OFF, ON}.

Any symbol can be placed in any register (by a rule or as part of the initialization of a run of the system). Many symbols have a specific, *permanent* representational function, such as denoting a particular person (e.g., John), or a particular set of situations (e.g., the set of conceivable situations in which someone is hungry, or the set of conceivable situations in which one person loves another). These denotations are merely part of the view of the system that we take as observers of it—the current Conposit versions have no causal connection with a world. The symbols are very much like the individual constants in a logic-based representation scheme that has a situation-based ontology.

---

[11] They are atomic at the register-machine level of description, but are patterns of activity at the connectionist level.

Apart from the "constant symbols" just discussed there is also a "null" symbol that does not denote anything, and a set of "unassigned" symbols that are very like the variables in a logic-based representation scheme. However, they are *not* much like the variables in an ordinary imperative programming language: the main difference being that it would be misleading to think of unassigned symbols as containers of values.

If a register contains a constant symbol *s* at some moment, then the register is deemed (by us as observers) to be denoting *at that moment* whatever it is that the symbol denotes. (If *s* is the null symbol, then the register is not denoting anything.) Thus, we say that a register containing the John symbol denotes John (temporarily).[12]

A register containing an unassigned symbol can acquire a denotation by virtue of the symbols and highlighting in adjacent registers. I defer the details of this for a little while. The important thing for now is that there is a further semantic rule, specifying that any two registers containing the same (non-null) symbol denote the same thing. Therefore, if register A acquires a denotation from its neighbor context, and register B contains the same unassigned symbol as A, then B also has that same denotation. We may also view the unassigned symbol itself as temporarily picking up that denotation, if we wish.[13]

One of the uses of highlighting will become apparent in the next subsection.

4.3. Traditional Symbolic Data Structures in the CM

The way Conposit realizes complex symbolic structures is illustrated by Figure 8.5. It shows a possible state of an 8 × 8 region within the CM, containing a

---

[12] As is common practice in typical writings in artificial intelligence (and connectionism, philosophy, etc.), I refer to *unique* people by mean of names that are in reality highly ambiguous. The JOHN symbol denotes some absolutely specific person that *we* simply call John for convenience. Actually, I think it would be more likely in a version of Conposit intended as a psychological theory for people to be referred to by means of descriptions, salient among which would be proper names and definite descriptions like "the person called John (and who . . .)," and which would be implicitly assumed to have unique referents in context. If a Conposit version followed this practice it would have a symbol for the *proper name* "John," not for John himself. The symbol could be automatically derived from some large activation pattern residing in sensorimotor networks and arising from hearing and/or speaking the word "John." This derivation might happen by means of something akin to the encoding networks assumed in connectionist systems using "reduced descriptions" (Hinton, 1988).

[13] The semantic rules are given largely because of the simplicity of simulated versions of Conposit and their lack of a causal embedding in a world. What I really subscribe to is an operational view of semantics, whereby the meaning of the symbols rests entirely in the way they take part in the internal and world-interfacing actions of the whole system. The rules concerning the unassigned symbols receive operational flesh below when the influence these symbols have on rule firing and execution is described.

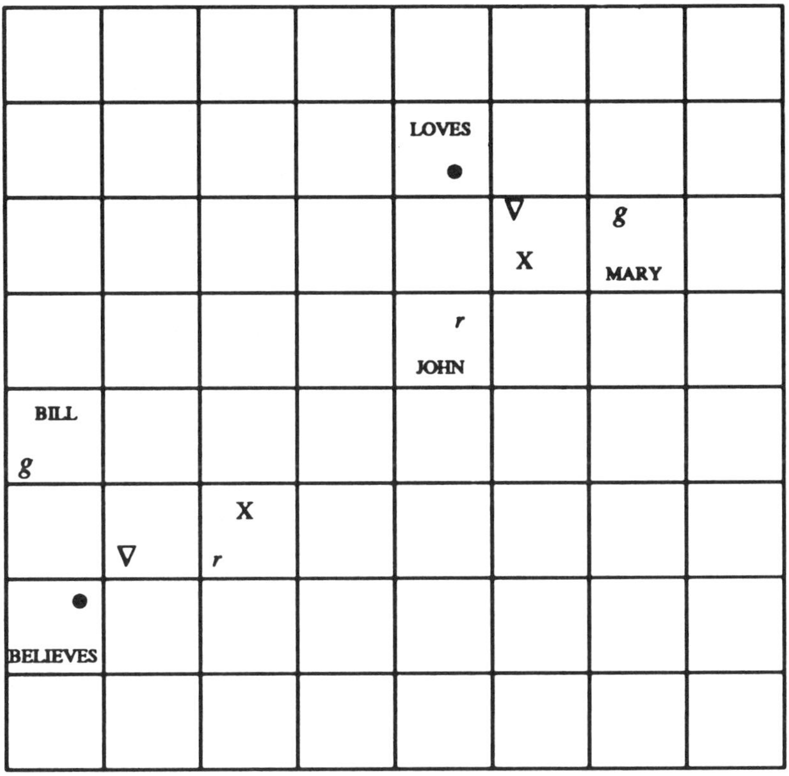

Figure 8.5.
CM subconfigurations for "Bill believes that John loves Mary."

realization of a traditional symbolic representation of the proposition that *Bill believes that John loves Mary*. Each square illustrates a register. The words and capital letter X indicate specific symbols *s*. Absence of a symbol word indicates an occurrence of the "null" symbol. The bullet (•), del (∇), "r" and "g" symbols indicate ONness of four specific highlighting flags, called black, white, red, and green respectively. The constant symbol LOVES permanently denotes the class of all possible situations in which one person loves another. Now, any white-highlighted register adjacent to a black-highlighted register containing a symbol denoting a *class* of things is deemed to denote, for the moment, a *member* of the class. Thus, in the example, the white register next to the black register containing the LOVES symbol denotes some loving situation or other, currently. Further, any red-highlighted register adjacent to a white-highlighted register denoting a loving situation is deemed to denote the agent of the loving; similarly for green highlighting and the object of the loving. Thus, the top-right "subconfiguration" of register states centered on the mentioned white register encodes the proposition that John loves Mary.[14]

So far, then, temporary association is a matter of exploiting the permanent, 2D structure of the CM, by having symbol occurrences and highlighting in suitable relative positions. In fact, the encoding of the structure of the John-loves-Mary proposition in the figure relies only on the *undirected adjacency* relationships in the CM, as refined by the use of highlighting of registers to differentiate their roles with respect to one another.

The symbol X in the figure is one of the "unassigned" symbols. This symbol appears in two places, one of them being the white register denoting the situation of John loving Mary. Therefore, by the semantic rule expressed earlier about symbol sharing, the other register containing X denotes that same loving situation. This register is within another subconfiguration which can be interpreted in a way analogous to the first one. The white register in it denotes some believing situation, with agent Bill. The object of the belief is denoted by the red register adjacent to the white register. Since this red register denotes the situation of John loving Mary, as we have just seen, we have an encoding of Bill's believing that John loves Mary.[15]

You will notice that in the believing subconfiguration green and red highlighting pick out the agent and the object of the believing respectively, whereas in the loving subconfiguration it was the other way around. This is no error; rather, I allow the meaning of highlighting (other than black and white) to be relative to the context in which it appears. Thus, red highlighting is not to be thought of as a universal AGENT label, although it does act as an AGENT label for all loving situations and an OBJECT label for all believing situations. The context relativity of the significance of highlighting is simply hardwired into the production rules that act on the CM. For instance, rules that detect or insert loving-situation representations are hardwired to respond to and manipulate red and green highlighting states in the right way. There would be no bar to designing a version of Conposit in which these highlighting flags did have universal significance, but nothing hangs on the issue in the current simulations anyway.

It is also not an error that the white-highlighted register denoting the belief situation contains the null symbol. It is unreasonable to postulate a constant symbol that permanently denotes this specific belief situation, and an unassigned symbol would only be needed for structure-linking purposes.

---

[14] It is good enough for the purposes of this article to switch freely between talking about propositions and relational situations. The subconfiguration under discussion can be said to encode either the proposition that John loves Mary or the situation of John loving Mary. In future work, however, a distinction may need to be drawn, especially in view of the philosophical tangles surrounding the representation of belief. (The present example involves Bill's belief.)

[15] This assumes an encoding of belief states as relationships between agents and situations. I am using this encoding mainly for illustration of how complex, nested structures can be set up. See Barnden (1989c) for my current views on how belief representation should be done.

In view of the possibly large number of different arguments (participants) that a situation might have, it might be preferable to use the sort of representation shown in Figure 8.6, to cut down on the number of highlighting flags and to allow more flexible representation and reasoning. Here we have subconfigurations amounting to the propositions that "loving is the type of the situation," "John is the agent of the loving situation," and "Mary is the object of the loving situation." We require, apart from black and white, only the two highlighting flags (red and green) used to differentiate the roles in TYPE, AGENT and OBJECT propositions. Of course, the representation is now much more cumbersome, and this might have an uncomfortably large effect on the speed of the system. Also, it would make the Subconfiguration Detection Module considerably more complicated.

The reader will no doubt have wondered about propositions that have more than seven participants, in view of the fact that a white register denoting a

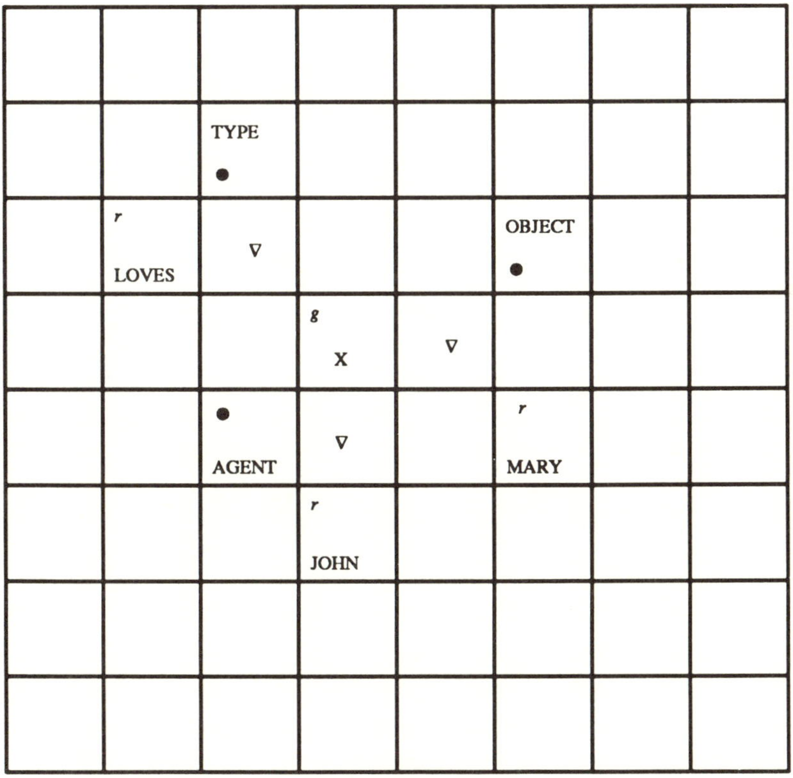

Figure 8.6.
Alternative representation (not used in simulations).

situation as in Figure 8.5 can only have seven neighbors other than the black, class-denoting one. The answer is that the technique of sharing unassigned symbols can be used to split up the representation of a single simple proposition (situation) into several pieces, as well as to associate large chunks of data structure together as was done in Figure 8.5. A split up of a loving situation is shown in Figure 8.7. Just as before, the white register containing X temporarily denotes the loving situation; and then so does every other register containing X, by the symbol-sharing semantic rule. The interpretation of the red and green registers is then *exactly* as it was in the case of the loving situation in Figure 8.5. The proposition-encoding data structures created by the current simulated versions of Conposit are sometimes split up in this way. When hardwired rules create split up propositions, the pieces are put into totally random unused areas of the CM. (This process is described below.)

It should be clear that the techniques presented enable Conposit to encode

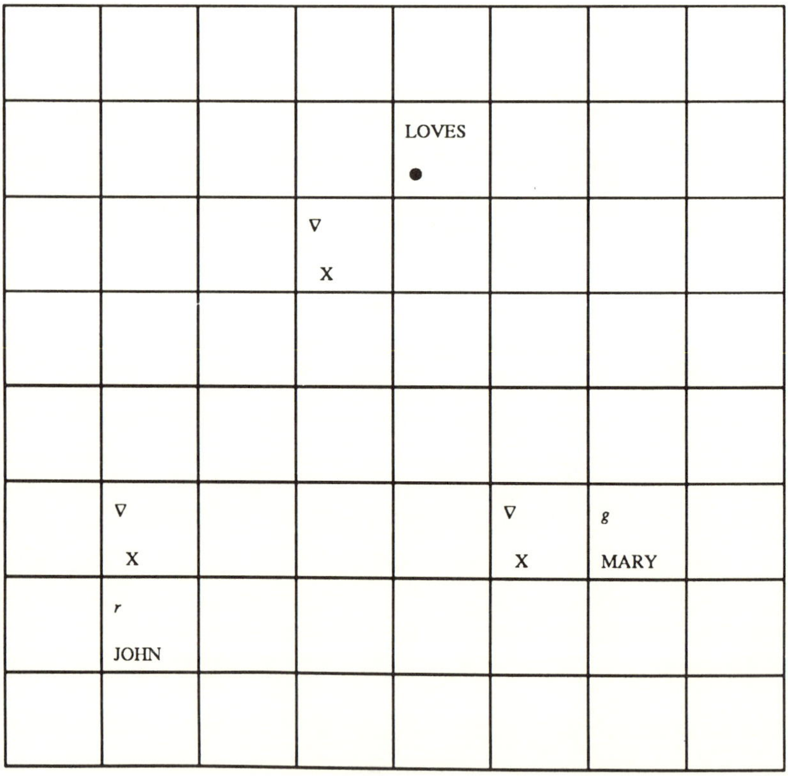

Figure 8.7.
A split-up subconfiguration for a loving situation.

more deeply nested propositions, such as that Tom hopes that Bill believes that John loves Mary. The only limitations are ones of resources: the size of the CM and the number of unassigned symbols available (current simulations provide for thirty). Also, the techniques presented can also be used to realize the equivalent of logical formulae involving connectives and quantifiers. Figure 8.8 illustrates a possible handling of connectives, relying on an OR symbol that denotes the set of all possible "disjunctive situations." This figure shows an encoding of the proposition that John loves Mary or Mary loves John. Note that there is no need to distinguish between the two roles of an OR situation, so that the same highlighting flag (red) is used for each. Figure 8.9 illustrates a possible handling of quantification, relying on a FORALL symbol that denotes the set of all possible "universal-generalization situations." The figure shows an encoding of the proposition that everyone is mortal. In this figure, P, S, X, and Y are unassigned symbols. P acts as the "bound variable" of the quantification. S comes to stand

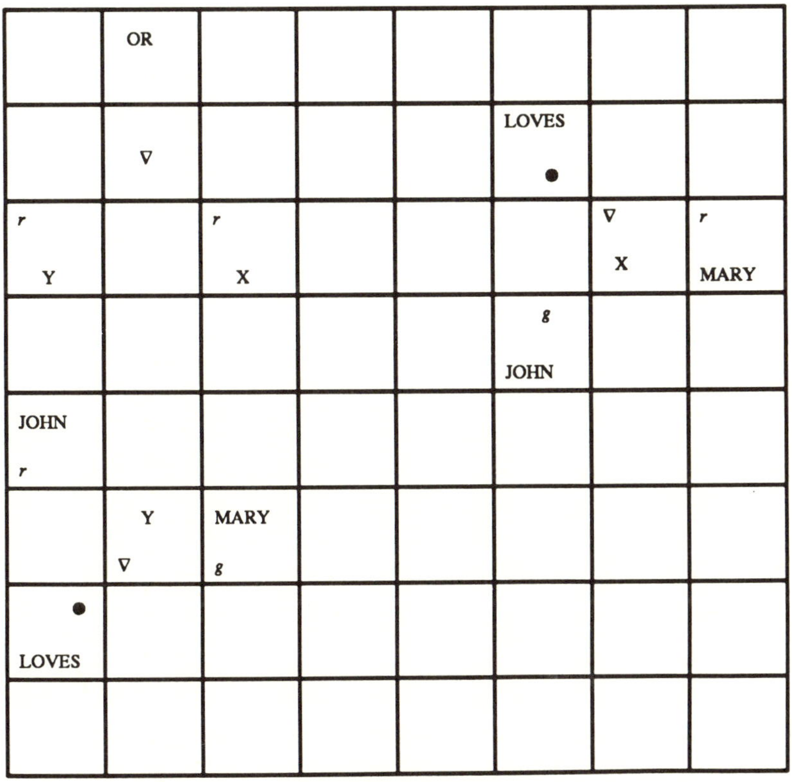

Figure 8.8.
"John loves Mary or Mary loves John".

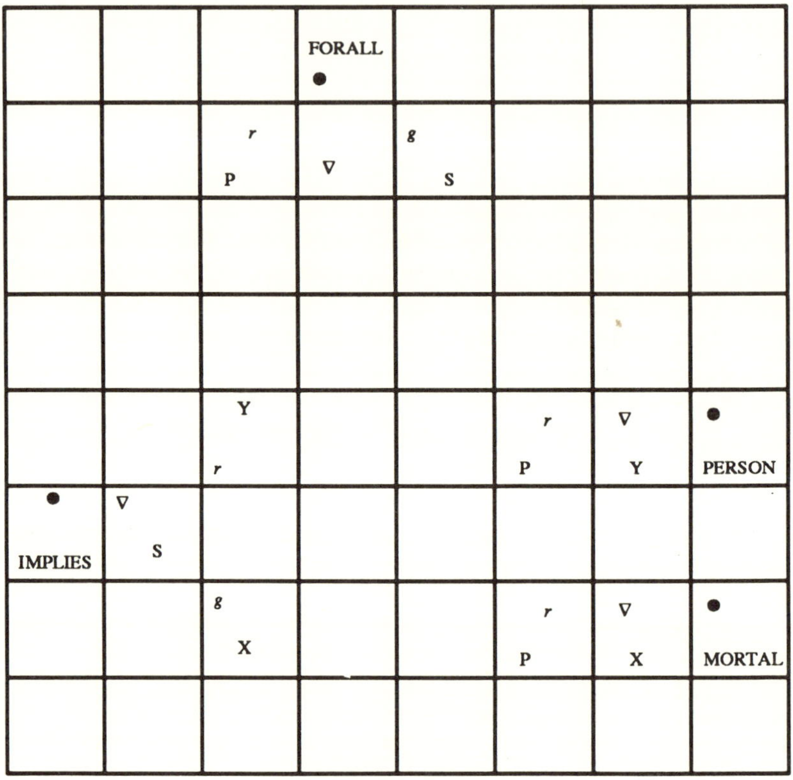

Figure 8.9.
"Everyone is mortal."

for the situation subject to quantification. The IMPLIES subconfiguration is analogous to the OR subconfiguration in the previous figure. I am not saying that connectives and quantification must be handled in the way suggested in the figures. The purpose of the presented treatment is to show that the representational tools presented can readily provide a realization of any logical expression or any semantic-network-like fragment. Of course, the tools are more general: they provide a way of setting up complex structures of very many different sorts. It is perfectly possible to design versions of Conposit that manipulate data structures that are not logic expressions or fragments of semantic network.

The reader should already have an inkling of how RPE and PSA are manifested in Conposit. I defer a full account of this manifestation until after the description of Conposit's processing, since RPE and PSA only make full sense in the light of the processing techniques which exploit them.

4.4. The Effect of Rules

In this subsection, I describe how hardwired rules can manipulate data structures of the sort exemplified above, and can thereby effect inferencing. I defer until a later subsection the question of how rules detect the presence of data structures of the right sort for them to work on. Suffice it to say for now that rules can detect particular configurations of symbols and highlighting states in the CM, by means of highly parallel detection circuitry in the Subconfiguration Detection Module (recall Figure 8.4). The effect of a detection is to start the firing of some rule (the execution of the action part of the rule). The first action of the rule is to switch on a certain special highlighting flag in a certain register of the data structure detected. The name of this flag is "detected."

In current versions of Conposit, rules fire one at a time. There is a fixed priority ordering of the rules, to take care of cases when more than one rule has its condition part satisfied. When a rule fires, it sends a sequence of complex "command signals" to the CM, each of which can cause one or more registers to change state. An individual command signal causes registers to change their highlighting states and/or their symbols. In general, only some of the registers are caused to react thus.

The next subsection describes command signals in detail, and explains how an action part can give rise to a sequence of them. In this subsection, I describe how one particular rule, in Conposit Version 1, effects data structure manipulation, in terms only of the sequences of highlighting/symbol changes they effect, rather than in terms of the detailed command signals themselves. The rule is called "Rule-H" and performs inferences describable in English as:

"If a man loves a woman then the man is hungry."

This rule is fired when the CM contains a proposition stating that a man loves a woman. Such a proposition could take the form shown in Figure 8.10. In this figure there is a white register that is deemed to denote an (indefinite) woman by virtue of being adjacent to a black register containing the WOMAN symbol (which denotes the class of all conceivable women). The unassigned symbol W temporarily denotes the woman. Note that the proposition can specify a particular man or woman by using a symbol like the JOHN symbol, or it can specify an indefinite man or woman. It could also include what is tantamount to a definite description of a man or woman, as shown in Figure 8.11. (An explicit statement that the object of the loving is a woman is still needed. It is only not needed if the object is specified by a symbol, like MARY, that permanently denotes a specific woman.) Our discussion will refer to the specific subconfiguration shown in Figure 8.10 as a source of illustration, but the same rule mechanism works for all the different types of proposition mentioned.

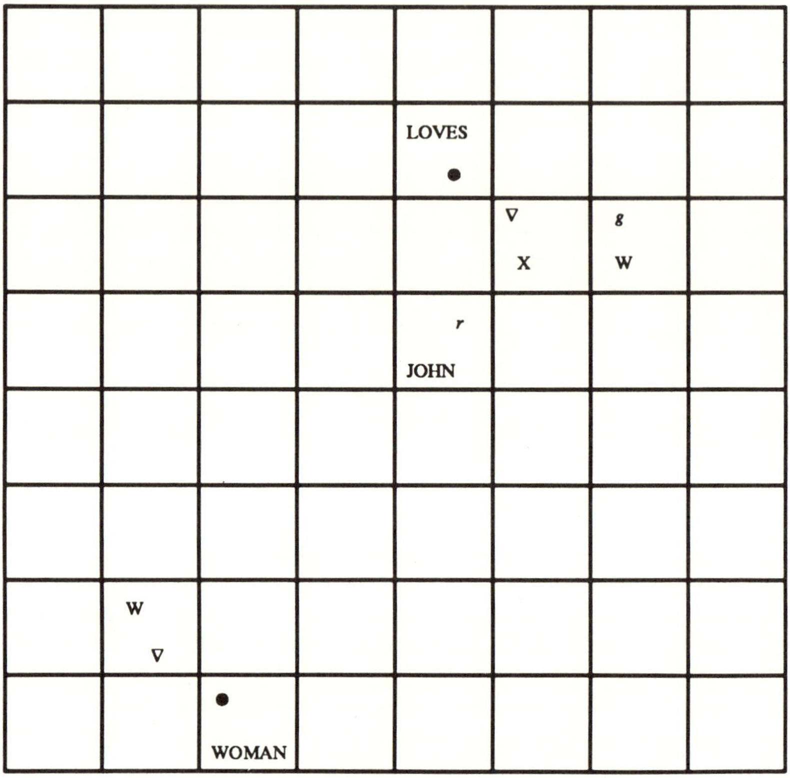

Figure 8.10.
Input "John loves some woman" for Rule-H.

In the case of the input in Figure 8.10, the effect of Rule-H will be to add a "John is hungry" proposition, possibly split up into two subconfigurations by means of an unassigned symbol Y, as shown in Figure 8.12. The rule's first action is to turn on the "detected" highlighting flag at the registers denoting the man-loves-woman situations in the CM. In Figure 8.10, there is only one such register, the white-highlighted one near the top of the figure. (If the subconfiguration had been split into pieces in the way described earlier in Figure 8.7, then there would have been several other registers also denoting the loving situation through containing the same unassigned symbol. All these registers would have had their "detected" flags turned on as well.) We call this action *Step A*. The remaining steps are as follows, in the case when the rule splits up the hungriness proposition it creates.

Step B: Mark an arbitrary one of the agents of the man-loves-woman

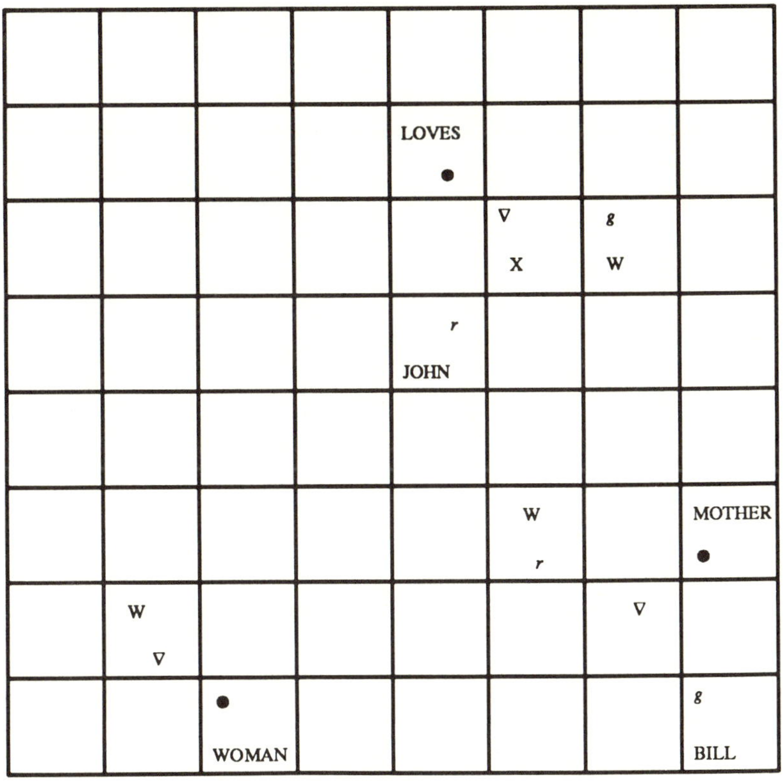

Figure 8.11.
Input "John loves Bill's mother" for Rule-H.

situations. {That is, for a certain highlighting flag *l,* turn *l* on at one arbitrary red register, R, that is adjacent to a "detected" white register.}

Step C: Make some register pair act as the black/white part of the desired hungriness proposition (cf. Figure 8.12). {That is, choose an arbitrary pair of adjacent registers that are "free" (i.e., contain the null symbol and have all their highlighting flags off) and are surrounded entirely by free registers; then make one of them contain the symbol HUNGRY and be black, and make the other one white and contain an arbitrary unassigned symbol, say Y, that is not currently in use.}

Step D: Complete the hungriness proposition by specifying the agent. {That is, choose an arbitrary pair of registers as in Step C, make one of them contain the unassigned symbol Y, and make the other be red and contain the symbol that is in the register whose *l* flag is on.}

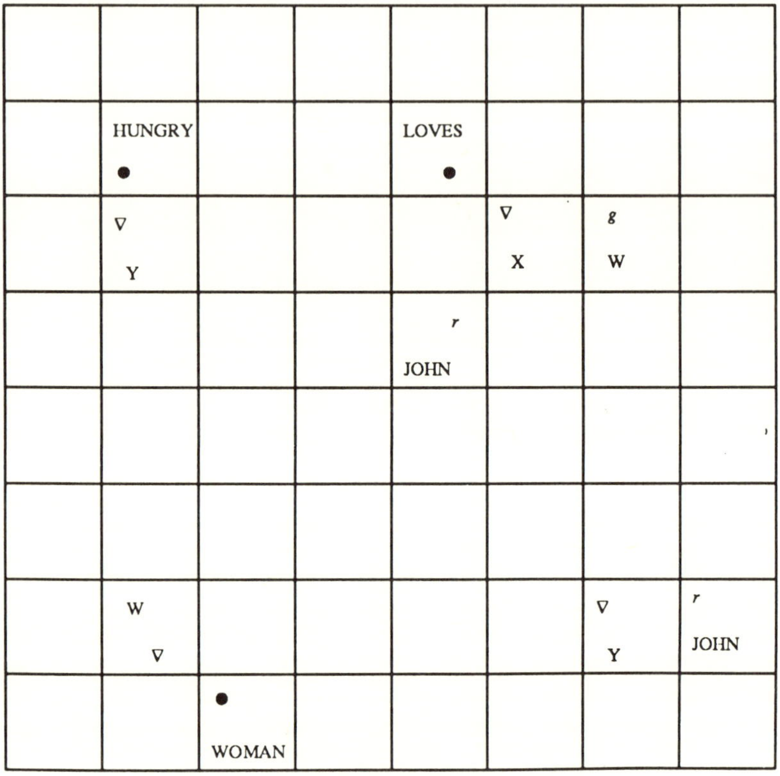

Figure 8.12.
After the firing of Rule-H on the input in Figure 8.10.

The desired effect has now been obtained. Notice that the rule just deals with one of the loving propositions detected in the CM. It would be straightforward to have the rule include a loop each iteration of which deals with an arbitrary one of the propositions.

The above account of the rule is simplified in two ways. First, we stated that the rule is fired when the Subconfiguration Detection Module detects a man-loves-woman proposition. In fact, the Module ignores propositions in which the man is already specified to be hungry by a hungriness proposition in the CM. Second, the rule as described would (erroneously) fire even if the man-loves-woman proposition were embedded within a larger proposition (saying, for instance, that Bill believes that John loves Mary). Although this possibility is not accounted for in Conposit Version 1, it would be straightforward to pay attention only to those situation-denoting registers that had a special highlighting flag called "asserted" on. Only top-level situation-denoting registers would have that flag on.

A more complex rule in Version 1 effects inferences describable in English as:

"If A loves B, and B loves C (not equal to A), then A is jealous of C."

Barnden (1988b) describes this rule in detail.

The subsection after next explains how rule steps, such as Steps A to D in Rule-H, are effected by means of sequences of command signals.

4.5. Space Allocation and Pair Installation in the CM

The creation of new pieces of data structure in the CM by rules requires the allocation of some "free" space for the purpose. Until recently, rules in Conposit only ever grabbed *pairs* of adjacent free registers. A register is "free" if it contains the null symbol and has all its highlighting flags OFF. Rule-H provides examples of pair-grabbing. The process of grabbing a pair of adjacent free registers and giving them new symbol and/or highlighting values is called "installing" a pair. Pair installation is done by means of a sequence of steps each of which is realized as one or two command signal transmissions. Barnden (1988b) gives one version of the sequence.

In order to avoid spurious and perhaps misleading associations being set up by the introduction of new data structures, Conposit's space-allocation mechanism actually grabs a pair of adjacent "superfree" registers. A superfree register is a free register all of whose neighbors are also free. Since what is wanted is an adjacent pair of superfree registers, each of these registers is "superduperfree," where a superduperfree register is a superfree register *at least one of* whose neighbors is also superfree. The command-signal sequence presented in Barnden (1988b) finds all the superduperfree registers in the CM, chooses an arbitrary one of them, R, and gives it the desired symbol and highlighting; it then chooses an arbitrary superduperfree neighbor of R and puts it into whatever state is required.

The most recent simulations of Conposit have allowed a rule to grab a 3×3 clump of registers, so that it can install a proposition without splitting it up.

4.6. Command Signals

Each of the steps outlined above for Rule-H is achieved by one or more command signals. First consider Step B of Rule-H. This is achieved by a command signal that turns on the *l* flag of an arbitrarily chosen register that has its red flag on and that has a neighbor with its "detected" flag on. Steps that create new pieces of data structure—for example, Steps C and D of Rule-H—are each performed by an execution of the installation routine described in the previous subsection. Step A of Rule-H involves the use of a special type of command signal that goes indirectly to the CM through the Subconfiguration Detection Module. Such a signal causes any CM register that is of a specified sort that that Module can detect to turn on the special "detected" flag. For Step A of Rule-H, the Subconfiguration Detection Module can detect registers denoting love situations that have, as agents, men who are not stated to be hungry; and the signal is used to put "detected" highlighting on all such registers.

All the direct command signals—the ones going directly to the CM—are instances of a single signal type. This type has a number of parameters controlling the effect of the signal on CM registers.[16] The effect of a command signal occurs in three stages. First, the signal is distributed *identically* to each CM register. Then, some registers are "selected" in accordance to information carried in the signal. Finally, each selected register reacts in the way specified by the signal. In detail:

Stage 1. the signal is distributed *identically to* each CM register.

Stage 2. ("which registers are selected?")

- Each register determines, independently from and in parallel with all others, whether it meets a "*satisfaction condition*" specified as part of the signal. This condition can require one or more of the following:
  - — that the register contain a particular symbol[17]
  - — that the register have ON values for specified highlighting flags
  - — that the register have OFF values for specified highlighting flags
  - — that *all* the register's *neighbors* have specific highlighting values
  - — that *at least one* of the register's neighbors have specific highlighting values.

  The registers satisfying the condition are called the "satisfying" registers.
- The signal may specify that (a) all the satisfying registers are selected, or (b) that only an arbitrarily chosen one of them is selected, or (c) that all of them *except* an arbitrarily chosen one is selected. In cases (b) and (c), the set of satisfying registers is accordingly reduced in order to produce the selected set.
- The signal may also specify that selection should be "spread by symbol sharing". What this means is that the selected set is now enlarged by including in it any register whose symbol is the same as one in an existing selected register.

Stage 3. ("what should the selected registers do?")

[16] On the other hand, in the system as described in Barnden (1986) there were several distinct types of command signal.

[17] This option is rarely used.

- All the selected registers independently and in parallel change state according to a "change specification" in the signal. This specification can state that some highlighting flags should be switched OFF (though they may be off already), and/or that some highlighting flags should be switched ON (though they may be on already), and/or that the symbol should be changed to one specified by the signal or to the one broadcast within the CM as the result of the previous signal (see next bullet paragraph).
- The signal may also specify that each of the selected registers broadcast its symbol to all other registers. In this case, there is an implicit assumption that all the selected registers contain the same symbol currently.

4.7. Position Independence, Locality, and Parallelism

From the previous subsection it is apparent that a command signal operates in a *position-independent* fashion, and that, were it not for the arbitrary-choice, selection-spread, and symbol-broadcasting features, it would operate over the array in a completely *register-local, register-parallel* fashion. These terms have the following meaning.

- By "position-independent" I mean that the signal in no way singles out any register for special treatment on the basis of which *position* it occupies in the array (although we have seen that it does pick out registers by virtue of their *states,* and possibly also by *arbitrary* selection).
- By "register-parallel" I mean that the processing in registers caused by the signal would proceed entirely in parallel.
- By "register-local" I mean that
  - (a) the *selection of* any register would be based entirely on the states of the register and possibly its neighbors,
  - (b) the *determination of the reaction* of a selected register would be based entirely on the state of the register (actually, selected registers all react in the same way, except in that a highlighting setting or symbol required by the signal may already exist in a register), and also
  - (c) the *effect* of a register's reaction would be confined to changing its own state.

The selection-spread feature in Stage 2 dilutes the register-parallel operation somewhat: this feature requires that each existing selected register broadcast its symbol to all the other registers, which then compare the broadcast symbol to their own symbols; since different registers may broadcast different symbols, the broadcasts are done sequentially. The arbitrary-choice and selection-spread features weaken aspect (a) of register-locality. The symbol-broadcast feature in Stage 3 weakens aspect (c).

Despite these dilutions of register-parallelism and register-locality, it is still fair to say that the processing caused by an individual command signal is fundamentally "SIMD-like." An SIMD (single-instruction multiple-data) computer operates essentially by sending instructions identically to each of a set of "processing elements", each of which then acts in a way that is defined entirely by local information and that affects only local information (except for sending back information to the special processor controlling the processing elements). The processing elements correspond to our registers, and the instructions correspond to our command signals.

4.8. Rule Action Flowcharts

A rule executes by sending a sequence of command signals to the CM. This sequence can be quite long—rules in the current Conposits can send up to a dozen or two signals. The rule's action part is much like a flowchart, as suggested in Figure 8.13. It consists of nodes that are joined to each other by directed links. There is a start node that is stimulated by the Subconfiguration Detection Module, and from there stimulation travels along directed links to other nodes. To simplify a little, each node sends a single command signal to the CM. The flowchart may include branchpoints and loops, as suggested by the figure. The decision as to which way to go at a branch point is based on further information delivered by the Subconfiguration Detection Module. This information can range from an indication of the presence of some specific highlighting state in the CM to the presence of a particular sort of subconfiguration. Actually, the node at a branch point sends stimulation to all its successors, but the successors also need the input from the Subconfiguration Detection Module in order to proceed. Currently, all the flowcharts are so organized as to ensure that no more than one successor is ever able to proceed. The decision at a branch point can also be based partially or entirely on the sampling of a random variable. The main use of this is to allow the rule to go round a loop a random number of times.

A flowchart node can send a signal not directly to the CM but rather to a "routine." A routine is a separate flowchart elsewhere that can be "called" by the action part of any rule. When the routine finishes its processing it sends a signal back to the successors of all nodes that can "call" it. Routines can call other routines, but no direct or indirect recursion is allowed. Routines provide two benefits, one obvious and the other not. The obvious benefit is that networks producing common sequences of actions do not need to be replicated. The non-obvious benefit is related to the fact that, in a biological implementation of Conposit, action parts may be physically far from the CM. However, certain fundamental routines may be much closer to the CM, allowing faster communication between the flowchart nodes and the CM. (At each signaling step a flowchart must wait for an "action-completed" signal to be received back from

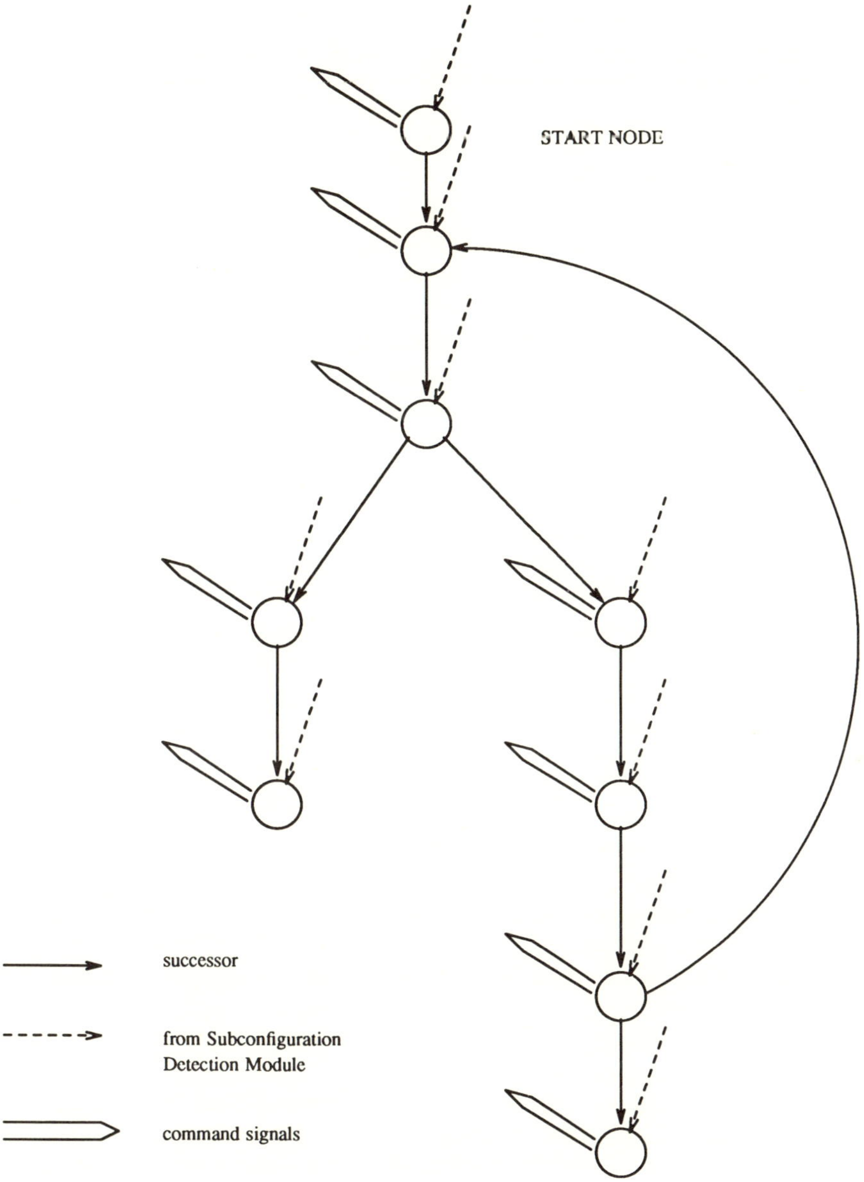

Figure 8.13.
A flowchart for a rule action part.

the CM.) In current Conposits, the main routine conceived of as being close to the CM is the one that installs a state in each of a pair of adjacent registers. This operation is fundamental to the building of data structures in the CM, and is used frequently. Having it done by a CM-local routine has a significant effect on the simulated running time of the model.

4.9. The Parallel Distributor

We have seen that command-signal processing involves the distribution of the signal to all registers (Stage 1 above), arbitrary register selection (in Stage 2), and two sorts of symbol broadcasting: one implicit in the optional "spreading" of register-selection on the basis of symbol sharing (in Stage 2), and one an option in Stage 3. All this is managed by a subsidiary module called the "parallel distributor" attached to the CM.

The parallel distributor is what directly receives a command signal. It then distributes the signal identically to the registers. In symbol broadcasting in Stage 2 or 3, each broadcasting register sends its symbol to the parallel distributor, which then distributes it identically to the registers; and, in the symbol broadcasting implicit in Stage 2, the parallel distributor also serializes the collection of symbols received from different registers to ensure that different symbols do not interfere with each other. In arbitrary selection in Stage 2, the parallel distributor receives an "I'm ready" signal from each register satisfying the command signal's satisfaction condition, and makes as its arbitrary choice the one that sent the signal that was received first. The serialization of broadcast symbols in Stage 2 is done by repeated applications of this mechanism.

4.10. Subconfiguration Detection Module

This module forms the bulkiest part of current Conposit versions. It consists of a large number of register arrays of the same size as the CM, but whose registers are somewhat simpler than those in the CM. The introduction of case-based reasoning (see concluding section of this chapter) would greatly reduce the size of the module, although its current size does not take it beyond biological plausibility (Barnden, 1986).

The register arrays in the Subconfiguration Detection Module are called "location matrices" (LMs). The purpose of any particular LM is to signal the presence of occurrences of "rule-relevant" information in the CM. By rule-relevant I mean that the information is important in the firing of one or more hardwired rules in the Action Part Module, or is needed to choose a direction at a branch-point in an action-part flowchart. For instance, because of the presence of Rule-H above, Conposit Version 1 contains an LM dedicated to signaling the presence of propositions stating that some man (who is not currently stated to be hungry) loves some woman. As another example, this LM receives part of its input indirectly from an LM dedicated to signaling the presence of loving propositions of any sort. There are also LMs signaling the presence merely of particular symbols. Ultimately, the state of any LM at any time step is defined by the state of the CM at that time step; and both the symbols and the highlighting in the CM affect the LMs.

An LM not only signals the *presence* of rule-relevant pieces of information, but also the *positions* in the CM of the pieces. For our purposes here, we can take each LM register to be binary valued, with ON and OFF as its possible values. An ON value at position (x,y) of an LM signals the presence of a piece of information (of the type to which the LM is dedicated) "at" the corresponding position (x,y) in the CM. For instance, if the LM is just signaling occurrences of some symbol s, then the ON value at (x,y) signifies that s occurs at register (x,y) in the CM. If, on the other hand, the LM signals the presence of love propositions of some sort, then the ON value at (x,y) signifies that the (x,y) CM register is acting as the "head" register of such a proposition, *or* contains the same symbol as the head register of this sort. (The head register of a love proposition is the white one adjacent to the black one containing the LOVES symbol, as in Figures 8.5, etc.)

The LM for detecting man-loves-woman propositions for the purpose of Rule-H provides direct input to the starting node of the flowchart for the rule's action part. This starting node becomes activated simply when at least one of the LM's registers is ON.

At this point I should emphasize three things:

1. An LM is only included if it detects CM state subconfigurations relevant to rule firing or action-part branching. It may well be that a rule *action part* can analyze and manipulate types of data structure that do not need to be detected for firing or branching purposes; in such a case there will be no LMs dedicated to detecting those data structures. Thus, the range of data structures that the system can *represent* and *manipulate* can be much larger than the range detectable by the Subconfiguration Detection Module. I believe this to be fundamental characteristic of the model that advantageously distinguishes it from more conventional connectionist models.
2. LMs can be shared by several rules: for instance, Rule-H shares the LM that detects love propositions of any sort with the more complex jealousy rule mentioned above. More radically, all LMs that just detect particular symbols are shared among all rules whose firing is sensitive to those symbols.
3. The symbol-sharing association technique (Conposit's realization of Pattern-Similarity Association) is given flesh partly by its embodiment in LMs: in any LM, if the register at (x,y) is ON and the corresponding register in the CM contains the same non-null symbol as does another CM register, say at position (u,v), then the (u,v) register in the LM is also ON. Some implementational consequences of this are discussed briefly in the Appendix.

LMs for Rule-H. I now detail the nature of LMs of the sort needed for rules like Rule-H. For each symbol *s* (except unassigned ones) to which some rule is firing-sensitive there is a location matrix *LM::s*. The presence of *s* in some CM register causes the corresponding register in *LM::s* to be ON. Conversely, the absence of *s* at a CM register causes the corresponding register in *LM::s* to be OFF.

If *s* is a symbol naming a *class* of entities—for example the symbols MAN and LOVES—then it is very likely that a rule that is firing-sensitive to it will actually be sensitive to the presence of registers denoting *members* of the class. In that case, there is a "member location matrix" *MLM::s* as well as the matrix *LM::s*. The task of *MLM::s* is to indicate the positions of CM registers denoting members of the class. Since the symbol LOVES names the class of conceivable loving situations, ON registers in *MLM::LOVES* identify CM registers currently representing individual loving situations (propositions). On the other hand, registers that are on in *LM::LOVES* identify registers containing the LOVES symbol itself; these registers currently denote the *class* of conceivable loving situations.

To be a little more precise, what an *MLM::s* identifies is any CM register that is white-highlighted and is adjacent to a black-highlighted register containing *s*. (And, as is standard, this LM also identifies the CM registers sharing a non-null symbol with such a register.) Recall that a white register of this sort is deemed to denote a member of the class denoted by the symbol. White highlighting at CM register (*x*,*y*) together with, for some position (*u*,*v*) adjacent to (*x*,*y*), black highlighting at the (*u*,*v*) CM register and an ON value at the (*u*,*v*) register of *LM::s* causes register (*x*,*y*) of *MLM::s* to be switched ON. (And, of course, all other registers related to that register by symbol-sharing in the CM are also switched ON.)

There is a further "taxonomic" mechanism whereby registers of *MLM::s* may be switched ON, if *s* denotes a class having a subclass that is also denoted by a symbol, *t* say. We want ON values in *MLM::t* to cause ON values at corresponding registers in *MLM::s*. Similarly, if symbol *u* denotes a particular member of the *s* class, then we want ON values in *LM::u* to cause ON values at corresponding registers in *MLM::s*. For example, an ON value at a register in *LM::JOHN* causes the corresponding register in *MLM::MAN* to turn ON, and an ON value at a register in *MLM::MAN* causes the corresponding register in *MLM::PERSON* to turn ON. Thus, there is a hardwired mechanism for effecting simple taxonomic inferences. This parallels the fact that many AI systems contain special provisions for dealing with taxonomic information in simple cases. It should be noted, however, that the technique does not deal with the embedded taxonomic information in statements like "Either Hilary is a cat or Hilary is a dog" and "Bill believes that anchovies are plants." For such cases, ordinary propositional data structures can be used in the CM for expressing the taxonomic relationships, and can appeal to MEMBER and SUBCLASS symbols deployed much as the LOVES symbol has been deployed in examples.

Since Rule-H must be sensitive to love propositions of a certain type, it requires the existence of *LM::LOVES* and *MLM::LOVES*. Further, since the love propositions may refer to people by symbols permanently denoting them, there must be an *LM::s* for all symbols *s* like JOHN and MARY. On the other hand, since the rule must respond to love propositions of the form "some man loves . . ." and ". . . loves some woman," which in the CM involve white/black pairs and the symbol MAN or WOMAN (see Figure 8.10), the system must also contain *LM::MAN* and *LM::WOMAN* and the corresponding MLMs. Further, since the rule must watch out for a proposition saying that the man is hungry, the system must contain *LM::HUNGRY* and *MLM::HUNGRY*.

I mentioned earlier that what fires Rule-H's action flowchart is an LM signifying the presence of man-love-woman propositions such that there is no proposition saying that the man is hungry. Let us call this location matrix *LM::umlw*. Here "umlw" stands for "unhungry man loves woman," although this is a little misleading, since the absence of the hungriness proposition does not actually mean that the man is taken to be nonhungry. This LM takes input from two other LMs, *LM::mlw* and *LM::ht*. The former identifies CM registers denoting man-loves propositions of any sort. The latter identifies CM registers denoting things that are stated to be hungry in the CM. (These registers are the red-highlighted, argument registers in hungriness propositions in the CM, and any registers sharing symbols with them.)

The functional relationships among the LMs needed to fire Rule-H, and between these LMs and the CM, are as follows. They are diagrammed in Figure 8.14.

- Register (*x,y*) in *LM::umlw* is switched ON if and only if the corresponding register in *LM::mlw* is ON, the corresponding CM register is white-highlighted, and there is no adjacent position at which *LM::ht* is ON and the CM has red highlighting ON.
- Register (*x,y*) of *LM::ht* is switched ON if register (*x,y*) in the CM is red and some register in *MLM::HUNGRY* that is *adjacent* to the (*x,y*) one is ON and corresponds to a white CM register.
- *LM::mlw* is fed by *LM::ml* and *LM::lw*. These identify, respectively, CM registers representing situations of some man loving some entity and situations of some entity loving some woman. Therefore, register (*x,y*) of *LM::mlw* is switched ON if the corresponding registers of *LM::ml* and *LM::lw* are both ON. Register (*x,y*) in *LM::ml* is switched ON if the (*x,y*) register in *MLM::LOVES* is ON, the (*x,y*) CM register is white, an *MLM::MAN* register in a position (*u,v*) adjacent to (*x,y*) is ON, and the (*u,v*) CM register is red-highlighted. ON values appear in *LM::lw* in a similar way, except that green takes the place of red and WOMAN takes the place of MAN.

Although a given rule requires a fair number of LMs—for example, Rule-H

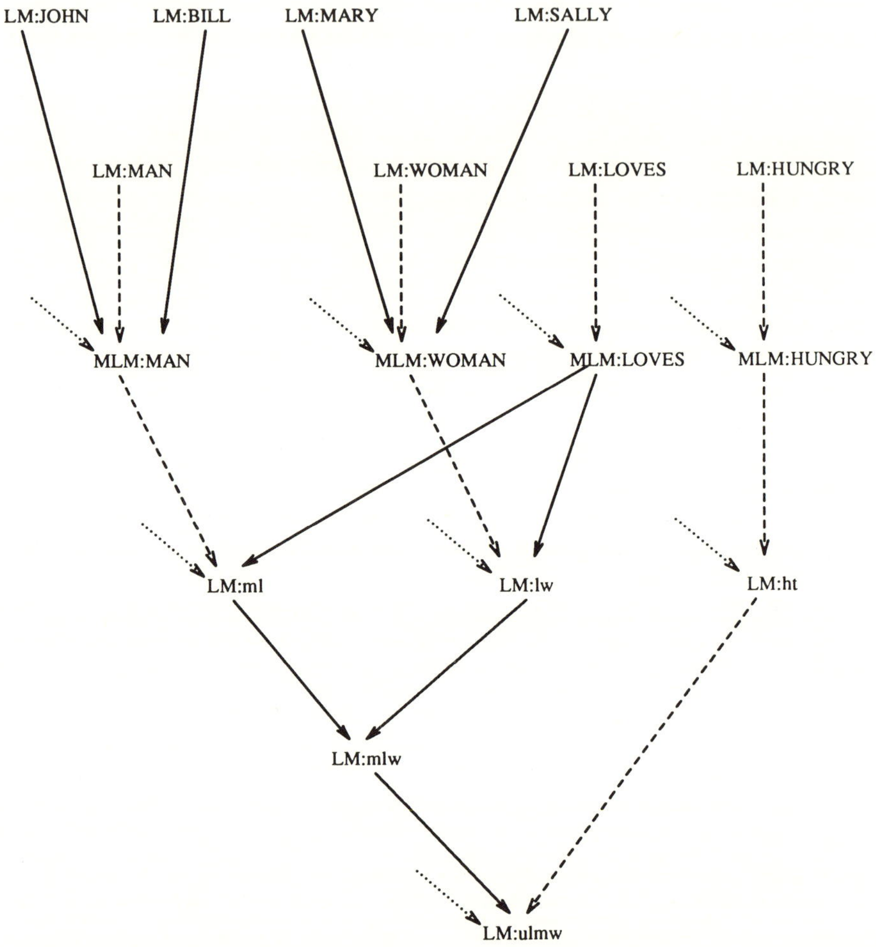

LEGEND

——→ each register gets input from register in *corresponding* position

- - - - → each register gets input from registers in *adjacent* positions

········→ each register gets highlighting input from corresponding or adjacent CM registers

(Each LM in top two rows also gets symbol input from CM)

Figure 8.14.
LMs for Rule-H.

requires nine apart from the *LM::s* for various symbols *s*—the sharing of LMs among rules, especially those that cooperate in some way on some inference task, promises to restrict the ratio of the number of LMs to the number of rules to an acceptable size in a version of Conposit that could operate in some realistically large common-sense reasoning domain. The figure of nine just given for Rule-H includes *MLM::HUNGRY, LM::ht, MLM::MAN* and *MLM::WOMAN, LM::LOVES, LM::ml, LM::lw* and *LM::mlw*. However, these LMs are likely to be needed for many other rules dealing with loving and hungriness. The *LM::s* for symbols *s* are also likely to be widely shared. That only leaves one LM, namely *LM::umlw,* that is rather specific to Rule-H. Even this one, of course, might be needed by some other rule.

In order to ensure that the states of the LMs are consistent with the state of the CM, the states of all LMs are refreshed after every change to the CM state. LMs are refreshed in parallel to the extent allowed by LM interdependencies. Thus the time taken for refreshing is proportional to the depth of the LM interdependency graph, not to the number of LMs. Also, within any given LM all registers are refreshed partially in parallel and partially in a serialized way, for reasons explained in the Appendix.

4.11. Indirect Command Signals

Recall that an indirect command signal was portrayed above as one that caused CM register (x,y) to turn its "detected" highlighting flag ON if register (x,y) of some specified LM is ON. An indirect command signal works as follows. A rule or routine flowchart node sends a simple signal to each register of the chosen LM. Any such register that is ON then sends a signal to its corresponding CM register. This signal causes that CM register to turn its "detected" highlighting flag ON.

5. RPE, PSA, AND TEMPORARY ASSOCIATIONS IN CONPOSIT

RPE is evident in the fact that two registers are deemed to be associated to each other if they are adjacent (the direction of adjacency being insignificant) and also have a suitable combination of highlighting states. Only some highlighting combinations at adjacent registers are deemed to set up associations. (For instance, a nonwhite register adjacent to a black class-denoting register is *not* taken to be associated to the latter register in any of the current Conposit versions.) Since the absolute position of subconfigurations within the CM is totally irrelevant in Conposit's realizations of traditional symbolic data structures, it is truly the *relative* positioning of symbol/highlighting states that has associational significance.

The operational significance of RPE within Conposit is that the Subconfiguration Detection Module and the command-signal processing within CM registers are sensitive to RPE-based associations. The sensitivity of the Subconfiguration Detection Module lies in the fact that a register in one LM can receive input from registers at *adjacent* positions in another LM as well as from the *corresponding* position. If it does so, it generally also receives information about highlighting from registers at adjacent positions in the CM. The sensitivity of command-signal processing to RPE-based associations lies in the fact that the effect of a command signal on a CM register can depend on the highlighting states of the register's neighbors.

Clearly, the highlighting combinations involved in RPE-based associations serve to "type" the associations. For example, a red register adjacent to a love-situation register denotes the agent of the situation, whereas a green register adjacent to the situation register denotes the object. The importance of this association-typing facility should not be underestimated: it is evidently a very important capability, but is one that is not trivial to realize in connectionist systems, especially those that seek to encode associations as facilitated connection paths (where the facilitation is by weight-enhancement or special values at intermediate units).

PSA is evident in the use of symbol-sharing to link pieces of data structure in the CM together, as in several examples above. Using the PSA terminology introduced in Section 3, the "associator patterns" are the shared unassigned symbols (implemented as neural activity patterns), and the pattern similarity is just equality of symbols.

PSA has operational significance because the Subconfiguration Detection Module and command-signal processing are sensitive to PSA-based associations. The sensitivity of the Subconfiguration Detection Module lies in spreading of ON values within individual LMs on the basis of symbol-sharing in the CM. (See point (3) near the beginning of Section 4.10.) Similarly, the sensitivity of command-signal processing lies in the (optional) spreading of register-selection on the same basis. (See Stage 2 in Section 4.6.) Both types of spreading are tantamount to the quasisimultaneous traversal of several or many PSA-based "links."

The sensitivity of the Subconfiguration Detection Module to RPE/PSA-based associations is what allows subconfigurations to be detected at all, and, moreover, to be detected *efficiently*. The sensitivity of command signal processing to the associations is what allows rule action parts to analyze and create data structures. Conposit's forms of RPE and PSA give it the same sort of data structuring power and flexibility that sequential allocation, pointers and associative addressing confer on existing computers. It is this sort of power that has been missing from other well worked out connectionist systems, one of the few exceptions being Touretzky's BoltzCONS system (1986).

An essential adjunct to PSA is the ability to insert unassigned symbols into CM registers. These allow large, complex data structures to be built up in the CM using PSA as the linking primitive. Of course, the size and complexity of data structures are bounded by the size of the CM and the number of available unassigned symbols. Simulations to date have allowed for thirty of these symbols, but there is no particular significance to that number and no reason why it could not be made much higher. Only up to about 15 unassigned symbols have actually been deployed in simulation runs (the maximum occurring in Version 3, which performs syllogistic reasoning based on Johnson-Laird mental models).

The use of shared unassigned symbols to link together different "chunks" (groups of registers) in the CM has a family resemblance to the use of "tags" in Touretzky's (1986) BoltzCONS system. There, data structures are constructed out of chunks that are symbol triples, in which the first symbol is a tag serving as a name for the triple. The tag in a triple T can also appear in non-first positions in other triples, and if it does so then those other triples are deemed to be linked to T. Conposit differs sharply from BoltzCONS, however, in the connectionist implementation of the chunks. Each triple in BoltzCONS is implemented as a pattern of activity distributed over some subset of the units in the system (where these units are generally shared with the implementations of other triples). The subset for a triple is monolithic in the sense that it is not divided into components corresponding to the three components of the triple; and there is no implementation of individual symbols. In Conposit, on the other hand, the different components of a chunk are separately represented, and individual symbols are implemented as patterns of activity; and, at any given time, neural units being used for one chunk are not shared with those used for other chunks, though a given unit can of course partake in the implementation of completely different chunks at different times.

The similarity of Conposit and BoltzCONS in respect of linking by symbol sharing is just a reflection that, at a moderately high level of description, both systems use simple extrapolations from the idea of associative addressing in computers.[18]

In discussion, a comment by Dyer led to the suggestion that one could entirely abolish Conposit's reliance on register adjacency as follows. One could replace Conposit's registers by more complex registers that contained two symbols, not just one. There would just be an unstructured set of registers, rather than an array. One of the two symbol fields in a register could be dedicated to linking by symbol sharing to other registers. (In fact, this is a direct realization of the basic PSA idea as introduced in Section 3.) What this accomplishes is to replace

[18] In discussion, Dyer was inclined to view the shared unassigned symbols as pointers. In a sense, they are pointers, albeit multidirectional ones, since they can be taken to "point" from one register to another. However, in common usage in computer science a pointer is taken to be an address of a memory cell. There are no addresses in Conposit. To say that unassigned symbols are pointers is as potentially misleading as saying that associative addressing keys in an associative computer are pointers.

adjacency of registers by the adjacency of the two symbol fields within the new type of register. I feel that this proposal is relatively undesirable, for several reasons. First, it requires the mechanisms that act upon registers to be more complex than Conposit's command signals, which only have to be concerned with a single symbol field. Secondly, from the point of view of a possible Conposit-based brain theory, if one is going to propose a system with limited, within-register adjacency of fields, one might as well go further and propose a more thorough-going use of adjacency that potentially corresponds well with the two-dimensional structure of cortex. (The assumption here is that the CM is implemented topographically in some small region of cortex, adjacent registers being implemented as adjacent subregions.) Thirdly, I have proposed that the two-dimensional structure of the CM could be exploited for the purposes of spatial imagery (Barnden, 1985, 1986, 1987), whereas the two-symbols-per-register approach does not lend itself to this.

5.1. Do Conposit's RPE and PSA Involve Binder Nodes?

"Binder nodes" are a popular way of attempting to achieve the connectionist implementation of temporary bindings (of variables, or of roles to fillers, and so forth). A binder node is an intermediate node on a path joining a node *implementing that which is bound* (a variable, role, etc.) to a node implementing the binding target (a variable value, role filler, etc.). We may ask whether Conposit's versions of the RPE and PSA temporary-association techniques bring in binder nodes in some way. The answer is that they might be seen as doing so, but only in a rather complex, forced and artificial sense.

To take RPE first, we observe that an adjacency relationship within the CM is construed as a temporary association only if the registers concerned have suitable highlighting. For example, a register A adjacent to a register S representing a love situation is only construed as representing the agent if it (A) is highlighted in red. Consider what happens if a rule wants to find the agent register A, on the assumption that S is already marked with "detected" highlighting, say. Let us say that the rule must mark A with highlighting *l*. Then what the rule does is to send a command signal to the CM, telling every red register adjacent to a detected register to turn highlighting *l* on. Some component signal in this command signal must therefore bring into play some sort of connection path P from S's "detected" highlighting flag to A's *l* highlighting flag. The details are not important: the point is that the ONness in S's "detected" flag is to cause ONness of A's *l* flag only if A's red flag is ON. Thus, ONness at A's red flag acts as temporary facilitation of some connection path that can be traced through the register-internal logic of A and S and the connections between A and S. In this sense we can say that the small subnetwork implementing A's red flag is acting (for the moment) as a binder node between A and S.

Moving now to PSA, suppose two CM registers contain the same unassigned symbol X, and recall that the way this association would actually be used within the CM is for a command signal to cause a symbol to be broadcast from one of the register, and subsequently some change to take place in the other registers, by virtue of its noticing that its own symbol is equal to the one just broadcast. The broadcast goes through the CM's parallel distributor, and involves indirect connection paths starting at each of the symbol-supporting subnetworks in a register, going through circuitry in the parallel distributor, and ending at the symbol-supporting subnetworks in every other register. Let us use the name B for the total subnetwork formed by all the symbol-supporting subnetworks and the connection paths just mentioned. A sharing of a symbol X by several registers therefore constitutes a particular activation pattern over part of B. Since any activation state of B that incorporates that pattern is deemed to define a temporary association among the X-sharing registers, we can say that B is a complex binding node which has a particular class of states that make it bind those registers. Other classes of states of B make it bind other registers together (or the same registers in a different way, because a different symbol is shared). Clearly, this view of Conposit's PSA as involving binder nodes is an extreme and highly complex one, at best.

6. VARIABLE BINDING IN CONPOSIT

RPE and PSA allow arbitrary temporary associations among information items to exist within the CM—recall that the problem of achieving such associations was identified as a major issue in the Introduction to this volume. In particular, the examples of the use of PSA and unassigned symbols in Section 4 show that PSA/RPE-based associations provide a sort of variable binding: if an unassigned symbol is regarded as a variable, then placing it, say, at the head register of a love proposition "binds" it to that proposition. Another particular effect of RPE and PSA is to allow role-filling: for example, the *agent* of a love proposition is represented by whatever red-highlighted register is adjacent to the proposition's head register or to a register linked to that head register by PSA. We could, if we wanted to, regard role-filling as a type of variable binding, because a role could be viewed as a sort of variable.

So, Conposit achieves a type of variable-binding (and role-filling) *within* the CM. But there is also the question of the variable-binding performed in the process of firing and executing hardwired rules: this is a type of binding operating between the CM and mechanisms *outside* the CM. We will look at how Conposit achieves variable-binding for rules, with specific reference to Rule-H, which was described in Section 4.

6.1. Variable Binding for Rule-H

Recall the English paraphrase of Rule-H:

"If a man loves a woman then the man is hungry."

We could express this in a form closer to the typical form of rules in a rule-based system:

"If a man M loves a woman W then M is hungry."

In the sense that the action part of Rule-H, when it acts upon a particular detected love situation, is able to access the registers representing the man and the woman, we can say that Conposit is binding the variables M and W to that man and woman. (It would be better to say that the system is binding the variables to the *registers representing* the man and woman.) However, these bindings are actually achieved in an indirect fashion, as we will see by considering the following alternative paraphrase:

"If there is a love situation S whose agent is a man and whose object is a woman, then the agent is hungry."

In this revised paraphrase there is only one variable, S, and the man and the woman are identified indirectly as filling roles in the situation bound to S. This new view is useful because it corresponds naturally to how the rule is fired by LMs. Recall that the rule's action part is only executed when there is at least one ON value within *LM::umlw*. This LM signals the presence of *all* man-loves-woman propositions in the CM such that the man is not stated to be hungry. Thus, the ON values can be viewed as *plurally* binding the variable S to all the possible alternative values it might achieve.

The first action of the rule is to send an indirect command signal via this LM, causing all the CM registers corresponding to the ON registers in the LM to acquire "detected" highlighting. The next action is, with only one command signal, to put *l* highlighting at just one, arbitrarily chosen, red register that is next to some register highlighted with white and with "detected." Such a register is therefore the agent register of an arbitrary one of the detected love propositions. Thus, the system has in effect chosen *one* of the alternative situations to which S is plurally bound *and* accessed the agent of that situation. This obtaining of access can be viewed as binding the variable M in the first rule paraphrase above. Rule-H does not access the object of the loving, but if it had done so we could view it as binding the variable W. The binding of M, and the hypothetical binding of W, are therefore only indirect: what is direct is the plural binding of S to all the detected love propositions.

The following paragraphs summarize some important features of Conposit's variable binding.

Representation, Establishment and Use of Bindings. The direct binding of S just discussed can be viewed as being realized *initially* as ON values in *LM::umlw,* and as a result being realized a moment *later* by "detected" highlighting at corresponding positions in the CM. Also, we saw that *l* highlighting is what realizes the later, indirect binding of the M variable. In sum, then, initial variable binding for a rule is effected by the Subconfiguration Detection Module and takes the form of ON values in the LM which is directly responsible for firing the rule, but the rule can then add extra flesh to that binding, and establish other bindings, by means of indirect and direct command signals that introduce certain highlighting states.

Indeed, the only way for the LM ONness to have an effect on the CM *is* for the rule to cause the introduction of some "detected" highlighting by means of an indirect command signal. Hence, the realization of bindings as highlighting is actually an essential feature. We may say that LM ON values do *represent* bindings (of a certain type), but that highlighting provides an alternative representation more directly involved in the *use* of bindings. In this regard, note that it is *l* highlighting that identifies the agent for the purposes of building the hungriness proposition: the installation of the register pair for the agent aspect of that proposition copies whatever symbol is in the *l*-highlighted register.

Since bindings are represented by highlighting, sooner or later, and since highlighting is an intrinsic part of the encoding scheme within the CM, the usage of bindings is just a special case of the way CM data structures are manipulated by command signals.

The Role of Registers. It is also important to observe that the binding represented by LM ON values and by highlighting is most simply viewed as a binding of variables to *CM registers* rather than either to the entities *denoted by* those registers or to the *symbols in* those registers. If we wish to view bindings as reaching out to the symbols (or denoted entities), as is often convenient, we must note the crucial played by the fact that a register can have different values at different times. That is, the system's capability to bind rule variables to different symbols (or denoted entities) on different occasions depends *both* upon the fact that the firing LM may have ON values in different places at different times (and thus identify different *CM registers*) *and* on the fact that a given register can have different values at different times. Hence, we may add the varying-value property of registers as being another aspect of Conposit's variable binding, suitably construed.

Processing-Locus Identification. In fact, variable-binding as construed as binding to *registers* is an example of what I have called "processing-locus identification" (Barnden, 1984b), in that highlighting and ON values in LMs are being used to identify CM registers as loci of processing. Variable-binding-to-symbols/entities can therefore be regarded as a combination of processing-locus identification and value settings of registers. The splitting of the issue into two parts is useful, because the same proposition can be realized in a large number of different ways within the CM (for instance, it can appear in different places in the CM): therefore, the *same* variable-binding (to a symbol/entity) can require *different* processing-locus identifications in different cases. The splitting of the issue would also be useful in discussing any other connectionist system in which the same piece of information can be represented in more than way. Most discussions of variable binding in connectionism fail to take proper account of this.

Plural Bindings of a Variable. The fact that ON values in an LM can represent the *plural* binding of a variable like S to several different values is not just an artificial route to a singular binding later. Rather, in some cases one can imagine a rule that *uses* those bindings simultaneously. For instance, if the job of the rule were to delete all the "detected" propositions, it could *simultaneously* delete white highlighting at all "detected" registers that are white. (This does not "release the space" used by those propositions, but in fact a more elaborate process could indeed do simultaneous freeing of all the register subconfigurations used by the propositions.) We therefore have a capability of within-rule parallelism resulting from the plural-binding capability.

LM Binding of Several Variables. Although the Subconfiguration Detection Module binds only one variable for the purposes of Rule-H, it is possible for it to bind several. Suppose for instance that there were a rule paraphrasable as

"If X is hungry and Y is tired then X is at least as unfortunate as Y".

This rule could be fired by the presence of ONness within both *MLM::hungry* and *MLM::tired.* It is clearer then to re-paraphrase the rule as

"If there is a hungriness situation H and a tiredness situation T, then the participant in H is at least as unfortunate as the participant in T.".

We then see that *MLM::hungry* and *MLM::tired* simultaneously provide (plural) bindings for variables H and T.

A Restriction on LM-Based Variable Binding. Although Rule-H's not-already-hungry constraint is obeyed by the Subconfiguration Detection Module, it is the action part of the jealousy rule mentioned in Section 4.4 ("If A loves B, and B loves C (not equal to A), then A is jealous of C") that observes the analogous not-already-jealous constraint and the A-different-from-C constraint. This arises from a general practical restriction on the complexity of variable binding that can be done *by the Subconfiguration Detection Module*. This restriction is, roughly speaking, that the constraints among the variables in the "subconfiguration-description" applied by the Subconfiguration Detection Module for the purposes of a given rule should form merely an (unoriented) "forest," rather than a more general form of graph. An unoriented forest is a collection of unoriented trees with no nodes in common, where an unoriented tree is an acyclic undirected connected graph. More perspicuously, an unoriented tree can be drawn in the usual tree-like fashion, with an arbitrary node chosen as the root and placed at the top. In our case the nodes are variables and the links are constraints.

6.2. On Circuitry Replication

A register at position (x,y) in an LM receives input only from registers at position (x,y) and neighboring positions in other LMs or the CM, and all registers in a given LM are driven by their inputs in exactly similar ways. Hence, if we view the Subconfiguration Detection Module as a binding mechanism, we see that the binding circuitry is identically replicated for all positions in the CM. Although this replication leads to a lot of circuitry, it is important to bear in mind that there is virtually *no* replication over the set of possible *symbols or data structures* to which variables can be bound. For instance, the circuitry that recognizes the proposition "John loves Mary" for the purposes of Rule-H, an establishes the bindings to the situation variable S and man variable M, is almost exactly the same as that which does the same thing in the case of the proposition "Bill loves some woman." (The circuitry I am referring to here is segments of the Rule-H action part as well as segments of the Subconfiguration Detection Module.) The only departure from exact identity here, and the reason for the "almost", is that recognition of the former proposition goes via *LM::JOHN* in order to place ON values in *MLM::MAN* and other LMs fed by this one, whereas recognition of the latter proposition goes via *LM::BILL* instead of *LM::JOHN*.

This point shows the usefulness as regarding Conposit's variable-binding-to-data as composed of a processing-locus identification leg and a register-contents leg (as explained above). Conposit's replication of binding circuitry, identically over all CM positions, is merely in the service of the processing-locus identification leg; and the replication required by this leg is tiny compared with what would result from replication over data.

6.3. Does Conposit Use Binder Nodes for Rule Variable Binding?

There is a sense in which the ON values in LMs define temporarily facilitated connection paths between components of rule action parts and CM registers, and a consequent sense in which some of Conposit's variable binding relies on temporarily facilitated connection paths. Recall that a rule's action part is stimulated into action by the presence of ON values in some LM. Typically, the first thing the action part does is to send an indirect command signal via this LM, in order to put "detected" highlighting at CM registers identified by the ON values. Thus, for each position (x,y), there is a connection path starting at the node in the rule's flowchart that sends the indirect command signal, going through register

(x,y) of the LM, and ending at register (x,y) of the CM. A message only gets through to this last register if the LM register is ON, showing that the ONness can be construed as temporary facilitation of the path (considered as a transmission path).

Although bindings created by the Subconfiguration Detection Module therefore involve connection path facilitation, the flowchart node that the path starts at is not an implementation of the variable bound. Rule variables in Conposit are best thought of as notional entities, but, if we like, we can view "detected" and other types of highlighting as variables for some of the time. The presence of highlighting at a CM register is not an example of connection path facilitation between something in the CM and something in the rule circuitry. At least, it is not so in any straightforward sense. Of course, connection circuitry is needed to implement the way in which highlighting affects a CM register's response to a command signal; and it is in fact possible to view an ON value for a highlighting flag in a register as facilitating multi-step paths from rule flowchart nodes to components within CM registers (in a way similar to but more complex than the way we viewed LM ON values as path facilitations). But again, the flowchart nodes are not implementations of variables.

The significance of these observations is that although variable-binding can be seen to involve path facilitation by means of ON values at various components of Conposit, these components are only loosely related to traditional "binder nodes". We could, however, say that LM registers that are ON can act as nodes that bind *flowchart nodes* in rules to CM registers.

7. CONCLUSION

Conposit is currently an exercise in showing how the manipulation of traditional but complex symbolic data structures can be performed in a connectionist system. Although no versions have yet been developed that retain the commonly advertised advantages of connectionism such as graceful degradation and similarity-based generalization, there is good reason to hope that these advantages can be reclaimed in a sophisticated future version of Conposit (see below).

Conposit maps symbolic processing down to the connectionist level through an intermediate register-machine level. This allows the task of crossing the symbolic/connectionist gulf to be much eased: it is not that difficult to see how to do symbolic processing in the register machine, and it is not very difficult to design a connectionist implementation of the register machine. Moreover, the multispan approach allows the details of one of the spans to be varied without affecting the other; in particular, different connectionist implementations of the register machine can be investigated without affecting the way that machine does symbol processing. Another benefit is that the mapping of high-level associations among information items down to connectionist structures can be much more sophisticated than those that tend to arise from a single-span approach. These advantages are no more than what is commonly obtained in computer science by proceeding through intermediate levels of description, but the exploitation of the idea is rare in connectionism for historical reasons.

Conposit's techniques for encoding complex data structures are novel, although they do have interesting relationships to existing techniques. The Relative-Position Encoding technique has a loose relationship to well-known retinotopic, tonotopic, etc., styles of representation. It is also closely related to a technique used by Charniak and Santos (Chapter 5), and can, with some stretching, be viewed as using a type of binder node. PSA has loose relationships to both the binder-node technique and the reduced-descriptions technique. Also, RPE and PSA are closely allied to the computer data structuring techniques of sequential allocation and associative addressing, respectively.

Conposit's techniques for processing complex data structures are based on marker-passing, the markers being highlighting states. The marker passing is somewhat unconventional in occurring within dynamically-constructed data structures rather than within permanent structures, although Lehnert (Chapter 6) also proposes marker passing and activation spread within dynamic structures. The variable-binding for hardwired rules is achieved by a combination of ON states in LMs and highlighting in the CM. The former type of binding is rapidly created by the Subconfiguration Detection Module, which uses fast parallel connectionist circuitry. There is a significant restriction on the types of multi-variable constraint that it is reasonable to ask the Subconfiguration Detection Module to respect: the graph induced by the constraints must not contain cycles. However, there is no restriction on the types of constraint that can be observed overall, because rule action parts can enforce constraints. Conposit's variable binding scheme is among the most advanced ones used in current connectionist systems. Better put: Conposit has an advanced ability to use the same piece of rule circuitry for different particular situations to which the rule should apply. Conposit's ability in this regard can be notionally cast as being a matter of variable binding, although rule variables are not a real part of the system at the register-machine level of description, in any strong sense.

Although the possible biological significance of Conposit is beyond the scope of this paper, I feel that Conposit's massively parallel nature combined with its reliance on arrays and *uniform* processing across those arrays lends it quite naturally to a biological implementation in which a CM or LM is implemented as a patch of cortical tissue. Indeed, this was one main motivation for taking CMs to be two-dimensional, since cortex is generally viewed as having two-dimensional replication of functional structure in the plane of its "horizontal" dimensions, at least within delineated regions of cortex, but no equivalent replication "vertically." (However, if an artificial physical realization of Conposit were to be devised, there might be good reason to choose another dimensionality for the CMs.) Current versions of Conposit are regarded at best as being tentative, partial, approximate and idealized hints about a possible future brain theory. However, it is still useful to hypothesize biological neural net implementations of current versions of Conposit, since if these operate fast enough and do not use too many neurons then there is more solid reason to hope that a future Conposit-based brain theory could be devised. Accordingly, current Conposit simulations have assumed various numerical timing parameters based on very crude assumptions about how Conposit could be realized as a biological neural net. The timings thereby obtained for rule applications and other tasks are quite promising (e.g., two-and-a-half seconds for a piece of mental-model-based syllogistic reasoning, and half a second for a commonsense inference rule such as the jealousy rule in Section 4.4).

Work is in progress on extending Conposit by incorporating a long-term memory for CM states and a way of using cased-based reasoning in place of rule-based reasoning.[19] I see these developments as being a way of evolving Conposit into a system that reclaims the commonly claimed advantages of connectionism such as graceful degradation and automatic generalization. (Recall the discussion of strategy early in this chapter.) The new version of Conposit would have numerous CMs, each capable of generating inferences by comparing cases (data structures describing present and past situations of interest, or generalizations of them). The system would thus be "distributed" in the sense of having a large number of CMs all performing similar jobs. Loss or malfunction of parts of the CM system would not cause dramatic changes in performance. Instead, the performance would gracefully degrade. (At a fine scale of analysis, ungraceful degradation may result from damage—for instance, localized damage to a CM's parallel distributor could cause major failure of that CM; but this would not have much effect on the total system.) Graceful degradation could also apply to the LTM system if long-term memory nodes were replicated, or were distributed networks of connectionist units. The case-based style of reasoning is inherently of a very flexible type, and automatically provides a form of generalization. This in itself may be as powerful as, or more powerful than, the types of automatic generalization currently advertised for connectionist systems. The types of similarity that could be included in case-matching could be more sophisticated and powerful than those currently achieved in connectionist systems on the simple basis of feature-sharing. In fact, feature-sharing could be introduced into the case-based system as a subsidiary method anyway: for instance, in matching two symbols in the course of matching a case against another data structure, it would not be necessary to require equality; instead, similarity could be measured indi-

---

[19] See Barnden (1986) for preliminary suggestions about the connectionist implementation of a long-term memory of CM states. For a selection of recent work on case-based reasoning see: Barletta and Mark (1988); Bradtke and Lehnert (1988); Hammond (1986); Kolodner (1987); Koton (1988); Ruby and Kibler (1988); Sycara (1988). Case-based reasoning is also strongly related to reasoning by analogy. See Kedar-Cabelli (1988) for a review of work on analogy in Artificial Intelligence.

rectly by stimulation of sets of microfeatures associated with the symbols. Memory recall would be done on an associative basis just as it is in current connectionist systems, although the style of association would be different in detail. Conposit would therefore not have lost the associative-recall advantage of conventional connectionist systems.

APPENDIX: CONNECTIONIST IMPLEMENTATION OF THE REGISTER MACHINE

Each of the three modules in Figure 8.4 is implemented as a large connectionist/neural network, by far the largest being the Subconfiguration Detection Module. These networks are of course connected together, the resulting flow of information being predominantly as shown by the arrows.

A.1. The Configuration Matrix

Each register in the CM is implemented as a small connectionist subnetwork, and each of these subnetworks is connected to each of its neighboring subnetworks (eight of them, except at the edges). As subnetworks, the registers are all isomorphic to each other, except for differences occurring at the edges. A symbol is implemented as an activation pattern that can be imposed on a subnetwork in any register. This arbitrary positioning of symbols within the CM is possible because of the network isomorphism between registers. The highlighting flags are represented in each register by means of a set of very small subnetworks, each of which can sustain either one level of activity called OFF or another level called ON.

In the current version of the connectionist implementation, the activation pattern for a symbol takes the simple form of a vector of on/off values on a set of units. The size of this vector is a parameter of the model.

A.2. Parallel Distributors

I describe only the implementation of the CM's parallel distributor, as the ones attached to LMs (see below) are very similar.

The connectionist implementation of the arbitration service provided by the parallel distributor assumes the existence of small random arrival-time differences among the messages sent from the CM registers to the parallel distributor. The parallel distributor informs the sender of the first message to arrive that it is the winner. When there is a sufficiently close tie among the arriving messages, the parallel distributor orders each of the tying registers to try again. If another quasi-tie occurs, another retry is ordered, and so on. This arbitration mechanism is very similar to mechanisms found in some current multi-processor computer systems, where several processors may need to affect a common piece of data or use a common resource, and one of the operations must be arbitrarily chosen (or they must be serialized). We call the mechanism a "temporal winner taker all" (TWTA) mechanism, and components similar to it could be of great use in other connectionist modeling efforts.

Almost always, only a small number of retries is needed, given the timing parameters currently in use. The time differences come from several sources, all appealing more to hypothetical implementation in biological neural networks than to artificially-implemented networks. First, because of small random differences in signal travel speeds along connections, the identical copies of a command signal that the parallel distributor sends to each CM register arrive at the registers at slightly different times, giving some a head start in the process of deciding whether they should react to the signal. Second, there are small random differences in the time taken by the network logic in different registers. Third, the travel speed differences also affect the travel times of messages from registers to parallel distributor, and the travel times of "retry" commands from parallel distributor to registers. Fourth, the registers are not all at the same distance from the parallel distributor, so that there is already a systematic relative bias among registers.

The TWTA mechanism is described in detail in Barnden, Srinivas, and Dharmavaratha (1990).

A.3. Direct Command Signals

Here we look only at the "direct" command signals, going direct to the CM from a flowchart node in a rule action part or in a routine. "Indirect" command signals, which go through the Subconfiguration Detection Module, are discussed below.

As we saw, a command signal conveys quite a lot of information to the CM. For the selection stage (Stage 2 in the account given in Section 4), the information consists of:

- a binary value saying whether or not a register has to contain a particular symbol in order to be selected
- that symbol (if required)
- the highlighting condition a register must satisfy in order to be selected
- a ternary value saying whether selection of a register requires a particular highlighting condition to hold at all its neighbors or at least at one of its neighbors, or does not require any neighboring register to satisfy a highlighting condition
- the highlighting condition, if any, for neighbors
- a ternary value saying whether no arbitrary selection is to be done, or one

arbitrary register is to be selected, or all except one are to be arbitrarily selected
- a binary value saying whether "spreading by symbol sharing" should occur.

For specifying what it is that selected registers should do, the information consists of:

- a specification of which highlighting flags should be turned OFF and which ON
- a ternary value saying whether the register should accept the symbol that was broadcast in the previous step, should accept the symbol transferred in the signal, or should not change its symbol
- the symbol to change to (in second case of previous clause)
- a binary value saying whether the register should broadcast its symbol.

All this information is conveyed to the CM's parallel distributor on a "cable" of connections, and thence to the CM registers by further cables. A cable contains of a connection pathway for each of the binary and ternary value mentioned above. For each of the two highlighting conditions listed (one to be satisfied by a selected register, another by one or more neighbors), the cable also contains a connection pathway for each highlighting flag. Each of these pathways is three-valued, one value requiring the corresponding flag to be ON, another requiring the flag to be OFF, and the remaining one saying that the setting of the flag does not matter. Similarly, the cable contains a connection pathway saying, for each highlighting flag, whether a selected register should turn that flag ON, turn it OFF, or leave it as it is. Finally, for each of the two symbols conveyed by the signal (one for selection, the other for action), the cable contains a connection pathway for each of the "bits" used in the activity pattern implementing the symbol.

The highlighting condition values, highlighting change values, and symbol bits coming in to a register on the cable from the parallel distributor are used in a straightforward way in "logic circuits" within the register. If the signal requires arbitrary selection, spread by symbol sharing, or symbol broadcast, the so-far selected registers send announcements to the parallel distributor. (In the spread and broadcast cases, such as announcement includes the symbol in the announcing register.) In the case of arbitrary selection, the parallel distributor chooses an arbitrary register out of the ones sending announcements, and either tells this register that it is the only chosen one, or tells all the other registers that they are chosen. In the case of spread by symbol sharing, the parallel distributor again chooses an arbitrary register out of the ones sending announcements, broadcasts its symbol to all registers (which then deem themselves selected if they contain that symbol), and then chooses another arbitrary register different from the one previously selected. Hence, the mechanisms in the parallel distributor subserving arbitrary selection and spread by symbol sharing have much in common, the mechanism for choosing one out of the announcing registers being the most significant from the point of view of connectionist implementation. In the case of symbol-broadcast in Stage 3 in Section 4.6, the parallel distributor simply ORs together the corresponding bits of the symbols in the announcements, and stores the result, which in fact should be the bit-pattern for each of those symbols since they are assumed to be identical.

A.4. Flowcharts in Rule Action Parts and Routines

The connectionist implementation of a Conposit flowchart is quite straightforward—each node being implemented as a small subnetwork—and is not unlike similar sorts of structure appearing in other connectionist systems concerned with the sequencing of actions. The random sampling mentioned in Section 4.8 is implemented by means of a unit that has some probability between zero and one of firing at any given time step.

A.5. Location Matrices

The way in which the presence of symbols and highlighting in the CM can contribute to ON values in LMs, and how ON values in LMs can contribute to ON values in other LMs, is straightforwardly implemented at the connectionist level. Each LM register is implemented as a small subnetwork part of which can either be in a high (ON) or low (OFF) state of activity. These values arise in the following way.

- For a symbol *s*, each register of *LM::s* receives a cable of connections from the corresponding CM register: one connection for the unit implementing each bit of the *s* activity pattern. The LM register contains a simple network of connectionist units acting as logic gates that checks whether the incoming symbol pattern is in fact *s*.
- If an LM register is simply turned ON by ON states in corresponding registers in other LMs, then a simple connection from those registers, and some simple AND/OR combinational logic, is adequate.
- If ONness at a register R in one LM is caused partly by ONness at any *adjacent* position in another LM, then R must contain circuitry to perform an OR operation on signals coming from connections from each position in the latter LM that is adjacent to R. Those signals might first have to be ANDed with signals on connections from highlighting flags at the corresponding CM positions. For instance, if R is register (x,y) in *MLM::MAN*, then it must AND the signal on a connection from the white highlighting flag unit in the (x,y) CM register network with the result of the OR operation on some other

signals. For each position (u,v) adjacent to (x,y), this OR'd set of signals includes one which is the AND of a signal on a connection from the black highlighting flag unit in the (u,v) CM-register network and a signal from the (u,v) register in *LM::MAN*.

- It remains to account for the required effect of symbol sharing in the CM. Recall that if register (x,y) of an LM is switched ON, and registers (x,y) and (u,v) of the CM contain the same non-null symbol, then register (u,v) of the LM must be switched on too. Obviously, no extra mechanism is needed to ensure this in the case of an *LM::s* for a symbol *s*. For other LMs, the effect is achieved by having each register receive a copy of the symbol in the corresponding CM register, and by attaching to the LM a Parallel Distributor similar to the one attached to the CM. When register (x,y) of the LM is turned ON, it broadcasts its symbol (if it is non-null) to all other registers in that LM. The broadcasts are serialized by the LM's parallel distributor to prevent confusion of symbols. Any LM register receiving in this manner a symbol equal to its own turns itself ON (but does not then broadcast its symbol). The spread of ON values in the LM on the basis of symbol-sharing is almost identical to the spread of register-selection in the CM on the basis of symbol-sharing.

As with the CM's parallel distributor, an LM's parallel distributor operates on the basis of time differences among the messages it receives from the registers. The time differences are likely to be larger in the LM case, however, because on top of the differences generated within the LM itself there are also differences generated by the connections from other LMs and the CM. Therefore, the probability that a broadcast retry will be needed in an LM is lower than it is in the CM.

In all the types of processing so far envisaged for Conposit, the number of registers that are ever ON at once in any one LM is quite small (two or three dozen at most, and typically far fewer than that). Therefore, the small time overheads caused by the serialization of symbol broadcasts do not add up to much. Hence, it is still true to say that the Subconfiguration Detection Module is an essentially parallel detection mechanism.

When a rule or routine flowchart node sends an indirect command signal through an LM, what happens is that a simple signal is sent on a connection to the LM's parallel distributor. This signal is identically distributed to all the registers in the LM, each of which then sends a binary value to its corresponding CM register along a special connection for that purpose. This value is just the ON/OFF value of the LM register itself. Any CM register receiving an ON value in this way turns its "detected" highlighting flag ON.

Clearly, at the connectionist implementational level, LMs and the CM are much more similar than they appear to be at the register-array level of description. Registers in both LMs and the CM contain symbols, and LMs and the CM both have parallel distributors, performing similar tasks of broadcast-serialization and command signal distribution. In effect, the components of the LM registers that hold ON/OFF values are like extra CM highlighting flags.

In current Conposit versions, the set of LMs and the way they are connected up is entirely fixed, just as all the rest of the system is fixed. It would be interesting to investigate ways of having the system develop and connect up its own new LMs by adaptive weight modification.[20] The way LMs are connected up is in essence very simple. The main problem here is the "translation invariance" across the CM (i.e., the fact that a given subconfiguration of the sort that the LM is meant to detect can appear anywhere in the CM). It would be undesirable to use a training procedure that required separate training to occur at all the different positions.

A.6. Unassigned Symbols

A rule must often cause a currently unused, but otherwise arbitrarily chosen, unassigned symbol to be inserted into a CM register. Since this action is done by means of a command signal, the selection of the destination register is performed by the normal register-selection capabilities of command signals. Hence, all that remains to be accounted for is the capability for selecting an unused unassigned symbol and transmitting it to the CM's parallel distributor. One crude connectionist implementation of this capability is as follows.

For each unassigned symbol there is a "Symbol Generator" unit and a "Symbol Inhibitor" unit. When activated, the Symbol Generator unit communicates its symbol to the CM's parallel distributor by means of suitable signals on a cable of connections. The unit also activates the corresponding Symbol Inhibitor unit, which in turn inhibits the Symbol Generator unit. The Symbol Inhibitor unit is capable of remaining active indefinitely, and vetoes any attempt to re-activate the Symbol Generator unit. The unassigned symbols are conceived as forming a linear sequence, and the Symbol Inhibitor unit for symbol i has an excitatory influence on the Symbol Generator unit for symbol $i + 1$. To select a unique unused unassigned symbol, a rule-flowchart node sends an identical excitatory signal to all the Symbol Generator units. Such a unit only becomes active if (a) it is not inhibited by its companion Inhibitor unit, and (b) either it is the first symbol in the sequence or it is excited by the Inhibitor unit for the preceding symbol.

Because of the limited nature of the tasks performed in current Conposit simulations, there is as yet no provision for freeing an unassigned symbol that ceases to be in use, but such a provision will ultimately be needed.

---

[20] As suggested by Cottrell in discussion.

REFERENCES

Barletta, R., & Mark, W. (1988). Explanation-based indexing of cases. *Proceedings of the 7th National Conference on Artificial Intelligence.* San Mateo, CA.: Morgan Kaufmann.

Barnden, J.A. (1983). On association techniques in neural representation schemes. *Proceedings of the 5th Conference of the Cognitive Science Society.* Rochester, NY.

Barnden, J.A. (1984a). Pattern-recognition in a pattern-based neurophysiological model of short-term information-processing. *Proceedings of the 6th European Conference on Artificial Intelligence.* Pisa, Italy.

Barnden, J.A. (1984b). On short-term information processing in connectionist theories. *Cognition and Brain Theory, 7*(1), 25–59.

Barnden, J.A. (1985). Diagrammatic short-term information processing by neural mechanisms. *Cognition and Brain Theory, 7* (3&4), 285–328.

Barnden, J.A. (1986). *Complex cognitive information-processing: A computational architecture with a connectionist implementation* (Tech. Rep. 211). Bloomington, IN: Computer Science Department, Indiana University.

Barnden, J.A. (1987). Simulation of an array-based neural net model. *Proceedings of the First Symposium on the Frontiers of Massively Parallel Scientific Computation* (NASA Conference Publication 2478). Washington, DC: NASA Scientific and Technical Information Office.

Barnden, J.A. (1988a). The right of free association: Relative-position encoding for connectionist data structures. *Proceedings of the 10th Annual Conference of the Cognitive Science Society.* Hillsdale, NJ: Lawrence Erlbaum.

Barnden, J.A. (1988b). Conposit, a neural net system for high-level symbolic processing: overview of research and description of register-machine level. *Memoranda in Computer and Cognitive Science* (No. MCCS-88-145). Las Cruces, NM: Computing Research Laboratory, New Mexico State University.

Barnden, J.A. (1989a). Simulations of Conposit, a supra-connectionist architecture for commonsense reasoning. *Proceedings of the 2nd Symposium on the Frontiers of Massively Parallel Scientific Computation.* Washington, DC: IEEE Computer Society Press.

Barnden, J.A. (1989b). Neural-net implementation of complex symbol-processing in a mental model approach to syllogistic reasoning. *Proceedings of the 11th International Joint Conference on Artificial Intelligence.* San Mateo, CA: Morgan Kaufmann.

Barnden, J.A. (1989c). Belief, metaphorically speaking. *Proceedings of the 1st International Conference on Principles of Knowledge Representation and Reasoning.* San Mateo, CA: Morgan Kaufmann.

Barnden, J.A., Srinivas, K., & Dharmavaratha, D. (1990). Winner-take-all networks: Time-based versus activation-based mechanisms for various selection goals. *Proceedings of the IEEE International Symposium on Circuits and Systems.* New Orleans, LA.

Bradtke, S., & Lehnert, W.G. (1988). Some experiments with case-based search. *Proceedings of the 7th National Conference on Artificial Intelligence.* San Mateo, CA.: Morgan Kaufmann.

Fodor, J.A., & Pylyshyn, Z.W. (1988). Connectionism and cognitive architecture: A critical analysis. In S. Pinker & J. Mehler (Eds.), *Connections and symbols* (pp. 3–71). Cambridge, MA: MIT Press, and Amsterdam: Elsevier. (Reprinted from *Cognition, 28,* 1988.)

Hammond, K. (1986). CHEF: A model of case-based planning. *Proceedings of the 5th National Conf. on Artificial Intelligence.* Los Altos, CA: Morgan Kaufmann.

Hinton, G.E. (1988). Representing part-whole hierarchies in connectionist networks. *Proceedings of the 10th Annual Conference of the Cognitive Science Society.* Hillsdale, NJ: Lawrence Erlbaum Associates.

Johnson-Laird, P.N. (1983). *Mental models.* Cambridge, MA.: Harvard University Press.

Johnson-Laird, P.N. (1988). Reasoning by rule or model? *Proceedings of the 10th Annual Conference of the Cognitive Science Society.* Hillsdale, NJ: Lawrence Erlbaum Associates.

Johnson-Laird, P.N., & Bara, B.G. (1984). Syllogistic inference. *Cognition, 16* (1), 1–61.

Kedar-Cabelli, S. (1988). Analogy—from a unified perspective. In D.H. Helman (Ed.), *Analogical reasoning* (pp. 65–103). Dordrecht: Kluwer Academic Publishers.

Kolodner, J.L. (1987). Capitalizing on failure through case-based inference. *Proceedings of the 9th Annual Conference of the Cognitive Science Society.* Hillsdale, NJ: Lawrence Erlbaum Associates.

Koton, P. (1988). Reasoning about evidence in causal explanations. *Proceedings of the 7th National Associates Conference on Artificial Intelligence.* San Mateo, CA.: Morgan Kaufmann.

Pinker, S., & Prince, A. (1988). On language and connectionism: Analysis of a parallel distributed processing model of language acquisition. In S. Pinker & J. Mehler (Eds.), *Connections and symbols* (pp. 73–193). Cambridge, MA: MIT Press, and Amsterdam: Elsevier. (Reprinted from *Cognition, 28,* 1988.)

Ruby, D., & Kibler, D. (1988). Exploration of case-based problem solving. *Proceedings of DARPA Case-Based Reasoning Workshop.* San Mateo, CA: Morgan Kaufmann.

Shastri, L., & Ajjanagadde, V. (1989). *A connectionist system for rule-based reasoning with multi-place predicates and variables* (Tech. Rep. MS-CIS-8905). Philadelphia, PA: Computer and Information Science Dept., University of Pennsylvania.

Smolensky, P. (1988). On the proper treatment of connectionism. *Behavioral and Brain Sciences, 11,* 1–74.

Sycara, K.P. (1988). Resolving goal conflicts via negotiation. *Proceedings of the 7th National Conference on Artificial Intelligence.* San Mateo, CA: Morgan Kaufmann.

Touretzky, D.S. (1986). Representing and transforming recursive objects in a neural network, or "Trees *Do* Grow on Boltzmann Machines." *Proceedings of the IEEE Conference on Systems, Man and Cybernetics.* Atlanta, GA.

Touretzky, D.S., & Hinton, G.E. (1988). A distributed connectionist production system. *Cognitive Science, 12* (3), 423–466.

9
Finding a Maximally Plausible Model of an Inconsistent Theory*

Mark Derthick

1. INTRODUCTION

1.1. Motivation

This chapter is concerned with finding a truth assignment for a set of propositional variables subject to constraints which might be inconsistent if expressed in classical logic. It does little to address the questions of why one would want to use an inconsistent theory, or why one would want to find a model of it. These questions are given more attention in (Derthick, 1988). Briefly, the answer to the first question is that it makes it easier for the knowledge engineer, and the answer to the second is that it makes it easier for the system:

The world is complicated enough that agents often make simplifying assumptions that do not hold universally—for instance, that birds fly. This general rule applies to many individual situations, and it is a useful heuristic when the current situation is not known to be one of the exceptional cases. In those situations, the agent may drop down to a more detailed theory which might, for instance, talk about lift and drag. All of the agent's theories, even the numerical ones, are just that—theories. The best way to cope with the mismatch between theory and reality may be to postulate rules that make the right predictions most of the time.

Default logic (Reiter, 1980) is one way to formulate this kind of rule. The

* This research was carried out while I was a graduate student at Carnegie Mellon University. It was sponsored in part by an Office of Naval Research Graduate Research Fellowship, and in part by the National Science Foundation under Contract Number EET-8716324. The views and conclusions contained in the document are those of the author and should not be interpreted as representing the official policies, either expressed or implied, of the U.S. Government. I thank Geoff Hinton and Dave Touretzky for their patient supervision.

truth value of a proposition in a default theory may be a function of many other propositions. For instance, in one of the canonical examples, to predict whether Dick is a pacifist it is helpful to know whether he is a Quaker, a Republican, or both. A theory may state that the default Quakers are pacifists, and Republicans aren't. Thus there may be multiple applicable default rules, and they may conflict. It will be impractical, in general, to give a default for every element of the power set of the rule antecedents. It therefore becomes necessary to use heuristics which combine the applicable default rules. One way to resolve interacting defaults is to prioritize them with certainties. The conclusion whose supporting defaults have the greatest total certainty wins. This paper presents a "Violation Counting Semantics" (VCS) for theories expressed in propositional calculus augmented with certainties.

The theories knowledge engineers formulate are usually expressed in a language at least as powerful as first-order logic. Question answering about such theories is undecidable. Even in VCS, question answering is NP-complete, so it is unlikely that there is a complete and correct algorithm which always returns an answer quickly. Finding a single most plausible model is a heuristic for guessing an answer quickly. This technique is also used in decision theory, where it is called "maximum likelihood estimation" (Chernoff & Moses, 1959). Also for reasons of efficiency, Levesque (1986) has suggested simplifying the knowledge representation problem by using "vivid knowledge bases," which are essentially models. Johnson-Laird (1983) advocates model-based reasoning on psychological grounds.

This paper gives an algorithm for constructing a connectionist network that finds maximally plausible models of VCS theories by gradient descent in model space. Global energy minima of the network correspond to maximally plausible models, but there may also be incorrect local minima. Much of the chapter concerns smoothing the search space of the network to reduce the impact of local minima. Extension to theories with quantification is discussed.

1.2. Implementation

Implementing model-based reasoning in a connectionist network is conceptually simple and elegant. There is one unit to represent each propositional variable, so each assignment of binary states to units represents a model. Every assertion corresponds to a constraint among a subset of the units. For instance the theory $\{a, a \rightarrow b\}$ has a corresponding network with two units and two constraints. The unit representing the proposition a is constrained to be on, and the unit representing b is constrained to be on if unit a is on.

Every constraint has an associated positive weight. There is an evaluation function, called the *energy function,* that sums the weights of all the constraints that are violated by a model. Therefore "energy" just means negative plausibility.

In the example network, there are four possible models, situated at the corners of the unit square. The value of the function is zero for correct models of the theory, and has a higher value otherwise. Using the Hopfield and Tank search method, described below, the search begins in the center of the state space and performs gradient descent. The search terminates in a corner of the space, which corresponds to a model. If the space is sufficiently smooth, the corner is a global energy minimum, and the model is one of the most plausible. Adding special-purpose energy functions to handle nested logical relations leads to much smoother search spaces than does the usual form of Hopfield and Tank energy equations, which sum pairwise products of unit states. The special-purpose energy functions do not fit the brain-like model of pairwise connections; hence, it may be less misleading to call VCS a parallel constraint satisfaction system and not label it "connectionist." To the extent that the energy function can be regarded as composed of independent contributions from many individual constraints, each involving only a small fraction of the units, the term "connectionist network" conveys the spirit of the approach.

During the search the constraints continually and in parallel exert pressure on the developing model to conform. Every proof that a syntactic system could find for a proposition corresponds to some causal web of constraints in the connectionist network. Determining satisfaction is intractable for propositional logic (Garey & Johnson, 1979), and having a parallel implementation is of no help in the worst case. However, it does make a big difference when good guesses are acceptable. In theorem provers, all possible paths are eventually searched, and there is no waste from checking the same path more than once. On the other hand, the rule application process is entirely local, and knowledge is only brought to bear when the control algorithm explicitly invokes it. If the most relevant knowledge is not invoked early, much of the search can be wasted.

2. DEFINING PLAUSIBLE MODELS

To a first approximation, the energy of a model in VCS is the number of assertions violated, weighted by their certainties. However even trivial changes to the form of the KB would then affect the energy. For instance, $\{a,b\}$ would mean something different from $\{a \wedge b\}$, because the model $\{a = F, b = F\}$ violates two assertions in the former, but only one in the latter.

There are a number of existing schemes for capturing the meaning of propositional formulas in arithmetic expressions. In Boolean algebra with positive logic, where one represents true and zero false, AND corresponds to min, OR to max, and NOT to $1 - x$. In fuzzy logic the same functions are used, but the domain is expanded to the continuous interval between zero and one, rather than only the endpoints (Zadeh, 1986). The truth value of an expression is meant to capture the likelihood of the whole as a function of the likelihoods of its composants.

The goal of VCS is very different. It does not need the exact likelihood of a formula being true, but only an ordering over models. This gives it the flexibility to use numbers outside the range [0, 1]. These numbers are proportional to log probabilities,[1] so they do in fact determine the probabilities of formulas. However a normalization step is required to find the proportionality constant, so it is impossible to compute the probability of a formula strictly from the probabilities of its constituents. Therefore this scheme is unsuitable for syntactic reasoning, as is usually done in fuzzy logic and expert systems. The ability to use numbers in the interval $[0, \infty)$ in model-based reasoning gives VCS more power to discriminate between models, as the following example shows. In boolean algebra or fuzzy logic, the sentences "Lincoln was buried in Grant's tomb" and "Lincoln was buried in Grant's tomb and violets are green" have the same likelihood, yet they impose different orderings on possible models. A KB containing the second sentence will rank the actual world lower than a KB containing only the first, because the actual world violates two constraints rather than just one.

A second difference between violation counting and most other schemes is the polarity of the mapping between truth values and numbers. In Boolean algebra, positive logic is conventional, but negative logic could equally well be used. In this case true is zero, false is one, AND is max, and OR is min. For counting constraint violation, it is crucial that zero constraint violation correspond to true. If the KB contains the single assertion that the atomic proposition p holds, the energy of models in which p fails to hold should be increased. The constraint expressing this is (ON p). The energy assigned to model α by the assertion p is $E_p^\alpha = s_p^\alpha$ where s_p^α is zero if p is true in model α and one otherwise. For convenience the distinction between the variable p and the state, s_p^α, of the unit representing the variable is dropped, as is the superscript indicating the model. The constraint (ON p) is also usually written simply p.

Like the negative logic version of Boolean algebra, VCS translates OR as min and NOT as $1 - x$. However to be able to distinguish pairs of sentences like the ones about Lincoln, it translates AND as + rather than max. The correct way to think about this is that models that violate multiple conjuncts of an assertion have a higher constraint violation. Being sloppy, it is also possible to think of the propositions themselves as having truth values that range from true to false to extra false. On this view, ANDing two false propositions results in a proposition that is even more false. A problem now arises with NOT when it is applied to these extra false propositions. If proposition p has energy 2, then (NOT p) has energy $1 - 2 = -1$, which is outside the domain of plausibilities, $[0, \infty)$.

---

[1] Derthick (1990) discusses the relationship between VCS and Bayesian inference.

Therefore a syntactic restriction is imposed on the language that NOT can never be applied to a proposition whose plausibility can be anything other than zero or one. Thus only disjunctions and other negations can appear inside the scope of a negation sign.[2] In logic, it is always possible to use de Morgan's laws to push in negation signs so they only apply to atoms, and this can at most double the size of the formula.

The search algorithm requires computing the derivative of the energy function in order to do gradient descent. Since min has discontinuous derivatives it is less than ideal for this search technique. Its derivative is zero for all arguments except the smallest, for which the derivative is one. If the two smallest arguments are close to one another, the derivative changes discontinuously for small changes in the state of each unit. It would be much better if the derivative could be divided among all the arguments, with the biggest share going to the lowest ones. Generalized mean values (Rivest, 1988) have the desired effect. One way to define the generalized mean value of a vector of positive numbers is

$$M_p(a) = \left(\frac{1}{n} \sum_{i=1}^{n} a_i^p \right)^{1/p} \tag{1}$$

For $p = 1$ this is just the ordinary arithmetic mean, and as $p \rightarrow \infty$ it becomes the max function. As $p \rightarrow -\infty$ it becomes the min function. The restriction to positive numbers is unfortunate, since the energy of component propositions may be zero. However if $p > 0$ the generalized mean value behaves appropriately for arguments of zero. Hence $\min(a,b,c)$ is rewritten $1 - \max((1 - a),(1 - b),(1 - c))$ and arguments to OR, like those to NOT, may only take on energies between zero and one.

Table 9.1 lists the value of the approximate max function for various p. Derthick (1990) uses $p = 16$. For smaller values the system would regard an OR constraint with one argument true, and the rest false, as partially unsatisfied. It would waste too much effort trying to satisfy more of the arguments. For larger values the energy barriers between states with different arguments satisfied would be too large, and the system would commit itself too soon. For simplicity, the theoretical analysis in this paper treats energy functions as if OR were translated as min. Keep in mind that the running system uses the generalized mean value approximation.

These constraints enable any propositional theory to be expressed as an energy function. To build in the formula $a \wedge (\neg\, b \vee c)$ requires an AND constraint with two components, an ON constraint and an OR constraint, which in turn has two components. The corresponding energy function is

[2] The appendix gives a grammar that incorporates the syntactic restrictions.

Table 9.1.
How the Approximate Max Function Behaves for the Vector a = (.80 .75 .60 .10), as p Approaches ∞, and How Much of the Derivative Is Attributable to the Largest Argument.

p	$M_p(a)$	$\frac{\partial M_p(a)}{\partial a_1} \Big/ \sum_i \frac{\partial M_p(a)}{\partial a_i}$
1	.56	.25
2	.63	.36
4	.68	.44
8	.72	.56
16	.75	.72
32	.77	.88
64	.78	.98
128	.79	.999

$$E = a + \min((1 - b),c)$$

A final constraint type is required to adjust the certainty of constraints. WITH-WEIGHT multiples the energy penalty for violating a constraint by a constant, w, the weight assigned to that constraint. For instance, the energy function for (WITH-WEIGHT w (ON a)) is $w \times a$. The name is "with-weight" rather than "with-certainty" because this is the traditional nomenclature in connectionist networks. In this paper "weight" and "certainty" have the same meaning. I tend to use the former when talking about implementation issues and the latter when talking at the functional level.

For consistent theories, the resulting semantics is compatible with that of classical logic. The classical models will all have zero energy, and all other models will have higher energy (the Appendix proves this). For inconsistent theories, which have no classical models, there will be no zero-energy models either, but there will still be a well defined set of minimum-energy models that least violate the weighted assertions.[3] It is usually desirable to consider only the minimal models in this set. This can be done by adding a "closed-world assumption" (Reiter, 1978), weak (NOT (ON p)) assertions for every propositional variable. As long as the certainty of these assertions is much smaller than that of the other assertions, adding them will only prune the set of most plausible models, and never introduce new models into the set. This numerical notion of minimality

[3] If the system cannot get the energy down to zero, it can figure out where the mistake lies, in the following sense. Each constraint contributes a term to the energy equation, and the system can establish which terms are non-zero.

is stronger than the subset notion usually used in defining minimal models, in that $\{p\ q\}$ is smaller than $\{q\ r\ s\}$ rather than incomparable.

Although the four constraint types, AND, OR, NOT, and WITH-WEIGHT, are sufficient to define an energy function that respects the semantics of any VCS theory, there exist many other mappings from KBs to energy functions that agree on the energy to assign every model. They only disagree when the atoms are assigned truth values intermediate between zero and one. For pragmatic reasons two other constraint types, introduced in Section 4, are used in VCS: IMPLIES and VERY.

The set of minimum-energy models of a knowledge base is unfortunately not invariant under the usual rules of logical inference. For example the meaning of $\{a,\ b\}$ is not the same as $\{a,\ a \rightarrow b\}$ because the empty model violates two assertions in the first theory, but only one in the second. Since VCS never performs syntactic inference anyway, this is less of a drawback than in deductive systems. Ginsberg has pointed out that this is a likely consequence of any system that does counterfactual reasoning (Ginsberg, 1986). The counterfactual consequences for b of $\neg a$ depend on the reasons for believing b in the first place. If it is believed only because a is believed, it should no longer be believed when a no longer is.

Thus there may be some justification in considering syntactic differences when reasoning. Systems that can semantically distinguish every pair of syntactically distinct entities probably go too far, however. In VCS there are semantically irrelevant syntactic distinctions. Propositions that can be derived from one another strictly by using the commutative, associative, and distributive laws are equivalent semantically.

Using de Morgan's laws also changes the meaning of a formula under the above translation. The energy contribution of the assertion $A \wedge B$ is $A + B$, while that of $\neg(\neg A \vee \neg B)$ is $1 - \min(1 - A, 1 - B) = \max(A,B)$. In the model where both a and b are false, the energy contribution of the first assertion is two, while that of the second is one. The two forms correspond to different beliefs about the independence of a and b. In the first, they are statistically independent, while in the second they are positively correlated. The expert system Prospector (Duda, Gaschnig, & Hart 1979) uses a similar mapping of logic onto logarithms of probabilities, and explicitly has two forms of AND available for the user, one corresponding to adding the log probabilities, and one corresponding to taking their maximum.

3. FINDING PLAUSIBLE MODELS

Well-defined models correspond to the corners of a unit hypercube, where each dimension represents the truth value of a propositional variable. By extrapolating the energy function defined over models to the interior of the hypercube, a continuous search space amenable to gradient descent results. The energy functions described above are expressed in terms of addition, subtraction, multiplication, division (by a positive constant), and exponentiation, and so they, as well as their derivatives, are well defined over the expanded space. By starting the search in the center of the space, where all states are $\frac{1}{2}$, gradient descent can be used. Since only corners correspond to models, interior local minima are potentially a problem. However, if all terms in the energy function are at most linear in the state of any given unit, no interior point will be a local minimum, so the search will always terminate at a corner.

To the extent that the energy space is smooth, there will be broad basins of attraction in the direction of the corners with the lowest energy. If the deepest basins are the broadest, then the basin for the best model will extend the farthest toward the center of the search space. This is the rationale for starting the search at the point where all states are $\frac{1}{2}$. In search spaces where there is a high degree of symmetry, there may be many equally good and similarly shaped basins of attraction, so a small random offset must be added to the initial states to break symmetry.

The energy function as defined above is less than ideal for searching because the "continental divides" of the various basins of attraction encroach far into the center of the search space, forcing the system to make decisions early. Hopfield (1984) introduced a technique for smoothing out the smaller basins, so as the search moves from the center of the search space toward the corners, its choice among the deep basins is not affected by less important issues, which can be sorted out later. This technique is the mean field approximation (Peterson & Anderson, 1987) to simulated annealing (Kirkpatrick, Gelatt, & Vecchi, 1983).

In a Hopfield and Tank network, another term is added to the VCS energy equation to smooth the space further:

$$E = E_{VCS} + \sum_i \int_0^{s_i} g^{-1}(s)ds$$

where $g(u) = \frac{1}{1 + e^{-\lambda u}}$, and so $g^{-1}(s) = \frac{1}{\lambda} \cdot \log \frac{s}{1 - s}$. λ determines the steepness of the transfer function, g, and is called the *gain*.

At low gains the second term dominates, but it goes to zero as λ increases. It is minimized at $s_i = \frac{1}{2}$, so early in the search states of units which are relatively unimportant in determining the global energy take on values near $\frac{1}{2}$. As λ is gradually raised, the first units whose states take on extreme values are those representing the most important propositions. By deferring commitments on less important propositions, shallow local minima resulting from their interactions are avoided.

Hopfield and Tank introduce another modification, which is intended to make their model more closely resemble neurons. Each unit is modeled as an amplifier with finite input resistance and capacitance, and with transfer function g. The "energy calculation" is done on the input side of the amplifier, and the trajectory of the circuit is given by the dot product of the energy gradient with the vector of derivatives of the transfer function. The circuit still monotonically decreases the energy function, and for the purposes of this chapter, the difference from steepest descent is unimportant.

4. SMOOTHER ENERGY FUNCTIONS

4.1. Making the Center of the Hypercube an Attractor

Even using the Hopfield and Tank algorithm, the basic energy functions discussed previously do not always give good performance. As the search moves away from the center of the space, it enters basins of attraction containing ever fewer models. The algorithm is most successful if committing to basins containing only a few models can be delayed as long as possible. By making the constraints' contribution to the energy function as flat as possible near the center of the space, the system can explore much of the space before making commitments. For instance if a short chain of inference makes p seem likely, that unit will become more active early on. If a longer chain of inference, which takes longer to assert itself, later negates the argument for p, it is desirable for the state of p to decay back to $\frac{1}{2}$. If the space is relatively flat, the extra energy term that adds a concave upward component to the whole space will be able to pull p back toward its uncommitted state.

Using the basic energy functions, the energy surface defined by implications is not flat in the center of the space. When $p \rightarrow q$ is implemented as $-p \vee q$, the energy function is $\min((1 \neg p), q)$, whose derivative is, using the generalized mean value approximation, $-\frac{1}{2}$ with respect to p and $\frac{1}{2}$ with respect to q. So the system will drift toward models where p is false, even though there are equally good models where p is true. The solution is to introduce a special IMPLIES constraint,[4] in which the energy contribution is a function of the difference in states: $E = [\max(0, p - q)]^k$ (see Figures 9.1 and 9.2). It is also convenient to define (EQUIV a b) $\equiv$ (AND (IMPLIES a b) (IMPLIES b a)). With this formulation, the states will decay back to $\frac{1}{2}$ from anywhere in the space, in the absence of other constraints. The effect of k is discussed below.

This same energy function can be used to implement ATLEAST, ATMOST, or EXACTLY constraints as well:

---

[4] Interestingly, possibility theory also has a special rule for implication, rather than relying on classical logic equivalence $a \rightarrow b \equiv \neg a \vee b$. The truth value for "if C_1 then C_2" is $1 \wedge (1 - \tau_1 + \tau_2)$, where the τ's are the truth values of the C's.

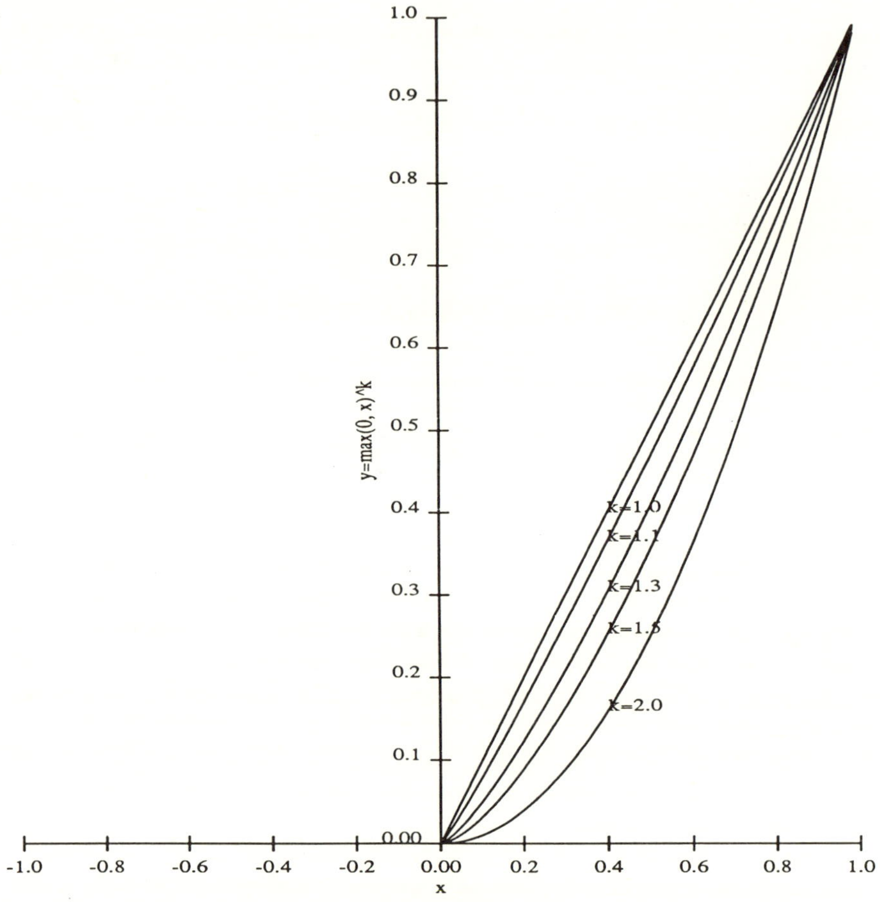

Figure 9.1.
Energy versus difference in state for IMPLIES constraints, for various exponents. (From Derthick, 1988.)

(ATLEAST n $p_1 \cdots p_k$) $\equiv$ (IMPLIES (AND(NOT p_1)$\cdots$(NOT p_k)) (WITH-WEIGHT n FALSE))
(ATMOST n $p_1 \cdots p_k$) $\equiv$ (IMPLIES (WITH-WEIGHT n FALSE) (AND (NOT p_1)$\cdots$(NOT p_k)))
(EXACTLY n $p_1 \cdots p_k$) $\equiv$ (EQUIV (AND (NOT p_1)$\cdots$(NOT p_k)) (WITH-WEIGHT n FALSE))
where FALSE is a constraint whose energy is always one.

There is another new constraint type, used to make the effect of a constraint felt more strongly in one direction than the other. Sometimes tentative evidence for proposition p should be taken as evidence for q, but tentative evidence against q should not affect belief in p. For instance if (ATLEAST $(n - 1)$ $a_1 \cdots a_n$), the equilibrium state of unit a_1 is close to $\frac{1}{n}$ (that is, nearly true). If a further

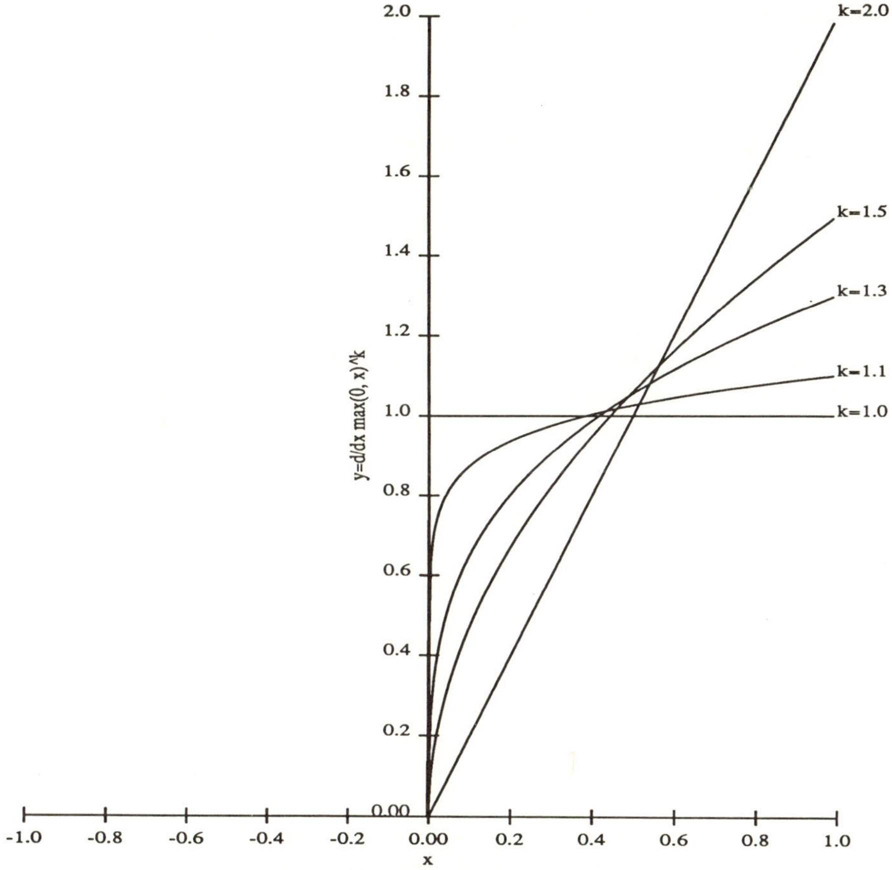

Figure 9.2.
Energy derivative versus difference in state for IMPLIES constraints, for various exponents. (From Derthick, 1988.)

constraint is added, (IMPLIES a_1 p), the equilibrium state of p would be forced to a similar value. Here the search is moving away from the center of the search space, and possibly making an irrevocable choice that p, when there are no constraints that can only be satisfied if p. Therefore the energy of units like a_1 is raised to a high power, so unless the system is very certain it should be on, it will have negligible effect.[5] This is done with a VERY constraint, and the energy is $1 - (1 - E_{component})^k$. In words, (VERY p) is false unless p is very nearly true. It is

[5] There is a similar operator in possibility theory where "very p" is translated by squaring the truth value of p.

also convenient to define the dual, (PRETTY p)≡(NOT (VERY (NOT p))), which is true unless p is very nearly false. The tables in the appendix summarize the constraints.

4.2. More Effective Inference Chaining

In logic, conclusions reached using long chains of inference are just as certain as the axioms themselves. In connectionist networks where truth values are replaced by activation strengths, it can be much more difficult to correctly propagate activation down long causal chains. The most obvious problems are attenuation and delay. If unit p is asserted to be on with unit strength, and the two implications $p \rightarrow q$ and $q \rightarrow r$ are also asserted with unit strength, the unit representing q will be on more than halfway, but less than fully on. Therefore q will have a smaller derivative than p, and its activation will be between one half and that of p's. The activation of each succeeding unit in the chain will decay exponentially to the resting activation, one half. Further, the time it takes for the states to rise from their initial values and begin to affect succeeding units introduces a delay that increases with the length of the chain.

There are also problems when different assertions in the chain have different weights. For instance if the assertion p has unit weight, but the implications have weight 10, the energy derivative of unit r will be 10 times as large as it "ought" to be. "Ought" is in quotes because no theory has yet been given for what the energy derivatives should be in the interior of the hypercube beyond the appeal for smoothness in the preceding section. A helpful physical analogy can be appealed to, however. The strength of a path should be like the strength of a physical chain: the strength of its weakest link. In the path $p \rightarrow q \rightarrow r$, if another assertion introduces a positive energy derivative for the unit p, that same "force" for asserting p should be transmitted to units q and r. From its initial state of $\frac{1}{2}$, the state of unit p will become more true until the derivative of the implication $p \rightarrow q$ exactly cancels the derivative of the outside force. Under these conditions the derivative of the implication with respect to q's state should be such that it feels the same force toward true that p feels. Mathematically, the sum of the derivatives of the units in an implication constraint should be zero. For the original implementation of implications this condition was not met in general: the energy of the constraint (OR (NOT p) q) is $(1 - p) \times q$, and

$$\frac{\partial E}{\partial p} + \frac{\partial E}{\partial q} = -q + (1 - p)$$

For the special IMPLIES constraint the condition does hold:

$$E = \max(0, p - q)^k = f(p - q)$$

$$\frac{\partial E}{\partial p} + \frac{\partial E}{\partial q} = \frac{\partial f}{\partial (p - q)} \cdot \frac{\partial (p - q)}{\partial p} + \frac{\partial f}{\partial (p - q)} \cdot \frac{\partial (p - q)}{\partial q} = \frac{\partial f}{\partial (p - q)} (1 - 1) = 0$$

Correct propagation depends on an equilibrium, or static, situation. If the forces are not yet balanced, the unit states will be changing and the sum of the derivatives is not necessarily zero. In order to reach equilibrium in this example, p's state must become more true than q's to the point where the energy derivative of the implication constraint (Figure 9.2) equals the external derivative. For values of k closer to 1.0, the curve is steeper, and so p's state will have to change less. The effect of k can be thought of as the elasticity of the chains. Low k's therefore result in "tighter" responses. Since the state of a unit is bounded, there is a limit to how much force an implication constraint can transmit, which is the certainty of the assertion times k. However up to that limit, the constraint will transmit exactly as much force as is applied to it. Thus the problem of non-uniform certainties has also been solved. A path really will be as strong as its weakest link.

In principle one would want k as close to 1.0 as possible so that forces can be transmitted while the unit states remain near $\frac{1}{2}$, and so the maximum force a constraint can transmit is not too much higher than its certainty. However the simulation proceeds in finite steps; each unit is probed and changes its state by a small constant times its derivative. As k gets smaller, the energy becomes ever more sensitive to small changes in state, so the constant has to shrink to prevent wild oscillations in the unit states. Derthick (1990) uses $k = 1.5$ as a compromise.

The analogy also extends to branching chains. If p implies (q and r and s), and there are forces trying to turn all three consequents off, the force on p should be the sum of the three forces. Mathematically, the sum of the forces should still equal zero. When this constraint is implemented as (IMPLIES p (AND q r s)) this relation is exactly true. When it is implemented using MAX instead of AND, the relation holds approximately.

5. CONCLUSION

5.1. Quantifiers

Propositional logic seems too weak for describing interesting domains. Expanding the quantifiers of a first order theory into repeated conjunctions or disjunctions over the domain is, in theory at least, a possible means of propositionalizing theories with finite models. Unfortunately, the propositional theory that results grows as d^n, where d is the size of the domain and n is the maximum depth of quantifier nesting.

However it may not be necessary to handle general purpose variables and quantification. Agre and Chapman (1987) argue that much of everyday behavior can be accomplished with state machines and special-purpose "routines," which incorporate a few deictic variables. μKLONE (Derthick, 1990) is a frame-based knowledge representation system which includes a deictic variable representing the subject of the current query. If Moby Dick is the subject, the system can simultaneously consider many facts about Moby Dick, such as his color or worst enemies, but it cannot simultaneously consider facts about other individuals, such as his worst enemy's religion. This lets it use propositions whose form is atomic, "the color," "the enemies," but whose semantics is parameterized, "Moby-Dick's color," "Moby-Dick's enemies." This has advantages because many of the inferences based on color or enemies are independent of whose color, or whose enemies.[6]

For every predicate argument which can be taken out of the explicit argument list, and made an implicit, deictic, variable instead, the size of the propositionalized theory decreases by a factor of d. In μKLONE, n was reduced from 2 to 1. In addition, it may be possible to argue that d does not have to be very large. The potential problem is the large, or even infinite, number of individuals generated by Skolem functions. In μKLONE, d is heuristically set only slightly larger than the individuals the KB explicitly knows about, because the way Skolem functions can chain together is limited by the fact that they must all refer to the current subject.

5.2. Special-Purpose Energy Functions

The Hopfield and Tank search method, in which units take on continuous values, is effective because the depth of an energy minimum is often reflected in the steepness of the gradient in that direction at the center of the search space. This is especially true in many of the classic connectionist testbed problems such as the traveling salesman problem (Hopfield, 1984), where the architecture is highly regular. The structural constraints ensuring that the solution is a tour do not favor any one solution over another, so the difference in the gradient in the direction of alternative syntactically correct solutions generally reflects differences in the data.

The structure of dependencies among propositions in a VCS theory may be highly irregular. An energy function that sums pairwise products of unit states is not very effective in this case. Not only are many extra units required to correctly implement the semantics of nested expressions, but also the if-then dependencies so skew the energy surface towards certain models, independent of the data, that the Hopfield and Tank search method was not successful. Rectifying the problems with the energy function to make it smoother and to make the center of the search space an attractor has worked well. For different problems, the particular

[6] Since μKLONE explicitly represents only a partial model, it cannot detect inconsistencies resulting from chains that involve facts not in the focus of attention. Like gradient descent itself, using partial models centered on the subject is only a heuristic. The working assumption is that the system can be tuned to give reasonable answers most of the time in familiar domains.

special-purpose energy functions required may be different. IMPLIES is just one example, which proved to be useful in a logic-like domain.

5.3. Probability, Default Logic, and VCS

Violation Counting Semantics applies only to sets of propositional sentences, each of which has an associated certainty. Default logic (Reiter, 1980) can also be used to define a set of maximally plausible models of sets of propositional sentences, by considering the sentences to be normal default rules with the interpretation, "If *p* is consistent with everything else currently believed, believe *p*." The potential advantage of VCS is that the numerical certainties offer a way to resolve conflicting default rules. In default logic, the only way to make sure that "Quakers are Pacifists" overrides "Republicans are not Pacifists" is to explicitly mention the exceptional case in the second rule: "Republicans who are not Quakers are not Pacifists." However, the simple prioritization scheme used in VCS cannot express all possible ways to resolve conflicting rules, so rules with explicit exceptions may still be necessary.

The main difference between VCS and probability theory is that numerical probabilities have a direct semantic interpretation, while certainties, being unnormalized log probabilities, do not. While this is a drawback of certainties, it allows the knowledge engineer to enter any combination of certainties with the assurance that the resultant theory will be consistent. When entering quantities which will not be automatically normalized, such as direct probabilities, it is up to the user to make sure the theory is consistent.

VCS arises from the attempt to do high level reasoning in connectionist architectures, and its usefulness will partly be determined by the success of that heuristic search method. The special-purpose energy functions described here produce sufficiently smooth search spaces for simple problems, but will probably not suffice for extremely complex domains. Hopefully, small connectionist modules, each of which has rather small search spaces, will play a useful part in a larger hybrid system combining knowledge-rich logical or probabilistic inference with knowledge-poor connectionist search.

APPENDIX: CONSTRAINTS

This appendix proves that any VCS constraint assigns an energy of zero to a model if the corresponding logical proposition is true in the model, and assigns it an energy greater than zero otherwise. This appendix treats the logically redundant, but pragmatically useful, constraints introduced in Section 4 as well as the basic ones described in Section 2. In translating a constraint into a proposition, the constraint types WITH-WEIGHT and VERY are ignored, and the differences between (IMPLIES p q) and (OR (NOT p) q) disappear. Therefore the mapping is many to one and onto. The proofs proceed by induction on the complexity of the constraint.

Lemma: ⟨0-1-constraint⟩'s assign an energy of zero to models consistent with the constraint, and an energy in (0,1] to other models.

Proof:
Base case: The constraint is an atomic proposition, TRUE, or FALSE. Table 3 shows the lemma to hold in this case.

Induction step: Assume that the arguments to any of the other ⟨0-1-constraint⟩'s in the constraint grammar (Table 9.2) satisfy the lemma. Then the energy function given in the table will also satisfy the lemma.

Theorem: Any μKLONE constraint assigns an energy of zero to a model if the corresponding logical proposition is true in the model, and assigns it an energy greater than zero otherwise.

Proof:
Base case: The assertion is a ⟨0-1-constraint⟩. By the lemma above, the

Table 9.2.
The Constraint Grammar. ⟨0-1-constraint⟩ Is a Subset of Constraint Types that Assign Every Model an Energy Penalty between Zero and One. (Reproduced from Derthick, 1990).

⟨0-1-constraint⟩	::=	TRUE
	|	FALSE
	|	⟨atomic-proposition⟩
	|	(NOT⟨0-1-constraint⟩)
	|	(OR⟨0-1-constraint⟩*)
	|	(IMPLIES⟨constraint⟩⟨0-1-constraint⟩)
	|	(EQUIV⟨0-1-constraint⟩⟨0-1-constraint⟩)
	|	(MAX⟨0-1-constraint⟩*)
	|	(PRETTY⟨0-1-constraint⟩)
	|	(VERY⟨0-1-constraint⟩)
⟨constraint⟩	::=	⟨0-1-constraint⟩
	|	(AND⟨constraint⟩*)
	|	(WITH-WEIGHT⟨positive-number⟩⟨constraint⟩)
	|	(ATLEAST⟨whole-number⟩⟨0-1-constraint⟩*)
	|	(ATMOST⟨whole-number⟩⟨0-1-constraint⟩*)
	|	(EXACTLY⟨whole-number⟩⟨0-1-constraint⟩*)

Table 9.3.
A Description of Each Constraint Type, and Its Energy Function.
(Reproduced from Derthick, 1990).

Constraint	$\mathbf{E^m_{constraint}}$	**Purpose**
$p(atomic)$	$\begin{cases} 0 \text{ if } p \text{ is true in } m \\ 1 \text{ otherwise} \end{cases}$	
(NOT p)	$1 - E^m_p$	Basic
(AND $p_1\ p_2 \ldots p_n$)	$\sum_{i=1}^{n} E^m_{pi}$	translations
(OR $p_1\ p_2 \cdots p_n$) $\equiv$ (NOT (MAX (NOT p_1)(NOT p_2) $\cdots$ (NOT p_n)))		
(IMPLIES $p\ q$)	$\max(0, E^m_q - E^m_p)^k,\ k > 1$	Results in flatter energy surface than $\neg p \vee q$
(EQUIV $p\ q$)	$\lvert E^m_p - E^m_q \rvert^k,\ k > 1$	More effecient than $p \rightarrow q \wedge q \rightarrow p$
(MAX $p_1\ p_2 \cdots p_n$)	$\lim_{p \to \infty} \left(\frac{1}{n} \sum_{i=1}^{n} (E^m_{pi})^p \right)^{1/p}$	Substitutes for AND when energy range must be zero to one
(PRETTY p)	$(E^m_p)^k,\ k > 1$	True unless argument is very nearly false
(VERY p) $\equiv$ (NOT (PRETTY (NOT p)))		False unless argument is very nearly true
(WITH-WEIGHT $w\ p$)	$w \cdot E^m_p,\ w > 0$	Changes importance of component constraint
FALSE	1	Of little use,
TRUE	0	except in proofs
(ATLEAST $n\ p_1 \cdots p_k$) $\equiv$ (IMPLIES (AND (NOT p_1) $\cdots$ (NOT p_k)) (WITH-WEIGHT n FALSE))		
(ATMOST $n\ p_1 \cdots p_k$) $\equiv$ (IMPLIES (WITH-WEIGHT n FALSE) (AND (NOT p_1) $\cdots$ (NOT p_k)))		
(EXACTLY $n\ p_1 \cdots p_k$) $\equiv$ (EQUIV (AND (NOT p_1) $\cdots$ (NOT p_k)) (WITH-WEIGHT n FALSE))		

energy assigned to a model is zero for models consistent with the constraint, and is greater than zero otherwise.

Induction step: Assume that the arguments to any of the other ⟨constraint⟩'s in the constraint grammar satisfy the theorem. Then the energy function given in the table will also satisfy the theorem.

REFERENCES

Agre, P., & Chapman, D. (1987). Pengi: An implementation of a theory of activity. *Proceedings of the Sixth National Conference on Artificial Intelligence* (pp. 268–272). Los Altos, CA: Morgan Kaufmann.

Chernoff, H., & Moses, L.E. (1959). *Elementary decision theory*. New York: John Wiley & Sons.

Derthick, M. (1990). *Mundane reasoning by parallel constraint satisfaction*. London: Pitman.

Duda, R.O., Gaschnig, J., & Hart, P.E. (1979). Model design in the Prospector consultant system for mineral exploration. In D. Michie (Ed.), *Expert systems in the micro-electronic age* (pp. 153–167). Edinburgh, Scotland: Edinburgh University Press.

Garey, M.R., & Johnson, D.S. (1979). *Computers and intractability: A guide to the theory of NP-completeness*. San Francisco, CA: W.H. Freeman.

Ginsberg, M. (1986). Counterfactuals. *Artificial Intelligence, 30,* 35–79.

Hopfield, J.J. (1984). Neurons with graded response have collective computational properties like those of two state neurons. *Proceedings of the National Academy of Sciences, 81,* 3088–3092.

Johnson-Laird, P.N. (1983). *Mental models*. Cambridge, MA: Harvard University Press.

Kirkpatrick, S., Gelatt, C.D., Jr., & Vecchi, M.P. (1983). Optimization by simulated annealing. *Science, 220,* 671–680.

Levesque, H.J. (1986). Making believers out of computers. *Artificial Intelligence, 30,* 81–108.

Peterson, C., & Anderson, J.R. (1987). *A mean field theory learning algorithm for neural networks* (Tech. Report MCC-EI-259-87). Austin, TX: Microelectronics and Computer Technology Corporation.

Reiter, R. (1978). On closed world data bases. In H. Gallaire & J. Minker (Eds.), *Logic and data bases* (pp. 55–76). New York: Plenum.

Reiter, R. (1980). A logic for default reasoning. *Artificial Intelligence, 13,* 81–132.

Rivest, R.L. (1988). Game tree searching by min/max approximation. *Artificial Intelligence, 34,* 77–96.

Zadeh, L.A. (1986). Test-score semantics as a basis for a computational approach to the representation of meaning. *Literary and Linguistic Computing, 1*(1), 24–35.

10
The Relevance of Connectionism to AI: A Representation and Reasoning Perspective*

Lokendra Shastri

1. INTRODUCTION

In this chapter we argue that not only is connectionism relevant to knowledge representation and reasoning, but it also provides an ideal computational architecture for intelligent systems. To justify this claim we first identify certain critical features that any computational architecture capable of supporting intelligent behavior must possess and then show that the core features of connectionism correspond exactly to these features. We also discuss how these core features influence the nature of representation and reasoning. Next, we briefly discuss some work on connectionist systems that can perform interesting reasoning tasks with extreme efficiency, and mention some constraints on the conceptual structure suggested by this work.

As the study of artificial intelligence has matured over three decades, it has become apparent that we had underestimated the complexity and intricacy of intelligent behavior. Today, we realize that it is one thing to build a system that performs "intelligently" in a limited domain, and yet another to design a system that displays the sort of natural intelligence we take for granted among humans and higher animals. The best available language understanding programs and vision systems do not even come close to matching the speed and versatility of an 8-year-old.

The major shortcomings of extant AI systems are their brittleness and their inability to meet real-time constraints. One insight gained by AI is that a wide range of knowledge is required for solving even the most commonplace cognitive

* The preparation of this document was supported by NSF grants IRI 88-05465, MCS-8219196-CER, MCS-83-05211, DARPA grants N00014-85-K-0018 and N00014-85-K-0807, and ARO grant ARO-DAA29-84-9-0027.

tasks. For instance, the mundane task of language understanding—a task that we perform effortlessly and in real time—requires access to a large body of knowledge and is the result of interactions between a variety of knowledge pertaining to phonetics, prosodics, syntax, semantics, pragmatics, discourse structure, facial expression of the speaker, and that nebulous variety conveniently characterized as commonsense knowledge. Today it is quite apparent that in order to avoid brittleness one will have to impart a great deal of knowledge to a system. In terms of standard terminology, the system will have to embody a sufficient number of facts and rules to cover all relevant aspects of the domain.[1]

Merely enumerating all the required rules and facts about a domain as broad as the domain of common sense is a formidable and unsolved problem and it has even been argued that it is *the central* problem of artificial intelligence (Hayes, 1983). The centrality of the enumeration problem cannot be overstated, but it is clearly not the *only* central problem in AI. An equally important and difficult problem is the specification of organizational principles for structuring this vast body of knowledge and the development of associated algorithms for providing efficient access to this information.

Although AI researchers have been successful in developing techniques and algorithms for structuring and accessing knowledge that work effectively in restricted domains, it has become abundantly clear that these techniques do not carry over to larger and more complex domains. In other words, the techniques do not scale. Very soon we run into the stone wall of computational effectiveness; the performance of the system degrades drastically and it can no longer solve interesting problems in acceptable time-scales.[2] It is not difficult to pinpoint the source of the problem. We have observed earlier that intelligent activity requires dense interactions between many pieces of information and in any system that encodes a vast body of knowledge about a complex domain, these interactions become too numerous to be carried out effectively using a von Neumann computer.

2. A COMPUTATIONAL ARCHITECTURE FOR INTELLIGENCE

A possible remedy to the problem of supporting and managing dense interactions suggests itself if one examines the architecture of a von Neumann computer. In such a computer the processing power—that is, the computational and inferential

---

[1] The choice of terminology is not critical. In the above comment the reader may replace "rules and facts" by scripts, schemas, frames, axioms, constraints, or whatever might happen to be the readers favorite form for representing a chunk of knowledge.

[2] To the uninitiated, such a behavior may seem paradoxical because one would expect a more informed system to behave more intelligently.

power—is concentrated in a *single* processing unit, while the information on which computations have to be performed is stored in the computer's memory. This memory simply acts as an *inert* repository of the system's knowledge. As a result of the single processor design, only one processing step can be executed at any point in time, and during each processing step the CPU can only access a tiny fraction of the memory. Therefore, at any given instant, only an insignificant portion of the system's knowledge participates in the processing. Given that intelligent behavior requires dense interactions between many pieces of information it would seem appropriate to treat each memory cell not as a mere repository of information, but rather as an *active* processing element capable of *interacting* with other such elements. This would result in a *massively parallel* computer made up of a large number of simple processing elements—as many as there are memory cells in a traditional computer—that would permit numerous interactions between various pieces of information to occur simultaneously.

In addition to massive parallelism what should be some other features of a computer suitable for realizing an intelligent system? First, it is essential that such a computer operate without a central controller because such a controller would simply introduce another information bottleneck—albeit at the level of control information. Other critical features that would lead to an optimal use of available parallelism may be identified by recognizing that the computing resources of any parallel system are used in two ways: task-related information processing and communication. The first of these involves computations directly relevant to the task at hand, while the second—the use of resources for communication—constitutes an overhead that does not contribute *directly* to the task. Clearly, minimizing communication costs would help in maximizing the use of parallelism.

Communication costs have two components: encoding/decoding costs and routing costs. The sender of a message must encode information in a form that is acceptable to the receiver who in turn must decode the message in order to extract the relevant information. This constitutes encoding/decoding costs. Sending a message also involves decoding the receiver's address and establishing a path between the sender and the receiver. This constitutes routing costs.

One may minimize routing costs by positing *fixed* connections between processors and stipulating that any message sent by a processor will always be transmitted along *all*—and only all—links emanating from the processor.[3] This would reduce routing costs to zero because sending a message would require neither the decoding of an address nor the setting up of a path. Stipulating fixed connections, however, would require that each processing element be connected to all processors with which it needs to communicate.

[3] Connectivity may of course change over longer time scales via learning and reorganization. What we are saying above is that solving a typical cognitive task such as language understanding in real-time, does not require new connections to be established.

But how can the decoding/encoding costs be minimized? A trivial way of reducing these costs to zero would be to stipulate that messages shall not have any content—if there is no content, there will be nothing to encode or decode and therefore the associated cost will be zero. Such a suggestion may sound frivolous but one can come very close to reducing the encoding/decoding costs to zero by restricting all messages to be *scalars,* that is, by requiring that a message not have any internal structure, its only information content being its *magnitude*.

To summarize, we have argued that an appropriate computational architecture for an intelligent knowledge-intensive system should have the following features:

- massive parallelism—large number of active processing elements
- no central controller
- hard wired links and a high degree of connectivity
- scalar messages with no internal structure, only a magnitude
- each processor computes a scalar output (a level of activation) based on the magnitudes of input messages (input levels of activation) and transmits it to all the processors to which it is connected.

The features listed above directly correspond to the core and defining features of connectionism, hence, the claim that connectionism is an ideal computational architecture for encoding intelligent systems.

The most compelling argument put forth in favor of connectionism is that it is neurobiologically plausible. However, we arrived at the core features of connectionism—without appealing to the architecture of the animal brain—by simply recognizing the characteristics of information processing that seem to underly intelligence. That nature has produced a computational device with a similar set of features is perhaps not an accident.

The above list of features does not make any reference to an important feature of connectionist models, namely, learning. The arguments offered above are independent of the question of learning and would hold even if learning were an issue. The point we wish to make is that there exists a strong case for connectionism even if learning is not a major issue.

3. IMPACT OF CORE FEATURES OF CONNECTIONISM

In this section we discuss the impact of the core features of connectionism on the nature of representation and reasoning. This impact may broadly be summarized as follows:

- Connectionism offers an extremely efficient metaphor for reasoning where inference is reduced to spreading activation in a parallel network.
- Restricting messages to only being scalars entails that messages do not have any direct symbolic content; the information content of a message is not in

"What is being said?" but rather in "Who is saying it?"[4] This requires that representations be explicit, multifaceted, and fine grained.

- In a connectionist system there is no *distinct* interpreter that mediates retrieval and reasoning. The connection pattern, the weights on links, and the computational characteristics of nodes not only represent domain knowledge but also encode the retrieval and inferential processes that operate on this knowledge. This state of affairs *forces* a strong coupling between a representation and the inferences that the representation is expected to support. It also requires that representations be vivid and directly mirror the inferential structure of the domain.
- Working within a massively parallel computational architecture helps in identifying novel classes of limited inference that can be performed with extreme efficiency and aids in discovering constraints that must be placed on the conceptual struture in order to support extreme efficiency.
- The connectionist approach suggests alternate formulations of information processing. Thus instead of viewing a knowledge-based system as a theorem prover or a production system, one may view it as a system that performs constraint satisfaction, energy minimization, or evidential and probabilistic reasoning. This encourages the use of alternate reasoning formalisms that have not received due attention within AI but may be appropriate for modeling a range of cognitive functions.

In the next section we discuss the connectionist metaphor for reasoning. Subsequently, we discuss how the nature of representations in a connectionist system is affected by the absence of an interpreter and the restriction that messages be scalars. Examples of constraints on conceptual structure suggested by connectionism are discussed later in the context of two connectionist systems for knowledge representation and reasoning. A discussion of issues relating to alternate formulation of information processing supported by connectionism is beyond the scope of this Chapter (but see Rumelhart & McClelland, 1986).

In the following sections we will often allude to the following three points. These points may be obvious but are, nevertheless, stated here because they are critical to our argument.

1. The notion of a representation is meaningful only in the context of the operations it is capable of supporting. In the case of knowledge representation, any representation must be accompanied by a specification of the retrieval and inferential operations it is expected to support. Unless this is

[4]A message has a magnitude and therefore actually encodes "Who is saying it and *how loudly?*" The magnitude does play an important role in encoding constraint strengths and evidential/probabilistic knowledge but is not critical in our discussion here.

done, one cannot establish the correctness of the representation, let alone judge its goodness.

2. Any computational model of intelligence must be computationally effective, that is, it should be capable of performing the specified tasks in realistic time frames—preferably in real-time.
3. In view of 2, the specification referred to in 1 must also specify the limits of acceptable performance for the retrieval and inference operations the representation is intended to support. Thus, a specification of the operations that a representation must support and the time frame within which these operations must to be performed, together constitute the *design constraints* for developing a representation.

3.1. Metaphor for Reasoning

Connectionism provides the following metaphor for reasoning: Assign a processing element to each unit of information and express each inferential dependency between pieces of information by explicitly linking the appropriate nodes. This suggests an extremely efficient way of performing inference because inference may now be viewed as parallel spreading activation in the network. As it requires that all inferential dependencies be made explicit, such a view of inference also leads to representations that are maximally vivid.[5] There are, however, two critical problems—convergence and control of spreading activation—that must be addressed before this metaphor can serve any useful purpose. The problem of convergence is discussed below while the problem of controlling spreading activation is discussed in Section 3.2.

Parallelism does not guarantee speed. In order to support extremely efficient inference, the spreading activation process must converge extremely fast. The computation performed by many connectionist systems corresponds to a *relaxation* process wherein activation circulates in a network until finally a stable network state is obtained (Derthick, 1988). Often it is difficult to place an upper bound on the convergence time of such systems and even in cases where it is possible to do so, it often turns out to be polynomial in the size of the knowledge base. In practice, such systems often require thousands of steps even for toy problems and their performance is clearly unacceptable given our concern for computational effectiveness. Ideally, we would like to establish that for an interesting class of problems, a system will converge in a *constant* number—preferably one—of sweeps of spreading activation across the network. Such a convergence behavior would ensure that the network can compute a solution in time proportional to the *diameter* of the network which is—in almost all cases—

[5] The connectionist metaphor may be contrasted with the *blackboard* architecture where the dependencies are essentially left implicit.

sublinear (and often *logarithmic*) in the size of the knowledge base. But for the connectionist network to compute solutions in a *single* pass of spreading activation, the dependencies among pieces of knowledge would have to be *acyclic*. This condition may be satisfied naturally in some domains that exhibit *directed* cause-effect relationships (much like an open loop system). In some other domains it may be possible to achieve this condition by carrying out a finer decomposition of the terms in the knowledge base so as to reduce the density of dependencies (where density is the ratio of the number of dependencies to the number of terms in the knowledge base). Cyclic dependencies may also be eliminated by identifying suitable constraints on the conceptual structure that in turn preclude certain types of cyclic dependencies. Such an approach has been adopted succesfully in developing connectionist systems for representation and reasoning and two such systems are reviewed in brief in Section 4.

3.2. Scalar Messages and the Absence of an Interpreter

The scalar nature of messages in a connectionist network entails that the messages have no direct symbolic content: The information content of a message is not "What is being said" but rather "Who is saying it?"[6,7,8]

The above restriction on the information content of a message does not pose a problem if one is only interested in encoding *associations* between concepts—storing associations simply requires spreading activation, for which scalar message suffice. This restriction, however, becomes critical if one wishes to represent structured knowledge and perform retrieval and inference on this knowledge. It requires that all relevant distinctions—no matter how subtle—be represented explicitly. Thus, every relevant facet of a concept and every role that a concept may play has to be distinguished and represented explicitly.[9] It also requires that concepts be represented at multiple levels of granularity (resolution) including extremely fine-grained levels as well as coarse-grained ones. For example, the concept "chair" must be represented at various levels of granularity including a level of detail that would be appropriate for inclusion in the description of a living room ("a chair"), a finer level of detail that would be appropriate

---

[6] As observed earlier, the content actually is "Who is saying it and how loudly," but for our purposes it suffices to describe the information content as being "Who is saying it?"

[7] The statement "messages do not have symbolic content" should be distinguished from the statement "connectionist systems do not have symbolic content." We do not subscribe to the latter view.

[8] In the discussion, Pollack raised the question of how it is possible for a neuron to know the few thousand sources of its input. In response, we may say that the neuron does not even have to "know who" is sending a particular message. All it needs to know is how to respond to the message, in the following sense: for each input line, the neuron knows how to modify its response if it receives activation along that input line.

[9] This corresponds to the idea of "exploded cases" discussed in (Cottrell, 1985).

if we were describing the chair itself ("an antique leather upholstered . . ."), and an even finer level where the details about the arm of the chair would become relevant, and so on. The concept "red" cannot be represented as a unitary concept and it must be represented using exploded values such as "apple red," "rose red," "brick red," and so on. Similarly, a role such as "patient" must be represented in an exploded manner by positing distinct roles such as "love-patient," "hit-patient," "give-patient," and so forth. In traditional knowledge based systems, such distinctions do not have to be *represented* explicitly as this burden may be shifted to the interpreter which may treat the role "patient" differently depending upon the action with which the role is associated.

When knowledge is encoded in a connectionist network the usual distinction between the representation (knowledge base) and the processes that operate on it (the inference engine) becomes blurred: the connection pattern, the weights on links, and the computational characteristics of nodes not only represent domain knowledge but also encode the retrieval and inferential processes that manipulate this knowledge. In a connectionist system there is no *distinct* interpreter that mediates the retrieval or reasoning process—the interactions among the nodes directly cause changes in the states of nodes that produce the appropriate results.

In the traditional framework, the availability of a distinct interpreter allows a certain latitude in choosing representations. This appears to be an advantage but it *allows* one to get away with inadequate and suboptimal representations—representations that are far less articulated and vivid than they ought to be, representations that leave implicit a lot of dependencies and structure that should have been made explicit. This happens because there is always the hope that one can salvage the situation by augmenting the interpreter and having it coax the necessary information out of the representation. Such an approach overlooks the fact that the resulting solution may be inefficient. The notion of an interpreter insulates one from performance issues by promoting the view that efficiency can be achieved by providing the requisite control information to the interpreter. Unfortunately, it may turn out that given the choice of representation, such control information simply may not exist.

The absence of an interpreter and the restriction on the nature of messages also *forces* a strong coupling between the nature of representation, the nature of inference that the representation is expected to support, and the degree of efficiency with which these inferences have to be carried out. This is not always the case in traditional approaches to knowledge representation where there is a tendency to isolate control issues (also referred to as performance/implementation issues) from issues of representation and expressiveness.

The coupling of issues related to content, organization, and inference that results from adopting the connectionist framework may seem misguided and at odds with conventional wisdom. Why should one conflate issues that have been decoupled, especially when such a decoupling leads to a neat division of problems? It is indeed true that the decoupling of issues serves an extremely important *pedagogical* and *analytical* purpose. Our goal however, is not simply to understand such systems, but to produce a detailed computational account of such systems. And in order to achieve this goal it may be essential to blur these distinctions and adopt an unified approach. As stated earlier, all representations have a purpose and the notion of a representation is meaningless unless accompanied by the specification of the operations it supports and the acceptable complexity of these operations. Thus understanding which inferences have to be made efficiently—that is, focusing on performance issues—may be essential for discovering the principles underlying the organization of knowledge, and this in turn may be essential for making the correct ontological distinctions and choices.

A coupled approach to choosing representations is commonplace in computer science where it is clearly understood that the development of *efficient* algorithms for solving a problem cannot be decoupled from the development of associated data structures. In fact, the design of an appropriate data structure is often the central step in the process and once the "correct" data structure is discovered, the algorithm follows by fiat.

The absence of an interpreter and the strong coupling between the structure of knowledge and inference is a mixed blessing. Although it is true that in any given connectionist knowledge representation system the class of inference wired-in can be performed with extreme efficiency, it is also the case that the remaining inferences can either not be performed at all or can only be "approximated." A similar limitation also exists in traditional implementations of knowledge representation systems. However, in traditional systems it is easier to augment the interpreter by adding appropriate procedures (for example, LISP code) to the system. This is not so in a connectionist encoding; the complete computational characteristics of nodes and their interconnections critically depend on the nature of inferences being wired-in, and introducing any changes in the *basic* inferential ability of a system may require a major reorganization of the system. In view of this, it is essential that we choose with great care the class of limited inference to be hardwired into the system and make explicit the nature of approximations made by the system.

We now consider a simple example that illustrates how the restriction on the nature of messages and the absence of an interpreter affects the choice of representations.

Let objects in the domain we wish to represent have two intrinsic properties: color (with values red and blue) and shape (with values square and circle), and let *left-of* be a binary relation defined between objects. Let obj-1 and obj-2 be two objects in the domain such that obj-1 is a red square, obj-2 is a blue circle, and obj-1 is to the left of obj-2.

For simplicity we assume that the representation is only expected to support the following simple operations:

- Retrieve an object given its (partial) description. For example, retrieve "obj-1" given "red color" or given "red color and square shape."
- Retrieve the value of a specific property of a specified object. For example, retrieve the color of obj-1 as "red."
- Test whether a given relational tuple is true or false. For example, test whether *left-of*(obj-1, obj-2) is true or false.

Let us develop a simple connectionist representation for this domain. We begin by assuming that the four property values red, blue, square, and circle are grounded in perception, and hence, are *primitive* concepts (or microfeatures). Thus we represent each of these property values with a distinct node (Figure 10.1a). Each node is a processing element and sends out activation when in an *active* state. One might suggest that the representation of obj-1 may be taken to be the pattern 1010—this being the pattern of activation over the set of property values (microfeatures) corresponding to obj-1, and similarly, the representation of obj-2 may be taken to be the pattern 0101. Such a representation, however, is inadequate for a number of reasons that are outlined below.

First, the proposed representation does not really *represent* the objects obj-1 and obj-2; the representation does not distinguish between patterns such as 1010 that correspond to objects explicitly represented in the system, and patterns such as 1001 (a red circle) that correspond to *potential* objects as yet unrepresented in the system. Moreover, the representation does not provide any way of associating a name with a stored object. For example, it is not possible to state that the pattern 1010 corresponds to the object obj-1. These are serious limitations because given the description "red square"—that is, given the pattern 1010—the system will be unable to *recognize* this pattern as being that of an *existing* concept—let alone recognize it as being the object obj-1.

Another problem with the current representation is that it makes the representation of composite concepts particularly difficult—if not impossible. The representation does not allow the system to refer to objects except by their *full* descriptions and therefore the representation of a composite object must include the full description of all its component parts. For example, as the system can only refer to obj-1 and obj-2 by their complete descriptions, the representation of *left-of*(obj-1, obj-2) will have to be *left-of*(red square, blue circle). Such a representation would soon become untenable as one tries to describe progressively complex structures—specially, if concepts have more than two property values.[10]

A simple solution to some of the problems listed above can be obtained by using the basic idea of abstraction. This involves positing a separate node for

[10] We discussed the above representation in spite of its serious limitations because such "distributed representation" schemes have been proposed and defended as viable representations (Rumelhart & McClelland, 1986). For a discussion of some other limitations of the distributed approach see Feldman, Fanty, and Goddard (1988).

Figure 10.1a.
An unstructured representation of obj-1 and obj-2.

obj-1: 'red square'

obj-2: 'blue circle'

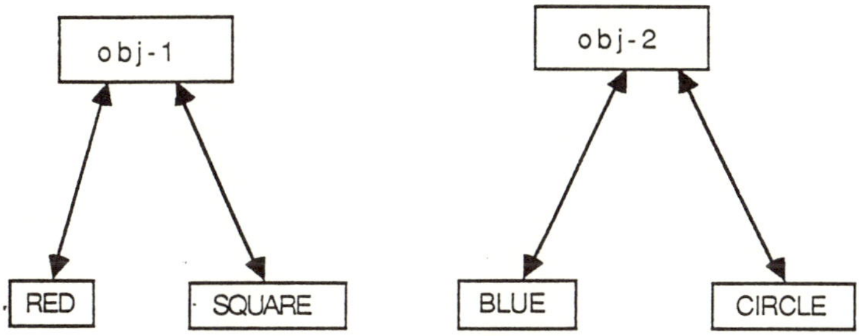

Figure 10.1b.
A representation with abstraction.

each object explicitly represented in the system and connecting such a node to all the property values of the corresponding object. Thus we would augment the representation of obj-1 by adding a node 'obj-1' and connecting it to the nodes 'red' and 'square'. The same can be done for obj-2 (Figure 10.1b). However, it must be remembered that the node 'obj-1' *does not in itself* represent the red square: obj-1. It represents obj-1 only by virtue of being connected to the nodes 'red' and 'square'; if we disconnect the node 'obj-1' from the nodes 'red' and 'square', it ceases to represent obj-1 (or for that matter, anything else).

The above needs to be emphasized because a lack of appreciation of this point leads to a prevalent misconception about "localist" representations. The presence of a node such as 'obj-1' provides a simple but effective way of distinguishing between the representation of explicitly represented (memorized) concepts such as "the red square: obj-1" and potential objects such as "a red circle." It also makes it possible to recognize and name the description "red square" as "obj-1." All we need to assume is that giving the description "red circle" amounts to activating the nodes "red" and "square" which—by virtue of their connections—will activate 'obj-1' but leave 'obj-2' inactive.

Our design, however, is still incomplete. The representation in Figure 10.1b does not allow us to distinguish between a "red-colored square shaped" object and a "red-shaped square colored" object. As far as the representation is concerned both are equivalent. Making this distinction is crucial, particularly, as we expect the representation to handle the task of answering questions such as

"What is the color of obj-1?" (this is one of the tasks we set for the representation). In response to this question we would like the system to say "red" (i.e., have the node "red" active without the node "square" also becoming active). However, the system cannot do so with the proposed representation. Starting with "obj-1" there is simply no way of activating "red" without activating "square" at the same time.

In a traditional semantic network the above problem does not arise because the links in the network can be labeled. In a semantic network, the link between "obj-1" and "red" would be labeled "has-color" and the link between 'obj-1' and 'square' would be labeled "has-shape" (refer to Figure 10.1b). During retrieval, an interpreter will read these labels and decide which link is appropriate for the given task. If the task is to find the color of obj-1, the interpreter would follow the link labeled "has-color" and arrive at the node "red."

In a connectionist network, however, we cannot have labels on links: This would amount to sending messages that encode more than a strength of activation Yet we need a mechanism that would allow messages from "obj-1" to selectively reach "red"—and not "square"—whenever the focus of attention is the color of "obj-1." This can be done in a straightforward manner by introducing an extra node that would associate "obj-1" and "red" only in the context of the property color, and "obj-1" and "square" only in the context of the property shape.

A possible solution along the above lines is given in Figure 10.2. The triangular nodes—called binder nodes—provide the required context. Each binder node associates an object, a property and a property value and becomes active on receiving simultaneous activation from a pair of nodes. To find the color of obj-1, one would activate the nodes "has-color" and "obj-1." The binder node linking "has-color" and "obj-1" to "red" will receive coincident activation

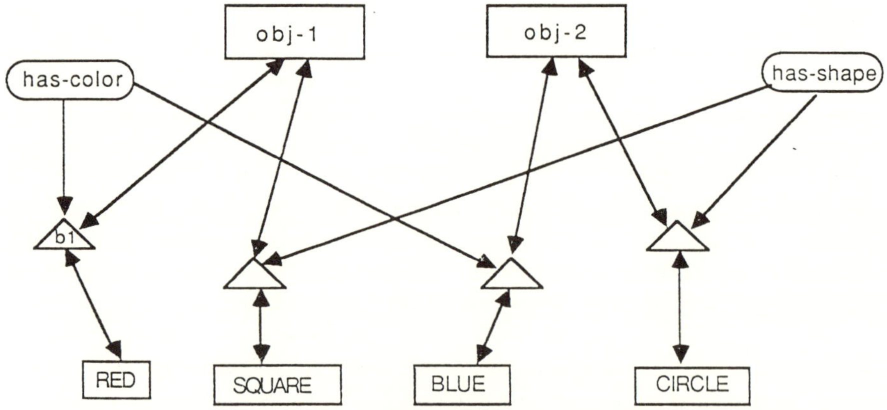

Figure 10.2.
A structured representation of obj-1 and obj-2.

along two of its links and become active. As a result, it will transmit activation to "red" which will then become active. If we need to find an object that is red in color we would activate the nodes "has-color" and "red." This will cause the appropriate binder node to become active and transmit activation to "obj-1" which will become active, thus completing the retrieval. Finding a "red square object" will involve activating the nodes "red" and "has-color" and "square" and "has-shape" which would also cause "obj-1" to become active.

Even the simple example discussed here illustrates how the restriction on the nature of messages and the absence of an interpreter forces certain ontological choices. For instance, it becomes necessary to represent attributes of objects as property value *pairs* instead of as *features*. Such a decision is not critical in an interpreted system; in such a system the fact "obj-1 is red in color" could have been represented by encoding "red" as a feature of "obj-1" and the information that "red is a color" could have been recorded separately. These two "isolated" pieces of information could have been put together by an interpreter during processing to ascertain that the object is red in color.

The representation of relations can be derived by applying techniques—similar to those outlined above. Figure 10.3 illustrates how *left-of*(obj-1, obj2) may be represented. We posit a generic node labeled "left-of" connected to two role nodes—one for each role of the relation (role nodes are depicted as diamond-shaped nodes). The actual instance of *left-of* is represented using the hexagonal *instancer* node labeled "left-of-1." This *instancer* node receives inputs from the role nodes of 'left-of' and the corresponding fillers of the roles—in this case "obj-1" and "obj-2". There is a link from "left-of-1" to "left-of." The *instancer* node performs the function of associating the correct role filler pairs. One can see how activating the two roles of "left-of" and the nodes "obj-1" and "obj-2" will lead to the activation of the node "left-of-1" and in turn of "left-of" indicating that *left-of*(obj-1,obj-2) has been asserted as an instance of the relation *left-of*.

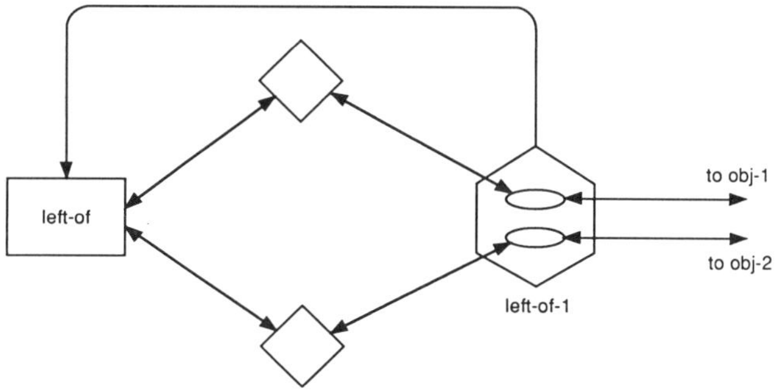

Figure 10.3.
A representation of left-of(obj-1,obj-2).

So far we have only considered the representation of relatively stable (long-term) knowledge. It is reasonable to assume that nodes such as "obj-1" and "left-of-1" exist (for example, they might be learned over time) in order to represent stable grouping of constituents. However, such a scheme is entirely inadequate if such groupings have to be created dynamically for short durations. The need for establishing such dynamic short-term bindings clearly arises in language understanding, vision, and reasoning. In fact it arises in any situation that involves reasoning with representations that include the use of variables. Consider the following example involving a simple reasoning step. Assume that a network encodes the rule:

$$\forall(x,y)\ (HIT(x,y) \rightarrow HURT(y))$$

and facts such as HIT(John,Susan) and HIT(Tom,John) among others. HURT(John) clearly follows from the above knowledge by instantiating the rule with the bindings "Tom" for "x" and "John" for "y" and applying modus ponens. If a connectionist network is to infer HURT(John) it must carry out an *equivalent* computation. In generic terms, it must have a way of activating the representation of HURT() given the activation of the representation of HIT(). Furthermore, it must have a mechanism for establishing bindings for variables "x" and "y" in the representation of HIT() and ensuring that the same bindings are induced in the representation of HURT(). The problem gets even more confounded if we wish to chain such inference steps and the bindings have to be propagated faithfully along the chain.

Note that any solution that requires such bindings to be pre-wired is unacceptable: prewiring these bindings would correspond to explicitly representing all possible instantiations of the rule. This is not feasible because the number of instantiations may be too numerous—potentially unbounded. Thus we need the ability to set up these bindings on the fly. As we cannot use links or nodes, it seems natural that we may have to use the temporal dimension to solve this problem, and indeed, in joint work with Venkat Ajjanagadde we have solved an interesting subclass of this problem (see Section 4.2).

The examples discussed above are simple and serve to point out how the restriction that all messages be scalar and the absence of a distinct interpreter, require that representational and inferential issues be coupled. In the next section we look at two connectionist systems that perform fairly complex reasoning tasks over structured information.

4. TWO CONNECTIONIST SYSTEMS FOR SOLVING COMPLEX PROBLEMS

In Section 3, we claimed that working within a connectionist framework would help in identifying classes of limited inference that can be performed with extreme efficiency, and suggest constraints that must be placed on the conceptual structure in order to achieve the desired efficiency. In this section we provide two examples in support of this claim. The connectionist systems mentioned below solve relatively complex tasks with extreme efficiency. The details of these systems are reported elsewhere (Shastri, 1988; Shastri & Ajjanagadde, 1990), here we simply describe the tasks that can be solved by these systems and state some of the constraints that emerge from this work.

4.1. A Connectionist Semantic Memory

Reasoning that may be characterized as *inheritance* and *recognition* (classification) within a semantic network plays a central role in language understanding, visual recognition, and common-sense reasoning. Inheritance and recognition are also significant because humans can perform these inferences effortlessly and extremely fast—to wit language understanding and visual perception in real time. A connectionist semantic memory that can solve the inheritance and recognition problems with the desired degree of efficiency has been proposed in (Shastri, 1988). This work prescribes a mapping from a formal specification of the knowledge to be encoded in a semantic network to a connectionist network that can solve an interesting class of inheritance as well as recognition problems in time proportional to the *depth* of the conceptual hierarchy (i.e., about 10 steps). As the response time is only proportional to the depth of the hierarchy, the system scales gracefully and can deal with large knowledge bases.

In addition to achieving efficient performance, adopting a connectionist approach to the design of a semantic memory lead to two other advantages.

- Attempts at formalizing inheritance and recognition in semantic networks have been confounded by the presence of conflicting property values among related concepts which gives rise to the problems of exceptions and multiple inheritance during inheritance, and partial matching during classification. Several formalizations of inheritance hierarchies have been proposed but none of them offer a uniform treatment of multiple inheritance as well as partial/best matching-based recognition. The connectionist approach suggested an evidential formalization of conceptual knowledge that lead to a principled treatment of exceptions, multiple inheritance, and recognition based on best/partial matching.
- The work resulted in the identification of constraints on the conceptual structure that lead to efficient solutions. One of these constraints specifies that the IS-A relationship between concepts cannot be an arbitrary partial ordering (though it may be more general than a strict hierarchy). Another constraint imposes a uniformity requirement on property value attachments in the conceptual structure and suggests that the conceptual hierarchy must comprise of

several alternate "views" of the underlying concepts if information about property values is to be used efficiently during recognition.

In order to state the above mentioned constraints in more detail we need to describe the representation language in brief.

4.1.1. An Evidential Representation Language. The knowledge in the semantic memory is expressed in terms of a partially ordered set of concepts (i.e., an *IS-A* hierarchy of concepts) together with a partial specification of the property values of these concepts. The set of concepts is referred to as *CSET*, the partial ordering as $\leqslant$, and the information about property values of a concept is specified using the distribution function $\delta(C,P)$ which specifies how instances of C are distributed with respect to the values of property P. For example, δ(*APPLE*,-*has-color*) may be {*RED* = 60,*GREEN* = 55,*YELLOW* = 23...}. Note that δ is only a partial mapping; an agent may not know δ for many concept property pairs. In general, for a given C and P, an agent may know $\delta(C,P)$ only if this information may prove useful in making inferences about C. In terms of a traditional representation language, knowing $\delta(C,P)$ amounts to knowing—explicitly—the values of P associated with C. For convenience we make use of the # notation. Thus, $\#C[P,V]$ equals the number of instances of C that are observed by the agent to have the value V for property P and $\#C[P_1,V_1]$ $[P_2,V_2]\ldots[P_n,V_n]$ = the number of instances of C observed to have the value V_1 for property P_1, . . . and value V_n for property P_n.

In terms of the above notation, the inheritance and recognition problems may be stated as follows:

Inheritance: Given a concept C, a property P, and a set of property values $X = \{V_1,V_2,\ldots V_n\}$, find a V_i that is the most likely value of property P for concept C. In other words, find V_i such that the most likely value of $\#C[P,V_i]$ equals or exceeds the most likely value of $\#C[P,V_j]$ for any other V_j in X. The inheritance problem: C = *BIRD*, P = *mode-of-transportation*, and X = {*FLY*,*SWIM*, *WALK*}, may be paraphrased as: Is the mode of transportation of a bird most likely to be flying, swimming, or walking.

Recognition: Given a set of concepts, $Z = \{C_1,C_2,\ldots C_n\}$, and a description consisting of a set of property value pairs, i.e., *DISCR* = $\{[P_1,V_1],[P_2,V_2],\ldots[P_m,V_m]\}$, find a C_i such that relative to the concepts specified in Z, C_i is the most likely concept described by *DISCR*. In other words, find C_i such that the most likely value of $\#C_i[P_1,V_1],[P_2,V_2],\ldots[P_m,V_m]$ exceeds the most likely value of $\#C_j[P_1,V_1],[P_2,V_2],\ldots[P_m,V_m]$ for any other C_j in Z. If Z = {*APPLE*,-*GRAPE*}, *DISCR* = {[*has-color*,*RED*],[*has-taste*,*SWEET*]} then the recognition problem may be paraphrased as: "Is something red in color and sweet in taste more likely to be an apple or a grape?"

4.1.2. Constraints on the Conceptual Structure. The following terms will be used in stating the constraints:

Relevance: Given a concept C and a property P, a concept B is relevant to C

with respect to P, if and only if i) $C \preccurlyeq B$ (i.e., B lies "above" C in the partial ordering), ii) $\delta(B,P)$ is known (i.e., distribution of instances of B with respect to values of property P is known) and iii) there exists no other concept A between C and B for which $\delta(A,P)$ is known.

Projection: Given a concept C and a property P, $CSET/C,P$, the projection of $CSET$ with respect to C and P, is defined to be the set of all concepts X_i such that $C \preccurlyeq X_i$ and $\delta(X_i,P)$ is known (that is, the projection $CSET/C,P$ is the set of all concepts above C whose distribution with respect to the property values of P is known).

The first constraint on the conceptual structure restricts the nature of the partial ordering of concepts. The restriction is predicated by the nature of property-value attachment in the conceptual structure.

Constraint-1: The conceptual structure must be such that the ordering induced by $\preccurlyeq$ on the projection $CSET/C,P$ results in a tree.

The above constraint does not require that all concepts be organized as a tree. It only requires that given a property P, all concepts that have values of property P explicitly associated with them should form a tree.

Before we state the second constraint we describe a particular conceptual structure that allows this constraint to be expressed in a relatively simple manner. The proposed conceptual structure also (trivially) satisfies Constraint-1 mentioned above.

In the proposed scheme (see Figure 10.4), concepts are organized in a three-tier structure. The topmost tier consists of a pure taxonomy that classifies the domain concepts into several distinct ontological categories. Such categories are derived using the principle of predicability (Keil, 1979; Sommers, 1965), which says that different sorts of things have different sorts of properties applicable to them, and one may classify things according to the predicates that apply, or do not apply, to them. Sommers has argued that ontological categories should form a strict taxonomy. The third or the lowest tier of the conceptual structure consists of instances. The second tier consists of a number of taxonomies called views. The root of a view is a leaf of the ontological tree, and the leaves of a view are instances. Multiple views may be defined with the same leaf of the ontological tree as their root, and therefore, there may be multiple views that have the same instance as one of their leaves. It follows that instances may have multiple parents, however, each parent must lie in a distinct view. The above organization offers advantages permitted by tangled hierarchies by allowing instances to have multiple parents, but retains certain tree like characteristics that help in simplifying the interactions between information represented in the conceptual structure and eventually leads to a parallelizable solution.

Constraint-2: If $\delta(C_i,P)$—i.e., distribution of instances of C_i with respect to property P—is known for some concept C_i in view H, then $\delta(C,P)$ should be known for as many concepts in H as may be necessary to ensure that given any token T_j under H, there exists a concept B_j in H that is relevant to T_j with respect to P.

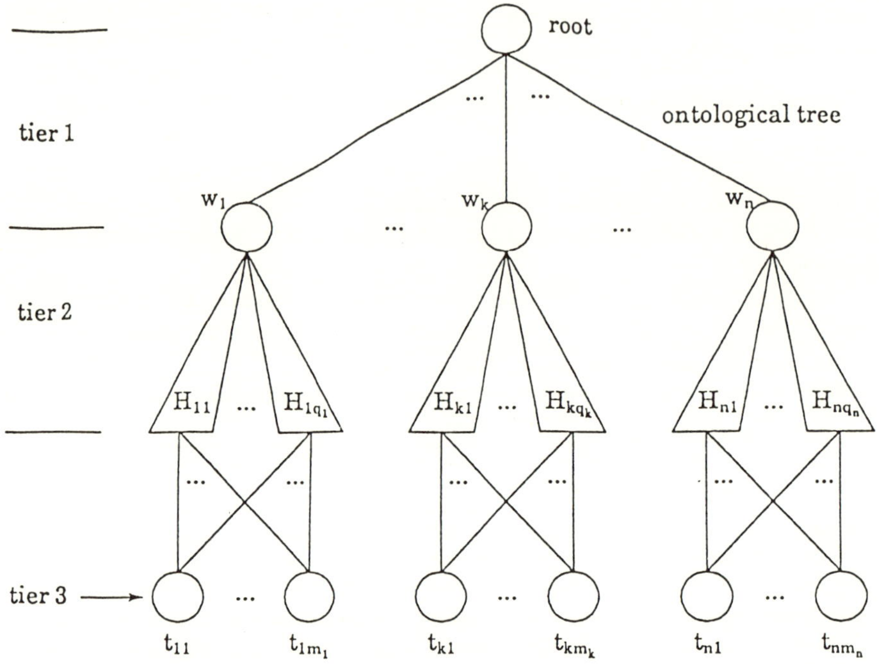

t_{11} ..., t_{nm_n} are tokens.
A token may have multiple parents but at most one parent per view.
w_1, ..., w_n are leaves of the ontological tree.
H_{i1}, ..., H_{iq_i} are q_i views defined over tokens of ontological type w_i.

Figure 10.4.
Multiple Views Organization.

Constraint-2 requires that if information about some property is stored within a view then such information must be stored at a sufficient number of concepts (sufficient in the sense specified in the constraint). This constraint also suggests that if a property value (or a cluster of property values) can be used to discriminate among a set of instances but is of no special significance as far as members outside this set are considered, then one must define a distinct view over this set of instances so that information about this property value may be used efficiently.

If either of the constraints mentioned above is violated, the system will produce anomalous results. These and other issues are discussed at length in (Shastri, 1988).

4.2. Deduction with Multi-Place Predicates and Variable Bindings

Shastri and Ajjanagadde (1990) describe the design of a connectionist system that can perform a broad class of deductive inference involving variables and multi-place predicates with extreme efficiency. Specifically, the system can represent knowledge expressed in the form of *rules* and *facts* and determine whether a given *query* follows from the facts and rules encoded in the system. The system responds to queries in *optimal* time, that is, the time taken to draw an inference is just proportional to the *length* of the proof and is independent of the size of the knowledge base.

As discussed earlier, reasoning with rules involving multi-place predicates and variables requires that the system be capable of maintaining and propagating variable bindings. The proposed system solves this problem in the following manner. Reasoning in the system corresponds to a transient but systematic propagation of *rhythmic* patterns of activation, where each *phase* in the rhythmic pattern corresponds to an object involved in the reasoning process and where variable bindings are represented as the *in-phase* (synchronous) firing of appropriate nodes. The system is described in detail in (Shastri & Ajjanagadde, 1990).

Rules in the system are assumed to be sentences of the form

$$\forall x_1,\ldots,x_m\ [P_1(\ldots) \wedge P_2(\ldots)\ldots\wedge P_n(\ldots) \rightarrow \exists z_1,\ldots z_l\ Q(\ldots)]$$

where arguments of P_i's are subsets of $\{x_1,x_2,\ldots x_m\}$, while the arguments of Q consist of any number of arguments from among the x_i's, any number of constants, and single occurrences of existentially quantified arguments.

Facts are assumed to be partial or complete instantiations of predicates. In other words, facts may be viewed as atomic formulae of the form $P(t_1,t_2\ldots t_k)$ where t_i's are either constants or distinct, existentially quantified variables. The system may also be extended so that the t_i's may refer to concepts in an *IS-A* hierarchy. A query has the same form as a fact. Some examples of rules, facts, and queries follow:

Rules:

$\forall x,y,z$ *give*$(x,y,z) \rightarrow$ *own*(y,z)
$\forall x,y$ *own*$(x,y) \rightarrow$ *can-sell*(x,y)
$\forall x$ *omnipresent*$(x) \rightarrow \forall y,t$ *present*(x,y,t)
$\forall x,y$ *born*$(x,y) \rightarrow \exists t$ *present*(x,y,t)
$\forall x$ *triangle*$(x) \rightarrow$ *number-of-sides*$(x,3)$
$\forall x,y$ *sibling*$(x,y) \wedge$ *born-at-the-same-time*$(x,y) \rightarrow$ *twins*(x,y)

Facts:
*give(John,Mary,Book*1); John gave Mary Book1.
*give(x,Susan,Ball*2); Someone gave Susan Ball2.
omnipresent(x); There exists someone who is omnipresent.
*triangle(A*3); A3 is a triangle.

Queries:

1. *own(Mary,Book*1); Does Mary own Book1?
2. *own(x,y)*; Does someone own something?
3. *can-sell(x,Ball*2); Can someone sell Ball2?
4. *present(x,Northpole,* 1/1/89); Was someone present at the north pole on 1/1/89?
5. *number-of-sides(A*3,4); Does A3 have 4 sides?
6. *can-sell(Mary,Ball*2); Can Mary sell Ball2?

All queries except 5 and 6 follow from the rules and facts and will be answered in the affirmative by the system.

Figure 10.5 illustrates the nature of the network encoding by depicting how the following knowledge is encoded:

- $\forall x,y,z\ [give(x,y,z) \rightarrow own(y,z)]$
- $\forall x,y\ [buy(x,y) \rightarrow own(x,y)]$
- $\forall x,y\ [own(x,y) \rightarrow can\text{-}sell(x,y)]$
- *give(John,Mary,Book*1)
- *buy(John,x)*
- *own(Mary,Ball*1)

The encoding shown in Figure 10.5 makes use of two types of nodes, namely, ρ-btu nodes (depicted as circles) and τ-and nodes (depicted as pentagons). When a ρ-btu node becomes active, it produces an oscillatory output in the form of a pulse train that has a period π and pulse width ω. The timing (or the *phase* of the output produced by a ρ-btu node) is precisely governed by the phase of the input to the node. τ-and nodes also oscillate with the same frequency as ρ-btu nodes except they become active only if they receive uninterrupted activation over a whole period of oscillation. Furthermore, the width of the pulses produced by these nodes is comparable to π.

Each constant in the domain is encoded by a ρ-btu node. An *n*-ary predicate is encoded by a pair of τ-and nodes and *n* ρ-btu nodes. One of the τ-and nodes is referred to as the *enabler* and the other as the *collector*. As a matter of convention, an *enabler* always points upwards while a *collector* always points downwards.

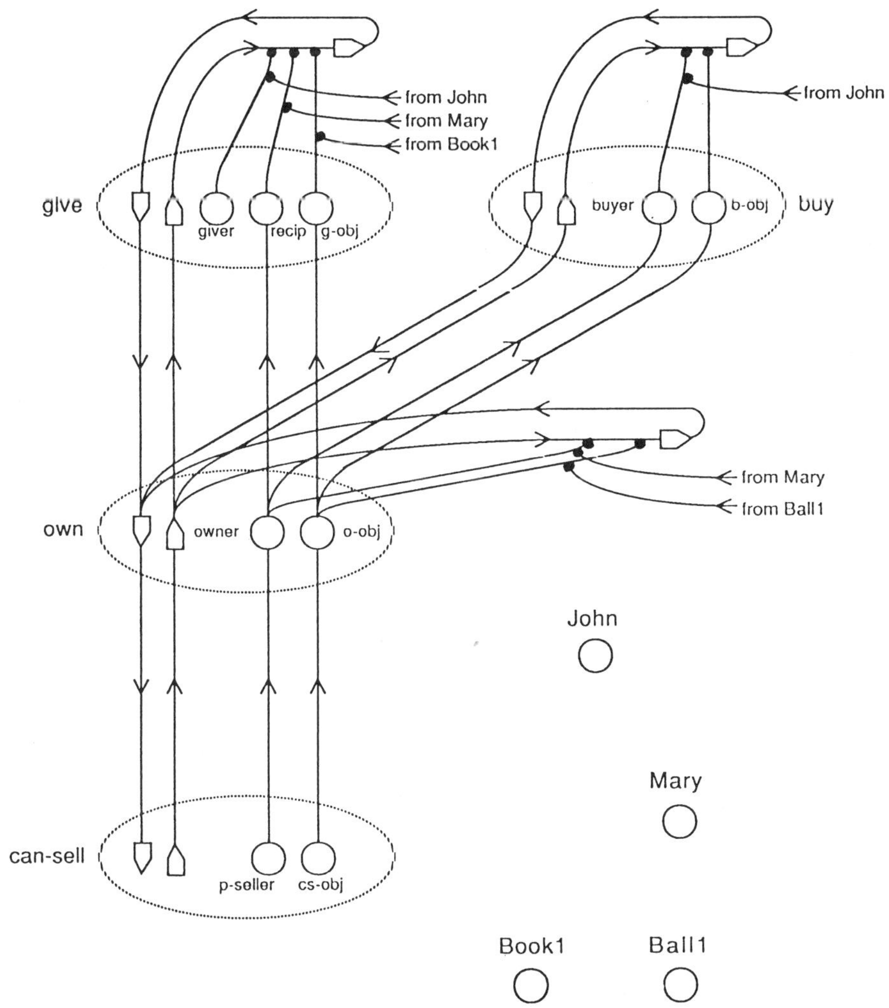

Figure 10.5.
An example encoding of rules and facts.

A fact is encoded using a τ-and node that receives an input from the enabler of the associated predicate. This input is modified by inhibitory links from argument nodes of the associated predicate. If an argument is bound to a constant in the fact then the modifier input from such an argument node is in turn modified by an inhibitory link from the appropriate constant node. The output of the τ-and node is connected to the *collector* of the associated predicate (refer to the encoding of the fact *give(John,Mary,Book1)* in Figure 10.5). Inhibitory links are depicted using a dark blob. If a link terminates on another link with a blob it means that a signal propagating down the former inhibits or blocks a signal propagating down the latter.

A rule is encoded by connecting the *collector* of the antecedent predicate to the *collector* of the consequent predicate, the *enabler* of the consequent predicate to the *enabler* of the antecedent predicate, and by connecting the argument nodes of the consequent predicate to the argument nodes of the antecedent predicate in accordance with the correspondence between these arguments specified in the rule (refer to Figure 10.5).

In the proposed system, reasoning is the transient but systematic propagation of *rhythmic* patterns of activation, where each *phase* in the rhythmic pattern corresponds to an object involved in the reasoning process, where variable bindings are represented as the *in-phase* firing of appropriate nodes, where facts are subnetworks that act as temporal pattern matchers, and where rules are interconnection patterns that cause the propagation and transformation of rhythmic patterns of activation. A detailed explanation of the encoding and the computations performed by nodes in the network are beyond the scope of this chapter, but may be found in (Shastri & Ajjanagadde, 1990).

If the argument structure of the rules satisfies certain constraints specified below, the system responds to queries in *optimal* time, that is, the time taken to draw an inference is just proportional to the *length* of the proof.

Figure 10.6 illustrates how the system processes the question *can-sell(Mary,Book1)* ('Can Mary sell Book1'). This query is posed to the system by providing inputs to the constants *Mary* and *Book1*, the arguments *p-seller, cs-obj* and *e:can-sell* (the *enabler* of the query predicate *can-sell*) as shown. Notice that *Mary* and *p-seller* receive *in-phase* activation and so do *Book1* and *cs-obj*. The eventual activation of *c:can-sell,* the *collector* of the query predicate *can-sell,* indicates that the answer to the query is *yes*.

4.3. Constraints on Rules and Derivations

The first constraint on the backward reasoning system is that only a bounded number of argument bindings may be specified in a query. A biologically, as well as psychologically, plausible estimate of this number appears to be about seven.

A second constraint is that a variable occurring in multiple argument positions in the *antecedent* of a rule that participates in the derivation of a query, should also appear in the consequent of the rule and get bound during the reasoning process.

In a restricted and simple version of the system (the one illustrated in Figure 10.5) any given predicate may only be instantiated once during the process of answering a query. This restriction only applies to dynamic or 'run-time' in-

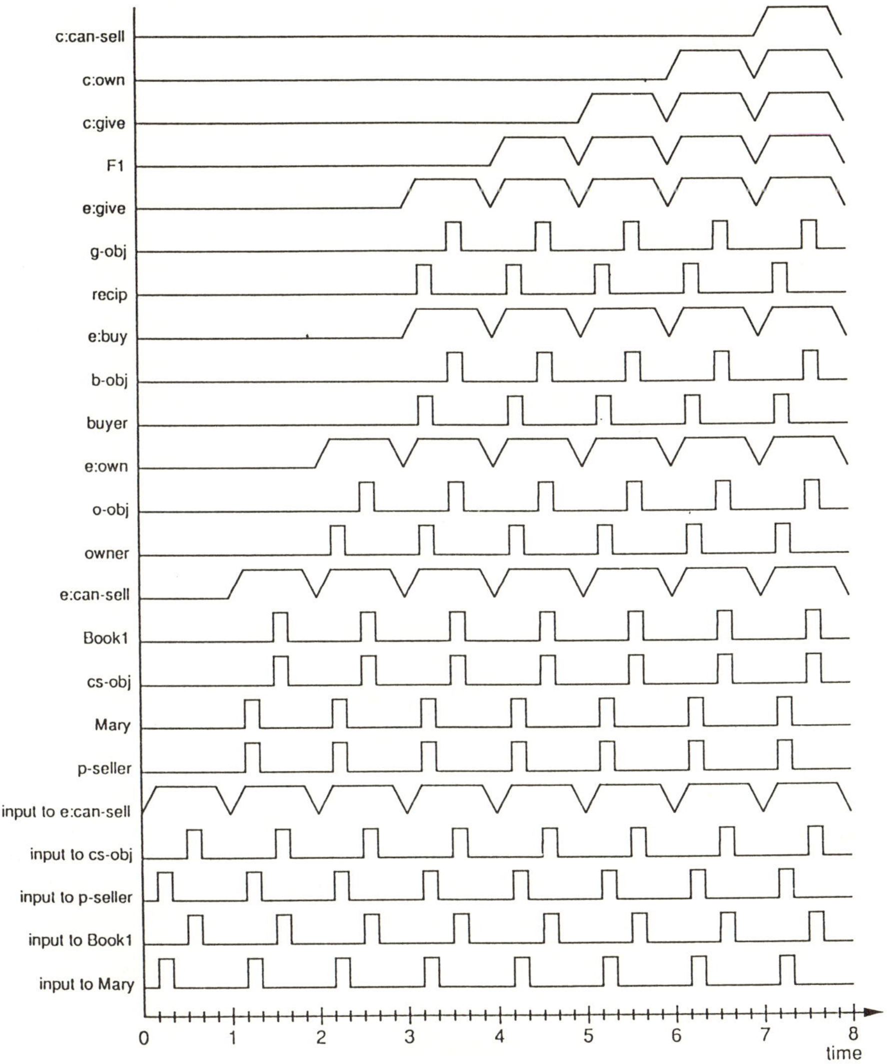

Figure 10.6.
Activation trace for the query *can-sell(Mary,Bookl)?*

stantiations of inferred facts pertaining to the same predicate. Any number of long-term facts pertaining to a predicate may be encoded in the network. The above restriction may be relaxed using a more elaborate encoding scheme so that a predicate may be instantiated several (but bounded) number of times (refer to Shastri & Ajjanagadde, 1990).

We believe that the above constraints admit an interesting class of inference, and it is significant that these inferences may be drawn in optimal time—that is, in time proportional to the length of the shortest derivation.

4.4. Extensions

The system described above is a *backward reasoner*. The same representation and binding mechanisms can be used to build a system that can perform *forward reasoning*, that is, make predictions based on its long-term knowledge (rules) and newly available facts. The reasoning and expressive power of the system can also be enhanced by interfacing it with a semantic network or as *IS-A* hierarchy. The rules in the reasoning system described above are hard logical rules. The system can also be modified to encode probabilistic rules by making use of link weights. In such a system, the weight on links between the *enablers* and *collectors* of antecedent and consequent predicates will encode the strength of rules.

5. CONCLUSION

We have tried to establish that connectionism provides an appropriate computational architecture for addressing problems in knowledge representation and inference. We have also tried to establish that connectionism should not be viewed merely as an implementation paradigm. For adopting the connectionist paradigm forces us to revise many of our views about representation and reasoning. The most significant revisions stem from the fact that a connectionist system must operate without an interpreter. There is clear evidence that some progress is being made in applying connectionist ideas to well defined problems in AI. The results thus far are promising and bolster our belief that connectionism will play a key role in the development of a detailed and computationally effective model of intelligence.

REFERENCES

Cottrell, G.W. (1985). *A connectionist approach to word-sense disambiguation*. Doctoral Dissertation, Department of Computer Science, University of Rochester.

Derthick, M. (1988). *Mundane reasoning by parallel constraint satisfaction* (Tech. Rep. CMU-CS-88-182). Pittsburgh, PA: Department of Computer Science, Carnegie Mellon University.

Feldman, J.A., Fanty, M.A., & N.H. Goddard. (1988, March). Computing with structured neural networks. *IEEE Computer, 21*(3), 91–103.

Hayes, P.J. (1983). *The second naive physics manifesto* (Cognitive Science Tech. Rep. URCS-10). Rochester, NY: University of Rochester.

Keil, F.C. (1979). *Semantic and conceptual development.* Cambridge, MA: Harvard University Press.

Rumelhart, D.E., & McClelland, J.L. (Eds.). (1986). *Parallel distributed processing, Vol 1: Explorations in the microstructure of cognition.* Cambridge, MA: Bradford Books/MIT Press.

Shastri, L. (1988). *Semantic networks: An evidential formalization and its connectionist realization.* London: Pitman/Los Altos: Morgan Kaufmann.

Shastri, L., & Ajjanagadde, V. (1990). *From simple associations to systematic reasoning: A connectionist encoding of rules, variables, and dynamic bindings* (Rep. MS-CIS-90-05). Philadelphia, PA: Computer & Information Science Department, University of Pennsylvania. *(Submitted to Behavioral and Brain Sciences).*

Sommers, F. (1965). Predicability. In M. Black (Ed.), *Philosophy of America.* Ithaca, NY: Cornell University Press.

11 Steps Toward Knowledge-Intensive Connectionist Learning*

Joachim Diederich

1. INTRODUCTION

1.1. Data- and Knowledge-Intensive Learning

An important classification in symbolic machine learning is the distinction between data- and knowledge-intensive learning methods. Data-intensive learning techniques require a set of training examples which is used to guide and constrain the search for possible generalizations. The notion of similarity-based generalization is used by Mitchell, Keller, and Kedar-Cabelli (1986) to refer to learning methods which search for similarities among positive examples, and differences between positive and negative examples in a training set.

The method described in this chapter is knowledge-intensive, that is, the technique uses knowledge which is already learned or built in. The motivation of this work is to explore connectionist learning methods which can use already available and structured knowledge to facilitate concept learning.

The built-in knowledge base is a connectionist semantic network which is used to recognize a single example. Recruitment learning is applied to build a new conceptual structure and to connect it to the existing knowledge representation system (constructive generalization). The new conceptual structure will improve the system's capability to recognize instances as described by the single example.

The kind of learning outlined in this paper can be described by the following "real world" example: a person sees a car and forms the hypothesis that this car

* Many thanks to Michael Braverman, Jerome Feldman, Wolfgang Klas, Bernd Neumann, and Lokendra Shastri for comments on earlier versions of this chapter, and to Alix Collison for her help in the preparation of the final version.

is a "Porsche." The hypothesis is verified by comparing the features of the perceived car with typical features of "Porsches." The person realizes that this is a special kind of "Porsche" with additional features which are not owned by "Porsches" in general. The new knowledge about this special kind of "Porsche" is added to the general knowledge about cars from this manufacturer.

1.2. Organization of the Chapter

This chapter is organized as follows. First, a brief introduction to connectionist recruitment learning is given. Second, the architecture of the built-in knowledge base is introduced, including a brief description of a simple form of connectionist inheritance. Essential parts of the learning algorithm are outlined next, including a formal description of the method. An example of knowledge-intensive connectionist learning is given, experimental results for the learning algorithm are presented and possible methods for the learning of multiple concepts and concepts with disjunctive attributes are outlined. Finally, the relation between the connectionist learning technique presented here and knowledge-intensive learning in symbolic artificial intelligence is discussed.

2. CONNECTIONIST RECRUITMENT LEARNING

The connectionist learning approach realized here applies a process for the recruitment of new units and assemblies of units to represent new conceptual information. In recruitment learning, a network consists of two classes of units:

- *Committed Units*. These are units which already represent some sort of information or function, that is, conceptual information. Committed units are connected to other committed units and their simultaneous activation must represent a meaningful state of the network. Committed units are also connected to
- *Free Units*. These form a kind of "primordial network" (Shastri, 1985) and are connected to other free units as well as to committed units.

Recruitment learning is the strengthening of the connection(s) between a group of committed units and one or more free units. This results in the transformation of free units into committed units. Shastri (1985) uses the term "chunking" if "a free node becomes committed and functions as a chunking node for the cluster (of committed units)—that is, the activation of node in the cluster results in the activation of the chunking node and conversely, the activation of the chunking node activates all the nodes in the cluster." It is possible to view the subnetwork of committed units embedded in the network of free units. Constructive generalization means acquiring units from the pool of free units.

3. THE ARCHITECTURE OF THE CONNECTIONIST KNOWLEDGE REPRESENTATION

The knowledge base is constructed by compilation from a symbolic representation language or by previous learning. The built-in representation system used *space,* and the *space of free* units. The concept space contains all learned or built-in concepts. The attribute space contains the possible values of attributes (called features). The instance space consists of single units, connected to concept units and feature units in the attribute space. The free space consists of uncommitted units which are recruited during learning.

All spaces are physically fully connected, that is, each unit is connected to all other units in the network. A 0-valued weight means "no association." Weights represent the strength of association. Throughout this chapter only the weight change between free space and concept space, and free space and attribute space is significant.

3.1. The Concept Space

The chosen representation of the concept space is similar to the one in Cottrell (1985).

The representation consists of 3-unit subnetworks for the representation of each concept (called "triple subnetworks" or "3-unit networks"), including the affirmative concept unit, the negative concept unit, and an additional intermediate unit. The affirmative and the negative unit have excitatory links to the intermediate unit, and the intermediate unit has inhibitory links to the affirmative and the negative unit. The intermediate unit guarantees that the subnetwork converges to one of three stable states (see Cottrell, 1985). Either the affirmative unit or the negative unit is on, or all units are off. See Figure 11.1 for an explanation.[1]

Subnetworks are connected in a hierarchy or heterarchy, reflecting the inheritance path. There are links from each affirmative unit to more general affirmative units, and from each negative unit to more specific negative units.

Units of the concept space are connected to units in the attribute space. Concepts are thereby associated with their properties. Inheritance can be described by the following example: an affirmative concept unit A is activated by some input. If A is strong enough, it becomes the winner in the 3-unit subnetwork of the concept space. It will therefore activate all units in the attribute space associated with A and the more general unit B. B itself will also activate its properties in the attribute space; therefore additional feature units become "on."

This process corresponds to simple inheritance in semantic networks. While

[1] It should be noted that the same effect can be achieved by a mutual inhibitory link with delay of propagation between two units only.

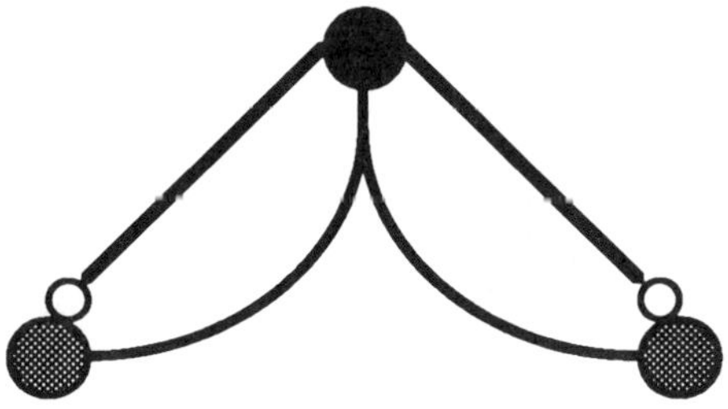

Figure 11.1.
A triple unit subnetwork.

the spreading activation process continues, more and more general concept units are activated and more and more relevant feature units are turning on. Multiple inheritance works with the same advantages and disadvantages as in standard semantic networks (see Touretzky, 1986, for examples).

Exceptions that would realize a nonmonotonic style of reasoning are built in by additional inhibitory links which modify the flow of activation from more general concept units to units in the attribute space. These links modify the inheritance process. More specific units can modify the effect that links from more general concept units have on units in the attribute space. So the connections between more specific concepts and their attributes become dominant. This realizes a basic assumption of semantic networks: the more specific should dominate the more general.

3.2. The Attribute Space

The attribute space is a network divided into subnets and each subnet contains the possible values of a single attribute. Subnets are a variant of "winner take all" (WTA) networks which use mutual inhibition (see Feldman & Ballard, 1982). Currently there is no explicit representation of an attribute itself; each subnetwork represents an attribute implicitly. Whenever a unit in a subnetwork of the attribute space is "on," the corresponding attribute is implicitly given.

In order to maintain likelihood information, a modification of WTA networks is used which adjusts competition among units according to the total input to a WTA network. This kind of approach is sometimes called "winner take more" (WTM) or "multiple winner take all" network. Our approach here is similar to the "network region" model in Chun, Bookman, and Afshartous (1987): Each

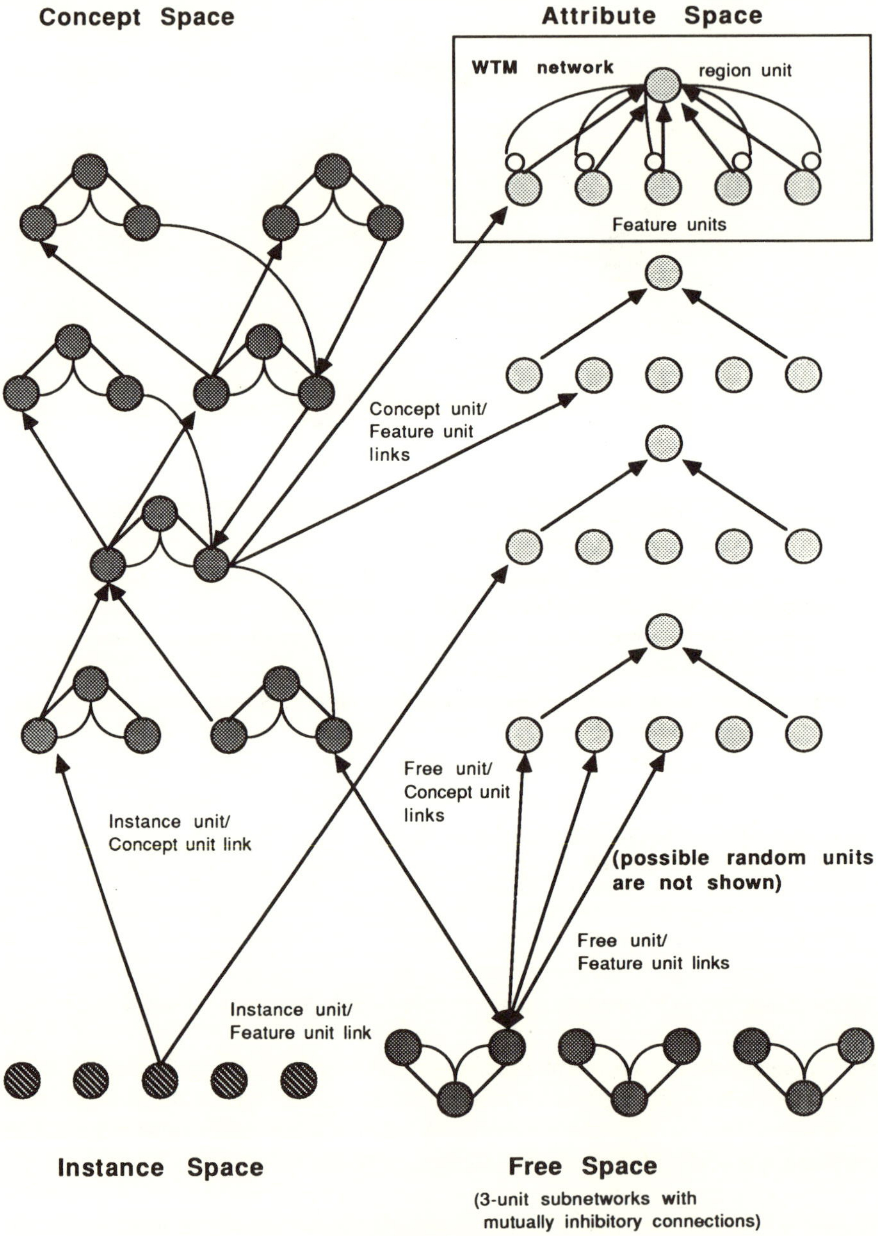

Figure 11.2.
The architecture of the system (not all links are shown).

unit in a WTM network receives the average of the total WTM network input as an inhibition signal, the result is the restriction of the dominance of winner units. All competing units with an input above average might stay active.

The total WTM network input is computed indirectly using the output values of all units in the WTM subnetwork. For each WTM network, an additional unit is built which receives the output of all units in the WTM net and computes the average. This additional unit, called "region unit," has inhibitory links to the units in the WTM net. The average signal is propagated to the WTM units via these inhibitory links.

3.3. The Instance Space

Instances are single units connected to concept units. Activation of an instance unit is followed by the activation of a concept unit. If an instance has additional properties or properties which are different from the attributes of the associated concept, explicit links to feature units in the attribute space are necessary. Presenting a training example to the system is done by clamping on an instance unit which activates its concept unit and additional units in the attribute space, but only if this training instance owns features not part of the concept definition.

3.4. The Free Space

The fourth space consists of free units. Parts of these free units become committed during recruitment learning. Free units are connected like concept units (triple subnetworks). The subnetworks of the free space are connected as a strict WTA network which allows only one unit of a triple subnetwork as a winner unit (with the single exception of the intermediate unit) while none of the other subnetworks in the free space has an active unit. Furthermore, there are bidirectional links between each feature unit in the attribute space and each free unit, and also between each affirmative or negative concept unit and each affirmative or negative free unit. These links initially have small random weights and are subject to weight change during recruitment learning.

Free units receive their own output as a strong positive reinforcing signal and the output of the competing free units as negative reinforcement (inhibition). This is similar to the competitive reinforcement learning in Lynne (1987). If a training example is presented to the system, the high activity in the attribute space will lead to nonspecific activation of the free space. The free unit with the highest potential will receive this activation (among others), and will thereby become a clear winner, in part through self-reinforcement. In the case of random connectivity (this connection pattern is described below), the unit with the strongest connections receives most of the activation and becomes the winner unit which is committed during recruitment learning.

This part of the learning process is similar to competitive learning (cf. Rumelhart & Zipser, 1985; Grossberg, 1987) where only the winner unit gets the chance to adjust weights. However, the weight change is different in competitive learning because there is a redistribution of weights over the input lines of a winner unit. In our approach, each input link of a newly committed unit becomes adjusted independently of other input-lines and features of the weight-vector. The weight change is based on the input-signal and the potential of the receiving unit (see Section 5).

Two patterns of connectivity are explored between concept space and free space, and attribute space and free space. The first case is full connectivity. There are links between each free unit and each concept/feature unit (with the exception of the intermediate units; furthermore, affirmative free units are only connected with affirmative concept units and negative free units are only connected to negative concept units).

Obviously, full connectivity is expensive when many free units, concept units and feature units are used. Random connections are therefore used as the second connectivity pattern. Additional random units are intermediate units between attribute space and free space. There is full connectivity between attribute space and random units, and there are random links between random units and units in the free space. During network construction, there is only a 50 percent chance for a link between a random unit and a free unit. As in the first case, each affirmative and negative free unit has links to each feature unit.

4. KNOWLEDGE-INTENSIVE LEARNING IN A STRUCTURED CONNECTIONIST SYSTEM

The following sources of information are used in our system: the *domain theory,* which is the total knowledge base minus the free space; the *goal concept,* which is an affirmative concept as part of the concept space; and the *training example,* which is a set of attribute/value pairs, describing an instance of the goal concept. The feature units in the attribute space which represent the values of an attribute as part of the training example are continuously activated by an instance unit. The *new concept* is defined in terms of all attribute/value pairs of the training example and attributes from the domain theory. Furthermore, we define as an operationality criterion that *mediated* inferences have to be transformed into *immediate* inferences, that is, an inference based on property values can be drawn in one inference step instead of a more complex chain of inferences (see Hollbach, 1988, for details). As an additional technical restriction we assume here that each attribute has only one individual value.

The algorithm has two parts, "Recognition" and "Constructive Generalization," which are *conceptual distinctions* and are not separated during processing:

Recognition

1. Let the instance unit which represents the training example activate all connected feature units in the attribute space.
2. Clamp on the goal concept unit in the concept space.
3. Run the total network until the pattern of activation stabilizes.

Constructive Generalization:

4. Recruit new triple structures for representing the new concept definition.
5. Run the total network to allow weight changes.

During recognition, an activation pattern is built in the attribute space which includes features of the training example necessary to describe the goal concept. In phase 3 of the algorithm above, less specific features from more general superconcepts of the goal concept also become active. A strong decay process is used in the concept space to restrict the influence of these less specific features. Strongly activated units represent features of the training example and the goal concept. Convergence is successful, if (a) all network regions in the attribute space (all WTM networks) have clear winners, and (b) the total network stabilizes.

The constructive generalization process is simple. The wiring between free and attribute space has been done already, but all weights have small random values. The weighted connections between the new concept unit and features represented by feature units in the attribute space are installed by using a modified Hebb rule with slow weight change. Because of this weight change rule, the new concept will get strong connections to features of the goal concept and/or the training instance, and weak connections to more general concepts on higher levels than the goal concept.

Furthermore, the new concept has weighted connections to units in the concept space. There will be a strong connection between the newly recruited unit and the goal-concept unit because the new concept unit is the winner unit in the free space and the goal-concept unit is clamped on. The new concept unit has small weighted connections to superconcepts of the goal concept also, but the decay process in the concept space is used to restrict the increase of these connections. The connection between the new concept unit and the goal-concept unit will be dominant.

Step 5 of the algorithm is used to allow these weight changes. Please note that it is the weight change rule which restricts the generalization process.

5. A FORMAL DESCRIPTION OF THE METHOD

We define the system in roughly the same way as Shastri (1985, p.56). However, the objective of this work is to define *recruitment learning* for a structured connectionist knowledge representation system.

The system is specified on two related levels: (a) on the conceptual level where generic concepts denote classes of individuals with common features and individuals represent instances of these concepts, and (b) on the network level units are organized in sets called "spaces" and interact via weighted links. Because we are using a localist approach, in most cases conceptual entities are represented by a single unit. However, it is important to distinguish between the conceptual level and the network realization. In contrast to similar approaches, such as Shastri (1985), Derthick (1987), and Touretzky and Geva (1987), the focus of attention here is on the enlargement of the network through recruitment learning.

The following notation is used throughout this section: capital letters (C, A,...F) denote sets. Lower-case letters denote individual members of sets.

5.1. The Conceptual Level

On the conceptual level the model is a n-tuple $W = \{C, A, V, I, F, \lambda, \alpha, \leftarrow\}$, where C is the set of all concepts, A is the set of all attributes, V is the set of all possible values of all elements in A (features), I is the set of all instances, F is the set of all free, uncommitted entities which become committed during learning, λ is a mapping from C to the power set of A, α is a mapping from A to the power set of V, and $\leftarrow$ is a partial ordering defined on C.

Furthermore, we define the function $\beta(c)$ which returns all values of all attributes of the concept $c \in C$:

$$\beta(c) = \cup\alpha(a_i)\ \forall a_i,\ a_i \in \lambda(c)$$

For each $c \in C$, $\lambda(c)$ is the subset of A which is owned by c; e.g. λ(car) might be {size, color}. For each $a \in A$, $\alpha(a)$ is the subset of V that consists of the values of a; e.g. α(color) might be {yellow, blue} and α(size) might be {big, medium, small}. If λ(car) = {size, color}, then β(car) = {big, medium, small, yellow, blue}.

C has a partial ordering, organized as a taxonomic heterarchy: if c_2 and c_3 subsume c_1:$(c_1 \leftarrow c_2) \wedge (c_1 \leftarrow c_3)$, then $\beta(c_1)$ contains $\beta(c_2) \cup \beta(c_3)$. $c_{gc} \in C$ is the *goal-concept*.

Free entities have no attributes and values, $\forall f_j,\ f_j \in F$: $\beta(f_j) = \{\}$.

In our system, $i_e \in I$ denotes the training example. i_e must be an instance of the goal-concept c_{gc}, i_e therefore inherits all attributes and values from c_{gc} as described above. Moreover, i_e might have attributes and values not shared by c_{gc}, but $\beta(c_{gc})$ is at least a subset of $\beta(i_e)$.

Recruitment learning means the transformation of free entities into concepts: $f_j \in F \wedge \neg(f_j \in C) ==> \neg(f_j \in F) \wedge f_j \in C$. The operator $==>$ refers to the process of transforming a free entity into a concept. In other words, $\beta(f_j) = \{\}$ is transformed into $\beta(f_j) = \beta(i_e) \cup \beta(c_{gc})$ after recruitment, where we note that $\beta(c_{gc})$ contains $\beta(c_n)$ when $c_{gc} \leftarrow c_n$. Note that f_j gets only weak connections to entities in $\beta(c_{gc} \leftarrow c_n)$ because these are accessible by inheritance.

5.2. The Network Level

On the network level the model is a n-tuple of elements $M = \{U, W\}$. U is the set of all units in the network and W is the set of all weights.

Members of U are sorted into four classes of elements which make up U. U^c denotes the class of all *concept units,* nodes which represent a generic concept: U^c_i represents $c_i \in C$. If U^c_i represents c_{gc} and $p_{gc} \in [0, 1000]$ is the potential of U^c_i, and if $(c_{gc} \leftarrow c_n)$, then $p_n < p_{gc}$ where p_n is the potential of c_n, the super-concept of the goal-concept. On the implementation level, this is guaranteed by the fixed weighted link between c_{gc} and c_n. Furthermore, U^v is the class of all *feature units* in the attribute space with U^v_i representing $v_i \in V$. U^i is the class of all *instance units* in the attribute space with U^i_i representing $i_i \in I$. The fourth and final class of units, U^f, consists of *free units* with U^f_i representing $f_i \in F$.

Each weight w_i is an integer $\in [-1000, 1000]$. Positive associated units have weights $w_i > 0$, negative associated units have weights $w_i < 0$, a zero weight means no association. Weights in both directions between all U^f and all U^v have initially small random values $w_i \in [0, 100]$.

We are particularly interested in the distribution of weights after recruitment, i.e. the distribution of weights between the newly recruited unit U^f_i and all $\beta(f_i)$. U^f_i always gets a link with maximum strength to U^c_{gc}, because U^f_i has a high potential as the winner of the competition among the free units, and because U^c_{gc} is clamped on.

The following weight change rule is applied (inputs and potentials are integers):

$$\Delta w_{ij} = \begin{array}{l} \text{if } (i_i >= 0 \wedge w_{ij} < p_j \wedge w_{ij} < i_i \wedge w_{ij} < \max) \text{ then } +1 \\ \text{else if } (w_{ij} > \min) \text{ then } -1 \end{array}$$

where i_i is the ith input to the receiving unit, p_j is the potential of the receiving unit, *max* is an upper limit for weights (= 990), and *min* is a lower limit for weights (= −990).
The simulations were done with this modified version:

$$\Delta w_{ij} = \begin{array}{l} \text{if } (i_i >= 250 \wedge w_{ij} < p_j \wedge w_{ij} < i_i \wedge w_{ij} < \max) \text{ then } +10 \\ \text{if } (i_i >= 100 \wedge w_{ij} < p_j \wedge w_{ij} < i_i \wedge w_{ij} < \max) \text{ then } +1 \\ \text{else if } (w_{ij} > \min) \text{ then } -1 \end{array}$$

The increase of weights depends on the receiving unit's potential and on the amount of the received input. Furthermore, the upper limit for this increase is the lower value of the potential p_j and the amount of transmitted activation i_i.

This weight change rule guarantees the appropriate distribution of weights from U^f_i to all U^v_i which represents $\beta(f_i)$; i.e. the newly recruited unit gets strong weights to highly activated elements in $\beta(f_i)$, medium weights to medium activated elements in $\beta(f_i)$, and smaller weights to weakly activated elements of $\beta(f_i)$.

U^f_j, representing $f_j \in F$, is the winner unit in the free space and is transformed in a new concept unit. U^f_j has links to all U^v, and all U^v have links to U^f_j in case of full connectivity between attribute and free space. Let p_i be the potential of U^v_i and p_j the potential of U^f_j. w_{ij} is the weight of the connecting link between U^v_i and U^f_j. According to the weight change rule above, $(w_{ij} < p_i) \wedge (w_{ij} < p_j)$. This means U^f_j gets stronger links to properties owned by the goal-concept than to properties of super-concepts of the goal-concept, because these are less activated.

6. AN EXAMPLE

The goal-concept (**Porsche**) has two features, **fast** and **imported.** The training example (**Porsche-914**) has four features: **fast, imported, yellow** and **owner: michael.** Furthermore, there are two features owned by the immediate and single super-concept (**Car**) of the goal-concept: **engine** and **gearbox.**

We have now specified a simple example as a training instance, a goal concept and an extremely simple domain. Still missing is the criterion for the new concept: the new concept definition must be expressed in terms of structural attributes of the example, the goal-concept or super-concepts of the goal-concept.

The training example can easily be recognized as an instance of **Porsche** because of its features **fast** and **imported.** Additional features of the training example can be inferred by use of the domain theory after a successful recognition.

In full detail the method works as follows. First, the recognition of the training example is done. The feature units **fast** and **imported** receive strong activation from the instance and goal-concept unit which causes high potentials for these units. **Yellow** and **owner:michael** are stimulated by the instance unit only and get medium activation. The affirmative concept unit **Porsche** stimulates the concept unit **Car** which in turn activates other feature units in the attribute space: **engine** and **gearbox.**

The features of the example receive continuous activation from the unit representing the instance. After 50 updates of the entire network, all units in the concept space are subject to a decay process. Because of this decay process, the concept unit **Car** looses activation. Note that there is only one source of stimulation for **Car,** namely the goal concept **Porsche.** The same happens to the feature units **engine** and **gearbox** in the attribute space, because these units receive their activation from the super-concept of the goal-concept.

After the decay process becomes effective, the second step of the method continues with the recruitment of the new structure. As mentioned above, triplets of units for the representation of concepts are already built in the free space. In the beginning, the connections have small random weights. The increase of weights between the new concept structure and features represented by active units in the attribute space is implemented by using the Hebb rule described above. The new concept therefore gets *strong connections* to the feature units **fast** and **imported,** and *small- or medium-weighted connections* to the feature units **engine** and **gearbox,** as well as to **yellow** and **owner:michael,** features of the training example which received no activation from the concept space.

The learning process is finished after installation of the weighted links. The new concept definition contains features of the training example as well as inferred features from domain knowledge. The new concept definition will improve the system's ability to recognize examples similar to the training example because of the distribution of weights between the new concept and its features in the attribute space.

7. EXPERIMENTAL RESULTS

The example above was tested and implemented by use of the Rochester Connectionist Simulator (RCS, Goddard, Lynne, & Mintz, 1987). Simulations were done using fair asynchrony (units are randomly chosen for update; in our simulations, each unit was updated at least once after 243 steps). See Diederich (1988) for experiments on recruitment learning with random connections.

7.1. The Generation of a Stable Activation Pattern in the Attribute Space

Figure 11.3 shows the development of the potentials of feature units in the attribute space during the first 200 steps (full connectivity). Note the effect of the decay process after 50 update steps. Features such as **engine** and **gearbox** lose activation after 50 steps because they are connected to concepts higher than the goal concept in the inheritance heterarchy. The results show a small oscillation in the potentials of the feature units caused by the ongoing competition of the winner units in the attribute space.

It is possible to distinguish between three classes of units in between the

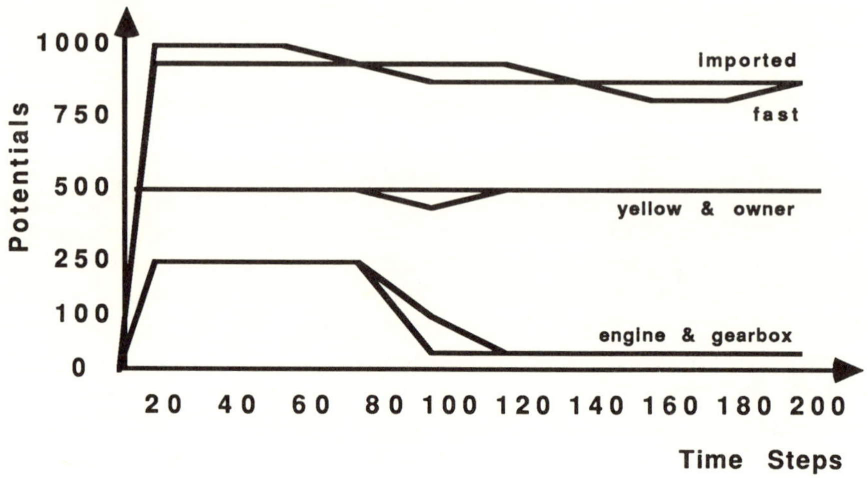

Figure 11.3.
The generation of a stable activation pattern in the attribute space.

attribute space after the network becomes stable. The first class consists of feature units which are stimulated through the instance unit *and* units in the concept space. These units get a high potential, and the new concept unit gets strong connections to these units. **Fast** and **imported** are members of the first class in our example. Members of the second class of feature units receive activation from the instance unit only. These have medium activation. The third class of feature units receives activation from super-concepts of the goal-concept. These have low activation and the new concept unit gets links with low weights to these units (**engine** and **gearbox** in the example).

7.2. Weight Developments Between a Newly Recruited Free Unit and the Attribute Space After the Presentation of a Single Example

Figure 11.4 shows the weight development between the newly committed unit and feature units in the attribute space when both spaces are fully connected. Note the decrease of some weights after 50 updates which is caused by the decay process in the concept space.

It makes sense to investigate recruitment learning when several examples are presented in a sequence. When more and more units of the free space become committed, the behavior of the system has the potential to change significantly, because newly committed units have well established weights to units in the attribute space and the concept space.

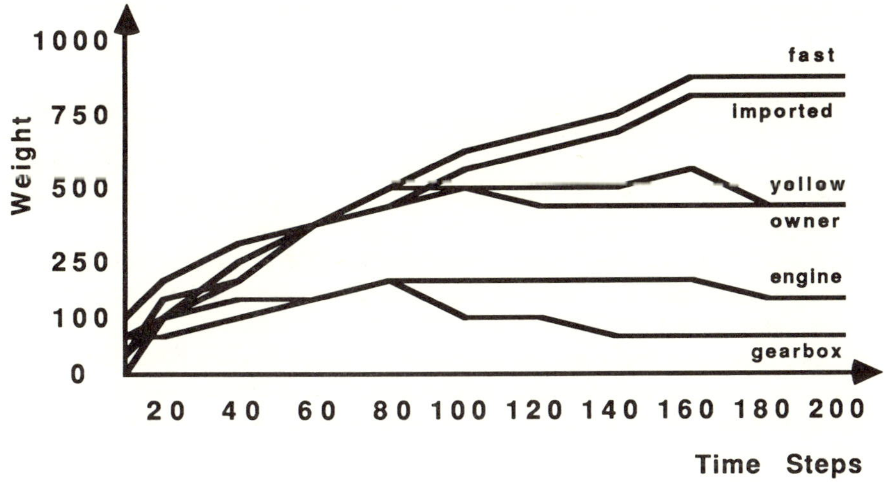

Figure 11.4.
Weight development between the free space winner unit and feature units in the attribute space (full connectivity).

7.3. Weight Development for a Second Example with High Similarity to the First Instance

It is important to understand the behavior of the free space when parts of this space are already recruited and therefore part of the concept space, because the network should have the ability to learn several concepts in a sequence. The recruitment of a triple-subnetwork might influence the competition between the remaining units in the free space and might interfere with further recruitment.

It is, of course, possible to free the newly recruited unit out of the free space by changing the inhibitory connections from and to this unit to 0-valued connections. This is no problem from a technical viewpoint, and will be necessary for large applications. However, there is at least one strike against this procedure: the newly recruited unit must change incoming and outgoing links (and not only the input-lines). The rest of this chapter investigates recruitment learning without such a procedure.

We are starting with the case where an instance has triggered recruitment learning and a new example is presented immediately after the end of this acquisition. This second example has high similarity with the first one: It shares all features with the first instance with the exception of one (which is not owned by the goal-concept). In order to understand the network's ability to acquire a new concept immediately after a first one, the following experimental procedure is used.

An instance is presented to the system, a goal concept is chosen, and the network runs for 200 update steps in the same way as described above. After 200 update steps all potentials and all output values in all spaces of the network are set to 0. Next, a new example is presented, a new goal concept is chosen, and the network runs for another 200 update steps. The weight development for the second example is recorded.

Figure 11.5 shows a typical result for the acquisition of a second new concept structure immediately after the first one. Note the weight development between the second recruited unit and features units in the attribute space.

This experiment was done 50 times (i.e., a second instance was presented immediately after a recruitment of a new concept), and the acquisition of a new unit failed only once: the system tried to recruit an already committed unit.

7.4. Learning Several Dissimilar Instances

The examples used in these experiments shared no features. The structure of the domain and the operationality criterion remained unchanged. An instance was presented to the system, a goal concept was chosen and the network was updated for 200 steps. After 200 steps all potentials and outputs were set to 0 to destroy activation patterns in concept, attribute, and free space. Next, a new example was presented, a new goal concept chosen, and the network was updated again

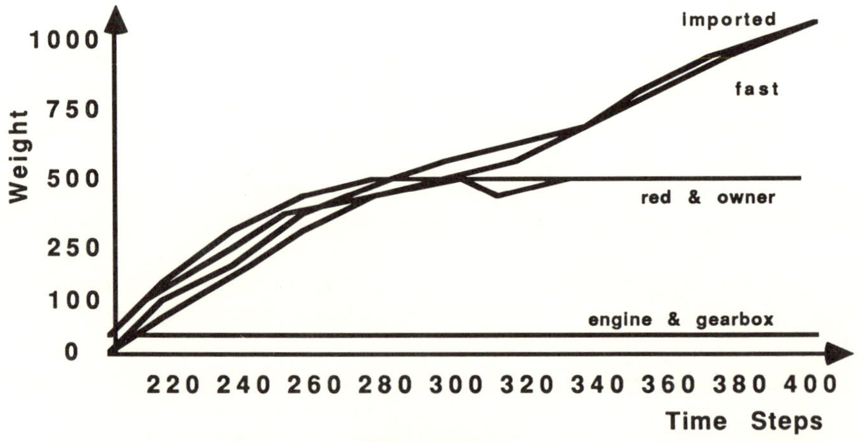

Figure 11.5.
Weight development between the free space winner unit and feature units in the attribute space (full connectivity) after the presentation of a second, similar example.

for 200 steps. In total, this procedure was performed three times. After each presentation of an instance, the weight change of links between the free and the attribute space was recorded.

Figures 11.6 and 11.7 show that the weight development is very similar for all instances independent of the time of presentation. However, because of the small size of the free space in our simulations, the network tends to pick an already-committed unit for the representation of a concept after the presentation of the third instance. This indicates that the free space must have a minimum size, or the recruitment of new units is affected by previous recruitment processes.

8. MULTIPLE CONCEPTS AND DISJUNCTIVE ATTRIBUTES

The example above describes a simulation with a single attribute space. If the goal is the recruitment of several new concepts with different attributes and values, two procedures are possible. First, a single attribute space is used and learning for each concept is done in different time intervals while all attributes and values shared by these concepts remain active. Second, more than one attribute space is used.

In many cases, disjunctive combinations of attributes are of interest. In order to learn these combinations, a direct connection between attribute and concept space, as proposed, is not sufficient and thus "hidden units" are necessary. See

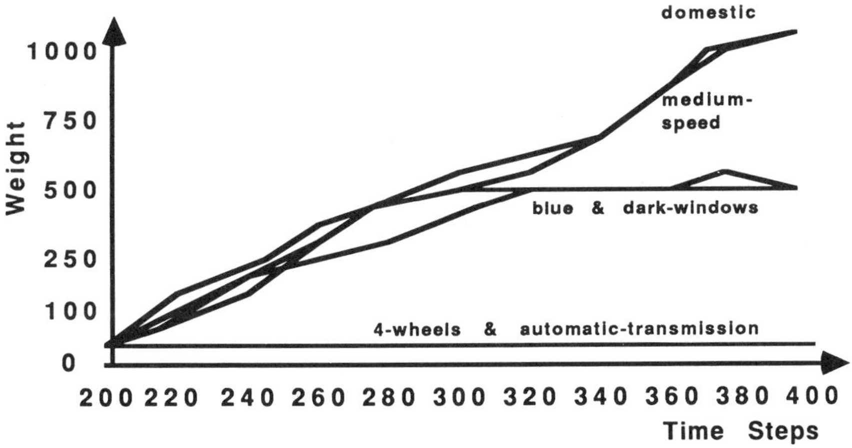

Figure 11.6.
Weight development between the free space winner unit and feature units in the attribute space (full connectivity) after the presentation of a second, dissimilar example.

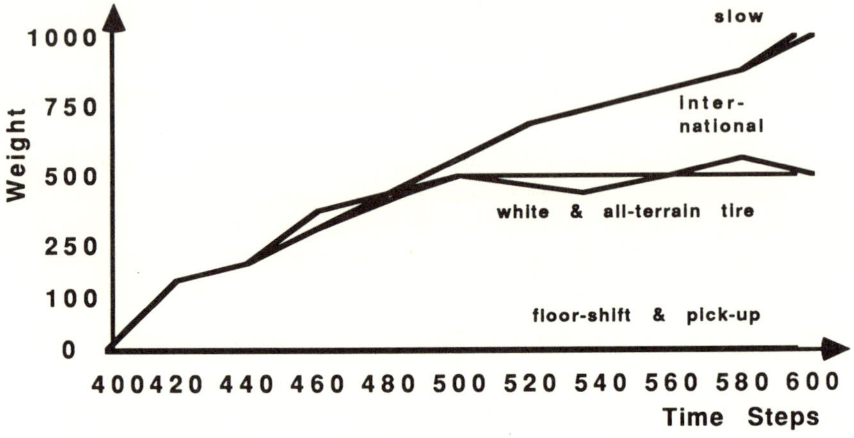

Figure 11.7.
Weight development between the free space winner unit and feature units in the attribute space (full connectivity) after the presentation of a third, dissimilar example.

Fanty (1988) for experiments on concept learning in structured connectionist systems and the use of sequential processing in massively parallel systems.

9. IDENTIFYING NECESSARY FEATURES FOR CONCEPT FORMATION

The most serious shortcoming of our system is the inability to distinguish between features of the training example which are necessary for the definition of the new concept, and those which are only relevant for the particular input instance presented to the system. In the example above, the features **yellow** and **owner:michael** are equally connected to the new concept, with respect to strength, although only one of them might be necessary for the definition of the new concept (yellow).

There are several ways to overcome this shortcoming:

1. A similarity-based learning component is added to the system to realize a combined knowledge- and data-intensive system which also captures the statistics of the input environment.
2. Another possibility is to use more knowledge to decide how specific or general a feature is. This would require detailed and explicit definitions of features.
3. It is possible to extend the method by telling the system which features are necessary for concept formation. The feature **yellow** in our example above

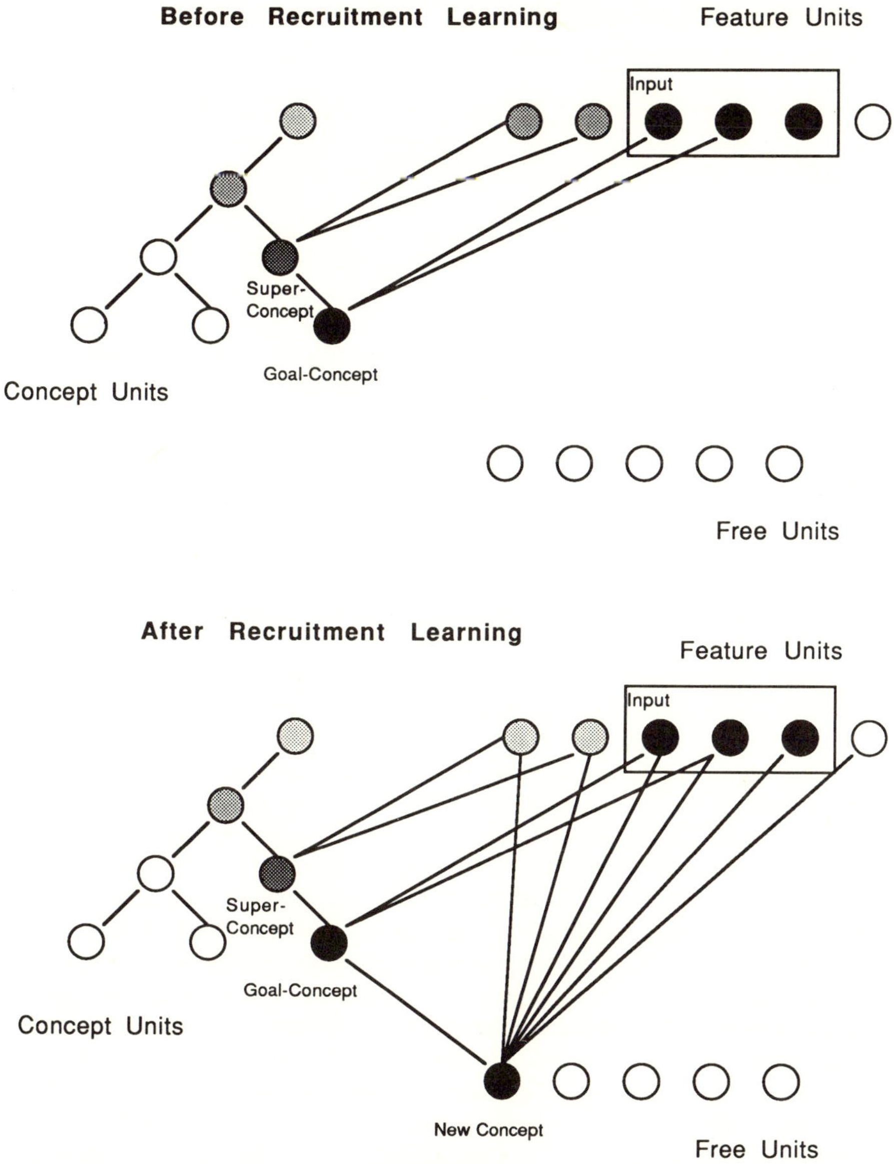

Figure 11.8.

Classification for and after recruitment. A set of features is the input in both cases. In the unmodified network before recruitment, the input feature units activate a generic concept, and additional feature units are getting "on" by stimulation of this concept unit or its super-concepts. After recruitment, the more specific newly recruited concept is getting the strongest input from the feature units and then primes additional feature units directly.

would be clamped on and the newly recruited unit would have strong connections to this feature.

4. Introduce a "generality" measurement in a similar way as certainty factors are used in evidential reasoning systems. Those features of the input example which are only owned by this particular instance would get small initial potentials and other features would get higher values.

10. CONCLUSION

A structured connectionist learning system is introduced which uses a built-in knowledge representation module for limited inferencing. Knowledge-intensive learning is possible in any stage of processing, it is efficient and robust. Furthermore, knowledge-intensive learning in connectionist systems can be used in addition to "learning from scratch" techniques to supply information if the input is incomplete or noisy.

On the implementation level, the system is an application of recruitment learning (Feldman, 1982). The new and essential contribution of the approach presented here is the *interaction* between constraints on the "knowledge level" and the connectionist implementation level. On the "knowledge level" the approach introduces the notion of goal concepts, restrictions for the new concept definition, and the use of a single instance. These are constraints for recruitment learning on the network level, and allow the connection of a new concept to a connectionist inheritance system.

The recruitment learning will make a connectionist inheritance system more *operational*. The system's ability to recognize instances as described by the training example will improve because of the newly recruited unit and the new concept it represents. During recognition, the presentation of another instance which belongs to the same class as the training example will cause the immediate activation of the newly recruited unit and therefore very efficient recognition (see Figure 11.8). Hollbach (1988) has introduced the distinction between immediate and mediated inferences. An inference is immediate if a conclusion is made based on a feature which is directly connected to a concept. A mediated inference is made when several inference steps are necessary for a final decision. The machine learning system described above will make a knowledge representation more operational by allowing more immediate inferences instead of mediated conclusions. The newly learned concept has weighted connections to its features, and activating these features results in the direct activation of the newly acquired concept.

Diederich (1989a, 1989b) describes an extension and modification of the approach outlined here. This new approach allows the modification of a connectionist knowledge representation system and the *integration* of a newly recruited unit in a conceptual hierarchy. In more detail, Diederich (1989a, 1989b) describes an implemented connectionist learning system that transforms an instruction expressed in a description language into an input for a connectionist knowledge representation system, which in turn changes the network in order to integrate new knowledge. This integration is always important when a single new fact causes changes in several parts of the knowledge base; it is an adjustment which cannot easily be done with learning-by-example techniques only. The new, integrated knowledge can be used in conjunction with prior knowledge.

The presented method should be applicable for connectionist inheritance networks in general. The necessary element is the distinction between concept, attribute, and free space.

REFERENCES

Chun, H.W., Bookman, L.A., & Afshartous, N. (1987). Network Regions: Alternatives to the Winner-Take-All Structure. *Proceedings of the 10th International Joint Conference on Artificial Intelligence,* pp. 380–387. Milan, Italy.

Cottrell, G.W. (1985). Parallelism in inheritance hierarchies with exceptions. *Proceedings of the 9th International Joint Conference on Artificial Intelligence,* pp. 194–202. Los Angeles, CA.

Derthick, M. (1987). A connectionist architecture for representing and reasoning about structured knowledge. *Proceedings of the 9th Conference of the Cognitive Science Society,* pp. 131–142. Seattle, WA.

Diederich, J. (1988). Connectionist recruitment learning. *Proceedings of the 8th European Conference on Artificial Intelligence*. Munich, Germany.

Diederich, J. (1989a). Instruction and Higher-Level Learning in Connectionist Networks. (Connection Science.) *Journal of Neural Computing, Artificial Intelligence and Cognitive Research, 1*(2), 163–182. Abingdon, U.K.: Carfax Publishing Company.

Diederich, J. (1989b): *"Learning by instruction" in connectionist systems*. In: Segre, A. (Ed.): Proceedings of the 6th International Workshop on Machine Learning, p.66–68. Morgan Kaufman Publ., Palo Alto, CA.

Fanty, M. (1988). *Learning in structured connectionist networks*. Doctoral thesis, Department of Computer Science, University of Rochester, NY.

Feldman, J.A. (1982). Dynamic connections in neural networks. *Biological Cybernetics, 46,* 27–39.

Feldman, J.A., & Ballard, D.H. (1982). Connectionist models and their properties. *Cognitive Science, 6,* 205–254.

Goddard, N., Lynne, K., & Mintz, T. (1988). *The Rochester Connectionist Simulator* (Tech. Rep. 233). Rochester, NY: Department of Computer Science, University of Rochester.

Grossberg, S. (1987). Competitive learning: From interactive activation to adaptive resonance. *Cognitive Science, 11,* 23–63.

Hollbach, S.A. (1988). *Automatic compilation of a connectionist knowledge base*. Internal Paper, Department of Computer Science, University of Rochester, NY.

Lynne, K. (1987). *Competitive reinforcement learning* (Internal Paper). Rochester, NY: Department of Computer Science, University of Rochester.

Mitchell, T.M., Keller, R.M., & Kedar-Cabelli, S.T. (1986). Explanation-based generalization: A unifying view. *Machine Learning 1,* 47–80.

Rumelhart, D.E., & Zipser, D. (1985). Feature discovery by competitive learning. *Cognitive Science, 9,* 75–112.

Shastri, L. (1985). *Evidential reasoning in semantic networks: A formal theory and its parallel implementation* (Doctoral thesis and TR 166). Rochester, NY: Department of Computer Science, University of Rochester.

Touretzky, D.S. (1986). *The mathematics of inheritance systems.* Los Altos, CA: Morgan Kaufman.

Touretzky, D.S., & Geva, S. (1987). A distributed connectionist representation for concept structures. *Ninth Conference of the Cognitive Science Society,* pp. 155–164. Seattle, WA.

12 Learning Simple Arithmetic Procedures

Garrison W. Cottrell
Fu-Sheng Tsung

1. INTRODUCTION AND MOTIVATION

One major criticism of artificial neural networks is that there is no obvious method for doing sequential, symbolic processing. Rumelhart, Smolensky, McClelland, and Hinton (1986) proposed that symbolic processing may be achieved by (a) creating physical representations of the problem, (b) processing the representations via pattern association, and (c) recording the result of the processing in the physical representation. The example they use is the problem of adding two three digit numbers. First the two numbers are written down in a standard format, for example:

```
327
865
───
```

This is now a pattern recognition problem, with the result being recorded by an action, that is, writing down the sum of the rightmost column. Then, a carry must be written as well. Now a new pattern presents itself,

```
  1
327
865
───
  2
```

and the process repeats. Similarly, they claim that a complex logical problem is solved by breaking it down into simpler problems and applying the above procedure repeatedly. Doing a problem "in your head" involves forming *internal representations* of the external representations used above. This latter aspect is beyond the scope of this research. For our part, we were interested in just what was involved in implementing the above description.

In this initial stage of research, the goal is to implement and test a neural network model of learning simple addition procedures. More specifically, we wanted to see if it were possible to learn to add two arbitrarily large numbers with currently existing sequential networks. We chose addition as our symbolic processing task because it is a simple example that everyone is familiar with, and yet it is nontrivial for parallel distributed processing (PDP) networks because it involves control issues as well. Addition involves sequential processing and looping, which are not traditional PDP tasks. Furthermore, it is a good problem to test for generalization, because we obviously can only train the network on a finite set of examples and yet there are infinitely many new cases to test it on; the network must learn the implicit, underlying rule in addition.

As an unexpected benefit of this research, we discovered a method for training networks with large training environments that, at least in this domain, is superior to giving the network a large subset of the environment initially. We found that our networks reached local minima when presented with large sets of examples. Instead, we developed an incremental method we call *combined subset training* that made the learning smooth and feasible. This method may be reasonable for other tasks, and may have implications for human learning.

Finally, we give the beginnings of a characterization of the dynamics of the network, by looking at the underlying space that the network operates in. At this level, we can see how states that are not reflected in the output are encoded internally.

In the following sections, we discuss the architecture of the model, the training strategy in more detail, the results obtained through combined subset training, some analysis of the network dynamics, and some implications of our model for PDP and cognitive modeling.

2. SETUP OF THE MODEL

In order to have a PDP network do sequences of actions, it has to have some way of knowing "where" it is in the sequence. This can only be accomplished by having the state of the network be different for different locations in the sequence. One way of accomplishing this is by explicitly having discrete states in the unit functions which change over time (Feldman & Ballard, 1982). An alternative is to have *recurrence* in the network, so that the state of the network is reflected in the activation levels of the units. We adopt the latter approach, following the work of Jordan (1986) and Elman (1988). Both of these approaches are restricted extensions of the basic feed-forward network used in most back propagation experiments (Le Cun, 1985; Parker, 1985; Rumelhart, Hinton, &

FIGURES

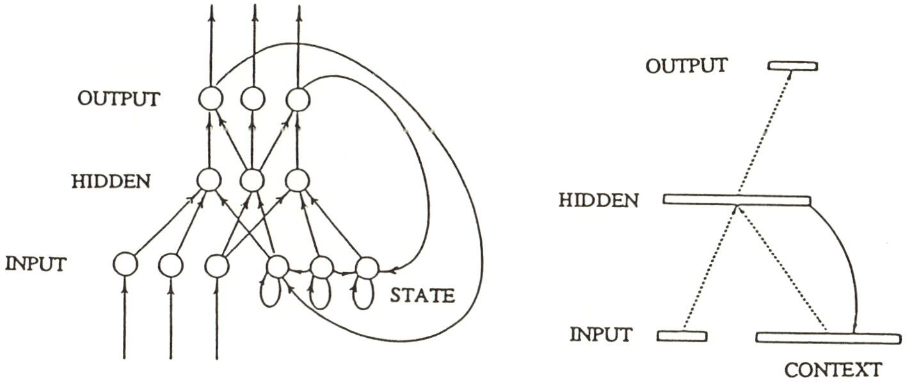

Figure 12.1.
(a) Jordan's recurrent network. The outputs are linearly summed over time in the state vector, lower right. (b) Elman's network. The context vector (lower right) is a copy of the hidden units from the previous time step.

Williams, 1986; Werbos, 1974), that nevertheless still allow the use of back propagation learning. In Jordan's approach (see Figure 12.1(a)), the output vector of the network is linearly averaged into a *state* vector (the same length as the output), which is given to the network as part of the input. The state vector at time t becomes some proportion (*mu*) of its value at time t − 1, plus the output vector at time t − 1. Thus the network has an exponentially decaying representation of its output history. In Elman's approach (see Figure 12.1(b)), the hidden unit activations at time t − 1 are copied into a *context* vector, which is given as input to the network at time t. This is equivalent to having the hidden units be completely recurrently connected, and back propagating one step in time along the recurrent links. We used both architectures in the following experiments.[1]

Regardless of whether we used the state network or the context network, the architecture of the model is as follows: We assume that the network is try to solve addition problems like the above example, and focuses its attention on one column of digits at a time. Thus the input to the network at any given time is one column of digits, plus the state or context vector, and one bit which signals the end of the input. We used a binary representation of the two digits. The network has two output fields: an *action* and a *result*. The *action* field is a localist encoding of four possible actions: WRITE the sum of the two digits, record the

[1] In deference to Jordan and Elman, we will call their network architectures *state* and *context* networks, respectively.

CARRY, shift the input window to the NEXT column of digits, and DONE. The result field only has meaning when the action is WRITE. In this case, the result field holds the sum of the two inputs. Otherwise, the result field is not important and no error is propagated back from it. One interesting aspect is the NEXT action; the network has control of when it is finished with this input and ready to move on to the next column of digits. An alternative would be to give the network a gray scale version of the problem, and force it to recognize the digits and shift its attention internally. For this preliminary research, we wanted to keep the problem as simple as possible. The network is trained to produce a sequence of outputs according to the program in Figure 12.2. Notice that the CARRY action is performed only when there is a carry (else it is skipped). If there is a carry, there is no explicit representation in the next input telling the network that 1 should be added to the sum. That is, the network must learn to "remember" the carry.

Some advantages of this set up are: Numbers of arbitrary lengths can be added; conditional branching, looping, sequence-following, and, of course, pattern association, are all inherent in the process. The inputs are the physical representation the network processes, and the action of the network both gives the result of the processing and controls its input, in a crude version of eye movement.

We simplified the addition problem by using base 4 numbers instead of decimal numbers, with each base 4 digit being given a two-digit binary representation. The use of base 4 vs. base 10 lessens the burden on the network of the number of basic pattern associations it must memorize. There are now 16 basic associations (4 × 4, although they are symmetric), plus special conditions as in the presence of carry and the "done" bit, an input that signals end-of-input. The

```
while not done do
begin
  output(WRITE, low_order_digit);
  if sum>radix then
       output(CARRY, ???);
  output(NEXT, ???);
end
if carry_on_previous_input then
           output(WRITE, '01');
output(DONE, ???);
```

Figure 12.2.
The "program" the network learns. There are two output fields, an *action* field and a *result* field. For most outputs, the *result* field is not trained ("???" in the figure).

carry actually complicates the situation quite a bit; an extreme way of counting the pattern associations the network has to learn would be to count 16 possible previous inputs (which determine whether or not a carry is added into the sum) times 16 possible current inputs for 256 associations. This is only counting the WRITE steps. A even more extreme way of counting the WRITE steps would recognize that the network has essentially an infinite set of different inputs depending on its processing history. This is reflected in the context or state vectors. Since most of this is irrelevant, one thing the network must learn is to *ignore* its distant history.

3. TRAINING STRATEGY AND RESULTS

The goal is to get the network to learn the addition process for an arbitrary number of digits. Immediate questions are: What makes a good training set? How many examples are enough for the net to generalize? We decided to restrict our attention (during training) to additions with numbers up to three digits. This set contains all the canonical situations, and therefore should be enough. However, there are 4096 additions (including all 1-digit, 2-digit, 3-digit combinations), and when translated to the network output sequences, there are more than 30,000 individual patterns. Learning is very difficult with such a large training set. To keep the net small (16 hidden units), and the training fairly fast (less than a minute per epoch on a Sun-4), we tried two training environments. One was a random subset consisting of 1 percent of the 4096 additions. This was learned within 3 to 5 thousand epochs. However, generalization was poor. We found if we tried a bigger subset, for example, 8 percent of the additions, the network would hit a local minimum (total sum squared error (tss) of 346 after 5000 epochs). Thus we have the following dilemma: If the training set is small enough to be learned in reasonable time, the network generalizes poorly. If the training set is large enough to insure good generalization, it does not learn in the time we are willing to wait. It seemed that another method of training was needed.

3.1. Combined Subset Training

Here we introduce the *combined subset training* (CST) method. The idea is very simple: We pick a manageable, randomly selected subset to train the network initially. When the network has learned it fairly well, we add another randomly selected subset of equal size to the first training set, and then train the network with the combined set. The net is now being trained with a set that is twice as large, but it already "knows" half of them. If this can be learned successfully, we double the training set in the same fashion. This procedure is repeated until the whole set is included, or until we find that the net is able to generalize to the rest of the original training set.

We found that it is important to start with a higher error criterion than desired in the final state, decreasing it with each subset doubling. For example, our goal is to have the total error be less than 0.05. On the first subset, we stop at a tss of 1.0, and then for each doubling, lower the error threshold by a small fixed amount. We stop when the network is generalizing sufficiently well. We should point out that throughout this procedure we use a single learning rate. Intuitively, this method should work for the following reason: When the net is only seeing a small subset of the total training set, many partial solutions *adequate for that subset* may be possible. Training to high precision may force the net to choose one of these local solutions, which may not generalize to the global solution desired. Stopping at a higher error criterion leaves the options open by preventing the network from diving too deeply into local minima.

For this initial experiment, we picked 1 percent (of the 4096 additions) as our initial set. We trained the networks (both types) to a low tss of around 1.0, and doubled to 2 percent. The tss for the 2 percent initially jumped up, but monotonically decreased fairly quickly. The same behavior was observed when we doubled to 4 percent and 8 percent. At 8 percent of the training set (close to 3000 individual patterns), we found that the net could already generalize very well to the rest of the 4096 additions.

Generalization is determined by dividing the entire four thousand additions randomly into 10 files, each containing 10 percent, and testing the net with all ten files. This allows us to see if the error is spread evenly over the entire set. In each case, the tss (over an individual file of about 400 additions) was between 0.4 and 0.7. That is, the average error for each addition (of up to 11 patterns in the sequence) was below 0.002. More importantly, this suggests that the error was spread very evenly among the sequences. There was no case in which the network output a 1 when it should have output a 0 (or vice versa), because that immediately adds about 1.0 to the total sum squared error (tss). The result is similar in both the state and context networks. See Figure 12.3(a). Each jump in the error corresponds to a doubling of the training set size. It is characteristic of a successful training regime that the peaks of these jumps are decreasing.

In Figure 12.3(b), we compare CST with training directly on subsets of size 2 percent, 4 percent and 8 percent. Notice that the CST curve falls under all of the others. More to the point, the 8 percent curve appears to have reached a local minima at tss 346, while the networks trained on 2 percent and 4 percent do not generalize well to the rest of the patterns (data not shown). This is evidence of the same dilemma we stated above: When training on *fixed* subsets, if we keep the set size small enough for the network to learn, it doesn't generalize well. If we start with bigger subsets, the network cannot learn.

To test the CST-trained network on longer additions, we next generated arbitrary numbers of lengths up to 14 (base 4) digits long (8 decimal digits). Even though the network has only been trained on additions of up to 3 digit numbers,

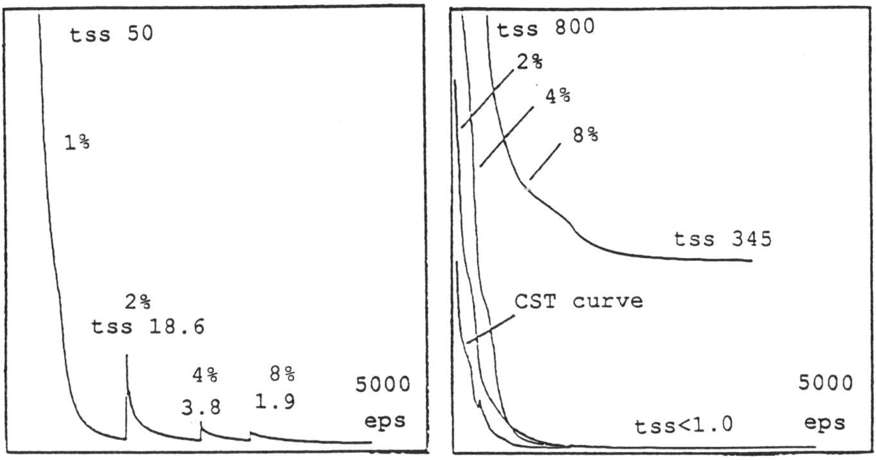

Figure 12.3.
(a) Error curve from combined subset training on the context net. Each jump in tss is where training sets are doubled. Beginning tss: 348.5; final tss: 0.399. (b) Comparison of CST to fixed set training for 2%, 4%, and 8% subsets (the y axis is much higher than in (a)).

on ten tests of ten additions (an example test set is shown in Figure 12.4), the net misses one addition out of ten on the average. Each mistake usually contributes most of the tss error in the statistics shown in Figure 12.5 before further training (first column). On the other 90 percent, the net gets each output almost perfectly, as evidenced by the very low tss in the other test files. We then trained the (context) net on test file 1 only, for 30 epochs, followed by 10 epochs with test file 9. The tss for all files, after every 10 epochs, are shown in Figure 12.5. We then tested the new weights on both the previous 3-digit additions and hundreds

78965	+	87	=	79052
9432080	+	92	=	9432172
40	+	76084	=	76124
7	+	8	=	15
94112	+	9133431	=	9227543
5078	+	83244	=	88322
94	+	9239650	=	9239744
30163504	+	6	=	30163510
74157	+	159	=	74316
389775	+	855	=	390630

Figure 12.4.
Example of a random addition test file.

Test Set	Initial tss	test1 10ep	test1 20ep	test1 30ep	test9 10ep
1	24.229	19.107	1.493	0.389	0.215
2	0.147	0.166	0.083	0.101	0.146
3	0.198	0.143	0.108	0.129	0.178
4	14.152	6.810	0.127	0.147	0.221
5	18.063	5.192	0.109	0.133	0.333
6	14.675	2.687	0.539	0.212	0.154
7	10.100	5.776	0.125	0.115	0.252
8	0.905	0.393	0.072	0.070	0.088
9	6.693	0.509	0.378	5.684	0.344
10	8.347	2.014	0.599	0.637	0.204

Figure 12.5.
Generalization behavior and weight refinement from mistakes. Each row corresponds to one test set of 10 arbitrary additions. The first column is the total sum squared error (tss) after the net has learned only on 3-digit additions. The weights are then refined by training on test set 1 for 30 epochs, which raised the tss for test set 9. The last 10 epochs are therefore trained on test set 9.

of the arbitrary, large additions. The errors for the latter are shown in Figure 12.6. In general, we find that:

1. Training on one or two test sets corrects performance on other test sets. This suggests that the net is prone to make only one, or few, classes of errors.
2. The net can always learn to correct the mistakes very easily (within tens of epochs of further training). Furthermore, the new weights do not upset the performance on the previous additions.
3. The new weights then rarely miss any arbitrary addition, on the order of one out of a few hundred.

From the patterns of error behavior and the observations listed above, it is clear that the network has learned the task, needing only small refinements.

The combined subset training procedure was not foolproof, since on one trial we tried it did not work. As with the example of non-learning to be given below, if the peaks in the error that occur with doubling are increasing, this is an indication that CST is not working. In our case, the problem could be in starting with too low of an initial error criterion. Further investigation is necessary to determine optimal parameters for "annealing" the error threshold and deciding the optimal subset size increase. If nothing else, then, this aspect of CST serves as an indicator of whether a particular simulation run will be successful or not. This can mean great savings in computation (and real) time when each run can take hours or days.

Test Sets	Before Refinement	After Refinement
11	60.328	0.807
12	69.133	0.688
13	84.252	0.637
14	42.185	1.361
15	51.162	1.054
16	108.05	0.909
17	80.287	0.864
18	35.224	0.858
19	56.477	1.273
20	97.135	0.682
2%	0.119	0.455
4%	0.216	0.882

Figure 12.6.
Tss errors from ten more tests, each containing 50 additions. Refinement refers to the 40 epoch training in Figure 12.5; no further learning is done on these tests. Refinement improved performance drastically for arbitrary additions, while degrading very little on random 2% and 4% subsets from the original 3-digit examples.

3.2. Differences between State and Context Nets

Both state and context networks behaved similarly on this project. We may ask the question: Is there some task that one can do, and not the other? Do they have important differences? The answer is yes, and a simple example is found by simply altering the output sequence in the sequential adder model. That is, instead of the original sequence of "write result-carry-next", the net is trained to output "write result-next-carry", as in Figure 12.7. A state network should not be able to solve this problem. This is because the state network has access to only the current input and the output history; it keeps no record of previous inputs or the internal states of the system. After writing the result, the NEXT action brings in the next pair of digits as input, so that the state net cannot possibly determine whether the next step should be CARRY or not. The context network has a transformed version of the input at the hidden layer which is recycled at each time step, thus it can "remember" input that is not reflected in its output.

Simulation results bear this out. The state network has a problem learning this task, as shown in Figure 12.8. It can achieve a low tss for each subset, but the error curve is not smooth and it does not generalize to the doubled subset. That is, it is memorizing the sequences rather than learning the task. Results with the context network show that this is a harder problem than the original problem. The context network takes about twice as long to learn it (~10,000 epochs) with CST.

```
while not done do
begin
  output(WRITE, low_order_digit);
  output(NEXT, ???);
  if sum(previous_input)>radix then
       output(CARRY, ???);
end
if carry_on_previous_input then
          output(WRITE, '01');
output(DONE, ???);
```

Figure 12.7.
A modified program that illustrates the difference between the context and the state networks. The state network has difficulty remembering inputs not reflected in its output.

3.3. Initial Analysis of the Internal Representation

We plan to apply the standard cluster analysis techniques to the hidden unit representations to see what the similarity structure the network imposes on its inputs. However, these are static representations of a dynamic process. It is more interesting in this case to look at the *dynamics* of the network as it moves through

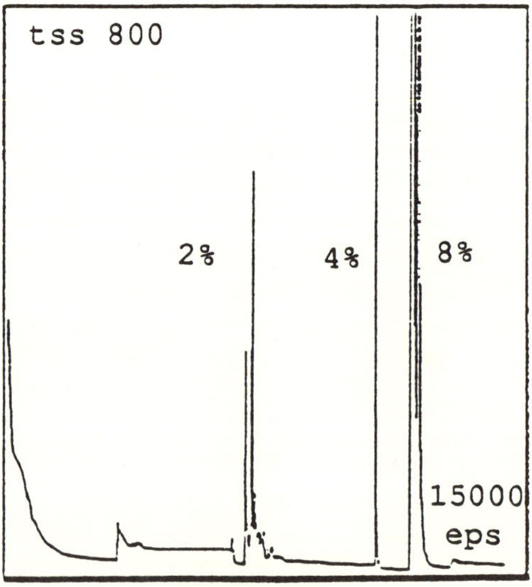

Figure 12.8.
Learning program 2 with the state network. CST doubling is indicated. The net is learning local solutions, and is unable to generalize.

the problem. Following a suggestion of Jeff Elman's, we found the principal components of the 16 hidden unit activations over time, as a context network processed 10 additions from one of the generalization test sets, as in Figure 12.4. This gives the directions of highest variance of the hidden unit activations over time. Basically, we can think of this as finding a new coordinate space for the hidden unit vectors, where the coordinate vectors are ordered in terms of how much "action" occurs along each one.

We show two kinds of plots from this. In Figure 12.9, we show the projection of the hidden units vectors onto the plane of the first two principal components as the network is doing a 30 step addition. Each point is labeled by the action that is produced on the output and the step in the entire computation. This shows how

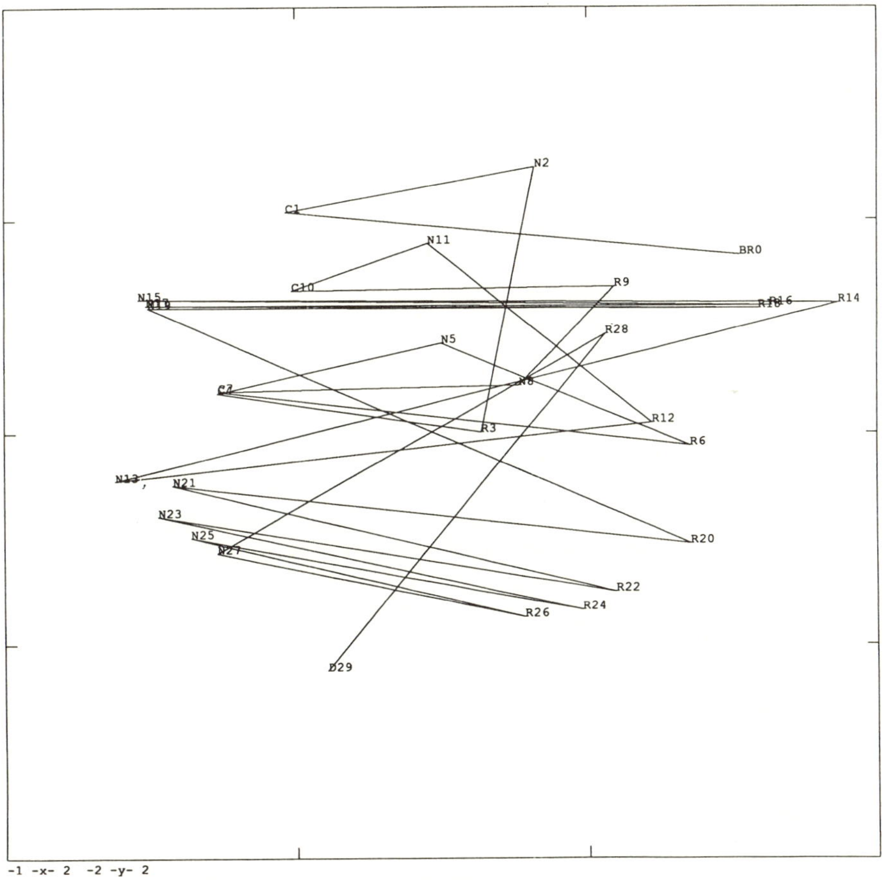

Figure 12.9.
Projections of the hidden units activation vector onto the first two principal components. The number in the point labels corresponds to the step in this addition. R: RESULT, C: CARRY, N: NEXT, D: DONE.

the network "moves" as it processes the input. There are several things to notice here. Basically, WRITE result actions (labeled R#) are generally in the right half of the space, NEXTs and CARRYs are in the left. Presumably differences that are not exhibited here will show up on other axes. A second observation is that the second component appears to be correlated with overall time within this problem, from top to bottom. There are exceptions, such as R28. It is interesting that the network represents this even though it doesn't need to in order to solve the problem. The more striking thing that comes out of this is that we can see that along the first principal component (the x axis) the network is distinguishing between a NEXT that follows a CARRY, versus one that follows a WRITE. All of the NEXTS following a carry are greater than 0 on this axis, all of those following a WRITE are less than 0. The significance of this is that following a NEXT that follows a CARRY, the network must output a result that is one more than the sum of the two inputs. It is "remembering" this fact in how it internally represents the state following a carry. This internal representation is available at the next iteration as the context vector. Hence, it can solve the problem.

This suggests another way of plotting the movement: the first principal component at time **t** vs. **t + 1.** This essentially gives the map from the context vector to the next hidden unit vector, since the context vector at time **t** is the hidden unit vector at time **t − 1.** It ignores the role of the input in this map. The fact that it looks sensible corresponds to the notion that the network learns the part of the problem that reduces the error in the output the most first. This is the **Action** field, since the **Result** field only gets trained every 3 or 4 iterations. In Figure 12.10 we show this plot for the same problem as in Figure 12.9. Here points are labeled by the transition being made. So N5 → R6 means we are plotting the point (N5,R6). Here the separation of the NEXT's following a CARRY really shows up—they are all in a "bump" above the main diagonal of the graph. This kind of graph gives us a better picture of a dynamic network than a cluster analysis does, because it gives us an idea of how the network makes transitions. More study of these will be needed to determine the extent of their usefulness.

4. DISCUSSION

4.1. Combined Subset Training

We suggest that the *combined subset training* (CST) method for large training sets is superior to the "all-at-once" method usually employed. Of course, application of this method to other problems is required to check out this claim. We applied it to a problem where the training set is large and unwieldy, yet the problem space is fairly "uniform." Experience with CST on this project shows that one can keep the same learning rate throughout the training, even when the training set is doubled. Also, the number of epochs necessary to reach error

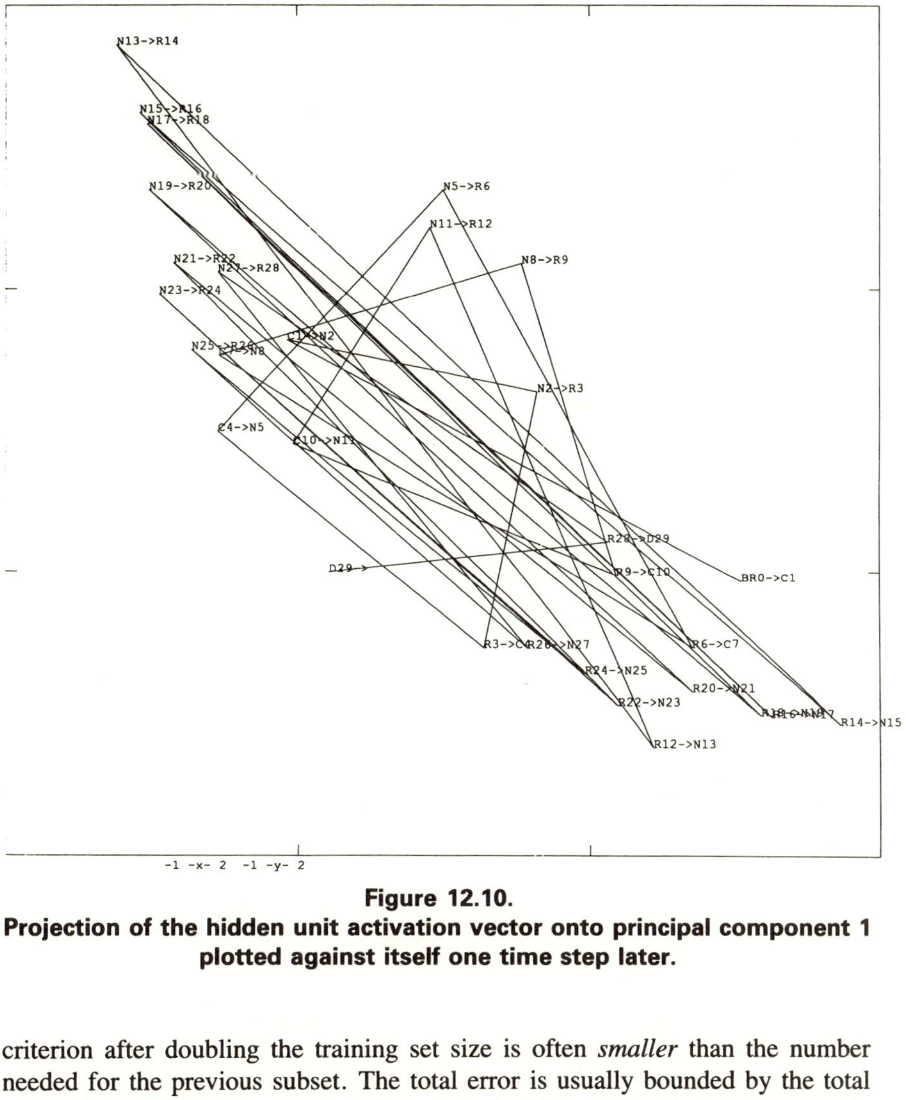

Figure 12.10.
Projection of the hidden unit activation vector onto principal component 1 plotted against itself one time step later.

criterion after doubling the training set size is often *smaller* than the number needed for the previous subset. The total error is usually bounded by the total error of the initial subset, and in fact each doubling raises the total error only slightly (if the net is converging to the right solution). The main point, of course, is that CST allows us to learn extremely large training sets.

4.2. Learning Programming Constructs

This project demonstrates the PDP nets can do simple sequencing, looping, and branching. Also, values necessary for future processing can be stored over short periods by the context network. Other recurrent network models are more powerful in this regard (Williams & Zipser, 1988), but require a prohibitively large amount of computer time to train. Since this takes a long time to learn (5000 more epochs for the context net) it suggests that memory for "variables" may require initial structures subserving this function that are easily refined by learning. Of course, this is what evolution does for us. We thus have simple versions of all of the mechanisms for a universal computer—except the ability to nest these constructs. We conjecture that nesting will not be able to be carried very deeply. Thus it would be very interesting to set up a problem with nested while-loops.

4.3. Is This a Good Cognitive Model of Addition?

We predict that in the literature on learning arithmetic, we will find several things. First, that children learn best by starting with small sets of examples and increasing the numbers until they have the concept. This sounds like a grandmother result (one my grandmother could have told me), but if one reads the connectionist literature for hints on training, most start with the complete training set. The work reported here suggests that there are reasons other than attention span why this might be a good idea. Specifically, learning a small number of special cases loosely allows the learning process to reduce the dimensionality of the search process by using a few examples to narrow the space.

Second, other partitions of the training space may speed up learning. We happened to double the size of the training set each time, and found that the network learned more earlier, although, asymptotically, the two versions (all at once vs. CST) flatten out around the same time. The difference was that CST ended up with significantly lower error. We may be able to achieve more speedup with different rates of increasing the set size. This would then be a testable process with children.

Third, we discovered that *it is easier to remember something if you're looking at it!* A bit facetious perhaps, but just as in humans, when a task requires a memory load, it takes longer to learn. The task in Figure 12.7 requires the network to "remember" input across one processing cycle, while the task in Figure 12.2 does not. The second task takes almost twice as many epochs to learn.

Some might argue that this network does not learn at all the way children do. Children are given an explicit rule to follow for addition. The basic issue is learning by personal experience versus learning by being told. It is certainly still an open question whether there are ways in which connectionist networks can learn facts and procedures by being explicitly given them. However, we feel that this aspect of learning is overemphasized and overrated. When someone tells me how to make coffee using the new coffee machine, it is often not enough for me to carry out the procedure perfectly, and I may forget the next time how I did it if enough time passes. The procedure is not really learned until *I have carried it out myself several times*. This fact is reflected in the common experience that students do not really learn concepts well without homework problems on them. The explanation of how someone learns something by being told again lies in the idea of *internalizing external representations*. Part of this process is internalizing linguistic expressions (external representations of commands) by learning what motor program they are indicating, then practicing the motor program.

4.4. Future Work

There is certainly more work to be done. For example, we would like to analyze the network representations developmentally, as it learns, and observe the bifurcation of the internal representation that is necessary to solve the problem. Perhaps by looking at the state space of the networks we can get a better idea of why CST works better than fixed subset training. Another thing to look at here is whether the subspace that corresponds to doing the procedure forms an attractor. If we start the network in an abnormal state, is it drawn to the space that corresponds to solving the problem?

Also, it would be a challenge to get a network to build internal representations once it has learned the external process. Simulating this process would require scanning the inputs (simulating receiving a verbal description of the problem), remembering them, and doing the problem. This would require shifting attention on internal representations, rather than the simple external shifts implemented here. It would also require larger memory capacity in terms of short term memory than that demonstrated here. Intermediate results need to be kept and combined for giving the final answer. This is difficult enough for humans. It would be a challenging task for a neural network.

5. CONCLUSIONS

In this chapter we presented a simple model of symbolic manipulation using a connectionist network that learned a procedure to add two multi-digit numbers. The model served as a catalyst for several other results. The most important one is a method for training networks to learn large training environments via Combined Subset Training. We found that without CST, the networks we studied could not learn the task. Further investigation is necessary to determine if this technique is suitable for other network architectures (such as standard feed-forward networks) and other problem types.

The second result is a clear demonstration of the capacity differences between the type of networks studied by Jordan and those studied by Elman by giving a simple program that one can learn that the other cannot. The basic notion may be stated as follows: Networks with only output histories cannot remember things about their input that are not reflected in their output. This is perfectly clear now; it was not when we started this research.

The third result is a demonstration that networks of this type can learn simple programming constructs that are not nested. It is conjectured that the ability to nest constructs will be severely limited. Related evidence can be found in work by Servan-Schreiber, Cleeremans, and McClelland (1988) on learning regular languages with context networks. They found that nesting one regular language inside another caused the network to "forget" where it was in the outer language. More powerful networks are needed to learn such languages (Zipser, personal communication).

Fourth, we have a simple cognitive model of learning addition. It is yet to be determined whether the types of errors made by our model are similar to those made by children. Another avenue to explore is whether there is an analogue to CST in the education literature. Also, this model is fertile ground for exploring other aspects of human procedural learning and symbolic processing.

Finally we have begun an analysis of the network by looking at its state space graph. This type of analysis is necessary when we are using recurrent networks to observe the dynamics of the system. We expect that the use of this kind of analysis will become more commonplace as more researchers study recurrent networks.

REFERENCES

Elman, J. (1988). *Finding structure in time* (Tech. Rep. 8801). La Jolla, CA: Center for Research in Language, University of California, San Diego.

Feldman, J.A., & Ballard, D. (1982). Connectionist models and their properties. *Cognitive Science, 6,* 205–254.

Jordan, M. (1986). *Serial order: A parallel distributed processing approach* (Tech. Rep. 8604). La Jolla, CA: Institute for Cognitive Science, University of California, San Diego.

Le Cun, Y. (1985). Une procedure d'apprentissage pour reseau a seuil assymetrique [A learning procedure for asymmetric threshold network]. *Proceedings of Cognitiva 85,* 599–604.

Parker, D.B. (1985). *Learning logic* (Tech. Rep. 47). Cambridge, MA: Center for Computational Research in Economics and Management Science, MIT.

Rumelhart, D.E., Hinton, G.E., & Williams, R.J. (1986). Learning internal representations by error propagation. In D.E. Rumelhart, J.L. McClelland, & the PDP Research Group (Eds.), *Parallel distributed processing: Explorations in the microstructure of cognition (Vol. 1, pp. 318–362). Foundations.* Cambridge: MIT Press/Bradford Books.

Rumelhart, D.E., Smolensky, P., McClelland, J.L., & Hinton, G.E. (1986). Schemata and sequential thought processes in PDP models. In J.L. McClelland, D.E. Rumelhart, and the PDP Research Group (Eds.), *Parallel distributed processing: Explorations in the microstructure of cognition. Vol. 2: Psychological and biological models* (pp. 7–57). Cambridge: MA.: MIT Press/Bradford.

Servan-Schreiber, D., Cleeremans, A., & McClelland, J.L. (1988, November). *Encoding sequential structure in simple recurrent networks,* (CMU-CS-88-183). Available from the Department of Computer Science, Carnegie Mellon University, Pittsburgh, PA.

Werbos, P. (1974). *Beyond regression: New tools for prediction and analysis in the behavioral sciences.* Unpublished doctoral dissertation, Harvard University, Cambridge, MA.

Williams, R., & Zipser, D. (1988). *A learning algorithm for continually running fully recurrent neural networks* (Tech. Rep. ICS-8805). La Jolla, CA: Institute of Cognitive Science, University of California, San Diego.

13
The Similarity Between Connectionist and Other Parallel Computation Models*

Jiawei Hong
Xiaonan Tan

1. INTRODUCTION

In 1985, when the Artificial Intelligence journal was publishing its 25th volume, the editors constructed a set of 10 questions and sent it to many experts in AI area (Bobrow & Hayes, 1985). Question 1 was: A.I. has developed rapidly in the last decade. What do you feel have been the most significant scientific and/or technological advances in that time scale? Of the dozen or so specific topics which people thought were significant, only two were mentioned more than twice: connectionism (massive parallelism) and expert system.

Some people mentioned that connectionist systems were an exciting recent idea with great promise, because they believed that many of the core problems of AI, such as pattern matching, context sensitivity, representation of real-world knowledge and plausible inference are better approached on a nonsymbolic computational basis. Massively parallel connectionist networks, spreading activation, and evidential inference appear to be a natural scientific paradigm for exploring fundamental questions of intelligence and to have a close correspondence to evolving understanding in psychology and neuroscience.

As people have expected, the rate of progress along the connectionism line is great. Connectionist techniques are now being more widely applied to the complex processing needs of "high-level cognitive processing." However, very little is known, as yet, about the computational potential and limitations of connectionist machines. The relationship between the connectionist model and existing computation models is not well understood. More theoretical work needs to be

* This work was supported by the National Science Foundation under NSF Grant DCI-87-96236.

done. Motivated by this, we make an analytic comparison of the connectionist model to the conventional computation models. We attempt to reveal the deep relation among them and to build a bridge that connects the connectionist model to the conventional ones.

The first author has proved that all the conventional computational models are not only equivalent in Turing's sense, but also similar in the sense that for the same problem class they need essentially the same parallel time, essentially the same space and essentially the same sequential time simultaneously (Hong, 1985, 1986). By essentially the same we mean polynomially related. This is called the similarity principle. Therefore the main problem in this paper is: Does the similarity principle hold good for the connectionist model? The answer is yes. We will prove that the connectionist model is similar to all other "non-uniform" computation models. In fact, we will prove that any weight in a connectionist machine of n neurons can be simulated by $\lceil (n + 2)log(n + 1)\rceil$ binary bits.

The connectionist model is certainly well suited for handling specialized problems in perception; it leads us to think about new ways of representing knowledge, new ways of organizing problem solving, and so on. However, like all computer systems, the connectionist model still provides no particular help in solving the problem of combinatorial explosion usually encountered in A.I. problems.

As a novel computation model, the connectionist model has great potential. We develop the current synchronous connectionist model into the asynchronous connectionist model, which is much stronger, and again into the superconnectionist model which is extremely strong. We prove that the asynchronous connectionist model, and more surprisingly, the superconnectionist model as well, are similar to all other nonuniform computation models. The difficulties of NP-completeness or NP-hardness (i.e., combinatorial explosion) cannot be overcome by these models either.

People might think that the expansion factor $\lceil (n + 2)log(n + 1)\rceil$ we get in converting from a connectionist machine to a Boolean aggregate is too large if n is a big number and therefore the connectionist machine could be much better in practice at dealing with exponential explosion. We argue that it is a false impression.

Assume that some group has already built up a connectionist machine. If the machine has been constructed using digital elements, then it is an aggregate. There is no expansion. If people are going to build up a connectionist machine using analog-valued elements, then the fundamental challenge is the precision of those analog elements. To simulate real analog-valued elements with limited precision, we do not need too many Boolean gates. If the precision is 1/1,000, then we need 10 Boolean gates to simulate each weight. If 1/1,000,000, we need 20. Only when the connectionist machine is constructed using analog elements which have no error at all (probably not feasible), we need $\lceil (n + 2)log(n + 1)\rceil$

bits. In practice, to simulate a real connectionist machine we need very reasonable amount of Boolean gates.

The theoretical results presented in this chapter build a bridge between the connectionist models and other computation models and point out the limitation. This is not to say that we should be pessimistic. In fact, the connectionist models are appropriate for AI problems. We do not believe that a human brain can solve combinatorial explosion problems, therefore we do not think AI should worry about NP-hardness too much. We do not see evidence for, nor can we imagine, limits to AI research possibilities.

2. CONCEPTS CONCERNING COMPLEXITY THEORY

In this section, we introduce some informal concepts of complexity. We hope they will be helpful to those readers who do not work in this field.

Whenever we talk about the complexity, we mean the complexity of a class of problems of different sizes. The larger the problem the more the computation time. For example, consider the problem of binary integer multiplication. We may define the total length m of two binary integers to be multiplied as the size of the problem (the binary length of an integer is the total number of bits in its binary expansion). By a straightforward method, the computation time is proportional to m^2. Therefore the time complexity of this method of multiplication is m^2, a function of the problem size m.

Apart from the sequential time, which is the total amount of primitive computation steps needed to solve the problem, we also consider other computational resources, such as parallel time and space. Roughly speaking, the space complexity is the total amount of storage used to store the intermediate results, another increasing function of the problem size. The parallel time is the time needed for solving the problem by many computers (or many gates) working together.

Usually these bounding functions are increasing. The commonly used functions are, according to their increasing rates,

$$log\ m,\ log^2 m,\ log^3 m,\ \ldots$$

$$m,\ m\ log\ m,\ m^2,\ m^3,\ \ldots$$

$$2^m,\ 3^m,\ \ldots,\ m!,\ 2^{m^2},\ m^2!, \ldots$$

$$2^{2^m},\ 10^{2^m}, \ldots$$

These four groups are called polylog functions, polynomial functions, exponential functions, and double exponential functions. In the second group, any pair of two functions are polynomially related in the sense that any function is bounded by a fixed polynomial of the other. The same is true for the first group. Each group is much much higher in increasing order than preceding groups. They are not polynomially related. In this chapter we use * to represent a constant (usually a small one). Therefore we use m^* to represent a (usually low degree) polynomial of m, and log^*m a polylog function.

For convenience sake, if the complexity bounding function (for sequential time, parallel time or space) is in the first group, we use the words "very efficiently." If the complexity bounding function is in the second group, we use the word "reasonable." If the complexity bounding function is in the third or even higher group, we use the word "intractable," because in this case, no matter how we waste our resources, we can hardly increase the size of the problem that can be solved. Therefore if a problem class can be solved in polynomial sequential time, we say that the problem class can be solved in reasonable time; if a problem can be solved in polylog parallel time, we say that it is solvable in parallel very efficiently; if a problem class needs exponential resource, we say that this class is intractable. If a problem class can be solved very efficiently in parallel using reasonable space, we say that this problem class is in NC (Nick Peppenger's class). We say that the two models are similar if they can simulate each other in such a way that both parallel time and space are polynomially related.

In practice, we often have problems of searching for a substructure with some special property in a large structure; for example, finding out if there is a clique of a certain size or a Hamiltonian path in a large graph. The large structure can be represented by a binary string of length m. We define the size of the problem to be m. Usually any substructure can be represented by a binary string of length m^*. We need only polynomial time to check if a substructure has this property. But the trouble is that there are exponentially many candidates to check. The total number of candidates will be doubled and doubled when the problem size is increased. This is the so-called combinatorial explosion. Usually these kinds of problems are called NP problems. Here P means polynomial—we need polynomial time to check if a substructure has the special property. The N means nondeterministic—we do not know which one. Therefore usually we do not have a reasonable algorithm to solve an NP problem. Most NP problems are intractable.

It was proved by Cook, Karp, and many others that some problems are NP-hard in the sense that if one of these problems can be solved in reasonable (polynomial) time, then any NP problem can be solved in reasonable time. If an NP-hard problem itself is an NP-problem, then we say it is NP-complete. Therefore do not try to solve an NP-complete or NP-hard problem in a reasonable amount of time, because this is impossible unless all NP problems can be solved in reasonable amount of time.

We have these NP-hard problems everywhere in the field of A.I. People might think that if we increase the speed and storage, some day we may solve these hard problems. We should point out that not only linear speed-up, but also polynomial speed-up can not provide significant help in solving exponential explosion problems.

We take the game of Go as an example. The problem is, given the positions of black and white pieces on a mesh of size m by m, to determine if there is a forced win for the first player. If we use a backtracking method, the total computation time is proportional to the total number of choices. At the beginning, the first player has m^2 possible choices. Then the second player has $m^2 - 1$ choices. Altogether, there are $m^2!$ choices. This is too high. By using some skills, we may reduce the complexity, say, to 2^m.

Now assume that you have a machine which can deal with 1,000,000 choices in one second, and I have another machine which is much slower than yours. If your machine runs t seconds, to simulate your machine, I have to run mine for t^2 seconds (a polynomial slow-down). Or in other words, if my machine runs for t seconds, yours needs only to run for $\sqrt{t}$ seconds.

If the size of the Go board is very small, say $m = 2,3$, a child knows how to win. When m becomes larger, the game becomes very difficult. We may define that a machine is of an m-degree-go-player if it can solve the game of size m in one year.

Assume that your machine is an m1-degree-go-player and mine is an m2-degree-go-player. Then,

$$2^{m1^2} = 365 \times 24 \times 60 \times 60 \times 1000000$$

$$2^{m2^2} = \sqrt{365 \times 24 \times 60 \times 60} \times 1000000$$

We have roughly $m1 = 6.5$ and $m2 = 5.6$. Remember that our Go board is of size $m = 19$. There is no big difference between your machine and my machine before the practically intractable goal $m = 19$.

In this Chapter, we shall compare the connectionist model with an aggregate. The input of an aggregate is a binary string consisting of m bits. For each number m, there is an aggregate. An aggregate is a set of Boolean gates (or, and, not gates) connecting to each other. The fan-in of each gate is at most 2 but fan-out is unbounded. Among them, there are m "input" gates where the m input bits are initially there. All these gates work synchronously in the obvious way. When the value of each gate does not change any more, we say the aggregate is stopped and the values stored in some gates are considered to be the final result. The total number of synchronous steps from the beginning to the end is the parallel time. The total number of gates is the space. The sequential time is the total number of primitive computation steps, therefore roughly the product of the space and the parallel time. Any digital computer, or any digital computing system consisting of many computers, is an aggregate.

If the space of an aggregate is s, then the parallel time can not be higher than 2^s. This is because, each gate has 2 states, 0 or 1, therefore the aggregate has at most 2^s different states. If the parallel time is longer than this number, then the aggregate will fall into an endless cycle, and therefore will not stop and we have no result. Later we will always assume that the parallel time is bounded by an exponential function of the space. In practice, it is also reasonable to assume that for any machine, the parallel time is bounded by an exponential function of the space. Otherwise the parallel time would be higher than some thing which is already intractable.

Some computation models, such as Turing machines, are uniform in the sense that for inputs of different lengths the program (the transition function of the Turing machine) is always the same. There is no extra information for longer and longer inputs. But for different input length *m,* we have a different aggregate, and there would be more and more extra information contained in the structure of the larger and larger aggregates for larger and larger input lengths. In this sense, we say that the aggregates for different input lengths are not uniform or non-uniform. The connectionist machine is another non-uniform model. More and more information may be stored in the weights for larger and larger number n of neurons. What is different here is that if the weights are some arbitrary real numbers, these real numbers could be infinitely long and therefore contain an infinite amount of information.

CONNECTIONIST MODELS

We now define a classical, standard sort of connectionist model in terms of linear threshold units. Quite a few connectionist models do not conform to the defined model, especially those defined in terms of nonlinear threshold units.

A connectionist machine consists of a set of n formal neurons, $Neuron_i$, $i = 1,2, \ldots n$, connecting to each other through formal nerves. Mathematically, we assume the formal nerve connecting the 2th neuron to the jth neuron is $Nerve_{ij}$, which is weighted by a real number w_{ij}. Each neuron has a threshold, a real number. The threshold of the jth neuron is denoted by T_j. At each time, a neuron may be in either an on state or an off state. We use a binary function $v(i,t)$ to represent the state of the ith neuron at time t, that is, if the ith neuron is on at time t then $v(i,t) = 1$, otherwise $v(i,t) = 0$. If the ith neuron is on, then it will affect the jth neuron through $Nerve_{ij}$ weighted by a real number w_{ij}. The jth neuron sums all the weights where the neuron is on. If the total sum is larger than its threshold T_j, then at time $t + 1$ the jth neuron will be on, otherwise the jth neuron will be off, as stated by the following formula:

$$v(j,t+1) = \begin{cases} 1, & \text{if } \sum_{i=1}^{n} w_{ij}v(i,t) > T_j, \\ 0, & \text{otherwise.} \end{cases} \tag{1}$$

We may put in the system another neuron, the $n + 1^{th}$, which is always on and disconnected from any other. Obviously the system is equivalent to the original one. Now we add a nerve connecting the $n + 1^{th}$ neuron to the jth neuron. We put a weight $-T_j$ on it and change the threshold of the jth neuron from T_j to 0. Because the $n + 1^{th}$ neuron is always on, the behavior of the jth neuron will remain the same as before. Therefore later we need only consider the case that all the threshold numbers are 0: $T_j = 0$ for all j. Thus, a connectionist machine of size n can be represented by a real matrix w_{ij} of size $n \times n$.

It is not difficult to see that the connectionist model can simulate other computation models, such as an aggregate. At the very beginning of the automata theory, people knew that any Boolean gate could be simulated by formal neurons. Because all conventional computation models are similar, if connectionist model can simulate aggregate, then it can simulate other conventional computation models with essentially the same efficiency.

But on the other hand, can the aggregate model simulate the connectionist model? In this section we will prove the following theorem, which was discovered by the first author in 1986.

Theorem 1 *A connectionist machine of n neurons defined by a real matrix of $n \times n$ real numbers can be simulated by an aggregate consisting of $O(n^3 \log n)$ Boolean gates with time slow down of only $O(\log n)$. Therefore, the connectionist model is similar to all other nonuniform computation models.*

The key point to prove the above theorem is a gap theorem which guarantees that though an arbitrary real number could be infinitely long, we need only $O(n \log n)$ bits for each weight to define an arbitrary connectionist machine of n neurons. The rigorous proof for n-dimensional case of the gap theorem can be found in (Hong, 1988). A simple proof of 2D case can be found in the appendix of this chapter, which should give the reader a good intuition.

We cite the gap theorem here.

Theorem 2 (Gap Theorem 1) *Assume that in n dimensional space we have many hyperplanes:*

$$P_\alpha\colon \sum_{i=1}^{n} a_{\alpha i} x_i = b_\alpha, \alpha \in S,$$

where S is an arbitrary set and $a_{\alpha i}$, b_α are integers satisfying $\sum_{i=1}^{n} |a_{\alpha i}| \leq K$ for some constant K. Then these hyperplanes divide the n-dimensional space into many regions. Some regions are degenerate, meaning that the volume of the region is 0. Otherwise the region is nondegenerate. If a region is nondegenerate, then we can inscribe an n-dimensional ball inside, such that the radius d of the ball is at least

$$d \geq \frac{1}{K^{n+1}(n + 1)}.$$

Theorem 3 (Gap Theorem 2) *If all* $b_\alpha = 0$, *then the hyperplanes divide the n-dimensional space into many cones. If a cone is not a degenerate one, then we can find an integer point inside the cone such that the binary length of the coordinates of the integer point is bounded by*

$$\lceil log(K^{n+1}(n + 1) + 1)\rceil.$$

Now we prove theorem 1. To simulate the connectionist model by the aggregate model, we should find some integers m_i, to simulate the real weights w_i such that

$$\sum_{i=1}^{n} w_i v(i, t) \geq 0 \tag{2}$$

if and only if

$$\sum_{i=1}^{n} m_i v(i, t) \geq 0 \tag{3}$$

for all possible $v(i, t)$. This would enable the replacement of each neuron by a formal neuron whose weights are all integers of length bounded in the way shown.

Anyhow, the value of $v(i, t)$ is either 0 or 1. The point $(w_1, w_2, \ldots w_n)$ is inside a cone divided by the hyperplanes:

$$\sum_{i=1}^{n} v(i, t)x_i = 0, \tag{4}$$

for all possible values of $v(i, t)$.

We can find an integer point $(m_1, m_2, \ldots, m_n)$ in the same cone. Since they are in the same cone divided by (4), inequality (2) holds if and only if inequality (3) holds. Since $v(i, t)$ is either 0 or 1, the summation of the coefficients (the $\sum_{i=1}^{n} |a_{\alpha i}|$ in Gap theorem 2) is bounded by n (the constant K in Gap theorem 2 is n):

$$\sum_{i=1}^{n} |v(i, t)| \leq n.$$

The binary lengths of coordinates of the integer point $(m_1,m_2,\ldots,m_n)$ are bounded by

$$\lceil log(K^{n+1}(n + 1) + 1)\rceil \leq \lceil log(n^{n+1}(n + 1) + 1)\rceil \leq \lceil log(n + 1)^{n+2}\rceil \leq \lceil (n + 2)log(n + 1)\rceil .$$

Therefore $n^2\lceil (n + 2)log(n + 1)\rceil$ bits will be enough to define a connectionist machine of n neurons. Since we have the conclusion that $\lceil (n + 2)log(n + 1)\rceil$ bits will be enough for each weight, we can use a standard parallel adder to add all the weighted inputs together. (The reader may consult Chapter 6 in Hong, 1986.) There are n numbers, each of length $\lceil (n + 2)log(n + 1)\rceil$. The total parallel time needed is $O(log\ n)$ (the slow down factor). The total number of gates to simulate one neuron is $O(n^2 log\ n)$. Therefore the total number of Boolean gates in the aggregate is $O(n^3 log\ n)$. (Note that this is only $O(n\ logn)$ times as large as the number of *links* in the original network.)

Therefore the space and the parallel time used by both machines are polynomially related simultaneously.

4. ASYNCHRONOUS CONNECTIONIST MODEL

The connectionist model described in the previous section is actually the synchronous one, where all neurons work synchronously. It is instructive to extend the connectionist model to an asynchronous one because working asynchronously seems to be the way that the brain gets jobs done. There are two kinds of meanings for asynchronism. The weak sense of asynchronism means that the computation result is always the same while the time schedules of the elements vary at random. Obviously, this kind of asynchronism does not help the computation. The strong sense of asynchronism means that the system is deterministic and the time schedules (for example, the time delays) of the computation elements are some different numbers.

We consider the case of the strong asynchronism. Merely changing the time schedules of the elements brings the synchronous connectionist model to the asynchronous one. In fact here we consider the strongest asynchronous model in which all these numbers are arbitrary real numbers. (For example, a signal can be sent from a gate to another in exactly π seconds.) We define an asynchronous connectionist model as follows:

We assume that there are n neurons as before. From the ith neuron to the jth neuron there is a nerve, $Nerve_{ij}$. This nerve has a time delay d_{ij}, an arbitrary real number. The information that the ith neuron is off or on (the value $v(i,t)$ is 0 or 1) will be weighted by a factor w_{ij}, delayed by a time equal to d_{ij}, and arrive at the jth neuron. The jth neuron sums the total delayed and weighted values among all its neighbors during the (continuous) time. If the summation is steadily greater than 0 (or steadily not greater than 0) during a period longer than some value δ_j, then the jth neuron should be on (or off). The number δ_j is an arbitrary real number and is called the time threshold of the jth neuron. All these time delays and time thresholds satisfy the following condition:

$$0 < \delta < \delta_j < \Delta \tag{5}$$

$$0 < \delta \leq d_{ij} \leq \Delta \tag{6}$$

where δ and Δ are two constants.

We attempt to probe deeply into the asynchronous connectionist model.

The history of a neuron during a period is a list of the following form:

$$(t_1, 0; t_2, 1; t_3, 0; t_4, 1; \ldots)$$

meaning that from time t_1 on the value of the neuron is 0, from time t_2 on, the value of the neuron is 1, . . . , and so forth.

It is not difficult to show that if we know the histories for all neurons during time period $[t - 2\Delta, t]$, then we can compute histories for all neurons during time period $[t - 2\Delta + \delta, t + \delta]$. The length of the time period is 2Δ, therefore there are only constant many terms in the history list. Of course, these numbers $t_1, t_2 \ldots$ might be arbitrary real numbers. If they are integers (later we will prove that all these numbers can be simulated by integers of length bounded by a polynomial of n), then we can think the history of a neuron during time period $[t - 2\Delta, t]$ as the state at time t. If we know the states for all neurons at time t, then we can compute the states of all neurons at time $t + \delta$. (In this way, we can treat the asynchronous connectionist model as a synchronous one.) This computation (to compute the state at time $t + \delta$ from the state at time t) can be very efficiently solved in parallel. In other words, this problem can be solved in polynomial space and polylog parallel time (this problem is in NC; consult Hong, 1986).

Now we concentrate ourselves on the problem of why these real time delays and time thresholds can be replaced by integers of polynomial lengths. If we change the time delays a little bit, the result of the computation might be changed, because a signal A now may arrive before signal B but it originally should arrive after signal B. But if we change the time delays and time thresholds in such a way that all time orderings remain unchanged, then the result of the computation will be the same.

As a very simple example, consider four neurons N_1, N_2, N_3, and N_4 connected as shown in Figure 13.1.

Here N_1 is the only neuron which carrys the input and N_4 is the only neuron which carrys the output. The numbers d_1, d_2, d_3, and d_4 are time delays on the corresponding connections. For simplicity, we have omitted other information. Now it is easy to see that if we change the time delays d_1, d_2, d_3, and d_4 in such a way that we always have

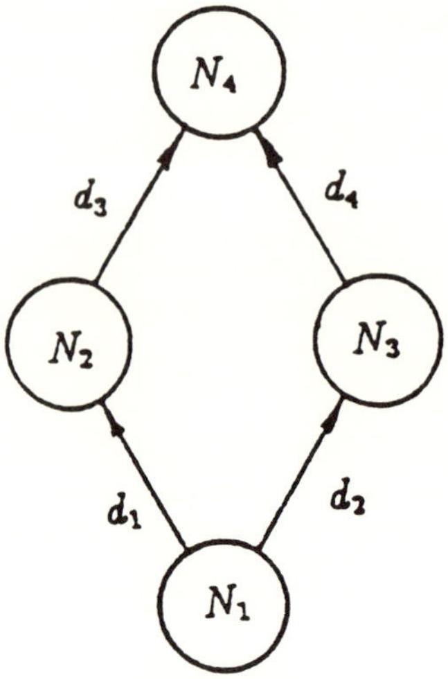

Figure 13.1.
A simple Neural Network.

$$d_1 + d_3 > d_2 + d_4,$$

that is, we always keep the time ordering, then the computation result at N_4 will be always the same. Generally, since there are many loops in the computation, any time ordering can be expressed in the following way:

$$\sum_{ij} a_{ij}d_{ij} + \sum_{j} b_j\delta_j > \sum_{ij} a'_{ij}d_{ij} + \sum_{j} b'_j\delta_j$$

where a_{ij}, b_j, are some integers representing the duplication of a connection or a neuron in one information route, while $a'_{i,j}$ and $b'_{i,j}$ are some integers representing the duplication of a connection or a neuron in the other information route. Therefore we have

$$\sum_{ij} |a_{ij}| + \sum_{j} |b_j| \leq t,$$

$$\sum_{ij} |a'_{ij}| + \sum_{j} |b'_j| \leq t,$$

where t is the total computation time. We can rewrite the inequality as

$$\sum_{ij} (a_{ij} - a'_{i,j})d_{ij} + \sum_{j} (b_j - b'_j)\delta_j > 0$$

and the coefficients satisfy

$$\sum_{ij} |a_{ij} - a'_{i,j}| + \sum_{j} |b_j - b'_j| \leq 2t.$$

By our Gap Theorems 2 and 3 again, we can simulate the real numbers d_{ij}, δ_j, by integers. Since the total number of variables (the dimension) is $n^2 + n$ instead of n, and the summation of the absolute values of the coefficients is bounded by $2t$ in stead of K, we know that the length of these integers found is bounded by

$$O(n^2 log\ t).$$

The computation time t cannot be much higher than an exponential function of n. Therefore $log\ t$, and the length of these integers found, is bounded by a polynomial of n.

When we replace the real values of delays and thresholds by integers, we have already obtained a synchronous model. The time now is discrete and enlarged by a factor $O(2^{n^*})$. Therefore, the "carving times" t_1, t_2, . . . in the history of a neuron during time period $[t - 2\Delta, t]$ are all integers of lengths n^*. Since there are only constant many these carving times in it, the history during time $[t - 2\Delta, t]$ (the state of the neuron at time t), can be represented by a binary string of length n^*.

We summarize the significant properties of the asynchronous connectionist model as follows:

1. The state of a neuron at time t (the history of the neuron during time period $[t - 2\delta, t]$) can be represented by a binary string of length n^*.
2. The states of all neurons at time $t + \delta$ can be computed from the states of all neurons at time t. The computation is in NC (can be very efficiently solved in parallel).

Based on these two points only, we can prove the following theorem (the proof will be given in the next section).

Theorem 4 *The asynchronous connectionist model is similar to all other non-uniform computation models.*

Therefore neither the asynchronous can help to solve the combinatorial explosion encountered with A.I. problems.

5. SUPERCONNECTIONIST MODEL

The fundamental importance of connectionist model lies in reflecting architectural considerations of the brain, building bridges to neurobiology. We may try to understand the architecture of the mind better by continuously developing the connectionist model.

We have extended a connectionist model from a synchronous model to an asynchronous one. In this section, the connectionist model will be strengthened in a tremendous way. We call the developed model superconnectionist model.

A superconnectionist model is a set of n neurons connecting to each other. At any time t, a neuron is in a state in S. At time $t + 1$, the state of neuron i is determined by the states of all neurons and a (maybe different) mapping

$$f_i: S^n \rightarrow S.$$

And we have the following assumptions for the superconnectionist model:

Assumption 1 *The size of set S is bounded by* 2^{n^*}.

Here * means a constant again, like 2 or 10, for example. This assumption says that the state of a single neuron can be represented by a binary string of length bounded by a polynomial of n. As mentioned in the last section, the asynchronous connectionist model satisfies this assumption. This assumption is very reasonable. The bound is large enough. Remember that n is the total number of neurons in the superconnectionist model. For example, we have 10^{12} or even more neurons. Let us say * is 2. The fact that a neuron has more than 2^{n^2} states means that a single neuron can remember more than 10^{24} binary bits!

We assume that the functions of different neurons are different. We did not put any restriction on the mapping f_i. But if the mapping is too strong, such as NP-hard or even nonrecursive, then the model is not interesting. Therefore we give another assumption:

Assumption 2 *The mapping f_i is in NC, i.e., the mapping can be realized in polynomial (reasonable) space and polylog (very efficient) parallel time.*

This assumption is also reasonable, because we can not expect that a single neuron can instantly solve a computation problem that cannot be solved very efficiently by any parallel computing system. As mentioned before, the asynchronous connectionist model satisfies this assumption. Therefore the asynchronous connectionist model is a special case of the superconnectionist model.

The superconnectionist model is very strong indeed. The limits put by Assumptions 1, 2 are in fact negligible. So far it is hard to imagine that the real neurons in the brain would be functionally beyond the above assumptions.

Surprisingly enough, even though the superconnectionist model looks enormously powerful, we can still prove that it is similar to all other non-uniform computation models.

Theorem 5 *The superconnectionist model is similar to all other non-uniform computation models. A superconnectionist model of n neurons can be simulated by a parallel machine within reasonable space (polynomial space) very efficiently (with polylog time slow down). Their information complexities are the same.*

This theorem is not difficult to prove. Since each mapping $f_i, i = 1,2,\ldots n$ is in NC, by definition there is a circuit C_i of polynomial width and polylog depth to accomplish the job. The whole design of the parallel computer to simulate the superconnectionist model is shown in Figure 13.2. Obviously, the width of the machine is n times a polynomial of n, still a polynomial of n. This machine can simulate one step of the superconnectionist model by accomplishing one cycle. The time slow down in the simulation is a polylog function of n, and therefore the parallel time of the simulating machine is also polynomially related to the parallel time of the superconnectionist model.

Since the asynchronous connectionist model is a special case of the superconnectionist model, Theorem 2 is also valid.

6. CONCLUSION

The connectionist model—encompassing neuron networks, spreading activation networks and evidential inference networks—is of fundamental importance. It reflects architectural considerations of the brain and exploits massive parallelism. It leads us to think about new ways of representing knowledge, new ways of

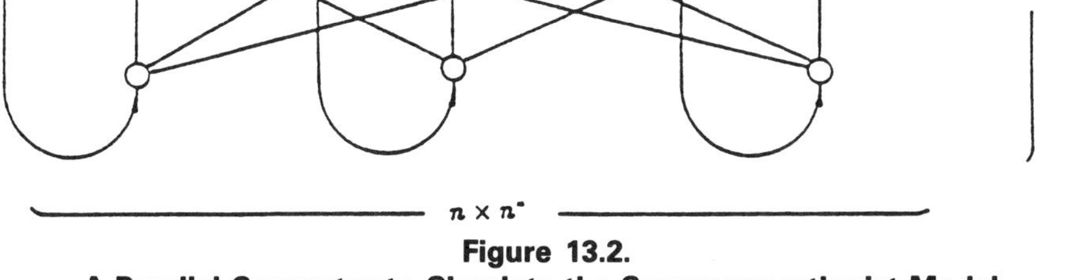

Figure 13.2.
A Parallel Computer to Simulate the Superconnectionist Model.

organizing problem solving and in particular new ways of thinking about low-level perceptual and memory mechanisms, and so on.

To understand the connectionist model in a deeper way, we analyse the computational potential and limitations by comparing it with other computation models; we develop the current connectionist model into the asynchronous model and the superconnectionist model. Our theoretical results indicate that the connectionist model of n neurons can be simulated by a nonuniform circuit of $O(n^3 \log n)$ Boolean gates with slow down factor of $O(\log n)$; further, the asynchronous connectionist model and superconnectionist model can be simulated by a parallel machine within reasonable space (polynomial space) very efficiently (with polylog time slow down). This means that the connectionist models are similar to all other nonuniform computation models. Our work builds a bridge that connects connectionist models to the conventional computation models and points out that like all computer systems, the connectionist model still cannot help to solve the problem of combinatorial explosion usually encountered in A.I.

Since analog-valued neurons are attracting increasing attention in the connectionist and neural net communities, we would like to make the following speculations:

The analog elements help the computation in a dramatic way only if:

1. A single analog element can solve a computation problem which is not in NC efficiently. That is, it can solve a problem which can not be solved by any parallel (digital) computer system very efficiently, or
2. The analog elements have very very high precision, in other words, have more than exponentially many significant bits.

Otherwise, if neither of the conditions is satisfied, then the network is a superconnectionist machine and is similar to all other machines. It cannot do any better to conquer the NP-hardness.

However, we can hardly imagine that a brain cell would be functionally stronger than a formal neuron defined in the superconnectionist model. If we agree that the function of the brain is the outcome of the functions of all its neuron cells, then the brain can not solve an NP-hard problem either. Therefore, we do not think that the problem of combinatorial explosion should be the real limit to AI.

REFERENCES

Bobrow, D., & Hayes, P. (1985). Artificial intelligence—Where are we? *Artificial Intelligence, 25*, 375–415.

Hong, J. (1985). On similarity and duality of computation. *FOCS 1980 and also Information and Control, 62*, 109–128.

Hong, J. (1986). *Computation: Computability, similarity and duality*. London: Pitman Publishing Ltd.
Hong, J. (1988, December). On connectionist models. *Communications on Pure and Applied Mathematics, XLI*(8), 1039–1050.

7. APPENDIX

The Proof of the Gap Theorem in 2D Case.

Theorem 6 *Assume there are many lines on the plane.*

$$a_{\alpha 1}x_1 + a_{\alpha 2}x_2 = b_\alpha \quad \alpha \in S$$

where $a_{\alpha i}$ *and* b_α *are some integers satisfying*

$$|a_{\alpha 1}| + |a_{\alpha 2}| \leq K$$

for some constant K. They divide the plane into many regions. If a region is non-degenerate, we can inscribe a disc inside, such that the radius d of the disc is at least $1/3K^3$.

Proof. Assume that the radius of the disc is d and its center is $\bar{y} = (y_1, y_2)$, that a line

$$a_1x_1 + a_2x_2 - b = 0$$

is tangent to this disc and the tangent point is $\bar{z} = (z_1, z_2)$. We use $N = \sqrt{a_1^2 + a_2^2}$ to denote the norm of the line. Then the unit normal vector of the line is $A_0 = (a_1, a_2)/N$ and

$$\begin{aligned} d &= A_0(\bar{y} - \bar{z}) \\ &= \frac{1}{N}(a_1y_1 + a_2y_2 - a_1z_1 - a_2z_2) \\ &= \frac{1}{N}(a_1y_1 + a_2y_2 - b) \end{aligned}$$

Therefore the coordinates of the center satisfy the following equation:

$$a_1y_1 + a_2y_2 - Nd = b$$

Assume that the disc is inscribed to three lines:

$$a_{i1}x_1 + a_{i2}x_2 - b_i = 0,\ i = 1,2,3,$$

and denote the norms of them by N_i, $i = 1,2,3$ respectively, then the coordinates of the center satisfy the following linear system of equations:

$$a_{11}y_1 + a_{12}y_2 - N_1 d = b_1$$

$$a_{21}y_1 + a_{22}y_2 - N_2 d = b_2$$

$$a_{31}y_1 + a_{32}y_2 - N_3 d = b_3$$

By our assumption of the gap theorem, we have $|a_{i1}| + |a_{i2}| \leq K$, $i = 1,2,3$, and therefore

$$N_i = \sqrt{a_{i1}^2 + a_{i2}^2} \leq |a_{i1}| + |a_{i2}| \leq K, i = 1,2,3,$$

we can solve the linear equation system for d: $|d| = \bar{D}/D$, where

$$\bar{D} = \begin{vmatrix} a_{11} & a_{12} & b_1 \\ a_{21} & a_{22} & b_2 \\ a_{31} & a_{32} & b_3 \end{vmatrix}$$

$$D = \begin{vmatrix} a_{11} & a_{12} & N_1 \\ a_{21} & a_{22} & N_2 \\ a_{31} & a_{32} & N_3 \end{vmatrix}$$

Since $d \neq 0$ and $\bar{D}$ is an integer, we have

$$|\bar{D}| \geq 1$$

Since

$$D = N_1 \begin{vmatrix} a_{21} & a_{22} \\ a_{31} & a_{32} \end{vmatrix} - N_2 \begin{vmatrix} a_{11} & a_{12} \\ a_{31} & a_{32} \end{vmatrix} + N_3 \begin{vmatrix} a_{11} & a_{12} \\ a_{21} & a_{22} \end{vmatrix}$$

we have $|D| \leq 3K^3$ and $d \geq 1/3K^3$.

Gap theorem 2. In case that $b_\alpha = 0$ for all α, the shape of any region is a cone. Then in any non-degenerate region we can find an integer point such that the binary length of its coordinates is bounded by $log(K^{n+1}(n + 1) + 1) = O(n \log K)$.

Proof. We add the following hyperplanes to the system:

$$|x_i| = 1, \qquad i = 1, 2, \ldots, n$$

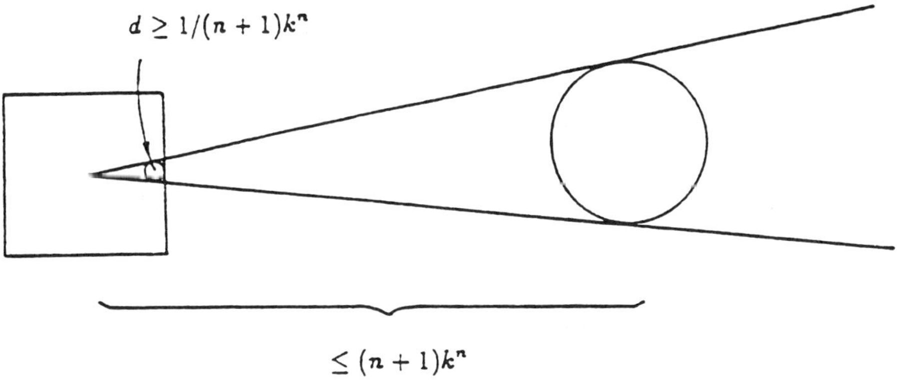

Figure 13.3.
An Illustration of the Bound Specified in Gap Theorem 3.

We inscribe a ball in the region as shown in Figure 13.3.

The radius d of this ball is at least $\frac{1}{K^{n+1}(n+1)}$. Scale and enlarge it alone the cone to a distance $K^{n+1}(n + 1)$ from the origin. Then we obtain a ball of radius 1. It is inside the cone. Since the radius of the ball is 1, we can find an integer point in the ball which is in turn inside the cone. The binary length of any coordinate of the integer point is bounded by

$$\lceil log(K^{n+1}(n + 1) + 1)\rceil = O(n \; log \; K).$$

14
Complex Features in Planning and Understanding: Problems and Opportunities for Connectionism*

Lawrence Birnbaum

1. INTRODUCTION

I will take advantage of my position as an appointed[1] "friendly critic" of connectionism to begin this chapter on a personal note. Much of the appeal of connectionist or neural network models to me—and, I suspect, to others as well—lies in the solution they apparently offer to problems of perception and interpretation, given certain simplifying assumptions. Even without going into the details, these models have driven home the point that boolean circuits can quickly compute, in parallel, a large number of features defined in terms of primitive inputs. Ambiguity, combinatorially intractable search, attention focusing—in short, all of the processing issues that have bedeviled artificial intelligence since its inception—seem irrelevant in the face of the massive parallelism that connectionist models offer. Perhaps these issues were all simply artifacts of serial computation.

But then again, perhaps not. From my perspective, as someone working in

* This chapter is based on a talk presented at the Workshop on High-Level Connectionist Models, hosted by the Computing Research Laboratory, New Mexico State University, Las Cruces, NM, in April 1988. I thank the organizers, John Barnden and Jordan Pollack, for their hospitality. For many useful discussions on these topics, I thank Anandan, Eugene Charniak, Jerry Feldman, Jim Hendler, Larry Hunter, Bruce Krulwich, Wendy Lehnert, Stan Letovsky, Charlie Martin, Drew McDermott, Eric Mjolsness, and Jordan Pollack. This work was supported in part by the Defense Advanced Research Projects Agency, monitored by the Office of Naval Research under contract N00014-85-K-0108 and by the Air Force Office of Scientific Research under contract F49620-88-C-0058. The Institute for the Learning Sciences was established in 1989 with the support of Andersen Consulting, part of The Arthur Andersen Worldwide Organization.

[1] Although not *self*-appointed—I was drafted.

planning and natural language processing, perception and interpretation don't actually *seem* to be solved problems. As a matter of fact, connectionist models have yet to seriously address the aspects of these problems that worry AI people. So we need to take a closer look at the assumptions upon which the connectionist solution is based.

The first major assumption is that we are not merely trading time for space, creating a combinatorial explosion in the size of the networks required. We cannot expect connectionist models to compute all possible boolean combinations of input features. The number of output features or units, and the number of units in intermediate layers, must be roughly proportional to (or at most, polynomial in) the number of inputs.[2]

The import of this constraint is that, since a connectionist network cannot compute *all* combinations of its inputs, it must compute only those combinations that are potentially *useful*. This requires either that the designer of the network specify those combinations which are useful for the task—in other words, that he construct what the rest of AI would call the vocabulary of a *representation theory*—or else a learning theory that will allow the model to pull out the useful combinations on its own. A lot of people in connectionism are betting on the latter, and it may be that such a theory will eventually be developed. But I think it is fair to say, and by now widely acknowledged, that the most impressive demonstrations of connectionist learning to date, for example, Sejnowski and Rosenberg's (1986) Nettalk model, have leaned rather heavily on the prior existence of representation theories in which the relevant features are easily expressed.

The second major simplifying assumption underlying the connectionist solution of perception and interpretation problems is that the complex features that must be computed are *propositional,* that is, that boolean combinations of input features will suffice. This raises two important questions: First, how realistic is this assumption? And second, can it be overcome in a way that preserves what is special and important about connectionism?

2. THE (NEGATIVE) EVIDENCE FROM NLP

Of all problems in perception and interpretation, language understanding poses what is probably the biggest challenge to connectionist models, especially those which attempt to dispense with explicit symbolic representations. Language is, after all, the prototypical symbol system. It should come as no surprise, then, that the evidence from natural language processing is largely negative with respect to the assumptions underlying connectionist approaches to perception and interpretation: The features that must be recognized in order to understand natural

[2] This was first pointed out to me by Jerry Feldman.

language are *not* simply boolean combinations of perceptually available features, and so propositional logic is *not* sufficient to represent the knowledge that must be employed.

The best way to see why this is the case is to look at some examples. Consider the following vignette:

> John walked up the steps with his arms full of groceries. Mary stepped around him and opened the door.

It should be clear that understanding this vignette involves recognizing that it describes an instance of a "helping" action—in fact, a rather stereotypical (or "scripty") instance. It is this recognition that renders the vignette coherent. Otherwise, it would simply be two separate and unrelated assertions. Thus, for example, if the story continued with "John told her about the party he was having that evening," we would probably interpret his action as an invitation reciprocating a friendly gesture. But such an interpretation depends on understanding how Mary's action could be seen as a friendly gesture in the first place.

More generally, it is now widely accepted that understanding linguistic input is fundamentally an issue of *explaining* that input in relation to its context and in terms of the understander's prior knowledge. In terms of the information processing paradigm underlying standard approaches to artificial intelligence, this entails deriving a representation of the input in which the causal relations among the actions and states it describes are made explicit (see, e.g., Charniak, 1972; Schank & Abelson, 1977; Wilensky, 1983), along with the reasons why the speaker alludes to them, and in the way that he does (see, e.g., Grice, 1975; Allen & Perrault, 1980). This process of "inference to the best explanation" is often called *abductive* inference, borrowing a term due to Pierce (see Pople, 1973).

There are two facts about explanatory inference that bear crucially on the assumptions of connectionism. First, it is fast: Determining the contextually appropriate meaning of an ambiguous word—which often depends upon explanatory inference of the sort illustrated above (see, e.g., Birnbaum, 1985)—usually takes people less than a half-second (see, e.g., Swinney, 1979). Thus, no "pokey" connectionist implementation of a combinatorially intractable forward- and back-chaining theorem-prover or production system will suffice—not because of any limitations of connectionism *per se,* but because such general models of symbolic computation, in and of themselves, offer no solution to the problem: The simple-minded application of such models to explanatory inference is inherently too slow for combinatorial reasons. Thus, connectionist implementations of standard symbolic computation paradigms may overcome the limitations of propositional reasoning, but at the cost of landing in the same pickle as the rest of us.

The second key fact about abduction is that it often involves the utilization of highly abstract explanatory structures, *especially in novel cases*. The simple vignette described above, obviously, is not such a novel instance of "helping." Thus, it seems plausible that the specific features involved in this case, or more accurately a description of the situation in terms of those features, already exists in memory as a scripty instance of the concept of "helping." Other specific exemplars of the concept might also be in memory, for example, "helping an old lady across the street." In these cases, it seems to me, connectionist models of situation recognition have some chance of success.

But can all instances of "helping" be recognized in this way? Consider the following example:

> Dukakis was worried about winning the New York primary without alienating the African-American vote in November. Gore started running commercials about Jackson's views on the Middle East. Dukakis won the primary, and carried the state in the general election.

Leaving aside the enormous amount of background knowledge of American politics that is necessary in order to understand this vignette, what makes it so problematic for models of understanding is that it describes a highly novel instance of "helping."[3] Unlike a case such as helping someone with their arms full of groceries by opening the door for them, it seems highly implausible that a description of this situation in terms of the specific features involved already exists in memory as a specialization of "helping." Recognizing this as a "helping" action, therefore, entails the representation and application of a description of "helping" actions in abstract, rather than specific, terms.

What does the concept of "helping" look like at such an abstract level? Well, roughly speaking, it looks like this:

```
(for-all (x, y) helps(x, y) <=>
(exists (a, b) action(a) &
        state(b) &
        actor-of(a, x) &
        precondition-of(b, goal-of(y)) &
        problematic-for(y, b) &
        causes(a, b)))
```

where, it should be noted, "causes" must be defined recursively, in order to handle both direct and indirect causation. In other words, an agent helps a recipient when there is a causal chain linking an action of the agent's with a problematic precondition for some goal of the recipient's. Thus, "helping" is

[3] If you are not sure that this story actually *is*, or could be, understood as Gore helping Dukakis, imagine a continuation in which Dukakis wins the election, and picks Gore to be Secretary of State.

a *thematic* concept, defined in terms of an abstract vocabulary of plan and goal relationships, rather than a vocabulary of domain-specific features. The importance of such abstract thematic concepts in language understanding, and more importantly their fundamental role in memory organization, are demonstrated by what Schank (1982) calls "cross-contextual remindings," in which an input situation reminds the understander of a thematically related episode sharing few, if any, specific features.[4] "Helping" is, in fact, a rather simple example of such a thematic concept.

Before I begin pointing the finger at connectionism, I must acknowledge that the representation and recognition of such concepts is difficult regardless of the approach taken. Although it is, in principle, possible to use rules like the above in a modified theorem-prover, such a crude and unstructured process is not merely combinatorially intractable, it is empirically vacuous: Because such mechanisms rely on nondeterminism to search through the space of possible explanations, they make no claims about how such a process should be carried out, beyond those inherent in the specification of the search space itself.[5]

Nevertheless, the problems posed by examples such as the above seem particularly difficult within a connectionist framework. For one thing, the recognition of each of the constituents of this concept, for example, determining that a given precondition is actually problematic for some agent, will often itself require considerable inference. For example, in this case the problem is that Dukakis cannot attack Jackson himself without alienating African-American voters. But this itself is a rather novel situation. We might, at best, presume that the understander knows that a politician cannot afford to attack another politician if he will later need the support of the latter's constituents, that is, that such an attack would be problematic under those circumstances. Even then, however, determining that such a situation holds in this case is far from simple, for example, it involves either recalling or inferring that African-American voters form the core of Jackson's constituency. Moreover, it must still be understood that, because Dukakis and Jackson are rivals, attacking Jackson is one way for Dukakis to achieve his goal of winning the primary. In sum, the recognition of such abstract structures seems to involve something like *chaining,* that is, transferring constraints over representations through several inferential steps.

Another difficult problem with "helping" is that all of its constituents are extremely *generic* (or, to use a colloquial expression, "vanilla")—almost all of the specific content of the concept lies in the structural relations among its components, and almost none in the particular predicates or features. This means, first, that a different arrangement of similar features might have a drastically different meaning, something that is obviously a problem for connec-

---

[4] Other important work on abstract thematic concepts includes Abelson (1973), Carbonell (1981), Lehnert (1982), Dyer (1983), Wilensky (1983), and Hammond (1989).

[5] See Birnbaum (1986) for a further discussion of this issue.

tionist approaches, given their well-known weaknesses in scoping attributes or binding variables. However, this is also the case with many concepts or schemas, perhaps even most. What makes abstract thematic concepts particularly problematic is that virtually *none* of their constituent features are specific: What story situations *don't* involve such elements as "problem," "causal chain," and so on? The problem of indexing and retrieving concepts built out of such generic elements when they might be appropriate is extremely thorny on anybody's account. But I think we are nevertheless entitled to be particularly demanding of connectionist models in regard to this problem, since it is by virtue of their content-addressable properties that they are alleged to be particularly suited to situation recognition tasks.

A third, and final, problem with "helping," particularly from a connectionist perspective, lies in establishing the causal relationship between the action taken by the helper, and the problematic precondition needed by the recipient of the help. The length of the causal chain between these two points is completely unspecified—in recognizing that a causal relationship exits, the understander must, in a sense, "traverse" its own mental representation of the situation, checking that all of the necessary constraints are met. One way to do this is to define "cause" recursively—for example, "A causes B if A immediately causes B or there exists a C such that A immediately causes C and C causes B"—which is what we have relied upon above. Alternatively, we might "reify" the concept of a "causal chain" so that it is no longer merely part of our theoretical vocabulary in describing the understanding process, but is actually something about which the understander itself can reason directly. In either case, one might be able to find, using purely associative methods, that some causal connection potentially obtains between the helper's action and the helpee's problematic precondition—but the connection between such a chain and "helping" must be established by pattern-matching of some sort. Both recursion and the explicit manipulation of structured representations seem necessary, and both pose severe challenges to connectionist models.

In sum, it seems clear that recognizing novel instances of "helping" requires complex, nonpropositional, inference and pattern matching over mental representations, tasks for which connectionist or neural network models, at least as currently conceived, do not seem inherently suited. Probably the most serious rejoinder to this argument is to take the position that I am expecting too much—it is, after all, arguable that *people* cannot handle serious novelty, and are limited to understanding only slight variations of previously understood cases.[6] Unfortunately, it seems all too easy to invent stories that seem, on the face of it, extremely novel, but are nevertheless easily understood.

Many of the problems identified above—the need for something like in-

---

[6] Much, though not all, current work in *case-based reasoning* takes this position; see Kolodner (1988) for a collection of papers representing a wide variety of research within this paradigm.

ference chaining with variable binding, the need for recursion, and the need for explicit representations—are of course well-known to critics and advocates of connectionist models alike. I would like, therefore, to concentrate more on the problems involved in indexing and retrieving concepts built from extremely generic component concepts, particularly since, as I noted above, this speaks to one of the alleged strengths of connectionist models, rather than their known weaknesses. Indeed, even within the standard symbolic AI paradigm, the belief has long been cherished that parallel associative methods must ultimately play an important, perhaps even crucial, role in memory retrieval and quasi-inferential reasoning (see, e.g., Quillian, 1968; Fahlman, 1979; Charniak, 1983; Stanfill & Waltz, 1986). In the following discussion, I focus on Charniak's (1983) theory of explanatory inference based on some form of "marker passing." Although it is not strictly speaking a connectionist model—at most, it might be considered a hybrid—I believe that the strengths and weaknesses of this model with respect to the problem of recognizing situations involving "vanilla" components are indicative of what can be expected from connectionist models in general.

Charniak's model is based on the following idea: Serial inference is great for nailing down the logic of a chain of reasoning, keeping track of variable bindings, and so on, but it's lousy at determining which chain of reasoning is likely to prove fruitful, and as a result it is combinatorially intractable. On the other hand, parallel associative reasoning is great for finding connections between concepts quickly, using noninferential methods, but it's lousy for nailing down the logic of such chains—for example, it has a hard time keeping track of variable bindings. Why not, then, combine them in some way?[7] In particular, inspired by Quillian's (1968) model of semantic memory, Charniak proposed that "markers," perhaps with activation levels, be spread through an associative network representing facts and inference rules, starting from certain given concepts. When markers from two different concepts land on the same node in memory, the intersection is noted, and the resulting path returned from memory. In this way, the model has the ability to quickly find potential inference paths between input concepts, or between inputs and hypotheses about them.

However, such methods alone are not capable of guaranteeing that the resulting path is in fact a valid explanation. Thus, Charniak's model uses a generate-and-test paradigm, in which the paths produced by marker-passing are checked over by a serial inference machine, to enforce logical consistency and compatible variable-bindings. For instance, consider Charniak's now-standard example:

Jack wanted to commit suicide. He got a rope.

---

[7] Both this tradeoff between "associative" and "logical" reasoning, and the possibility of combining them in some way, were pointed out some time ago (in rather general terms, to be sure) by Minsky (1968).

Spreading markers from "suicide" marks, among other things, known ways of killing or dying. Spreading marks from "rope" marks, among other things, known uses of rope. Markers from these two sources eventually intersect, and as a result the path "suicide—hanging—noose—rope" is generated. Once this path is retrieved from memory, it is a relatively simple matter to check over the actual rules containing the nodes in this path, and determine that a consistent set of variable bindings is possible, resulting in the following causal chain: "Jack wanted to commit suicide. Jack decided to hang himself. Jack needed to make a noose. Jack needed to get a rope. Jack got a rope."

It should be clear that the use of marker passing and serial inference in a generate-and-test paradigm depends on two key assumptions: First, the cost of checking over the paths retrieved must be relatively low; second, the *number* of paths retrieved must be relatively small. The latter assumption is particularly crucial, for the larger the number of paths that must be checked by the serial inference mechanism, the more the entire process begins to look like undirected inference again.

Unfortunately, this is exactly where abstract explanatory structures pose a problem. Consider the following variant on Charniak's rope example:

> Jack the detective was trailing a suspect. The suspect went into a hardware store, and Jack followed him inside. The suspect looked at gardening tools. Jack stood in another aisle, in front of the rope display. All of a sudden, the suspect looked up and eyed Jack suspiciously. Quickly, Jack got a rope and went to the checkout counter.

If we now ask why Jack got the rope, it should be clear that the answer has nothing to do with rope *per se*. Rather, Jack's goal is to allay suspicion and appear inconspicuous. The reasoning involved appears to be something like this: "One way to look inconspicuous is to appear to have a good alternative reason to be where you are. A good reason to be where you are is to do the scripty thing there. The scripty thing to do in a hardware store is to buy hardware. Rope is hardware. To buy something, you have to get it and take it to the checkout counter of the store. So, to buy the rope, you have to get it and take it to the checkout counter of the store."

This example poses several difficult problems for any purely associative reasoning methods, including both marker passing and more orthodox connectionist approaches. For one thing, it raises the problem of representing and reasoning about the reasoning processes of another agent, that is, what would allay the subject's suspicion, and why—and this, in turn, is likely to rest on the ability to represent and reason about one's *own* reasoning processes. However, here I want to focus on the problem of how to recognize the relationship between Jack's goal of avoiding suspicion and his behavior in getting the rope, for it is this problem that marker passing was intended to solve.

What path can we expect a marker-passing scheme to return from memory given the above example? Roughly speaking, it must be something like this: "inconspicuous—scripty action—buy—get." Regardless of the details, however, the key point here is that any path connecting the goal in this case (remaining inconspicuous) with the behavior (buying rope) must include a node corresponding to the rule that mentions performing a scripty action in order to look inconspicuous. This, however, raises a difficult problem: After all, what action *isn't* scripty under some circumstances? If we allow marker passing to employ such a node, then, because almost every action is stereotypical in some context, a path through that node will be generated for almost every action taken in our story. As a result, the path "inconspicuous—scripty action—script *x*—action *y*" will be generated for *every* action *y* that takes place in the story. So, a marker-passing approach is faced with the following dilemma: Either it cannot generate paths of this sort, or else it will massively overgenerate them.

Now, it might be argued that there are ways around the problems posed by this particular example. One plausible approach, for instance, would be to put a high threshold on the node for "scripty thing," so that markers were only passed through it in cases when the goal of looking inconspicuous were highly salient—as it is above because of the subject's "suspicious look." Unfortunately, however, this will not work in general, since it is quite possible to construct stories which rely on the same reasoning, but without such an additional clue.[8] Consider, for example, the following vignette:

> Jack the detective was trailing a suspect. The suspect went into a grocery store, and Jack followed him inside. The suspect took a cart and started walking down the aisles. Jack followed suit, taking items off the shelf from time to time and putting them in his cart.

In this story, it is again apparent that Jack is putting groceries in his cart in order to look inconspicuous (since that is the stereotypical thing to do in grocery stores), despite the fact that there is no "suspicious look" by the subject to prime our interest in Jack's goal of remaining undetected. In sum, the basic problem remains: If one is going to use associative methods to recognize instances of abstractions such as "looking inconspicuous," or "helping," or any of a large number of thematic concepts, then one has to live with either false positives, or false negatives, or both.

3. OPPORTUNITIES

This chapter has been fairly negative about the prospects for connectionist and neural net models to handle fundamental problems in natural language process-

---

[8] Which is not to say that this clue does not play an important role in facilitating our understanding of the above story.

ing: Language understanding requires complex inference, and propositional features and rules will not suffice. It should come as no surprise that exactly the same problems also manifest themselves in planning and intentional behavior. Consider, for example, how Jack determined what to do when he was spotted. Why did he choose to get *rope* in the hardware store, as opposed to something else? The answer seems clear: He chose rope because of the *opportunity* presented by its immediate presence. The recognition of such an opportunity is an act of perception just as complex as—in fact, more complex than—the comprehension of a story involving such a recognition (Birnbaum, 1986). Thus, the problem of recognizing complex, abstract features is a key issue in planning as well as understanding, because planning in a situation *depends upon* understanding that situation.

However, in all of this daunting inferential complexity, which seems so incompatible with connectionism, I see an important opportunity for connectionist and neural network models. For if perception and interpretation really *do* require complex inference, as I have argued here, then there remains the crucial problem of directing and focussing the comparatively limited computational resources available. Using relatively cheap, parallel, "associative" network methods to direct the attention of more sophisticated computational mechanisms may be a way to approach this problem while avoiding the infinite regress of "meta-level" reasoning.

REFERENCES

Abelson, R. (1973). The structure of belief systems. In R. Schank & K. Colby (Eds.), *Computer models of thought and language* (pp. 287–339). San Francisco: Freeman.

Allen, J., & Perrault, C. (1980). Analyzing intention in utterances. *Artificial Intelligence. 15,* 143–178.

Birnbaum, L. (1985). Lexical ambiguity as a touchstone for theories of language analysis. *Proceedings of the Ninth IJCAI,* pp. 815–820. Los Angeles, CA.

Birnbaum, L. (1986). *Integrated processing in planning and understanding* (Research rep. No. 489). New Haven, CT: Yale University, Department of Computer Science.

Carbonell, J. (1981). *Subjective understanding: Computer models of belief systems.* Ann Arbor, MI: UMI Research Press.

Charniak, E. (1972). *Towards a model of children's story understanding* (Tech. rep. No. 266). Cambridge, MA: Artificial Intelligence Laboratory, MIT.

Charniak, E. (1983). Passing markers: A theory of contextual inference in language comprehension. *Cognitive Science, 7,* 171–190.

Dyer, M. (1983). *In-depth understanding: A computer model of integrated processing for narrative comprehension.* Cambridge, MA: MIT Press.

Fahlman, S. (1979). *NETL: A system for representing and using real-world knowledge.* Cambridge, MA: MIT Press.

Grice, H. (1975). Logic and conversation. In P. Cole & J. Morgan (Eds.). *Syntax and Semantics, Vol. 3: Speech acts* (pp. 41–58). New York: Academic Press.

Hammond, K. (1989). *Case-based planning: Viewing planning as a memory task.* San Diego: Academic Press.

Kolodner, J. (Ed.). (1988). *Proceedings of the 1988 Workshop on Case-Based Reasoning.* San Mateo, CA: Morgan Kaufmann.

Lehnert, W. (1981). Plot units and narrative summarization. *Cognitive Science, 5,* 293–331.

Minsky, M. (1968). Introduction. In *Semantic information processing.* Cambridge, MA: MIT Press.

Pople, H. (1973). On the mechanization of abductive logic. *Proceedings of the Third IJCAI,* pp. 147–152. Stanford, CA.

Quillian, M. (1968). Semantic memory. In M. Minsky (Ed.), *Semantic information processing* (pp. 227–270). Cambridge, MA: MIT Press.

Schank, R. (1982). *Dynamic memory: A theory of reminding and learning in computers and people.* Cambridge, England: Cambridge University Press.

Schank, R., & Abelson, R. (1977). *Scripts, plans, goals, and understanding.* Hillsdale, NJ: Erlbaum.

Sejnowski, T., & Rosenberg, C. (1986). *Nettalk: A parallel network that learns to read aloud.* (Tech. Report No. JIIU/EECS/86-01). Baltimore, MD: Johns Hopkins University, Department of Electrical Engineering and Computer Science.

Stanfill, C., & Waltz, D. (1986). Toward memory-based reasoning. *Communications of the ACM, 12,* 1213–1228.

Swinney, D. (1979). Lexical access during sentence comprehension: (Re)consideration of context effects. *Journal of Verbal Learning and Verbal Behavior, 18,* 645–660.

Wilensky, R. (1983). *Planning and understanding: A computational approach to human understanding.* Reading, MA: Addison-Wesley.

15
Conclusion

Jordan Pollack
John Barnden

This final chapter completes the book with detailed discussion of topics which arose at our workshop on high-level connectionist models (see Preface). Many of these topics are linked to long standing issues in philosophy and AI. Some of them have been addressed previously by various proponents and opponents of connectionism, while others are the emergent products of isolating a group of ardent symbolists and connectionists in the New Mexico Sun for several days. We recorded and subsequently transcribed the discussions which took place, but, in the interest of the reader, we have taken editorial privilege with the often colorful prose. We have tried to stay faithful to what was expressed, but, nonetheless, it is best to regard this chapter as our impressions of and extrapolations from the participants' views.

1. LEVELS AND MODES OF DESCRIPTION

Hendler presented the view (attributed to Geoffrey Hinton) that comparing AI and Connectionism was analogous to comparing zoology and molecular biology. AI engages in the study and description of the various "animals" of intelligent activities, while connectionism focuses on understanding the principles which make the common "cells" work. It is, of course, not clear that a detailed understanding of cells will lead to an understanding of animals.

However, the comparison goes deeper than this reductionist humor, and asks questions about the orthogonal concerns of differing fields of inquiry. On the one hand, Dyer suggested that while a single researcher may work at many different descriptive levels in a single field, his or her evaluation criteria remain the same across these levels; for example, a computer scientist who is developing a model of a neuron may ask if it performs an efficient algorithm. On the other hand, in moving between research fields the "sociology" changes, and different evaluation metrics apply; for example, a biologist may view the computerized neuron from an organic chemistry perspective as totally inadequate. This is certainly of concern to interdisciplinarians.

On the other hand, Pollack questioned the degree of orthogonality that Hendler saw between the concerns of different levels or fields. He pointed out that molecular biologists study DNA and protein sequences to understand growth and metabolic processes in living beings; AI researchers study knowledge representation and interrelated processing techniques like machine learning and explanation-formation; and connectionists study distributed representations, statistical associations, and numerical relaxation algorithms. All of these types of investigator are thus, at some level, studying data structures and algorithms, and therefore have more common concerns than they are often given credit for. Further, if one reduces conventional implementations of standard AI systems to boolean circuitry, symbolic and numeric AI are less different than many people imagine. The chapter by Hong and Tan is quite relevant to this point. Indeed, many discussions of traditional symbolic processing versus connectionism may be confounded by assessing them at disparate levels of description. What connectionist architectures should be compared to is not high-level abstractions, such as LISP interpreters, but, rather, the lower-level computational architectures used to implement them.

Hendler pointed out that the notion of descriptive levels seems to imply the existence of systematic translators between levels, analogous to programming-language compilers. Dyer denied the need for such compilers, since his symbolic neuroengineering approach works at various levels of description without them. The point here is that, in order to save years of network evolution, it is profitable to build a connectionist system which relies upon the results of years of AI research. The fact, however, that one's connectionist system was *engineered* from a prior symbolic description, such as a semantic network, by no means implies that its behavior can be described fully in terms of manipulations of the symbolic structures one started with—the symbolic description may be just end up being an approximate description of a finer-grain connectionist process.

Moreover, as Pollack pointed out, the problem of "transformational incompleteness" makes the question of equivalence between high-level "source" and low-level "object" processes quite thorny. Compilation improves time or storage costs at the expense of *information* about the source. For example, most conventional language compilers forget the symbol table or the formulaic definitions of constants (unless operating in a special debugging mode). Thus, even if one has a systematic translator, the amount of information lost by the compilation process renders the "decompilation" of compiled programs problematical. Furthermore, a given low-level program may not be one that the compiler could generate from any possible high-level program.

A related idea (emphasized by Jeffrey Elman) is that one cannot, in general, have an adequate appreciation of high-level accounts of behavior without some knowledge of how they are implemented at a low level. We concur with this, and we note that most high-level accounts make some assumptions about the complexity profile of low-level primitives, ascribing high efficiency to many of them. For instance, a high-level psychological model that involves a process of sequencing through a list of memory items in short-term memory might rest on a widely held assumption that each shift of attention from one item to the next is quite a fast operation. This is a significant assumption, since it would be easy to devise an implementation of attention-shift that made it slow. Yet originators of high-level accounts rarely spell out their tacit efficiency assumptions, tending instead to share them quietly with their own community. These low-level assumptions are nevertheless crucial in guiding the research pursued by that community.

On the other hand, according to Dyer, having a low-level description does not mean that higher-level descriptions can be dispensed with. We do not really know much about what a successful low-level account of, say, emotions, will be like, but it is very probable that it will still have to satisfy certain constraints at higher levels which can already be described, using notions like beliefs, goals and plans. For instance, if you believe that somebody has obstructed one of your goals then you are likely to be angry with that person. Even the originator of a future connectionist implementation of emotional behavior is likely to want to appeal to the high-level constraints in describing the behavior of the system.

A major point of contention at the workshop regarded the value of directly implementing symbolic systems in connectionist terms (as opposed to merely using symbolic systems as a *guide* to the construction of connectionist systems—cf. a point above attributed to Dyer). In the Introduction we claimed that such "implementational connectionism" could be valuable for several enterprises, including the study of how the brain could implement high-level reasoning, the study of middle-level mental architectures, the engineering of hybrid models, and the development of new connectionist representations and mechanisms.

At the workshop, however, the idea of the further study of connectionist implementations of classical symbolic processes such as resolution theorem provers, production systems, syntactic parsers and LISP-like list-manipulations was largely rejected. Birnbaum coined the colorful epithet "Pokey Connectionist Models" to critically capture the ineffectiveness of many existing connectionist models of symbolic processes.

We note here a double standard, that the drive to build such connectionist models is generally stimulated by criticisms of the form "Connectionism surely cannot do X." When someone finally demonstrates a connectionist model of X, it is often not very natural or very efficient. This, of course, leads to the further criticism of the sort: "Connectionism does X, but poorly!"

Nevertheless, we must continue to explore implementational connectionism, especially when a connectionist model can achieve the *function* of a symbolic system without directly implementing its "*moving parts.*" For example, even if it does logical deduction it need not do it in the same way as existing theorem provers do it; if it runs production rules, those rules do not have to be structurally or behaviorally similar to rules in traditional rule-based systems; and if it uses compositional representations, it does not have to rely on any simple notion of concatenation of symbols. What is of continuing interest are connectionist implementations which maintain the power of symbolic systems while adding more psychological or biological constraints, or which add new low-level concepts that change the tacit efficiency assumptions of AI researchers.

2. ON THE NATURE OF SYMBOLS

One of the more extended and interesting discussions at the workshop concerned symbols, as was to be expected in a meeting of connectionists and symbolists. According to Elman, the reason that many people think that certain things cannot be done without symbols is that they have worked with them for so long; the effect of working with symbolic systems is subtle, because it causes one to think about problems in a particular, restricted way. Although this point may be valid, most participants agreed that at least some of the powerful aspects of symbols are indeed desirable if not inevitable in high-level models. Of course, the issues depend very much on what one takes a symbol to be. In this section we try to capture and expand upon the discussion which took place at the workshop. After some discussion on what symbols may be, we discuss their implementation and use, and how this relates to the representational adequacy problem for connectionism.

The word "symbol" has rather different connotations for different intellectual communities. On the one hand, a poet or playwright might assume that a symbol communicates by virtue of its preexisting connotations—perhaps, we may say, by being iconic in a general sense, such as when a physically stark stage setting is used to symbolize laçk of emotional comfort. On the other hand, a computer scientist tends to view, as a symbol, any member of an enumerable set of items out of which complex structures can be built, such as the tokens of a formal (or natural) language. Such tokens need not individually have any meaning at all. However, in AI and cognitive science, symbols are indeed often correlated with the *meaningful* primitives of content theories for particular domains, and merely implemented as tokens.

A well-known though possibly spurious issue is whether the relationship between a representation (e.g., a meaningful symbol) and what it represents is, or should be, "stipulative" (that is, somewhat arbitrarily assigned by human beings), or whether it can be in some sense "naturalistic," in the sense of being created naturally and automatically by the system by a process of slow adaptation based on the way the system is embedded in its environment. One might take the traditional notion of symbol, as found in logic and AI, to imply or assume that the relationship is stipulative. Consider then a connectionist who views the representations in his/her system as being naturalistic in their meanings. Jeffrey Elman adhered to this view in the discussion, and Dyer also attested to the value of such representations. A connectionist such as Elman (but not Dyer) is likely to take such naturalistic representations to be nonsymbolic. However, despite the undoubted importance of naturalistic representations—for they engage in representational relationships that are particularly complex, flexible, rich, and principled, as Elman pointed out—there may not be any deep reason for refusing to call them "symbols." After all, the stipulative quality in the traditional notion of symbol may be a relatively superficial and dispensable feature. It is certainly true that, in a typical symbolic system implemented on a computer, an atomic symbol for a person John would in essence be some arbitrarily assigned bit-string. However, one could imagine the system, S, being connected to a sensory module in such a way that when a new person is encountered a new bit-string is invented by some sort of transformation of the output of the sensory module. It would seem undesirable to refuse to view such a bit-string as a symbol just because it arose "naturally," since it plays exactly the same sort of role within S as a John bit-string with a stipulative meaning. Perhaps we may say that the stipulative quality of symbols in standard AI systems is a superficial and temporary consequence of the fact that such systems are *currently* not properly embedded in the world. In fact, in view of these arguments and others[1] we tend to feel that the distinction between naturalistic and stipulative representation is ill-defined if not illusory.

The physical implementation of semantically primitive symbols as wordlike tokens requires machinery which is quite easy to build out of the basic elements of computer programs and data-structures. Characters need to be stored as bytes, variable-length vectors of bytes need to be manipulable, and, to complete the picture, arbitrary associations between these vectors and random memory addresses need to be efficiently accessed. One difference between a conventional programming language like FORTRAN and a "symbolic programming language" like LISP is that programs in the latter can crucially depend on efficiently using a word-like symbol at run-time to gain access to its associated memory address. Such access was made very efficient with the invention of hashing.

Thus, in traditional AI implementations, wordlike tokens are used as *pointers* into memory, and the memory areas pointed to can contain large data-structures. This organization leads directly to a great flexibility in memory allocation, since the data structures can be moved around, as long as the symbol table is kept updated.

It is worth asking why it is that there is a strong tendency in connectionist and neural net research to shy away from the idea of using something like pointers: that is, of allowing a part of the network to contain a name of a part of that same

---

[1] C.A. Fields (personal communication) argues that this putative distinction is invalid, being based on equivocating two distinct forms of semantic question.

network. After all, pointers are a very important mechanism in computers for setting up temporary associations. The avoidance of pointers in connectionism may have less to do with substantive technical considerations then with the sociopolitics of research—intellectual rebellions often seek to throw out all ideas that came before, regardless of value.

In fact, to fail to *consider* pointers is inconsistent with connectionism. The circuitry in a conventional computer that does the addressing (pointer following) is broadly very similar to connectionist associative-memory networks. The real contrast is in the fact that the addressing circuitry in a conventional computer uses a key (a location name) to access *a place in which* information resides, whereas a connectionist associative memory uses a key (a partial or distorted pattern) to recall the information itself, directly. But, no good argument for why a connectionist or neural system should *not* deal in place-names for information, at least for *some purposes,* has to our knowledge been put forward. For a system to so deal for the purposes of *short-term,* high-level cognitive processing would not even conflict, in principle, with the typical connectionist precept that all the *long-term* information in a connectionist network is encoded in the connection weights. The chapters by Barnden, Dyer (ROBIN), and Shastri shed further light on connectionist approaches to pointing.

This "pointer" use of symbols is perhaps the most basic, but not the only use. Others have outlined the desirable uses and operations on symbols and symbol structures [e.g., Newell (1980)]. In the workshop discussions, many uses of "symbols" were discussed, in the context of understanding and overcoming the shortcomings of current connectionist models.

The pointer use of symbol is a special case of the more general notion of "reconstructive" use, under which a symbol is a small code used in some way or other to reconstruct a large amount of information. (In fact, Shastri was in favor of defining a symbol in this way. Also, Derthick reminded us that the reconstructed information might be a procedural entity rather than a declarative data structure.) If the symbol is a pointer in the usual computer-science sense of the term, the symbol provides a memory address and the reconstruction takes the simple form of a mere retrieval of the information from the addressed memory area (although it may be that further pointer-following is initiated). A more sophisticated type of symbol could be the result of applying some compression transformation to the very information that is meant to be reconstructed. This case includes the reduced-description techniques of Hinton (1988) and Pollack (1988, 1990). Touretzky threw some interesting light on the issue in talking about the omnipresent metonymy in natural language, reminding us that the notion of something "pointing to" something else can take on very elaborate forms.

There is also the "transportation" use of symbols: symbols may be transmitted through limited bandwidth channels (as in a multiprocessor). The ability to copy symbols from place to place was viewed as crucial in the workshop discussions, because it allows distributed accessing of large bodies of information. Hendler argued that the ability to pass a representation from place to place makes it into something that is quite like a symbol, even if it is, say, a distributed pattern of activation. Shastri claimed that the need for passing around representations arises as soon as one tackles a task that requires creating structures in a flexible way; most current connectionist systems do not engage in this sort of task, so that their representations may appear to be in some sense "nonsymbolic," but this appellation will become untenable the moment one tries to modify the system to handle dynamic structures.

Finally, there are the "structural primitive" and "identification" uses for symbols. Since symbols can be combined into complex structures, they serve as the most basic or "atomic" elements in many languages. And since symbols are subject to equality tests, and in some cases to ordering tests (e.g., alphabetically), they can form the basis for similarity comparisons between complex structures.

As Elman pointed out, it is very important to tease apart the necessary abilities of cognitive representations from the aspects of symbols which are granted by virtue of either existing technology or long-held philosophy. It is important that connectionist representations support the operations of complex thought, not that they be equivalent to traditional implementations of symbols. In some cases, connectionist representations do not yet afford the requisite abilities; in others, some of these abilities are all mixed together and difficult to see. Major limitations have arisen out of connectionists' own rhetorical successes.

For example, Pollack referred to the constraint promulgated by Feldman and Ballard (1982), that in a connectionist system, one is not passing around symbols or symbol structures, but only numbers (activation levels of nodes). But, if this is taken to mean that only large, distributed activation patterns qualify as symbols, then it is difficult to regard these symbols as compressed codes, so that they lose some of the advantages of conventional symbols, such as being able to be easily transported and composed into larger structures.

Furthermore, we must assume that physical systems cannot communicate real numbers in finite time, so activations are only allowed to take on a limited number of significant digits. Combined with the constraint that the network structure adapts slowly over time, the net effect is to impose a finiteness condition on the activation states of a network. The representations available to theories involving a finite set of finite-state units, of course, fail to compare with representations which can assume an infinite tape.

Complementing a point by Shastri that was referred to above, Dyer noted that because neural network researchers often work on toy problems which do not require the complex representations and processes (such as trees and bindings) that are easily dealt with by means of symbol processing, they make claims that symbolic methods are not needed. Similarly, Lehnert reported that it was only when she found how hard it was to do variable binding in connectionist systems that she realized how important it really was, having previously always taken it for granted.

By admitting that complex representations are necessary for cognition, however, we do not mean that existing types of connectionist processing, originally designed for perceptual vector representations, must be thrown away. To crib from Simon's (1969) parable of the ant: simple processes (such as connectionist memories and pattern associators) can exhibit complex phenomena when applied to complex structures. The representation problem for connectionism has been how to get complex structures to conform with its simple processes. Some of the research presented at the workshop (Dyer, Elman, Pollack) bears directly on this aspect of the question of complex structures.

For a concrete example, Pollack's (1988, 1990) work uses a recursive modification of back-propagation on auto-associative memory to develop fixed-width analog representations for finite sets of symbolic trees, along with two simple translation mechanisms, the compressor and reconstructor. This work elaborates Hinton's (1988) notion of *reduced descriptions.*

The *Compressor* encodes small sets of fixed-width patterns into single patterns of the same size. It is recursively applied, from the bottom up, to a fixed-valence tree with labeled terminals (leaves), resulting in a fixed-width pattern representing the entire structure. For the binary tree $((A\ B)(C\ D))$, where each of the terminals is a fixed-width binary pattern, this would take three steps. First A and B would be compressed into a pattern, R_1. Then C and D would be compressed into a pattern, R_2. Finally, R_1 and R_2 would be compressed into R_3.

The *Reconstructor* decodes these fixed-width patterns back into facsimiles of their parts, and determines when the parts should be further decoded. It is recursively applied, from the top down, resulting in a reconstruction of the original tree. Thus, for this example, R_3 would be decoded into R_1' and R_2'. R_1' would be decoded into A' and B', and R_2' into C' and D'.

For binary trees with k-bit patterns as the leaves, the compressor could be a single-layer network with $2k$ inputs and k outputs. The reconstructor could be a single-layer network with k inputs and $2k$ outputs. Consider simultaneously training, using back-propagation (Rumelhart, Hinton, & Williams, 1986), these two mechanisms as a single $2k$-k-$2k$ network, as shown in Figure 15.1. An encoder network (Ackley, Hinton, & Sejnowski, 1985) is trained to reproduce a set of input patterns, and, in learning to do so, develops a compressed code on the hidden units for each of the input patterns. The classic example trains an 8-3-8 network to reproduce the eight 1-bit-in-8 codes and develops some permutation of the 3-bit binary code on the hidden units. In order to find codes for trees, however, this auto-associative architecture must be used recursively. Extending the simple example from above, if A, B, C, and D were k-bit patterns, the network could be trained to reproduce (A B), (C D), *and* ((A B)(C D)) as follows:

input pattern	hidden pattern	output pattern
$(A \quad B)$	$\rightarrow R_1(t)$	$\rightarrow (A'(t) \quad B'(t))$
$(C \quad D)$	$\rightarrow R_2(t)$	$\rightarrow (C'(t) \quad D'(t))$
$(R_1(t) \quad R_2(t))$	$\rightarrow R_3(t)$	$\rightarrow (R_1(t)' \quad R_2(t)')$

where t represents the time, or epoch, of training. Assuming that back-propagation converges in the limit, the sum of the squares of the differences between the desired and actual outputs would go to 0, and:

$$A' = A$$
$$B' = B$$
$$C' = C$$
$$D' = D$$
$$R_1' = R_1$$
$$R_2' = R_2$$

Therefore, R_3, would, in fact, be a representation for the tree ((A B)(C D)), by virtue of the fact that the compressor would be a deterministic algorithm which transforms the tree to its representation, and the reconstructor a deter-

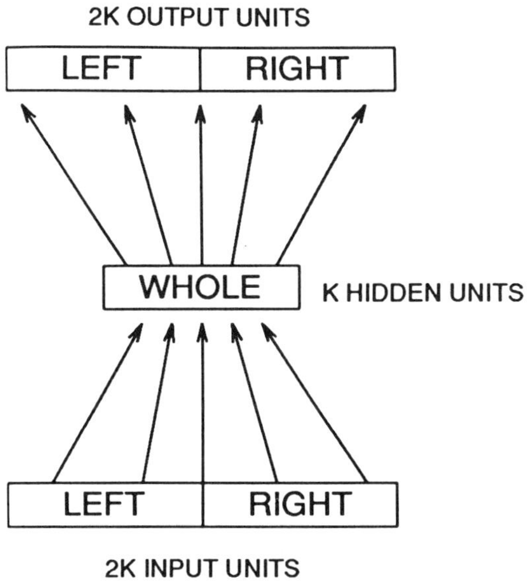

Figure 15.1.
Single network composed of both compressor and reconstructor.

ministic algorithm which transforms the representation back to the tree. Along the way, representations will also be devised for all subtrees, in this case, (A B) and (C D).

This strategy works on a collection of trees just as it does on a single tree. A 48-16-48 network was trained to represent a finite set of schematic conceptual ternary trees. These are listed in Table 15.1. Every terminal is represented as a vertex, and every subtree is "assigned" a point inside the 16-dimensional unit hypercube. These vectors achieve some of the attributes of symbols as outlined above: They are compressed codes for larger information structures which can be reconstructed, thus acting like pointers. They may be transmitted (at least over parallel bus structures). They act as primitives, combining into complex structures. What is more interesting is that similar syntactic structures are assigned points near each other (by Euclidean distance) in this space; this is demonstrated by Figure 15.2, which shows the hierarchal clustering of the 16-dimensional patterns.

This question of how similarity is physically captured is central to the contention between tokenistic and connectionistic symbols. During the workshop, Elman pointed out that distributed representations (say, for JOHN and MARY) allow similar concepts to share their identity, since the reason that two points are "close" in concept space is because they have similar values along many featural dimensions.

Table 15.1.
Ternary trees used for 48-16-48 network experiment.

1	(LOVED PAT MARY)
2	(LOVED JOHN PAT)
3	((WITH SAW TELESCOPE) JOHN (ON MAN HILL))
4	((WITH ATE CHOPSTICKS) MARY SPAGHETTI)
5	(ATE MARY (WITH SPAGHETTI MEAT))
6	(ATE PAT MEAT)
7	(KNEW PAT (LOVED JOHN MARY))
8	(THOUGHT PAT (KNEW JOHN (LOVED MARY JOHN)))
9	(HOPED PAT (THOUGHT JOHN (ATE MARY SPAGHETTI)))
10	((WITH HIT (MOD TELESCOPE LONG)) JOHN MAN)
11	(HIT JOHN (WITH MAN (MOD TELESCOPE LONG)))
12	(HOPED PAT (SAW (WITH MAN TELESCOPE) PAT))
13	(HIT PAT (IS MAN (THOUGHT MAN (LOVED MARY JOHN))))
14	(SAW (IS (MOD MAN SHORT) (THOUGHT MAN (SAW MAN JOHN))) PAT)

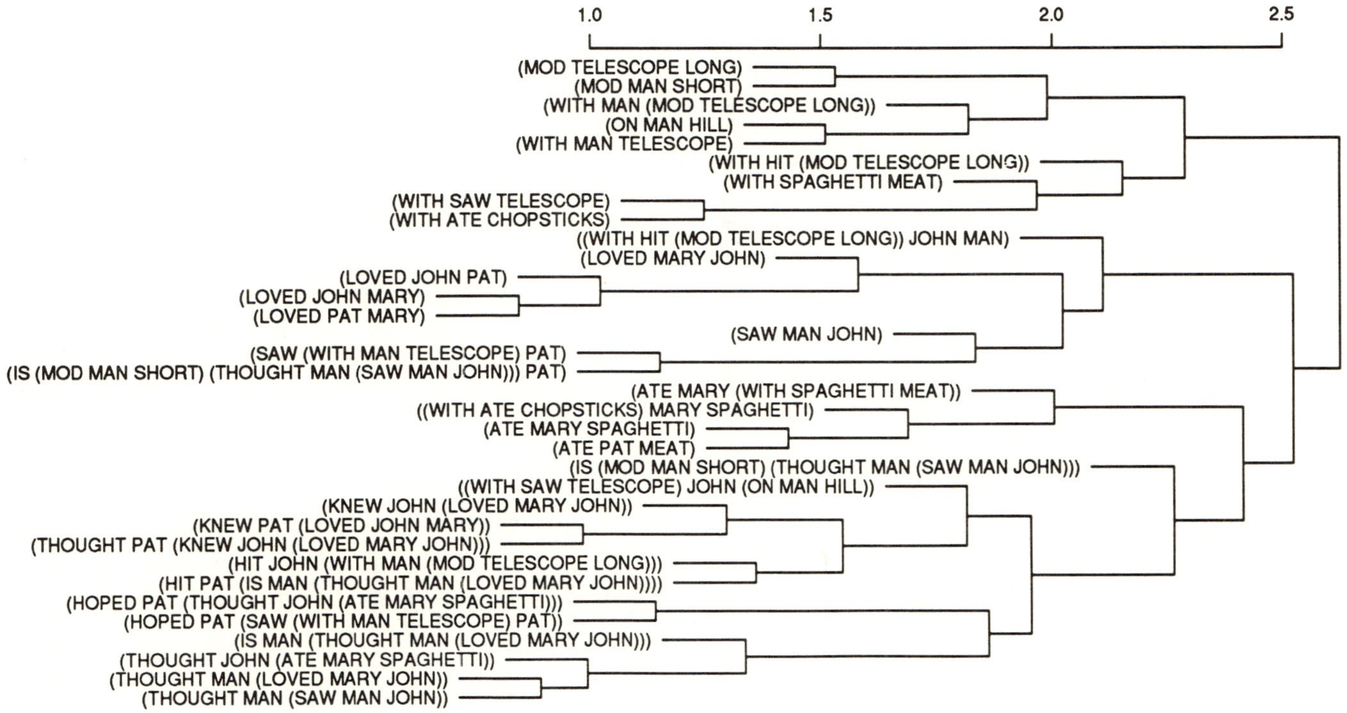

Figure 15.2.
Hierarchal Clustering of points corresponding to ternary trees.

However, Shastri pointed out that in a standard AI system the symbols for JOHN and MARY, even if atomic, also share something—the way they are connected into the entire representational and inferential web of the system. Both of the symbols will allow access in some way to a common set of aspects of the concept of, say, living people. Both will be substitutable in axiom schemata or rules that encode generalities about people, physical objects, and so on. The claimed difference between this sharing and the sharing among naturalistic connectionist representations would presumably have to be that the latter share by virtue of having similar internal "syntax" (as complex activation patterns). However, we may add that this is not a clear-cut difference, because it is not fair to compare connectionist representations merely with traditional *atomic* symbols. *Complex* symbols like formal structures corresponding to the linguistic descriptions "the mother of Mary" and "the mother of John" do of course share internal syntax. Indeed, the way in which similar such representations are meant to lead to similar activity in the network and the way in which similar traditional symbolic structures are meant to be subject to similar processing by procedural entities (e.g., rules) are closely related, and are just special cases of the same broad issue of *systematicity of processing* we discussed in the Introduction.

The ability to distribute symbolic structures, or pointers to them, to multiple processes leads to a symbolic similarity-based generalization ability that is a sort of converse or dual to the familiar connectionist type. The latter is to do with generality possessed by a given *single processing mechanism* (a subnetwork) in virtue of its being able to deal with many similar representations (activation patterns); while the converse symbolic type we are pointing out is the generality possessed by a given *single representation* (symbolic structure) in virtue of its being able to be acted upon by many "similar" processing mechanisms. We say "similar" here by appeal to the notion that any mechanisms that are capable of dealing with the particular sort of syntax possessed by the single representation are to that extent similar.

We should also note that the ability to pass a single symbolic representation to multiple modules provides an important contrast with connectionist systems. In a typical connectionist system, one often finds activity patterns whose significance is highly local to a specific area in the network and which can only be usefully manipulated by processes already implemented in the wiring in that area. Also, in almost all connectionist systems, the weights developed in one area through training, and therefore embodying useful learned information, are not accessible in any direct sense by other areas. The problem presented by these two types of locality is not usually noticed, since most systems are so simple architecturally that they do not even have communicating subsystems. Once one starts building complex architectures, communication issues arise. These issues emerge in the chapters by Bookman, Barnden, Dyer, and Lehnert.

3. SOME TOPICS FOR FURTHER INVESTIGATION

In this section we briefly point towards areas in which more connectionist research could profitably be done.

Combinator-Based Processing. One direction which has not been fully explored by connectionists and may prove fruitful is a long-established technique for avoiding explicit variables. First, let us assume that we have a symbolic processing system that works by manipulating lambda-calculus expressions (see, e.g., Barendregt, 1984). These involve explicit occurrences of variables. Such processing has completely general computational power (it is Turing equivalent), and in particular can take the place of the manipulation of conventional logical formulae. These expressions can be rewritten into a form in which there are no variables, but only constants, ordinary functions, and certain special functions called "*logical combinators*" (Curry & Feys, 1958; Turner, 1979).

Some computer programming languages are compiled into a lower level combinator-based language, so that a running program manipulates combinator-based expressions. The processing of an individual combinator causes some rearrangement of the expression. These manipulations can be executed by specialized computers [see, e.g., Turner, 1979]. This suggests the possibility of designing a connectionist system that manipulates combinator expressions and thus in some sense avoids the use of variables.[2]

We say that the use of variables is avoided only "in some sense" because the application of a particular manipulation step to a combinator expression is tantamount to a rule application involving the hidden binding of variables in the rule to pieces of combinator-based expression that need to be shifted around. Further, combinator expressions count as complex data structures, and we know that these present problems for connectionism. However, the confinement of variable binding into a highly constrained, standardized form within a small set of simple combinator manipulation rules could be beneficial. Further, combinators are useful to consider because they tend to concentrate one's mind on the issue of *getting the effect* that variables allow one to get. That effect is the processing of a large class of data structures without needing a concomitantly large amount of mechanism.

Meta-Level Processing. Birnbaum's chapter brings up the important issue of meta-level processing, which came out also in workshop discussion, and includes, for example, systems which can reason about themselves and their own knowledge. This issue has been largely ignored in connectionist theories, mainly

[2] As an aside, Barnden (1983) has proposed a nonstandard set of combinators for the symbolic representation of propositional attitudes, as a way of avoiding the notorious problems that variables give rise to in that domain. In saying this, however, we do not mean to imply that these problems are identical to the difficulties presented by variables in connectionism.

because it is normally conditioned on the existence of explicit structured representations, which has not been a priority for connectionists until recently. Pollack pointed out that the fact that it has not been worked on does not mean it is antithetical to or impossible for connectionism. (One must remember, though, as Cottrell pointed out, that most "low-level" processes, such as reading or riding a bicycle, are not available for introspection; and a crucial issue this raises is that of explaining the process and means by which high-level descriptions of these tasks eventually become hidden from introspection as we get skilled.)

Birnbaum holds that for a system to do introspection it needs complex representations and long chains of inferences (although he also holds that connectionists should not construct what he calls "pokey connectionist implementations" of traditional symbolic AI inference processes). Dyer pointed out that AI researchers have not spent enough time building primitives and representations for facilitating introspection. For instance, in the planning domain, one should consider the use of specific structured concepts like the injunction, "Don't burn your bridges behind you" (your plan might fail, so you had better have the ability to recover). These structures have not been looked at very much by connectionists. Dyer mentioned Dolan's system for manipulating such thematic structures using tensor manipulation networks (Dolan, 1989).

An important, *standard* aspect of rule-based systems in cognitive psychology and AI has for a long time been the ability of rules themselves to inspect, manipulate, and/or create rules, and to treat a rule as a data-object in its own right.[3] Yet, in current debates about the similarities and differences between symbolic and connectionist systems, people rarely consider whether a connectionist system that can be said to exhibit rule-based behavior, either precisely or approximately, has (or appears to have) the ability to inspect and modify those rules as data in their own right.

Certainly, any connectionist system which has some logic to its behavior and has the ability to modify its own weights can be viewed as both "rule-based" and "self-modifying", but these adjectives are not linked as they are in symbolic systems. The insistence on *explicit* rule-representation and manipulation is a stronger constraint since it involves this linkage. A system that can engage in such activity could be said to be *strongly* rule-based, and the crucial point is that its behavior must be somehow dependent on explicitly represented rules, and thus be affected by their modification.

However, this path to meta-level reasoning for connectionist systems does not require system to have a perfect self-model or to execute rules in any direct way. Instead, it could have an approximate self-model based on rules that are approximate descriptors of its behavior, and a feedback system whereby changes that the

---

[3] Consider, for instance, the meta-rules of MYCIN (Davis, Buchanan, & Shortliffe, 1977) and rule-manipulation in production-system languages such as OPS-5 or YAPS (Allen, 1983).

system effects in this model ultimately affect the connection weights on which the system's behavior is directly based.

Dynamically Created Subnetworks. It has often been proposed that connectionist systems be able to recruit "unused" nodes for the purposes of rapidly building new subnetworks, by raising the weights on the node's connections to those nodes with which it is now to interact. However, few detailed systems actually incorporate such a mechanism. The system described in Diederich's chapter is one such exception.[4] The "storage management" problem of how to recruit nodes efficiently has not been studied in much detail, despite the extreme importance of storage management issues for the practicality of symbol processing on ordinary computers. Also, by and large, in detailed systems that do create new subnetworks, these become a permanent part of the system. If the pieces of network are only temporary, however, we have further storage management problems such as the analogue of "garbage collection" in ordinary computer systems.

The system described in Lehnert's chapter is one of the few detailed systems that rapidly create temporary pieces of connectionist network. This chapter, as well as some workshop discussion arising from Birnbaum's presentation, suggests the importance of further study of such behavior. Now, Lehnert's system is a hybrid one, having major portions that work by symbol processing that is not given a connectionist implementation; and of course the dynamic construction and discarding of networks poses no fundamental problem for traditional symbol processing. However, it is much more difficult to see in detail how a fully connectionist system could create new pieces of network, even when the creation is just a matter of creating or facilitating links between existing nodes.

The issue connects with another observation we can make about levels of system description. Marker passing or activation spreading in a connectionist system is usually cast as being over the base-level, connectionist networks themselves. But another possibility is that marker passing or activation spreading might take place on abstract networks, lying at higher "virtual" levels of system description. Moreover, these networks could be rapidly-created, temporary networks not requiring dynamic link creation at the concrete level. For example, in the Conposit system described in Barnden's chapter, the way in which "highlighting" states are moved around within the configuration matrix (a connectionistically implemented register array) amounts to fairly traditional marker passing; yet, the networks over which this marker passing occurs are rapidly created, temporary and abstract, being defined in a complex way in terms of temporary activation states of the connectionist network implementing the register array. This observation underlines the potential importance of multiple levels of description in connectionist systems.

[4] See also Feldman (1982) and Ash (1989).

Speed of Processing. A general agreement arose between Barnden and Shastri that insufficient attention is given in connectionism to the speed of the processing, especially in the common case of processing that involves many relaxation stages. Shastri holds that humans are fast in certain kinds of reasoning tasks and slow in others, and he has been especially concerned with providing connectionist accounts of the former. In his chapter he argues against the use of relaxation-based connectionist systems for fast kinds of reasoning, although he agrees with an observation of Touretzky's that in some cases the relaxation may be fast enough to be practical. However, some tasks that we assume to be suitable for relaxation-based treatment may in fact be handled better—more quickly and accurately—by nonrelaxation approaches (cf. Marr, 1982, p.107). Barnden asserted that in connectionist modeling which has any relevance to biological neural networks one should pay serious attention to the time delays involved in signal travel along connections. In particular, such delays could become very significant in relaxation processes over biological neural networks that have large physical extension. Given the slowness of neural pulse transmission in the brain (at best, about one centimeter per millisecond, and more typically about one millimeter per millisecond: an order of magnitude or two slower than in peripheral nerves), a network that is geographically widely distributed in the brain may not be a suitable substrate for a relaxation process that requires a large number of cycles.

A different type of significance is accorded to time delays in recent work of Barnden, Srinivas, and Dharmavaratha (1990), where signal timing differences are exploited in a new approach to achieving "winner-take-all" behavior (Feldman & Ballard, 1982), an important aspect of many connectionist systems.

Moving Target Learning. An interesting commonality emerged in the DUAL work of Dyer, the recurrent prediction networks of Elman (1989), and the recursive auto-associative memory of Pollack (in press) (which was sketched above). All three use recurrent back-propagation on simple feedforward networks, with the additional feedback loop that the activations of hidden unit vectors are copied into the training environment. This environment therefore evolves with the network, and can be said to be a "moving target."

Dyer's system learns to represent small labeled graphs, Elman's net learns to represent critical previous context in predicting sequences of tokens, and Pollack's network learns to represent symbolic tree structures. Since these are the first connectionist models to learn to represent complex, variable-size structures, the moving target strategy may be a valuable one.

Final Thought

On the one hand, we may conjecture that the mental objects and processes that have been developed through biological evolution are too complex to be matched by anything that conventional Artificial Intelligence could manually devise. (Surely mental representations are of the same order of biological complexity as antibodies or genes!) On the other hand, neither connectionism nor other number-crunching varieties of machine learning have yet evolved any data structures as complex as the (excessively rigid) symbolic structures typed in by AI programmers.

John McCarthy has been quoted as saying that AI and connectionism are two horses in the same race and should both be permitted to run the course. We can assert (modifying a sentiment of Hendler's) that there is really only one horse, but that it has two heads. One head assumes clearcut symbolic representations and explores the complex space of heuristic algorithms. The other head assumes simple algorithms and explores the complex space of neural representations. Ultimately, the wire may be broken by the horse's neck—mathematical principles which, regardless of physical instantiation, account for the development of all systems of complex objects, from organic chemicals through life forms, to language, and thought.

REFERENCES

Ackley, D.H., Hinton, G.E., & Sejnowski, T.J. (1985). A learning algorithm for Boltzmann Machines. *Cognitive Science, 9,* 147–169.

Allen, E.M. (1983). *YAPS: Yet another production system* (Tech. Rep. TR-1146). College Park, MD: Department of Computer Science, University of Maryland.

Ash, T. (1989). *Dynamic node creation in back propagation networks* (Tech. Report 8901). La Jolla, CA: Institute for Cognitive Science, University of California at San Diego.

Barendregt, H.P. (1984). *The lambda calculus: Its syntax and semantics* (Revised ed.). Amsterdam: North-Holland.

Barnden, J.A. (1983). Intensions as such: an outline. *Proceedings of the 8th International Joint Conference on Artificial Intelligence.* Los Altos, CA: Morgan Kaufmann.

Barnden, J.A, Srinivas, K., & Dharmavaratha, D. (1990). Winner-take-all networks: Time-based versus activation-based mechanisms for various selection goals. *Proceedings of the ICEE International Symposium on Circuits and Systems.* New Orleans, LA.

Curry, H.B., & Feys, R. (1958). *Combinatory logic.* Amsterdam: North-Holland.

Davis, R., Buchanan, B., & Shortliffe, E. (1977). Production rules as a representation for a knowledge-based consultation program. *Artificial Intelligence, 8*(1), 15–45.

Dolan, C.P. (1989). *Tensor manipulation networks: Connectionist and symbolic approaches to comprehension, learning, and planning* (Tech. Rep. UCLA-AI-89-06). Los Angeles: UCLA.

Elman, J.L. (1990). Finding structure in time. *Cognitive Science, 14*(2), 179–212.

Feldman, J.A. (1982). Dynamic connections in neural networks. *Biological Cybernetics, 46,* 27–39.

Feldman, J.A., & Ballard, D.H. (1982). Connectionist models and their properties. *Cognitive Science, 6,* 205–254.

Hinton, G.E. (1988). Representing part-whole hierarchies in connectionist networks. *Proceedings of the 10th Annual Conference of the Cognitive Science Society.* Hillsdale, NJ: Lawrence Erlbaum Associates.

Marr, D. (1982). *Vision.* San Francisco: W.H. Freeman.

Newell, A. (1980). Physical symbol systems. *Cognitive Science, 4,* 135–183.

Pollack, J.B. (1990). Recursive auto-associative memory. *Proceedings of the Tenth Annual Conference of the Cognitive Science Society* (pp. 33–39). Hillsdale, NJ: Lawrence Erlbaum Associates.

Rumelhart, D.E., Hinton, G.E., & Williams, R.J. (1986). Learning internal representations through error propagation. In D.E. Rumelhart, J.L. McClelland, & The PDP research Group (Eds.), *Parallel distributed processing: Experiments in the microstructure of cognition,* (Vol. 1, pp. 25–40.) Cambridge: MIT Press.

Simon, H.A. (1969). *The sciences of the artificial.* Cambridge: MIT Press.

Turner, D.A. (1979). A new implementation technique for applicative languages. *Software Practice and Experience, 9,* 31–49.

Author Index

Subject Index

Notes to the reader:

1. Entries including numbers and Greek letters are alphabetized as if those letters and numbers were spelled out. Thus, "3-unit subnetworks" and "ρ-btu nodes" are treated as if they were "Three-unit subnetworks" and "Rho-btu nodes" respectively.

2. The page number list for a given entry does not necessarily include the numbers for its sub-entries. For example, the number list for "Learning" does not include the "41" listed for the "explanation-based" sub-entry of "Learning".

3. In cross-references to sub-entries, a colon is used to separate the sub-entry name from the main entry name, as for example in "*see* Energy: landscapes".

4. In a sub-entry name, the main entry name sometimes appears abbreviated to a single letter. Example: the "Knowledge" entry has a sub-entry called "k. bases (KBs)". (These abbreviations are ignored in the alphabetization of sub-entries, and are usually omitted in cross-references.)

5. A page number list may contain Chapter references, when the (sub-)entry is discussed throughout the chapter. A Chapter reference may, however, be followed by a bracketed list of numbers of particularly significant pages.